North Africa: nation, state and region

North Africa:
nation, state, and region

Edited by George Joffé

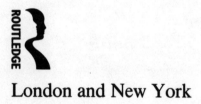

London and New York

First published 1993
by Routledge
11 New Fetter Lane, London EC4P 4EE

Simultaneously published in the USA and Canada
by Routledge
29 West 35th Street, New York, NY 10001

Typeset in Times by Leaper & Gard Ltd, Bristol
Printed and bound in Great Britain by
Mackays of Chatham PLC, Chatham, Kent

British Library Cataloguing-in-Publication Data
A catalogue record for this book is available from the British
Library.
ISBN 0-415-09162-4

Library of Congress Cataloging in Publication Data
North Africa : nation, state, and region / edited by George
Joffé.
        p.   cm.
    Includes bibliographical references and index.
    ISBN 0-415-09162-4
    1. Africa, North.   I. Joffé, George.
DT185.N6   1993
961–dc20   92-31338
                                                    CIP

Contents

Part III Independent states

Part IV The region today

Contributors

Dr Ali Bahaijoub is the London director of the Maghreb Arabe Presse press agency. He has specialised in EC affairs and in the Western Saharan question, which formed the subject of his Ph.D.

Dr Jerome Bookin-Weiner is programme director at Bentley College. He has specialised in sixteenth-century Moroccan history, particularly in the Saʿādīan period, and in the history of corsairing in Morocco. Recently he has edited (with Dr Mohamed El-Mansour) a study of Moroccan–American relations.

Dr Mohamed Chtatou is in charge of the educational and bibliographic section of ISESCO (the Islamic Educational, Cultural and Scientific Organisation) in Rabat. His academic interest is primarily in linguistics and he has specialised in Berber languages.

Professor John Damis is a member of the politics department of Oregon State University. His major interest in the Maghreb has been the Western Sahara issue and, more recently, the issue of regional integration.

Professor William Hoisington Jun. teaches history at the University of Illinois and has specialised in French colonial policy. He is the author of a book on General Noguès: *The Casablanca Connection*.

Dr Mohammed Kenbib is a member of the Faculté des Lettres of Mohammed V University in Rabat. He has specialised in the nineteenth- and twentieth-century history of Morocco.

Dr Remy Leveau was, for a long time, employed in the Moroccan administration. He is now a sociologist at CERI in Paris and the author of a standard work on Moroccan political structures, *Le fellah marocain, defenseur du Trône.*

Jon Marks reports on North African affairs for *Middle East Economic Digest* and for other publications concerned with the area. His research work was originally carried out in the Algerian Mzab.

Salem Mezhoud, who originates from Kabylia in Algeria, now works for the Minority Rights Group. He has made a special study of Berber problems in North Africa.

Dr Henry Munson Jun teaches social anthropology at the University of Maine. He is the author of a study on the role of Islam in the Middle East and of another study on social attitudes in Morocco.

Dr Richard Pennell teaches history at the University of Singapore. He is the author of a study on the Rif War: *A Country with a Government and a Flag*. Currently he is investigating the role of corsairing and piracy in the nineteenth-century Maghrib.

Dr Hugh Roberts has specialised in the politics and sociology of independent Algeria. His original work was carried out in Kabylia and he is currently writing a book on recent developments in Algerian political life.

Dr Youssef Selmane is attached to the English Department at Algiers University. His doctoral thesis was devoted to contemporary Algerian theatre and he has been active in recent developments in drama in Algeria.

Claire Spencer has investigated the history of Tangier during the colonial period, with particular emphasis on Spanish interests there. She is currently attached to the Rockefeller Foundation.

Dr Abdeljelil Temimi is the director of CEROMDI, an independent research centre devoted to the history of the Arab world during the Ottoman period and located in Zaghouan in Tunisia.

John Wright works for the BBC Arabic Service and has long been interested in Libya. He is the author of two standard histories of Libya and, most recently, of a history of the Central Sahara.

Dr Rachida Yacine is at the University of Wahran (Oran) in Algeria. She specialises in the historical development of linguistic and cultural policy in North Africa.

Foreword

North Africa differs from the Middle East in several significant ways. It was subject to a uniform colonial experience as part of the French empire; its populations are far more culturally homogeneous than those of the Middle East; and, since the *Reconquista*, it has always been far more susceptible to European influences than has the Middle East. It has thus had a far better basis for regional integration and for effective state formation than has the Middle East itself.

This book endeavours to investigate the background to the political developments of modern North Africa. It not only looks at the pre-colonial past but also investigates the effect of the colonial period itself on the developments since independence. Particular emphasis is laid on the regional dimension in view of the creation of the UMA, a confederal regional organisation, in early 1989.

The contributors to this volume are all persons with long experience of the North African political and historical scene. Their contributions are drawn from a conference – the first major conference held in Britain on North Africa for many years – that took place in late 1989. Many of the contributions have been updated since then to take account of more recent developments.

In the new post-Cold War world, North Africa takes on a new significance for Europe as issues of migration and regional trade begin to dominate the European agenda. However, in the non-Francophone part of Europe, North Africa is still a relatively unknown region. The appearance of this book is, therefore, timely. It is edited by George Joffé, of the Centre for Geopolitics and International Boundaries Research at the School of Oriental and African Studies, who also convened the original conference on which it is based.

Acknowledgements

I would like to thank the former director, Professor J. A. Allan, the current director, Dr R. Tapper, and the staff of the Centre for Near and Middle Eastern Studies at the School of Oriental and African Studies in London for their help and forebearance which made the original conference on which this publication is based possible. I am also very grateful to Diana Gur for her tireless work in handling the administrative and secretarial tasks involved in preparing the publication itself. Without their collective committment – and that of the original participants at the conference – this book could not have been published.

A note on transliteration

Transliteration of proper names has always presented a major problem in North Africa because the French tranliterations have become the officially registered versions of proper names, even since independence. As a result, in this volume, geographical names are given in their generally accepted form, personal names in correct transliteration for the pre-colonial period and in the officially registered form thereafter. Technical terms, as far as possible, are transliterated according to standard norms.

Introduction

George Joffé

The contributions gathered together in this book were originally prepared for a conference, held at the School of Oriental and African Studies (London University) under the auspices of the Centre for Near and Middle Eastern Studies, on the topic of 'North Africa and the Nation-State' at the end of 1989. This was the first major university-sponsored conference on North Africa to be held in Britain and was held at a time when the political outlook in North Africa appeared to be more hopeful than it had been for many years. Several months before, in February 1989, the Maghreb Arab Union had been inaugurated at a Maghrebi heads-of-state meeting in Marrakesh; in the wake of severe rioting in October 1988, Algeria had, in March 1989, begun the process of political liberalisation which was to lead to multiparty municipal elections in June 1990 and to legislative elections in December 1991; Tunisia was still seeking a path to political liberalisation in the wake of the removal of President Bourguiba from power in November 1987; Libya was beginning its own process of political liberalisation after the collapse of its military intervention in Northern Chad in March 1987; and Morocco, by then well along the path to economic reform, was anticipating a final solution to the Western Saharan conflict.

All the states concerned had spent the intervening period since independence engrossed in the process of nation-building as a means of buttressing the legitimacy of the regimes that controlled them. The crumbling of the single-party systems that had controlled Algeria and Tunisia – a process which was to prove to be rapid in Algeria but much slower in Tunisia – was partnered by the easing of the radical ideological rigours of the *jamāhiriyyah* in Libya and by the growing awareness in Morocco that the devolution of power would be essential to preserve the state, particularly if the Western Saharan conflict were resolved in its favour. In short, it seemed clear that the maximal political unit in North Africa was to be the nation-state, particularly when North African leaders demonstrated considerable constitutional caution in designing the Maghreb Arab Union as a confederation of states. It thus seemed an appropriate moment to consider the status of the concept of the nation-state in the region.

Of course, events since the conference was held have not fully accorded with those earlier hopes. Tunisia has still not found a suitable formula for integrating different currents within its national political life, particularly those linked to Islam, and the Ben Ali regime cannot, therefore, relax its grip on the political process there. In Libya, despite the generally liberalised atmosphere, the Qadhdhāfī regime seems as dependent as ever on the retribalisation of political life as its own guarantee of survival, with the result that issues of legitimacy and nation-building have stagnated. In Algeria, the unanticipated electoral successes of the Front Islamique du Salut, with the implied threat that it would create an 'Islamic state' once it had achieved power, produced an army-backed coup which was designed to re-assert the original sovereign assumptions for which the Algerian War of Independence had been fought. In Morocco, international pressure had persuaded the government to address claims of human rights abuses, but the crisis over the Western Sahara lingered on.

Behind all these specific circumstances loomed the still uncertain implications of the United Nations-sponsored and United States-led intervention against Iraq's invasion and annexation of Kuwait between August 1990 and March 1991. Although Morocco had initially warmly supported the initiatives of the Bush administration, a position which – surprisingly enough – was later more cautiously endorsed by Libya, the Moroccan government soon backed off from open involvement and, eventually, joined with its partners in the Maghreb Arab Union in unsuccessfully seeking a negotiated settlement to the crisis. Indeed, Tunisia had been openly critical of the American initiative and Algeria preserved a chilly silence. This general reticence over the crisis in the Gulf was the result of the virtually universal popular rejection of the actions of the United Nations and the West and its conservative Arab allies and indicated the degree to which North African governments had become susceptible to public opinion by the beginning of the 1990s. In other words, the role of the nation-state as a vehicle of political legitimisation has not waned in North Africa and, although recent events were not anticipated by the participants in the original conference, the issues that they addressed remain as acute as ever.

The chapters in this volume fall into four discrete groups relating to the pre-colonial and colonial periods of state formation in North Africa and to the independence period – Libya obtained independence through United Nations action in 1951, Tunisia and Morocco achieved independence from their statuses as French protectorates in 1956 and Algeria, which had been politically integrated into France after 1870, endured an eight-year war to force the French government under Charles de Gaulle to grant it independence in 1962. Since independence, however, the development of the independent states has culminated since 1989 in the creation of a regional framework for political and economic collaboration. It is still not clear whether this will ripen into full integration; indeed, an earlier experience, sponsored by the United Nations Economic Commission for Africa and placed under the auspices of the Permanent Maghreb Consultative Committee during the 1960s which collapsed in 1969, offers plenty of grounds for caution. None the less, it is clear that the motivations behind the Maghreb Arab Union involve a common desire to confront the growing economic power of Europe through the EEC and the development of the Single European Market and a realisation that struggles between the two major states of North Africa – Algeria and Morocco – for regional hegemony will be in the long run to the disadvantage of all states involved. These considerations alone provide some hope that the latest experiment in regional collaboration will be more successful than its predecessor, largely, no doubt, because those involved are prepared to exercise far more caution.

Four of the chapters deal directly with these issues. Dr Mohamed Chtatou outlines the background to the formation of the Union and indicates the popular hopes embodied in the initiative undertaken in February 1989. Dr John Damis, who has devoted much of his attention in the past to issues involving regional tensions, turns his attention here to the potential for the Union as a vehicle for the defusing of regional tension. Indeed, it could be argued that this should ultimately be the most important outcome of the Maghreb Arab Union experiment and, as such, would have the greatest significance for the states of North Africa. If, indeed, the Union becomes a permanent element within the political and diplomatic structures of the region and serves primarily as a legitimate forum for dissipating intra-regional tensions and conflict, it will have done so only because the four states involved in it have been prepared to cede to it a portion of their national sovereignty; namely, the absolute right of states to handle their external affairs in whatever way they see fit. Normally, only states with complete confidence in their individual domestic

political and economic stability are prepared to make such concessions in any meaningful sense and such a move on the part of North
Africa's emerging states would, therefore, be a very significant
comment on the success of the process of state formation in the
region.

Another chapter in this section, by Professor Remy Leveau, investigates the actual nature of the state in the Maghreb in terms of
colonial influences and the threats to its survival since independence.
Professor Leveau is particularly anxious to demonstrate that the
nascent Islamic movements do not necessarily threaten the North
African state, particularly if they are prepared to participate in the
democratic process. Indeed, he argues that the innate role of Islamic
values inside the regions should make moderate political Islam a
peculiarly appropriate vehicle for pluralistic political systems in the
future in what he calls the 'arbitrator-state'. The final contribution, by
Dr Ali Bahaijoub, seeks to explain an alternative approach to the
problem of state stability – namely, Morocco's attempt to join the
EEC. This, he points out, is not only an attempt to counter the economic consequences of the development of the Single European
Market after 1992 – which will penalise south Mediterranean expor-
ters to Europe, such as Morocco and Tunisia. It is also a statement
over official views of the stability of the state and over the success of
Morocco's pluralistic political system, since member-states of the
EEC must have democratic political systems with proper legal guarantees of human rights.

Indeed, the success of the processes of nation-building and state
formation in independent North Africa have preoccupied several
contributors. Salem Mezhoud describes the role played by the Berberist movement in Algeria in forcing the Chadli Ben Jedid regime to
recognise the pluralism inherent in Algerian society at a cultural level
and, implicitly, at a political level as well. This consideration is underlined by Dr Youssef Selmane in his description of the role of popular
theatre in Algeria as a vehicle of cultural and political protest which
uses techniques that stretch back to the early days of Islam in the
Fertile Crescent. The longevity of the Front de Libération Nationale
(FLN) as a forum for Algerian political aspirations and the role of the
army as guarantor of the Algerian state, both depending on the
informal political culture of Kabylia, is the theme of Dr Hugh
Roberts's analysis of the political significance of the recent changes in
Algeria's domestic political scene. Similarly, Dr Rachida Yacine
examines the way in which the language debate has influenced the
process of nation-building throughout the region.

Another aspect of the role of indigenous culture on the political process is highlighted by Dr Henry Munson in his analysis of the significance of political Islam in Morocco. He points out that political Islam in Morocco – whether radical or moderate – is unable to threaten the position of the monarchy because it, too, is a formidable competitor for religious legitimacy as '*Amir al-mu'minīn*' and '*Imām*' and because of his innate *baraka*. By implication, therefore, he underlines the problems faced by government in Algeria and Tunisia, which enjoys no such innate legitimacy and raises questions over the accuracy of Professor Leveau's thesis of the potentially positive role for political Islam within a pluralistic political process. Unhappily, recent events in Algeria seem to bear out Dr Munson's implied critique, although the collective presidency in Algeria may well contemplate the re-introduction of a restricted democratic process along the lines proposed by Professor Leveau. At the same time, Dr Richard Pennell in an interesting comparison of the evolution of the development of the state in Libya and Morocco, underlines the role played by history in determining modern political behaviour. He thereby emphasises the role of a traditional political culture of the kind found in Morocco but which is missing in Algeria in ensuring political stability – a point also made by Dr Munson.

Indeed, it is the issue of continuity that links the remaining chapters in this volume to those described above that deal with the postcolonial era. Jon Marks, in an analysis of the resistance of the Beni Mzab to integration into French-controlled Algeria after 1882, points out that, although there may not have been fully-fledged nationalist movements until relatively late in the twentieth century (although this was not the case in Tunisia, where the Neo-Destour began to operate before the Second World War), there were continuing traditions of rejection of French rule and a growing sense of protonationalist identification that mirrored the dual patterns of primary and secondary resistance identified in Africa south of the Sahara. Perhaps the best-known example of this – and not discussed in this volume for precisely that reason – was the Rif war in Morocco between 1921 and 1926.

There was, however, another side to the process of state formation and to the development of modernist nationalist movements in the region during the colonial period – namely, the attitudes adopted towards the indigenous populations and to their increasingly overt aspirations towards independence by the colonial powers involved. These reactions are the concern of three other chapters. John Wright discusses the complex evolution of British policy towards Libyan independence after 1943 which was determined by London's perceptions of Libya's strategic significance. These, in the end, persuaded the British government that Libyan independence under a Sanusi monarchy would be the best option. It was a fateful decision, for it contributed directly to the radicalisation of the Libyan political scene and the creation of the *jamāhiriyyah*. Professor William Hoisington underlines how French colonial politicians failed to understand the nature of popular rejection of assimilation into France and the French 'Mission Civilisatrice'. It was this rejection throughout the French colonial empire in North Africa that not only made the development of national movements of independence possible, but also set the scene, ultimately, for Maghrebi assumptions of a regional identity that were eventually to surface in the creation of the Maghreb Arab Union. Claire Spencer, in an intriguing analysis of the Spanish decision in 1940 to occupy the international city of Tangier, underlines how quarrels between colonial powers also had a role to play in the formulation of indigenous demands for independence.

The North African state, however, often pre-dates the colonial period, as the remaining three chapters in this book illustrate. Dr Jerome Bookin-Weiner discusses the role played by the corsairing centres along the Moroccan coastline during the latter years of the Saʿādian dynasty in forging a resistance to the European presence there. He also describes the general state of *fitnā* within Morocco at the time, which the Alawite sultanate crushed in the late seventeenth century as part of its own contribution to state-formation in Morocco, a tradition that has continued up to the present day. Dr Mohammed Kenbib turns his attention to Moroccan reactions to the French occupation of Western Algeria, particularly to the consequences of Morocco's defeat at the battle of Isly in 1845. He suggests that, after the initial Moroccan response in support of the Emir Adbelkader, the presence of a large body of Algerian immigrants on Moroccan territory between 1845 and 1912 caused a political alienation between the two communities and the growth of a more modern sense of secular nationalism. Dr Abdeljelil Temimi, in discussing the role played by Tunisian diplomatic representatives abroad in the formulation of Tunisian foreign and commercial policy in the early years of the nineteenth century, highlights the level of interaction that already existed in the pre-colonial period with the otherwise alien Christian Mediterranean world. He also points out that European ideas had begun to percolate throughout the area long before colonialism arrived and that this aspect of North Africa's precolonial history requires more objective historical study.

In short, the processes of nation-building and state formation had begun in North Africa long before colonialism. In some areas, such as Morocco, coastal Algeria and Tunisia, this process had been evolving for several centuries beforehand. There is little doubt, however, that the colonial experience gave a powerful impetus to both processes and, at the same time defined the modern states that were to develop there after the colonial period had ended. Since independence, each of the states has evolved in a unique fashion, although all of them have continued to be profoundly marked by the colonial experience and have had to give priority attention to the process of nation-building in order to legitimise the regimes that had been created. At the same time, as the early hopes of independence faded, the concept of regional identity has been revived as a means of allowing the independent states to collaborate in solving their own problems and in presenting a common front to an increasingly difficult international environment. This book is designed to be a small contribution to the understanding of this process.

Part I
The pre-colonial period

1 Corsairing in the economy and politics of North Africa

Jerome Bookin-Weiner

Corsair raiding by the so-called 'Barbary pirates' in the early modern period has long been the subject of romantic tales, popular fiction, and popular history. Blood-curdling tales of rape, pillage and slavery by the 'Mussulmans' of North Africa were standard fare in Europe and North America from the sixteenth century right up to our own day. In the late nineteenth century first-hand and fictionalised tales of woe gave way to popular histories, and even today one finds accounts of the 'Barbary pirates' on remainder lists. The overall impression created by this body of literature has created the popular view that North African history from the sixteenth century through the Napoleonic era is primarily, if not exclusively, that of the corsairs. Moreover, the popular histories lead their readers to the conclusion that the corsairs dominated the politics and economic life in North Africa during that period.

In this chapter we shall examine these issues with special reference to the situation in Morocco, particularly during the period of greatest corsair activity there; the middle years of the seventeenth century. Relations between the corsairs and the economic and political life of the hinterland will be considered, as will comparative examples from Algiers, Tunis, and Tripoli.

Corsair raiding from Moroccan ports, specifically out of Rabat–Salé, was a product of a conjuncture of circumstances in the second quarter of the seventeenth century. The meeting of Mediterranean corsairs, European pirates, and a group of people expelled from their homeland and unable to gain acceptance from their new neighbours, combined with increasing naval traffic in the Atlantic to favour the corsairs and their activities. Yet, the decisive factors governing the scope and intensity of corsair activity were the corsairs' relationship to other political forces in Morocco, the interrelationship of the various groups inhabiting Rabat–Salé, and the type and efficacy of

3

European diplomacy and countermeasures. The corsairs' periods of greatest activity coincided with the periods of their greatest independence from outside political forces and least internal strife in Rabat-Salé. Periods of decreased activity generally coincided with strong domination or discord in Rabat-Salé or followed forceful English, Dutch, or French diplomacy and countermeasures.

In this chapter we shall examine the relationship of Rabat-Salé with the Saʿādī dynasty and the regional and political-religious factions which affected developments there. The relations between the three groups inhabiting Rabat-Salé will be examined further, with special reference to their effect on corsair activity and Rabat-Salé's relations with the Moroccan polity in general. Similarly, we shall look at the European interventions and their effect on internal relations in Rabat-Salé, the corsairs, and Rabat-Salé's position in Morocco generally.

UNDER THE SAʿADIS (TO 1626)

Under Mulay ʿAbd al-Malik and Mulay Ahmad al-Mansur a small corsair fleet existed in Rabat-Salé. European sources speak of seven or eight ships operating in that period. Presumably this official corsair fleet engaged in *jihād* against the Spanish. Financed and outfitted by the *makhzan*, they probably paid the sultan his Qurʾānic due of 20 per cent of the booty and slaves.[1]

With the accession of England's King James I in 1603, and his outlawing of piracy from English ports, the European freebooters of all nationalities who had sheltered on the English and Irish coasts collected along the Moroccan coast. Their activities flourished without interference because of Saʿādī preoccupation with the succession struggle following al-Mansur's death. These pirates, animated by a hatred for Spain, knew no life other than privateering and harassing Spanish naval activity.[23] Unwilling to abandon the fight against Spain or to renounce piracy, they continued to capture Spanish ships and sell their cargoes in Moroccan ports. The pirates' acts frequently prejudiced their governments' relations with the Saʿādī's *makhzan* and led to repeated requests to curb their activities.[2] In March 1606, Mulay Abu Faris warned the Dutch ambassador to Marrakesh that he must stop the Dutch from committing 'acts of insolence in the harbours of the Moroccan coast which cause complaints from other nations,'[3] presumably Spain, whom the Moroccans did not wish to offend. The Spanish meanwhile, apparently carried out raids – either privateering or on land – against Morocco. The galley rowers on a

Spanish ship seized by the Dutch in 1604 were Moroccans whom the Dutch returned to the Saʿādīs when they sent an ambassador to Marrakesh in 1605.[4]

In the spring of 1607, the States General of the United Provinces of The Netherlands sent a fleet to chase the pirates from the Moroccan coast. They met no great success with the English pirates, and the States General complained to the English king in 1607 and sent another squadron to the Moroccan coast the following summer.[5] The English themselves also tried to act against the English pirates. In June 1610, Samuel Cade was imprisoned at Southwark for piracy after he seized and looted the *Suzan* of Bristol in Safi harbour.[6] Englishmen and Dutchmen constituted a majority of the European pirates along the Moroccan coast in the first decade and a half of the seventeenth century. The case of Samuel Cade, who seized an English ship, would appear to be a rare exception to the rule that the pirates spared the ships of their own nations. The Dutch pirates concentrated on Spanish and English ships and the English on Spanish and Dutch, while both also took French prizes.[7] The English pirates headquartered at al-Maʿmūra on the mouth of the Wadi Sabu. In 1610, John Harrison reported that twenty-two pirate ships arrived there at one time along with their prizes. The following year, Sir Ferdinando Gorges reported more than forty pirate ships with over 2,000 men. At the time Spain seized al-Maʿmūra in 1614, the pirates' leader was Henry Maynwaringe, who began his naval career in 1611 cruising against the pirates in the Bristol Channel under commission from the Lord Admiral. Two years later he became a pirate himself, operating out of al-Maʿmūra for two years. His stated intention was to 'carry on an indiscriminate warfare against the Spaniards'. Maynwaringe remained true to his native land, restricting his attacks to the ships of other nations. He even went so far as to restore booty proved to be taken from the English.[8]

On 8 August 1614, the Spanish seized al-Maʿmūra while Maynwaringe and his cohorts were on a cruise which took them to Newfoundland.[9] The Saʿādī *makhzan* was by now so weakened by more than a decade of succession struggle and so engrossed in its own struggle for survival that it was powerless to oppose either the pirates who sheltered at al-Maʿmūra or Spain's seizure of the port in 1614. Mulay Zaydan could only attempt to counter Spain's designs by encouraging the Dutch to move in before the Spanish. Spain, in fact, seized al-Maʿmūra only a few weeks before a projected joint Dutch–Moroccan action.[10] At this point the Saʿādī *makhzan* had no navy of its own. One of Mulay Zaydan's objectives in promoting friendly relations with the Dutch in 1610 was to secure the construction of several ships in The Netherlands and create a navy.[11] Although the States General permitted three ships to be built for Zaydan, the Spanish destroyed them before he could use them.[12] When Mulay Zaydan fled from Abu Mahalli to the coast in the spring of 1612 he still had no ships of his own and had to charter French and Dutch ships to carry his entourage and possessions to Agadir.

Thus, during the first decade and a half of the seventeenth century, the naval raiding conducted from Moroccan shores had no direct relation to the *makhzan* or any other internal Moroccan political faction. They also played no role in Moroccan economic life other than to provide a rather minor source of foreign goods. In this period the raiders were European pirates, many of them former privateers. They continued to practise the only vocation they knew: naval raiding. They sheltered and sold their prizes to European and Moroccan Jewish merchants in ports along the Moroccan coast, but had no connection with Morocco.

As a result of their expulsion from Spain, a large influx of Morisco refugees arrived in Morocco during the years 1609–14. The exact sequence of events which brought a large number of them to Rabat–Salé is unclear, but in 1619 Moriscos guided corsairs in their raids along the Spanish coasts.[13] When Zaydan regained Marrakesh from Abu Mahalli in 1614, the people of Salé immediately sought his assistance against the Spanish in al-Ma'mūra. According to the *Chronique anonyme de la dynastie Sa'dienne*, the Slawis soon despaired of getting meaningful aid, despite Zaydan's promises, and turned to Sidi Mahammad al-Ayyāshī instead.[14] So it seems likely that the Moriscos were installed in Rabat before 1614, because al-Ifrani mentions that Zaydan tried to use them to capture al-Ayyāshī after he evaded capture at Azammur and assumed leadership of the *jihad* against al-Ma'mūra. Zaydan's *qā'id* in Rabat's *qaṣba*, Abd al-Aziz az-Za'rūrī warned the Morisco sheikhs who forewarned and protected al-Ayyāshī. Zaydan levied 400 troops from among the Moriscos at Rabat and sent them to the Dra'a valley, probably during Abu Mahalli's rebellion, but perhaps as late as 1617. When that campaign dragged on, the majority of the Moriscos deserted Zaydan, returned to Rabat, and, according to al-Ifrani, developed a dislike for az-Za'rūrī and Mulay Zaydan. We know that the final break between Zaydan and the Moriscos in Rabat, which al-Ifrani ascribes to another levy of troops for a new Dra'a campaign, took place in the period 1626–7.[15]

In the intervening years, the corsairs of Rabat–Salé established themselves and made their initial impact on naval traffic in the Atlantic. Although Rabat–Salé pledged allegiance to Mulay Zaydan, it is evident that he did not exercise effective control there. On 8 August 1617, when corsair raiding from Rabat–Salé, under the joint leadership of European renegades and Moriscos, was just beginning, the Dutchman, Abbé Willemzoon noted that 'not placing any value on the King's authority, they will take possession of everything they can seize'.[16] When another Dutch captain, Albert Ruyl, visited Rabat–Salé a little more than five years later he found that people there bluntly told him they did not hold the sultan in high regard.[17] Zaydan himself credited the Moriscos and Andalusians he had installed in the *qaṣba* – 1,500 of them according to Ruyl[18] – with preserving Rabat–Salé as part of his territory.[19] Yet Zaydan did not meet his obligations to pay them, and they, in turn, kept all the revenue from their corsair raiding. Occasionally they sent him a few slaves. The Qurʾānic twenty per cent of the booty due to the sultan went to his *qāʾid* az-Zaʿrūrī, who also collected taxes on merchandise sold in Rabat–Salé and harvests in the neighbouring fields. Renegade corsairs in Rabat–Salé told Ruyl that the large share of the booty collected by the *qāʾid* and his secretary meant that they would encourage increased corsair activity.[20] Later, in 1623, Ruyl learned in Marrakesh that when Mulay Zaydan asked az-Zaʿrūrī to send him some Christian slaves the *qāʾid* responded, 'if his majesty wants to have slaves he must first send some money'.[21]

In August 1624, Mulay Zaydan lost whatever residual control he may have had over the corsairs when he named Dutch renegade Morat Rais *qabṭān* of the fleet. That this act should have cost him any control is not as strange as it seems, because Morat demanded and received a letter patent from Zaydan granting him complete freedom of action.[22] Almost immediately Rabat–Salé became a more active corsair centre. Morat used his far-reaching powers to protect his Dutch countrymen from the corsairs. As a result, Dutch sources do not reflect the increase in the extent and intensity of corsair activity. The French, on the other hand, noted that a large portion of the damage done by the corsairs, in terms of ships and men captured and trade disrupted, affected them. The English records detail the severe disruption caused in the Newfoundland fishing fleet in 1625 and 1626. Spain must also have suffered greatly from the increase in corsair activity.[23]

In addition to the corsairs who set out from Rabat–Salé in the years 1625–7, Algerine corsairs and European pirates also brought their prizes and captives there. They came and went freely without any obligations other than payment of the established taxes on the prizes they sold.[24] During the period of Saʿādī control, the corsairs and pirates operating from Morocco's Atlantic ports had no direct connection with the events going on around them. Saʿādī weakness prevented the *makhzan* from taking any concerted action against the European pirates in the first two decades of the century. By the early 1620s, the *makhzan*'s representatives in Rabat–Salé nominally controlled the corsairs and their activities, but the control was more form than substance. The *makhzan* could not impose its will on the corsairs. They accepted Saʿādī suzerainty passively and did not actively participate in the tribal and factional alliance system which formed the basis of the Moroccan political system. Consequently the corsairs could act entirely on their own, without reference to the *makhzan* or its representatives.

ESTABLISHMENT OF THE INDEPENDENT DIWAN IN RABAT (1626–9)

When the *makhzan* attempted to assert itself in Rabat, the people revolted. The Moriscos living in the *qaṣba*, dominated by former residents of the Spanish town of Hornachos, played an active role in the outfitting of corsair ships and served as Zaydan's garrison. When the Sultan tried to levy troops from among them in 1625 to fight in the south, they revolted against him.[25] Several months later the Moriscos expelled az-Zaʿrūrī after sending John Harrison a letter telling him that they would 'shake off Mully Sidan's tyrannous government' if he would come to talk to them.[26] Sidi Mahammad al-Ayyāshī helped to spirit Harrison from Titwan to Salé. He travelled overland, dressed in Moroccan-style clothing, mostly on foot and by night, as a series of guides allied to al-Ayyāshī led him to Salé. When Harrison arrived there, the Moriscos asked him to wait while they deposed az-Zaʿrūrī.

The most obvious explanation for the break is that it resulted from the Moriscos' refusal to supply the troops levied for service in the Draʿa valley. None the less, two other factors may have contributed. Ruyl mentioned that in 1622 and 1623 Mulay Zaydan had failed to pay his garrisons regularly, and this may have antagonised them. Ruyl cited this as a cause of tension then. Conflict may also have arisen over booty and revenue from corsair activity. Az-Zaʿrūrī took 20 per cent of the booty and a 15 per cent tax on merchandise sold in Rabat. The Moriscos still apparently owed him tax monies when they expelled him, because one of Zaydan's reasons for sending the Spanish renegade *qāʾid* Ajib to Rabat the following year was to collect debts owed to az-Za'rūrī. When Harrison returned to Rabat in the spring of 1627, Ajib was there trying to reassert Mulay Zaydan's authority. Zaydan, according to Harrison, wanted the Moriscos to send Harrison to him, but they refused. Zaydan insisted, making the issue a test of the Moriscos' allegiance. They 'thereupon immediatlie dispatched his [Zaydan's] Alkaid [Ajib] awaie, who not far from the towne was robbed and slaine by the Lerbies [Arabs]'.[27]

The last formal tie between the Moriscos in Rabat and the Sa'ādī *makhzan* now broken, they established an independent government in the *qaṣba*, modelled after a Spanish town council and called *dīwān* in Arabic. The *dīwān*, composed entirely of residents of the *qaṣba*, assumed responsibility for control of the corsairs' activities, and Morat Rais seems to have retained his position as *qabṭān* for several years. On 10 May 1627, the *dīwān* and John Harrison initialled a draft treaty which prohibited the seizure of English ships and seamen.[28] As a consequence, French and Spanish ships suffered the majority of the losses to the corsairs in the next two years.

Mulay Zaydan died on 20 September 1627, shortly after the Moriscos threw his *qā'id-s* out of Rabat.[29] Until this revolt Rabat–Salé had been one of the rare areas which continually acknowledged his authority and did not require frequent pacification. Al-Ayyāshī already controlled much of the Gharb and areas to the north near Titwan. The Sa'ādī *makhzan*'s decay was well advanced. The loss of Rabat did not hasten the process. It is significant to note that the Moriscos established an autonomous city-state rather than joining with al-Ayyāshī. They chose to remain outside the traditional Moroccan alliance structure and continued to play a passive role in Moroccan politics.

The people of Salé remained hostile to the newcomers. They continued to regard the Moriscos as Christians. Al-Ayyāshī, on the other hand, maintained good relations with them. During the first half of May 1627, he raised a large army in the hope of getting English and Dutch assistance for an all-out land and sea attack on the Spanish *presidio* at al-Ma'mūra. When the Europeans begged off, he mounted a land attack anyhow. The attack failed to dislodge the Spaniards, but in the process al-Ayyāshī's men ran two Spanish supply galleys aground in Wadi Sabu and captured 800 men, arms, munitions, and other provisions. The Moriscos apparently participated in the attack, for they helped him remove eight artillery pieces and attempted to move them back to the *qaṣba*. When the Slawis heard this they attempted to bar the way, and a fight developed on the outskirts of Salé. The Moriscos routed their neighbours but, before they could sack Salé, al-Ayyāshī returned. He made peace, allowing the Moriscos to take the artillery. Harrison, who had taken six cannons to Rabat–Salé when he returned from London that spring, added to his account of the incident, tongue in cheek: 'So the King of Spaine can not now challenge Your Majesty for sending ordinance to Sallie, for he himsellff hath sent them ordinance against his will'.[30]

During the first years of the Morisco *dīwān*, corsair raiding from Rabat–Salé continued on an intensive level. English West Country mariners held a deep grudge against the Rabati corsairs for their attacks on Newfoundland fishing fleets in 1625 and 1626, and they occasionally attacked the corsairs in the Atlantic.[31] Yet the corsairs abstained from attacks on English ships and pleaded their case with the King. Charles I responded by issuing a proclamation putting English sailors on notice to cease attacking 'the persons, shipps, or goodes belonginge or which shall belong to Algier, Tunis, Tituan, Sallie, or anie other porte or parte of all the countries which are under the same government'.[32] The Dutch also escaped attack. Morat Rais remained *qabṭān* of the corsairs under the Morisco *dīwān*. Previously he had done his utmost to protect Dutch shipping and sailors from seizure and captivity and he continued to do so. On 12 August 1627, he wrote to the States General, 'until my death, I particularly want to favour my homeland, to help it, and to honour it. But I can do no more than I have done because the people here are in revolt against the King'.[33] Morat's influence combined with Dutch diplomacy and the Dutch reputation as an enemy of Spain to prevent the corsairs from carrying out any concerted actions against them.

BLOCKADE AND CIVIL STRIFE (1629–30)

While the corsairs generally spared the English and Dutch before 1630, they ravaged Spanish and French shipping and towns on the Spanish and French coasts, bringing prizes and captives back to Rabat.[34] Spain, deeply involved in European conflicts and in serious financial difficulties, did not, or could not, react against the corsairs. But in 1629 France did, with important consequences for the corsairs and internal affairs at Rabat–Salé. On 27 June 1629, Isaac de Razilly sailed with ten ships for the Moroccan coast under instructions to obtain the release of French captives. He arrived at Rabat–Salé on 20 July.[35] The *dīwān* in Rabat refused to deal with Razilly unless he presented them with arms and money – 100 cannons and one million livres. Hearing this, Razilly deployed his ships and blockaded the port cities. Razilly's squadron seized and burned seven corsair ships during the first month and a half of the blockade. It also freed a number of French and Spanish captives and took Moroccan captives as well.[36]

Civil war erupted in Rabat as a consequence of the losses Razilly and his squadron inflicted, the shortage of foodstuffs caused by the blockade, and the *dīwān*'s refusal to deal with Razilly in spite of the hardships he caused. After the Moriscos in the *qaṣba* seized control and declared themselves independent in 1627, word spread, and other Moriscos and Andalusians came to Rabat. These people depended on the trade and the commerce which corsair prizes brought to Rabat–Salé for their livelihoods, and on shipments from Asila and elsewhere for their food because independent Rabat lacked a hinterland. The blockade had choked off their livelihood and their lifeline by preventing entry of the English and Dutch traders and the supply ships from Asila. The *dīwān*'s refusal to consider their interests in this situation fomented violence by the Andalusians living outside the *qaṣba*.

But without heavy artillery they could not conquer the fortress. In order to repel the attacks, the *qaṣba*'s defenders opened fire on the city with their cannons. They fired intermittently for four days.[37] Nevertheless, circumstances forced the *dīwān* to face reality, and at the next opportunity they agreed to negotiate a truce with Razilly. On 2 October 1629, they signed a truce of five-months' duration. The terms included release of all French captives in Rabat–Salé, an end to the blockade and French harassment of Rabat–Salé's shipping, an end to corsair raids against the French, and free trading privileges for the French in Rabat and for Rabatis in France.[38]

Razilly's blockade had been successful. The English and Dutch had obtained peace by providing the *dīwān* with arms and munitions. At first the *dīwān* had attempted to extract similar terms from Razilly, but without success. Further, the blockade seriously weakened the corsairs in two ways. First, by seizing and burning some of their ships and imprisoning some of the corsairs, he effectively reduced the size of the fleet. The following year they armed only seventeen ships, the lowest number in years.[39] Second, the conflict Razilly's blockade triggered between the residents of the *qaṣba*, led by the *dīwān*, and those living outside the *qaṣba* intensified. It led to a change in the nature of the local government and continued strife until the Dila'is took over in 1641.

The following spring, when John Harrison returned, it became evident that the civil war had much deeper roots. The Moriscos from San Lucar, Cadiz, Llerena, and Hornachos dominated the *qaṣba*, with the Hornacheros as the single dominant element. After the

Moriscos seized control of the *qaṣba* in 1627 they had invited other refugees to join them in Rabat. But in Rabat the new arrivals found that the Moriscos in the *qaṣba* had no intention of sharing the fruits of their joint labours. The newcomers settled outside the *qaṣba*, built a new wall to enclose a section of the vast area encircled by the five-century-old Almohad wall, and shared with the Moriscos 'a proporcionable parte ... in all publique charges'.[40]

When Harrison arrived on 8 April 1630, he 'found all in *rebueltas*, the Castle and the Raval or town in cyvill dissencions one against the other'. The Andalusians now living in the city outnumbered the Moriscos in the *qaṣba* and demanded

> equall share and part with them of the Castle, both in the govern-
> ment, customs, and other profittes and priviledges ... [and that] 50
> of the chief of the Castle to come and live with them in the towne,
> and 50 of their owne in the towne...

The Moriscos refused these demands and trained their cannons on the city again, thinking they could 'bring the towne altogether into subjection and to their owne bowe'. But the construction of the houses made cannon-fire minimally effective. Meanwhile the Andalusians, who had only one small cannon, used it effectively against boats plying between the *qaṣba* and Salé, which supplied the *qaṣba* with food. The Moriscos, in turn, had sent all their horses across to Salé, and now paid some of Salé's horsemen as well. They 'often sallied over at a forde up the river, and offended the towne, taking their cattle and other provisions with them'.[41]

Harrison found himself welcomed by both factions in Rabat. At the suggestion of some of the leaders of both factions he attempted to arrange a settlement. Aware that one of the functions of *murābiṭ-s* was peacemaking, he wrote to Sidi Mahammad al-Ayyāshī asking him to mediate. But the *'ulamā'* was engaged in an attack against Tangier and could not respond quickly. A short time later, Morat Rais returned from Tunis, bringing with him a *murābiṭ* who lived in the old Roman settlement and Marini *qaṣba* of Shalla just outside the Almohad wall. This *murābiṭ* assumed the role of mediator and arranged a settlement between Moriscos and Andalusians. The mediation took the form of binding arbitration in which the *murābiṭ* gained the assent of both sides to his decision before issuing it. He did so by threatening that whichever party broke the agreement would become his enemy and that the neighbouring Arab tribes would subject them to attacks. Henceforth each faction elected a *qā'id* and eight members of the *dīwān* for a total of two *qā'id-s* and sixteen members of the *dīwān*. The *qāʾid-s* both lived in the *qaṣba*, where the *dīwān* held its sessions. They shared taxes and revenues and burdens and profits proportionally.[42] For the next six years this system apparently worked well, for the sources report no further internal troubles in Rabat until 1636.

SIDI MAHAMMAD AL-AYYASHI AND THE CORSAIRS (1630–5)

No sooner had the internal problems between the Moriscos and Andalusians in Rabat been resolved than difficulties began with Sidi Mahammad al-Ayyāshī. The *mujāhid* had welcomed the Moriscos' rebellion against Mulay Zaydan from 1626–7 because he himself refused to recognise Mulay Zaydan's authority. His role in the Moriscos' break with Zaydan was such that Harrison informed Charles I that by al-Ayyāshī's 'countenance and assistance the Andaluzes have prevailed at Salley'.[43] Yet in 1630, Harrison wrote that the *murābiṭ* was 'no great frinde to Salley'.[44]

In the interim, al-Ayyāshī, for whom *jihād* against the Spanish *presidios* was an obsession, must have discovered the Rabatis' ambivalence towards Spain. In fact, the Moriscos never despaired of returning to their former homes. Early in 1619, Jorge Mascarenhas, Spanish governor of Mazagan, met one of them who came to the *presidio* on a ship sent by Mulay Zaydan. When he asked the Morisco about Spain, it brought tears to the man's eyes as he told the governor that he was a Christian and still wanted to die in Spain. Mascarenhas also felt from his discussion that the Moriscos were prepared to cede Rabat to the Spaniards.[45] Every European who discussed their beliefs with them came away with the impression that the Moriscos still felt more Christian than Muslim, an impression that their Muslim neighbours in Salé turned into an accusation. A French priest wrote to the Vatican in 1625 that many of the Moriscos remained Christians.[46] The same year, John Harrison in Titwan found the Moriscos there 'alreadie Christians in heart, most of them'.[47] Two years later, in Rabat, he had much the same feeling about the Moriscos there who faced death for professing Christianity, 'yet manie have to me'.[48] In 1630, Francois d'Angers, a Redemptionist priest, wrote that 'the majority of them were still Christians in their souls'.[49]

Harrison noted in 1627 that Mulay Zaydan aroused the Slawis against the Moriscos by alleging 'that they have a secrette plot to deliver the Castle into Your Majesties [Charles I] hands and become Christians, and Sallie to be the rendevous for all the Moriscos dispersed in all Barbarie'.[50] No available evidence supports Zaydan's claim at that date, but by 1631 the Moriscos showed a desire to return to Spain. It seems possible that this desire was a prime motive force behind an important aspect of their corsair raiding. They hoped to induce Spain to permit them to return to their former homes by becoming so bothersome that the Spanish king would be forced to permit their return in order to put a stop to their raids.

Another factor in their desire to return to Spain was the state of their relations with Sidi Mahammad al-Ayyāshī after the settlement of the civil war in Rabat in 1630. According to Arab and European sources, they refused to aid the *mujāhid* in attacks against al-Ma'mūra and al-Araish. Al-Ifrani says they procrastinated in complying with his request to build ladders for an assault on the walls of al-Ma'mūra until reinforcements arrived in the garrison, making it useless to attempt the action. Furthermore, al-Ayyāshī accused the Moriscos of giving intelligence information to the Spaniards defending al-Ma'mūra. A Spanish source also tells us that the Moriscos of the *qaṣba* did not help al-Ayyāshī during his siege of al-Ma'mūra in 1631. This gave the *mujāhid* further incentive to conquer the *presidio* in order to use it to diminish the wealth and power of the Moriscos.[51]

Over the next several years, the conflicts between al-Ayyāshī and the Rabatis grew as he gained new evidence of their aid to the Spaniards. He consulted the *'ulamā'* to determine whether the passing of intelligence to the Christians constituted sufficient grounds to fight against the Rabatis. In delivering his *fatwa* (Islamic legal opinion) against the Rabatis, one of the *'ulamā'* added to the enumeration of their sins the fact that they kept all the revenues from corsair activity, restricted others' participation in trade, and helped the Christians by supplying them with food. Other *'ulamā'* concurred, and violence broke out between al-Ayyāshī and the Rabatis. In July 1631, al-Ayyāshī laid siege to the *qaṣba* from his own fortress south-west of Salé. Al-Ayyāshī's cannons served two purposes: besieging the *qaṣba* and controlling the entry of ships into the harbour. Meanwhile his son 'Abd Allah led attacks against the city and *qaṣba* from the area of Shalla. Al-Ayyāshī's initial clash with the *qaṣba* and city continued for about a year without a decisive result.[52]

In 1631, the Moriscos and Andalusians also came into renewed contact with the Sa'ādī *makhzen.* When Mulay Zaydan died in September 1627, and his son Mulay 'Abd al-Malik succeeded him in Marrakesh, Mulay al-Walid, another of Zaydan's sons, fled Marrakesh after a defeat at his brother's hands.[53] Al-Walid's mother was a Morisco, expelled from Spain and taken as a wife by Mulay Zaydan.

For this reason, when he went to seek refuge with al-Ayyāshī, the *mujāhid* had sent him to Rabat 'to receive him for their King ... but they refused, making excuse his elder brother was King of Morocco and they durst not, or rather intending (as before) to make themselves a free state'.[54] Soon after leaving Rabat–Salé, al-Walid was betrayed to his brother who imprisoned him in the *qaṣba* of Marrakesh for the remainder of his reign. When a French renegade killed Mulay ʿAbd al-Malik in March 1631, al-Walid succeeded him. The Rabatis feared that after Mulay al-Walid became sultan he would ally with al-Ayyāshī to destroy them in order to repay their lack of kindness.[55]

The Moriscos faced the hostility of their neighbours in Salé, of the surrounding Arab tribes who treated them as Christians, of Sidi Mahammad al-Ayyāshī, and Mulay al-Walid. This hostility coupled with their Christian sentiments and desire to return to their former homes in Spain led the Rabatis, particularly the Hornacheros, to enter into negotiations with the Spanish. They wanted to return to Spain and deliver the *qaṣba* into Spanish hands. In 1631 the Hornacheros proposed a treaty to King Felipe IV (1621–65). It envisioned their return to Hornachos, active membership in the Roman Catholic Church (subject to the regulations and judgments of the Inquisition), and return of their children taken from them at the time of their expulsion. They proposed to turn the *qaṣba* over to Spain, complete with its artillery and any merchandise in it at the time, and to bring themselves and their possessions to Seville in their corsair ships, which they would turn over to the King for his navy.[56]

Although these plans never came to fruition, negotiations did not cease. By June 1633 they had reached agreement on a secret treaty. Arthur Hopton, the English ambassador in Madrid, wrote on 6 June 1633 that such a treaty had been concluded and that the Spaniards had written to the Pope to ask for his assent to taking back the recently expelled Moriscos.[57] Evidently the Pope did not give his assent, for in 1637 we still find the Moriscos negotiating 'to deliver the towne into the King of Spaines hands'.[58] The negotiations with Spain came at a time when the Rabatis and their corsairs fell under pressures from al-Ayyāshī, neighbouring tribes, and the Saʿādī sultan Mulay al-Walid. The latter tried to reassert his ultimate authority over them throughout his reign, but had only one notable success: in 1635 he compelled them to accept the treaty he signed with the French.[59]

In this period of turmoil, the corsairs were almost totally inactive. Dutch sources reveal two prizes of Dutch origin taken by the corsairs – and later released – and two corsair vessels taken by Dutch ships between 1630 and 1634.[60] Before 1635, the English were definitely more sinning than sinned against by the corsairs. Repeated attacks against corsair ships by English pirates threatened to bring the corsairs down on English shipping once again. The most serious incident took place in 1631. In accordance with Charles I's 1628 proclamation forbidding hostile acts against the Rabat–Salé corsairs, Harrison had given certificates to the corsairs along with copies of the proclamation. When Thomas Maddock stopped a corsair in 1631 the latter showed him Harrison's certificate and the King's proclamation. Maddock took the 'certyficat and wiped his tayle with it', according to Dutch and English renegades in Rabat.[61] He then proceeded to seize the corsair ship and crew, selling them into bondage in Spain for a small sum of money.[62] Despite repeated protests and threats, four years passed before the corsairs began to take revenge by renewing their attacks on English ships.[63]

The long period of inactivity, particularly the tardy response to English provocation, indicates that the corsairs felt the effects of the Moriscos' conflict with al-Ayyāshī and their neighbours. Between 1630 and 1635 the size of the fleet changed little – Captain Pallot reported seventeen ships in 1630 and Pierre-Priam du Chalard twenty-two in 1635.[64] Given the conflict with al-Ayyāshī and the decline in activity, it seems probable that the numbers were much lower in the intervening years. Only France, and undoubtedly Spain as well, seems to have suffered at all from attacks, for in July 1634 Antoine Cabiron reported more than 300 French captives in Rabat–Salé.[65]

CALM AND THE FINAL STORM (1635–40)

By 1635, peace reigned in Rabat–Salé. The corsairs began to return to the seas in force. English shipping, spared reprisal for long-standing grievances, felt their muscle. In 1635 and 1636, large numbers of Rabat–Salé corsairs came to England's coasts. They renewed their attacks on the Newfoundland fishing fleets after a hiatus of nine years. In 1635 they took between 150 and 200 captives, and many more the following year. Estimates of the number of English captives in Rabat–Salé in 1636 ran as high as 1,200, which may be two and half times the actual number. At the same time Dutch seizures of Rabat–Salé ships showed a dramatic increase in 1635, with at least seven cases recorded. The French joined in the following year, capturing at least two corsair ships.[66]

Thus, for a second time corsair activity reached a peak in a period of peace among the factions in Rabat–Salé. For eight years internal strife, a blockade, and conflict with Sidi Mahammad al-Ayyāshī diverted attention and energy from corsair raiding. The fleet could not operate freely. Now the corsairs could again cruise the Atlantic with a large degree of freedom. By March 1637, the fleet that du Chalard had placed at twenty-two in 1635 had more than doubled in size, with twenty-four earmarked for a cruise off the English and Irish coasts.[67]

But once again the corsairs flourished only briefly. In August or September 1636, renewed trouble broke out in Rabat. The Andalusians of the town once again pressed grievances against the Hornachero-dominated population of the *qaṣba*. The cause of the trouble is not clear, but probably related once again to the distribution of revenues and booty from corsair raiding. The conflict resumed when a group from the city, led by ʿAbd Allah bin ʿAlī al-Qasari, expelled the Hornacheros from the *qaṣba* and set themselves up there. According to one report, the rebels banished the leaders of the Hornachero community who fled to Algiers and Tunis. Apparently drunk with his newly won power, al-Qasari soon laid siege to Salé. He crossed the river with his cannons on a bridge of boats. But Sidi-Mahammad al-Ayyāshī quickly returned from one of his campaigns to repulse the initial attack, sending al-Qasari back across the Bu Raqraq. Then, together with forces supplied by Muhammad al-Hajj ad-Dilai, al-Ayyāshī laid siege to Rabat, destroying crops in the surrounding areas as well.[68]

On 3 April 1637, an English squadron commanded by William Rainsborough arrived in Rabat–Salé. Its purpose was to suppress the corsairs and secure the release of English captives. In addition to attempting to blockade the estuary, Rainsborough entered into negotiations with al-Ayyāshī, which led to a treaty which they signed on 18 Dhu al-Hijja 1046/13 May 1637.[69] In the treaty Rainsborough agreed to aid the *murābiṭ* during the siege of Rabat. He blockaded the port and sent men into Salé to aid movement and make use of his artillery. Faced with al-Ayyāshī's force of 15,000–20,000 men assaulting them by land, burning and cutting off food supplies, and Rainsborough's blockade which prevented relief from the Atlantic side, the people in Rabat began to divide into three groups: those supporting al-Qasari; those supporting rapprochement with al-Ayyāshī; and those favouring submission to the Saʿādī Sultan Mulay Muhammad ash-Sheikh al-Asghar. For twenty days they debated their options before deciding to send al-Qasari to the Sultan, who had already made a futile attempt to come to his aid against al-Ayyāshī.

On 2 July 1637, the people of Rabat took over the *qaṣba* and sent al-Qasari to Muhammad ash-Sheikh al-Asghar camped near Azammur.[70]

While al-Qasari was away, the people of Rabat once again entered into negotiations with the Spanish to deliver Rabat to them. Presumably they still wanted to return to Spain, as they had proposed six years before. They reached an agreement with Don Juan de Toledo late in July and he returned to al-Maʿmūra to get 500 men to occupy the *qaṣba*, but high seas delayed their return. In the interim, on 7 August 1637, al-Qasari returned to Rabat on a ship commanded by Robert Blake, an English merchant who held the customs concession at Safi by a grant from Mulay Muhammad ash-Sheikh al-Asghar. Six days earlier, word had come that the Sultan had pardoned al-Qasari and the people of Rabat, and he sent the *qāʾid* back as his appointee in the port. Blake and al-Qasari brought a cargo of grain with them to appease the Rabatis, many of whom fled after al-Qasari executed the leaders of the movement which had expelled him a few weeks before.[71]

Al-Ayyāshī continued his siege of Rabat after al-Qasari returned. He refused to accept Saʿādī suzerainty or al-Qasari, who had personally insulted him. Before the English squadron under Robert Blake arrived in mid-June 1638, al-Qasari had been killed, either by a Titwani merchant detained in Rabat by al-Qasari or by one of al-Ayyāshī's men. After al-Qasari's death, his son succeeded him, but the Sultan sent a French renegade *qāʾid* named Morat with 250–450 men as a garrison for the *qaṣba*. Al-Qasari's son remained *qāʾid* in name, but Morat commanded the sultan's garrison and held effective power. Al-Ayyāshī in a turnabout, welcomed the *makhzan*'s renewed presence. He sent the Hornacheros, who had sought refuge with him, back to Rabat where they took up residence in the city below the *qaṣba*. He himself took his men north to the outskirts of al-Maʿmūra, and it seemed that calm had returned to Rabat–Salé. Only four corsair ships remained in Rabat after more than two years of strife, and they prepared to resume their raids.[72]

But peace lasted only five or six days. The Hornacheros 'thought to have resumed the power they had had before, by makinge themselves masters of all'.[73] Warfare broke out once again. The Hornacheros, aided by neighbouring tribesmen, besieged the *qaṣba*'s garrison commanded by Morat. The Sultan and the Spanish at al-Maʿmūra sent relief ships with supplies of food to help the garrison. Al-Ayyāshī did not take part in the renewed hostilities, but set off for Fez to relieve his son ʿAbd Allah who had lost a battle to Mulay

Ahmad al-Asghar, the sultan's younger brother. But the Hornacheros besieging the *qaṣba* incurred the *mujāhid*'s wrath. Al-Ayyāshī intercepted a letter they wrote to Mulay Ahmad al-Asghar asking for help. Meanwhile, the garrison and Andalusians in the *qaṣba* once again renewed contacts with the Spaniards in al-Maʿmūra when it seemed unlikely that the Sultan would come to their aid.[74]

After al-Ayyāshī surrounded Mulay Ahmad al-Asghar in the mountains near Fez, he returned to Rabat–Salé early in 1639. There he seized control of the city of Rabat, 'continued the siege of the Chateau; and banished the rest of the Andalusians who had stayed in ... [the] city and in that of Olde Salé, except for a few artisans who the two cities can not do without'.[75] The Hornacheros he banished spread out from Rabat, finding refuge in Marrakesh, Algiers, Europe, and Dila.[76] In Rabat, the siege of the *qaṣba* and its Saʿādī garrison continued through 1640. The inhabitants, seeing no hope of relief by land, offered 'to deliver the Castle to anie Christian prince that would transport them and their estates to some partes where they might spend their remainder of dayes in peace and quiett'.[77] But the siege did end that year when Muhammad al-Hajj ad-Dila'i, leader of the Dila'iyya religious brotherhood from the Middle Atlas, took up the Hornacheros' case against al-Ayyāshī and marched against him. The ultimate result was al-Ayyāshī's death on 30 April 1641, after which the Dila'is assumed control of Rabat–Salé until 1664.

Corsair raiding all but ceased during the four years of civil strife in Rabat–Salé. The fleet, which had numbered fifty or more ships, declined to less than five because the Morisco and Andalusian financers, outfitters, captains, and crewmen were preoccupied with the internal political and military problems of Rabat–Salé. Renegade captains continued to sail, but took their prizes and made their preparations elsewhere: most frequently Titwan, Algiers, and Tunis. Only after the Dila'is re-established order and calm in Rabat–Salé did corsair raiding resume, but never again with the intensity of 1625–6 and 1635–6.

RABAT–SALE UNDER THE DILAIS (1641–64)

Precise details of the Dila'i takeover of Rabat–Salé are lacking. For three years after al-Ayyāshī's death the *qaṣba* remained in the hands of Mulay Muhammad al-Sheikh al-Asghar's garrison. Corsair raiding resumed in these three years, but it seems that many of the corsairs returning to Rabat–Salé to sell prizes originated from Algiers. The Dila'is definitively asserted their power in Rabat–Salé in 1644 during a period of renewed civil strife in Rabat. Ostensibly supporting the Hornacheros, they succeeded in expelling other groups from the *qaṣba* and established their headquarters there.[78] In this period the corsairs remained largely inactive. Their principal backers, the Moriscos and Andalusians, were fully occupied defending their own positions and had no funds, time, or energy to spare for outfitting and supporting corsair activities. It therefore seems probable that what corsair activity did exist in the early days of the revival was based mainly in Algiers and used Rabat–Salé as an entrepôt for prizes and captives.

After the Dila'is restored order in 1644, corsair raiding enjoyed a revival. By 1648 the fleet had grown to twenty-four ships, and the corsairs again ranged far and wide in the Atlantic. Corsair activity became so bothersome to the Dutch that in 1649 they sent a squadron to deal with the problem. It captured several ships and took them to Cadiz where the crews were sold as slaves. In 1650, the Admiralty of Amsterdam sent a squadron of four ships and a yacht to blockade the Bu Raqraq and force the authorities there into negotiations for a treaty.[79] The Dutch blockade in 1650 succeeded not only in its primary purpose of bringing the corsairs to task, but also in decimating the corsair fleet. The twenty-four ships of 1648 dwindled to only ten four years later. But other factors also contributed to the decline. In the early 1650s Rabat–Salé suffered from the effects of a drought which increased the price of wheat by 1,200 per cent and left potential outfitters of corsair cruises without adequate funds. In 1650, another revolt took place, this one only by the residents of Rabat.[80] Whether this short-lived disturbance resulted from the effects of the blockade, the onset of the drought-fuelled inflation in food prices, or other causes is not clear. It certainly contributed to the corsairs' decline.

Until 1651, the *qaṣba*, town of Rabat, and Salé each had separate administrations and separate *qāʾid-s*. Saʿīd al-Janāwī dominated the others from his position on the north bank in Salé. In 1651, Muhammad al-Hajj ad-Dila'i received the *bayʿa* as sultan from the people of Fez and most of the other cities and towns in central and northern Morocco, and decided to reorganize the government in Rabat–Salé. He installed his son ʿAbd Allah as governor. ʿAbd Allah took up residence in the *qaṣba* and made Saʿīd al-Janāwī his chief aide and deputy. Major decisions were taken only after consultation with local notables, one of whom became ʿAbd Allah's private secretary. ʿAbd Allah left internal affairs largely in al-Janāwī's hands until the latter's death in 1655. Then Ahmad al-Janāwī (the relationship between the two is not clear) took over those functions. ʿAbd Allah's principal role was in foreign affairs. Rabat–Salé was the Dilaʾi window to the outside world. ʿAbd Allah and his *dīwān* conducted their foreign relations.[81]

Statements by Henry de Castries and Roger Coindreau that the period from 1651 to 1660 was filled with a succession of acts of piracy, creating all sorts of difficulties for European consuls in Rabat–Salé seem to greatly overstate the case.[82] While the corsairs did resume their raids in this period, it is clear that their numbers and the scope of their activity never approached the high points reached during 1625–6 and 1635–6, or even 1644–9. This decrease in corsair activity occurred despite the fact that to all appearances local conditions at Rabat–Salé were more settled than at any time since Mulay Ahmad al-Mansur's death. The explanation lies in a multitude of local and international factors.

The Dilaʾi governor Abd Allah ad-Dilaʾi does not seem to have encouraged corsair raiding and may well have discouraged it. Saʿīd al-Janāwī apparently also discouraged corsairs from using Rabat–Salé as a home port. Both engaged in trade with Mediterranean North Africa, particularly Tunis. So did the ship captains of Rabat-Salé.[83] Corsair raiding could have upset this profitable trade, and was therefore discouraged, but by no means outlawed. In 1647, al-Janāwī was said to be awaiting the departure of the ships in order to seal them out of Rabat–Salé and turn entirely to trade.[84] The Moriscos no longer held the *qaṣba*, the most important point in Rabat–Salé for corsair raiding because of its position overlooking the sand bar and harbour. Those who remained now lived in the town. In any case, their zeal had waned, tempered by forty years in exile, the measure of acceptance they had gained in Rabat–Salé, and the maturing of a new generation. Corsair raiding from the Bu Raqraq, always a highly profitable activity, had lost its guerrilla warfare overtones and become a pure business proposition. The many years of internal strife had sapped the Moriscos' economic resources, making it more difficult for them to finance corsair voyages except as economic ventures.

The conclusion of the Thirty Years' War and signing of the Peace of Westphalia ended general European conflict for a time. Therefore, the emerging national navies of the important maritime states could be, and were, used against the North African corsairs in the Mediterranean and to convoy merchant ships. This made corsair life more dangerous and less attractive. Consequently, Europeans no longer came to Rabat–Salé, Algiers, Tunis, and Tripoli in the numbers they had in the sixteenth century and first half of the seventeenth century.

If life in the navy was not sufficiently exciting, adventurous, or remunerative, the pirate bands in the Caribbean offered an alternative: becoming a renegade and sailing under Muslim colours. The period of direct Dila'i rule in Rabat–Salé therefore was not a period of unsurpassed corsair activity. From the evidence in Dutch sources – the only ones with any detail for the period – they appear to have been pliant to the desires of their political masters and certainly not a major political factor. The size of the fleet never exceeded two dozen ships and generally remained under ten.

When a revolt broke out against ʿAbd Allah ad-Dila'i in February 1660 it was general, with participation by the inhabitants of Rabat and Salé. The available evidence offers few clues as to the origins of this revolt, which resulted in an eighteen month siege of the Dila'is in the *qaṣba*. Arabic sources make no mention of it whatsoever. The only European eyewitness to write about the events, Dutch consul David de Vries, merely described them.[85] But 1660 was a bad year for the Dila'is. A revolt in Fez and defeat at the hands of Ahmad al-Khadir bin ʿAlī Ghaylan accompanied the events in Rabat–Salé. Ghaylan may well have instigated the revolt in Rabat–Salé in hopes of further weakening his adversaries. Muhammad Hajji has also pointed out that hostility toward the Dila'is had deep roots, particularly among the Moriscos, and that they required only the slightest encouragement from Ghaylan to rise up.[86] Castries's assertion that 'the domination of Dila finally weighed on the Hornacheros and Andalusians; it seemed humiliating to them, of Arab origin, to be subjects of these Berbers of the upper Muluya'[87] may have some validity, but it seems more likely that this would have motivated the Slawis who had such a cultured and pious self-image. The Slawis, moreover, had always stood behind Sidi Mahammad al-Ayyāshī, and doubtless resented the Dila'is because they had ended his career.

In any event, the siege ended in 1661 when help arrived from Algiers. At the same time, Ghaylan's chief lieutenant in charge of the siege was killed, and ʿAbd Allah fled the *qaṣba* for Tamasna, possibly on an English ship. ʿAbd Allah left Ahmad al-Janāwī in command of the *qaṣba*. He managed to hold out until 3 May 1664, when Ghaylan's brother Tahir entered the fortress. Throughout the long siege the English, fearful of the havoc Ghaylan could wreak on their shipping if he held the *qaṣba*, supported the Dila'is from their newly occupied garrison in Tangier.[88]

GHAYLAN AND THE 'ALAWI-S (1664–72)

The end of Dila'i rule in the *qaṣba* came about when the members of 'Abd Allah's *dīwān*, led by Ahmad al-Janāwī, surrendered to Ghaylan's brother. Ghaylan himself went to Rabat–Salé in October 1664, but only for a brief time. The real ruler of Rabat–Salé remained Ahmad al-Janāwī and his aide Ahmad Himi. Late in March 1665, another of Ghaylan's lieutenants came to Rabat–Salé, touching off a series of changes. The remaining soldiers from Mulay Muhammad ash-Shaykh al-Asghar's garrison were expelled from the *qaṣba*, 'Abd al-Qadir Marinu elected *qāʾid* by the Andalusians, the Hornacheros and *qāʾid* of Salé made prisoners of the *qaṣba*, al-Hajj Muhammad Fannish (descendant of renegades) made *qāʾid* of Salé, and Ahmad al-Janāwī stripped of his powers and killed before the end of April. Several months later, in August 1665, 'Abd al-Qadir Roxo and one of 'Abd al-Qadir Sirun's sons replaced 'Abd al-Qadir Marinu as *qāʾid-s* in Rabat. Along with al-Hajj Muhammad Fannish they continued to pledge their loyalty to Ghaylan, who by now faced the growing power of Mulay ar-Rashid al-'Alawī. In June 1666, Ghaylan's forces were defeated and put to rout by ar-Rashid. The 'Alawi *sharīf* took control of Rabat–Salé shortly thereafter. He retained al-Hajj Muhammad Fannish as *qāʾid* of Salé and restored 'Abd al-Qadir Marinu as *qāʾid* of Rabat.[89]

After Ghaylan became suzerain of Rabat–Salé, corsair raiding, which had all but ceased during the four years of local strife (1660–4), resumed on a small scale.[90] Ghaylan's tenure as overlord was so short that little is known of the relationship between the corsairs and the political authority, except that they adhered to the truce negotiated with English agent Thomas Warren in April 1666 for the short time it was in force. After Mulay ar-Rashid defeated Ghaylan in June 1666, the corsairs resumed their attacks on the English and other nationalities, although their numbers remained small. In 1669 it became clear that Mulay ar-Rashid had little, if any, control over the authorities at Rabat–Salé or the corsairs. They invoked his name when refusing to formally conclude a truce with the English, but later they interfered with the execution of his orders for the return of English captives to Tangier. The sultan had to send a personal representative to see that his orders were carried out and that the *qāʾid-s*, who had personal financial interests in the outfitting of corsairs, did not interfere.[91]

After these incidents, the 'Alawī sultans, first Mulay ar-Rashid and, after his death in 1672, Mulay Ismāʿīl, began to assume direct control over the corsairs in a process which soon transformed them from the independent corsairs of Rabat–Salé into the naval arm of the 'Alawī *makhzan*. During these years, the size of the fleet fluctuated in the range of seven to eleven ships.[92] In 1670, captives brought to Rabat–Salé were being taken from there to Mulay ar-Rashid in Fez, where about 300 Christians in leg irons did manual labour for the sultan. The following year there were reports of corsair ships outfitted by Mulay ar-Rashid – two out of a total of seven according to one report. In 1672, a French report from Lisbon said the Sultan was arming four out of nine ships, while William Sedgwick, writing from Rabat–Salé, spoke of 'the 2 Kings men of warre'. Sedgwick said that the sultan's 'Ships are easily knowne, the one having three Flower de luces, and the other three roses in their sternes'.[93] A clear trend of *makhzan* participation in the outfitting of corsair ships was established before Mulay ar-Rashid's death in mid-1672. With relatively firm political control of Morocco, the 'Alawī-s could and did concern themselves with manifestations of independence such as those evidenced by the corsairs in 1669 and 1670, in a way that had been impossible in Morocco since the death of Mulay Ahmad al-Mansur nearly seventy years before. The corsairs and *qāʾid-s* of Rabat–Salé, who now had to contend with a strong *makhzan*, could no longer act on their own account and reluctantly, but gradually came under *makhzan* control.

In the period of *fitna* the corsairs benefited from the political fragmentation of Morocco, but they in no way caused or contributed to it. The corsairs and their Morisco and Andalusian sponsors remained outside the mainstream of Moroccan political events. They did not directly participate in the upheaval going on around them. To do so would have required that they become involved in the constantly changing mosaic of tribal and factional alliances. They never did. As a consequence they could not influence political events in Morocco, or even in the area around Rabat–Salé. But events did affect the corsairs. The political leaders who controlled Rabat–Salé influenced corsair activity. When the *dīwān* encouraged the corsairs, they flourished. When the Dila'is and 'Alawīs strictly controlled their activity, they languished.

The corsairs themselves did not play an important role in the periodic upheavals in Rabat–Salé. Division of the profits from their raids provoked some of the troubles, but for the most part local political disputes between the Andalusians and Morisco factions in Rabat and the Slawis across the Bu Raqraq caused the difficulties. Local factions succeeded in allying with outside groups to their own advantage on numerous occasions, but they never proved valuable partners for their allies. The corsairs, in the microcosm of Rabat–Salé, and the Moriscos and Andalusians, in the macrocosm of Morocco, remained outside the main flow of events. The conditions in the microcosm had a strong bearing on corsair activity, yet the corsairs played no appreciable role in creating the conditions or working to change them. Similarly, the political conditions in Morocco had an important influence on the corsairs and their backers, but they remained outside the tribal and factional alliances which determined them.

Under Mulay Ismāʿil and his successors, the corsairs never regained the prominence they held during the *fitna* period. Even during the recurrent strife between Ismail's death in 1727 and his son Mulay ʿAbd Allah's death thirty years later, there was no serious revival of corsair raiding from Moroccan ports. Under Sidi Muhammad bin ʿAbd Allah (1757–90) there was something of a revival, but not of the corsairs as an independent force. Indeed, the cornerstone of Sidi Muhammad's foreign policy was promotion of trade with Europe, and even America, and the corsairs were merely the naval side of his military apparatus. Occasionally he made use of the corsairs to harrass the shipping of states he wished to do business with or whose attention he needed to capture – the infant United States for example. But by now the Moroccan corsairs had become an instrument of state policy rather than an independent force. Under his son Mulay Sulayman (1792–1822) there was a brief attempt to revive the corsairs once again, but Sulayman quickly came to the realization that they posed as much of a threat to him as to their intended victims – the European navies were now so strong that their vengeance was a very real threat to the stability of his rule.

Therefore, the corsairs and corsairing played little, if any, role in the economy and politics of Morocco. In the earlier period it was the upheavals of the political system as a whole which allowed them to flourish, not they who played a role in the upheavals themselves. Later they became an instrument of state policy, operating in an analogous fashion to the privateers used by virtually every maritime state during the period.

COMPARISONS WITH ALGIERS, TUNIS, AND TRIPOLI

When we think of the 'Barbary pirates' it is more those based in Mediterranean North Africa than those based in Morocco who come to mind. Intensive corsairing was far more prevalent in the Mediterranean than in the Atlantic, which was the primary field of operations for Morocco's corsairs. Indeed, corsairing had been a prominent feature of Mediterranean seafaring since the early sixteenth century, with attacks coming with almost equal intensity from Muslim corsairs and Christian corsairs based in Malta. In Algiers in particular there were considerable periods in the sixteenth century when the corsair captains controlled the political life of the city, and Khayr ad-Din and his brother Uruj, known popularly as the Barbarossas, were the corsairing Turks who brought Algiers into the Ottoman sphere.

Nevertheless, Ottoman Algeria was far more than the capital city of Algiers, and available evidence points to the fact that while the corsairs may have played a significant role in Algerine politics from time to time (especially in the sixteenth and seventeenth centuries), they were not always the dominant element. Corsairing was a major economic activity, occupying perhaps as much as 25 per cent of the economically active population of Algiers at certain periods. Revenues from corsairing played a significant role in the finances of the Ottoman administration in Algiers, but had little direct impact on the economy of the hinterland where most Ottoman Algerians lived. Much research still needs to be done before we can have a clear picture, but the conclusions one can draw from works such as Lucette Valensi's *Le maghreb avant la prise d'Alger* lead to the belief that the corsairs' economic and political role in pre-colonial Algeria has been greatly over-emphasized, especially if one looks at the territory as a whole and not just at the port city of Algiers.[94]

Tunis and Tripoli present a similar, yet different picture from Algiers. In both cases there were periods, particularly in the sixteenth and early seventeenth centuries, when the corsairs played a fairly prominent role, as they did in Algiers. However, unlike Algiers, which never saw the establishment of hereditary dynasties of Turkish rulers, Tunis was ruled by the Husaynids from 1705 and Tripoli by the Karamanlis from 1711. In both cases a symbiosis between the ruling elite and the corsairs emerged, with the corsairs playing a relatively minor political role. Economically, corsairing occasionally played a major role in state finances, but only in periods when international conditions allowed them relatively free rein at sea. At other times the state had to rely on customs duties levied on legitimate trade (frequently far more important than corsairing revenues even when they were very active, especially in Tunisia) and taxation of the peasantry and tribes to support its activities. Indeed, in many ways the situations in these two states were more similar in the 18th century to that in Morocco.[95]

The overwhelming conclusions of an examination of the economic and political role of corsairing in North Africa are that:

1 those roles have been greatly over-emphasized in popular literature, largely because their European victims saw North Africa essentially in terms of the corsairs, and
2 there is a great deal of research which needs to be done before a clear picture can emerge of how the corsairs in Algiers, Tunis, and Tripoli interacted with the local political and economic scene.

NOTES

1 Pedro de Herrera to Mateo Vasques (Sibta, 16 August 1588), British Museum (BM), Additional Manuscripts (add Mss) 28348, fol. 292; also in Henry de Castries (ed.), *Sources inédites de l'histoire du Maroc. Angleterre* (SIHMA) (Paris, 1918), I, p. 504; and Khadduri, *War and Peace in the Law of Islam* (Baltimore, 1955), p. 121.
2 M. Coy to the States General (Safi, 19 June 1605) in Henry de Castries (ed.), *Sources inédites de l'histoire du Maroc. Pays-Bas* (SIHMPB) (Paris, 1906), I, pp. 82–7; same to same (Marrakesh, 7 September 1605) in SIHMPB, I, pp. 97–102; same to same (Marrakesh, 18 March 1606) in SIHMPB, I, pp. 132–40; same to same (Marrakesh, 21 June 1606) in SIHMPB, I, pp. 151–3; same to same (Marrakesh, 28 November 1606) in SIHMPB, I, pp. 166–9; and R. Cocks to Thomas Wilson (Bayonne, 31 March 1607), Public Record Office, London (PRO), State Papers (SP) 94/13, fol. 181, also in SIHMA, II, pp. 308–9.
3 P. M. Coy to the States General (Marrakesh, 18 March 1606) in SIHMPB, I, pp. 132–40.
4 Instructions for P. M. Coy (The Hague, 11 May 1605) in SIHMPB, I, pp. 74–81.
5 Resolution of the States General (The Hague, 8 February 1607) in SIHMPB, I, pp. 181–2; States General to Admiral van Heemskert (The Hague, 6 March 1607) in SIHMPB, I, pp. 183–5; Instructions for Joris van Spilbergen (near Cape St Vincent, 9 May 1607) in SIHMPB, I, pp. 222–3; Resolution of the States General (The Hague, 3 August 1607) in SIHMPB, I, pp. 249–50; and Resolution of the States General (The Hague, 19 April 1608) in SIHMPB, I, pp. 276–7.
6 BM, Lansdowne Mss 145, fol. 52. See also SIHMA, II, p. 556, note 1.
7 Arnoult de Lisle to Villeroy (Marrakesh, 12 January 1607) in Henry de Castries (ed.), *Sources inédites de l'histoire du Maroc. France, première serie* (SIHMFl), (Paris 1907), II, p. 359; Henri IV to Mulay Muhammad ash-Shaykh al-Mamun (before 26 March 1607) in SIHMFl, II, pp. 363–4; and Henri IV to Arnoult de Lisle (no place, no date, but before 26 March 1607) in SIHMFl, II, pp. 365–6.
8 John Harrison to Lord Salisbury (Safi, 10/20 June 1610), PRO, SP 71/12, fol. 82; also in SIHMA, II, p. 450; Sir Ferdinando Gorges to Lord Salisbury (Plymouth, 5/15 July 1611), PRO, SP 14/65, no. 16; also in SIHMA, II, pp. 463–4; Mainwaring (ed.), *The Life and Works of Sir*

Henry Mainwaring, vol. 1 (London, 1920), pp. 6–7 and 11–13, quote from p. 11

9   SIHMPB, II, pp. 334–41; and SIHMFl, II, pp. 566–71.
10 Jan Evertsen to the States General (al-Ma'mūra Roadstead, 10 July 1614) in SIHMPB, II, pp. 306–8; same to same (Safi, 15 September 1614) in SIHMPB, II, p. 340; and Jan Lievens's Journal (9 August 1614) in SIHMPB, II, p. 355.
11 Mulay Zaydan to the States General (from his camp, 18 Dhu al-Hijja 1020/6 March 1610) in SIHMPB, I, pp. 498–501.
12 The States General approved construction of 'three or four vessels' but the Spanish attacked and destroyed them within six months of their delivery to Mulay Zaydan at Safi in March 1611. See Resolution of the States General (The Hague, 26 June 1610) in SIHMPB, I, pp. 519–20; SIHMPB, I, p. 672; and Mulay Zaydan to the States General (Marrakesh, 20 Rajab 1020/28 September 1611) in SIHMPB, I, pp. 673–4.
13 John Digby to Lord Buckingham (n.p., 5/15 April 1619), BM, Harleian Mss 1580, fols. 106–9; also in SIHMA, II, p. 512.
14 Georges S. Colin (ed.), *Chronique anonyme de la dynastie Sa'dienne* (Rabat, 1934), p. 103.
15 Muhammad as-Saghir bin al-Hajj bin Abd Allah al-Ifrani, *Nuzhat al-Hādī bi-Akhbār li-Mulūk al-Qarn al-Hādī* (Fez, n.d. [about 1890]). Also available in French translation *Nozhet-Elhadi. Histoire de la dynastie Saadienne (1511–1670)* edited by Octave Houdas (Paris, 1889), and another Arabic edition edited by Houdas (Paris, 1888). French translation (F): pp. 438–9, Houdas Arabic edition (A): p. 264, Fez: p. 226; John Harrison, 'An accounte: to His Majesty of my last two imployments into Barbarie' (n.p., 1/11 September 1627), PRO, SP 71/12, fols. 125 and 127–9; also in SIHMA, III, pp. 32–3, 39–40, and 43; and John Harrison to the Commander of the Fleet (Titwan, 20/30 July 1625), BM, Harleian Mss 1518, fol. 321; also in SIHMA, II, p. 575. Neither al-Ifrani nor Harrison gives dates for these events.
16 Abbé Willemzoon to the Admiralty of Rotterdam (off the Moroccan coast, 8 August 1617) in SIHMPB, III, p. 65.
17 Letter from Albert Ruyl (Safi, 17 February 1623) in SIHMPB, III, p. 270, n.3.
18 Albert Ruyl's Journal (Salé, 16 December 1622) in SIHMPB, III, p. 272.
19 *Ibid.* (Marrakesh, 6 October 1623) in SIHMPB, III, pp. 419–20.
20 *Ibid.* (Salé, 15 December 1622) in SIHMPB, III, p. 217; and Letter from Albert Ruyl (Safi, 17 February 1623) in SIHMPB, III, p. 270, n.3.
21 Albert Ruyl's Journal (Marrakesh, 19 October 1623) in SIHMPB, III, p. 429.
22 Moses Pallache to the States General (From Mulay Zaydan's camp, 18 August 1624) in SIHMPB, IV, pp. 10–11.
23 Albert Ruyl's Journal (Salé, 15 December 1622), in SIHMPB, III, p. 271; Isaac de Razilly to Cardinal Richelieu (Pontoise, 26 November 1626) in SIHMFl, III, pp. 115–16; SIHMPB, IV, for 1624–7, *passim.*; SIHMA, II, pp. 558–96; and SIHMA, III, pp. 1–9.
24 Johan de Mortaigne to the States General (den Briele, 21 January 1625) in SIHMPB, IV, pp. 99–100; Statement of Yusuf Biskaynu in Resolution of the States General (The Hague, 25 January 1625) in SIHMPB, IV, p.

105; States General to Mulay Zaydan (The Hague, 8 November 1624) in SIHMPB, IV, pp. 36–7; Albert Ruyl to the States General (Safi, 11 December 1623) in SIHMPB, III, pp. 490–1; and SIHMPB, IV, p. 513, n.2.

25 al-Ifrani, F: p. 439, A: p. 264, Fez: p. 226; and John Harrison to the Commander of the Fleet (Titwan 20/30 July 1625) BM, Harleian Mss 1581, fol. 321; also in SIHMA, II, p. 575.

26 John Harrison, 'An accounte …' (n.p., 1/11 September 1627), PRO, SP 71/12, fol. 128; also in SIHMA, III, pp. 39–40.

27 John Harrison, 'An accounte …' (n.p., 1/11 September 1627), PRO, SP 71/12, fol. 128; and Albert Ruyl's Journal (Marrakesh, 19 October 1623) in SIHMPB, III, p. 429.

28 Capitulacion att Sallie (Qasba of Salé, 24 Sha'bān 1036/10 May 1627), PRO, SP 103/1, Spanish copy also in SIHMA, III, pp. 14–24.

29 al-Ifrani, F: pp. 403–4, A: p. 243, Fez: p. 208.

30 John Harrison, 'An accounte …' (n.p., 1/11 September 1627), PRO, SP 71/12, fols. 129–31; also in SIHMA, III, pp. 45–7. Quote from fol. 131, p. 47. See also al-Ifrani, F: p. 442, A: p. 266, Fez: pp. 227–8.

31 Muhammad bin Ahmad to Charles I (n.p., 21 June/1 July 1628), PRO, SP 102/2, fol. 78; also in SIHMA, III, pp. 73–4; and Diwan to Charles I (Qasba of Salé, 8 July 1628), PRO, SP 102/2, fol. 76 (English translation), and fol. 77 (Spanish copy), fol. 77 also in SIHMA, III, pp. 75–7.

32 Proclamation of Charles I (Whitehall, 22 October/1 November 1628), PRO, C 66/2474, no. 10, also in SIHMA, III, pp. 80–1.

33 Morat Rais to the States General (Salé, 12 August 1627), in SIHMPB, IV, pp. 169–70.

34 See, for instance, Diwan to Charles I (Qasba of Salé, 8 July 1628), PRO, SP 102/2, fol. 76 (English translation), and fol. 77 (Spanish copy), fol. 77 also in SIHMA, III, pp. 75–7; Muhammad Vanegas to the States General (The Hague, 23 October 1629) in SIHMPB, IV, p. 235; and Isaac de Razilly to Cardinal Richelieu (Port Louis, 25 November 1629) in SIHMFl, III, p. 200.

35 Procès-verbal d'André Chemin (n.p., 1629) in SIHMFl, III, pp. 206–8; and Instructions for Isaac de Razilly (Grenoble, 18 February 1629) in SIHMFI, III, pp. 184–5.

36 Procès-verbal d'André Chemin (n.p., 1629) in SIHMFl, III, pp. 217–18; and Isaac de Razilly to the Duke of Medina-Sidonia (Salé Roadstead, 12 September 1629) in SIHMFl, III, p. 232.

37 Isaac de Razilly to Cardinal Richelieu (Port Louis, 25 November 1629) in SIHMFl, III, pp. 201–2; and Procès-verbal d'André Chemin (n.p., 1629) in SIHMFl, III, p. 243.

38 Truce between Louis XIII and the Diwan of Rabat (Salé, 2 October 1629) in SIHMFl, III, pp. 244–6.

39 Relation de Capitain Pallot (n.p., early September 1630) in SIHMFl, III, p. 290.

40 John Harrison, 'An accounte …' (n.p., 28 September/8 October 1630), PRO, SP 71/12, fol. 181, also in SIHMA, III, p. 105.

41 John Harrison, 'An accounte …' (n.p., 28 September/8 October 1630), PRO, SP 71/12, fol. 181, also in SIHMA, III, p. 105–6.

42 John Harrison, 'An accounte …' (n.p., 28 September/8 October 1630),

PRO, SP 71/12, fol. 181, also in SIHMA, III, p. 105–7. See also al-Ifrani, F: pp. 443–4, A: p. 267, Fez: p. 228; and Rélation d'une sortie des troupes de Tanger (n.p., 10–11 January 1630) in SIHMFl, III, pp. 275–81.

43   Charles I to Sidi Mahammad al-'Ayyāshī (Westminster, 12/22 October 1627), PRO, SP 71/12, fol. 137, also in SIHMA, III, pp. 60–1. See also Sidi Mahammad al-'Ayyāshī to Charles I (from his camp near Salé, 2 Ramadan 1036/17 May 1627), PRO, SP 102/2, fol. 104, also in SIHMA, III, pp. 23–4.

44   John Harrison, 'An accounte ...' (n.p., 28 September/8 October 1630), PRO, SP 71/12, fol. 181, also in SIHMA, III, p. 107.

45   Jorge Mascarenhas to Felipe III (Mazagan, 4 February 1619), BM, Add Mss 28461, fol. 40, also in SIHMFl, III, p. 49.

46   SIHMFl, III, p. 97.

47   John Harrison to the Commander of the Fleet (Titwan, 20/30 July 1625), BM, Harleian Mss 1581, also in SIHMA, II, p. 579.

48   John Harrison, 'An accounte ...' (n.p. 1/11 September 1627), PRO, SP 71/12, fols 128–9, also in SIHMA, III, p. 42. See also 'Mr Harrisons relations of his proceedings in barbarie for peace with Sallie and Tituan' (n.p., end of 1627), PRO, SP 71/12, fol. 146, also in SIHMA, III, p. 70; and John Harrison, 'The State of Barbary' (n.p., 15/25 July 1631), PRO, SP 71/12, fol. 190, also in SIHMA, III, p. 145.

49   SIHMFl, III, p. 341.

50   John Harrison, 'An accounte ...' (n.p., 1/11 September 1627), PRO, SP 71/12, fol. 129, also in SIHMA, III, p. 43.

51   al-Ifrani, F, p. 444; A. p. 267; Fez, pp. 228–9; and Georges S. Colin, 'Project de traité entre les Morisques de la Casba de Rabat et le Roi d'Espagne, en 1631' in *Hesopéris*, vol. XLII (Paris, 1955), pp. 18 and 21. The document appears to be a communication from the Duke of Medina-Sidonia to King Felipe IV.

52   al-Ifrani, F: pp. 444–5, A: p. 267, Fez: p. 229, and SIHMFl, III, p. 195.

53   *The tragicall life and death of Mulav 'Abdala Melek, the late King of Barbarie* (Delph, 1633), also in SIHMA, III, p. 194.

54   John Harrison, 'The State of Barbary' (n.p., 15/25 July 1631), PRO, SP 71/12, fol. 191, also in SIHMA, III, p. 149.

55   *The tragicall life ...*, also in SIHMA, III, p. 204; al-Ifrani, F: pp. 405–6, A: pp. 244–5, Fez: p. 209; and Colin, *op. cit.*, pp. 18 and 21–2.

56   Colin, *op. cit.*, pp. 18–20 and 22–4.

57   Arthur Hopton to Sir John Coke (Madrid, 6 June 1633), PRO, SP 94/36, fol. 292, also in SIHMA, III, pp. 189–90, line 48.

58   William Rainsborough to the Lords of the Admiralty (Salé Roadstead, 8/18 August 1637) PR, SP 71/13, fol. 23, also in SIHMA, III, p. 324.

59   Acceptance of the Articles of Peace by the Slawis (Salé, 1 September 1635) in SIHMFl, III, pp. 499–501; and Pierre-Priam du Chalard to Louis XIII (Salé Roadstead, 13 October 1635) in SIHMFl, III, pp. 503–4.

60   Joseph Pallache to the States General (The Hague, 6 July 1633) in SIHMPB, IV, pp. 326–7; same to same (The Hague, 5 August 1633) in SIHMPB, IV, pp. 330–2; Ahmad bin 'Ali 'Abd Allah bin 'Ali al-Qasari to the States General (Qasba of Salé, 12 June 1634) in SIHMPB, IV, pp.

352–3; and ʿAbd Allah bin ʿAli al-Qasari and Muhammad bin Amar to the States General (Qasba of Salé, 10 August 1634) in SIHMPB, IV, pp. 354–5.

61 John Harrison to A. A. Carnwath (Salé Roadstead, 5/15 October 1631), PRO, SP 71/12, fol. 197, also in SIHMA, III, p. 164.

62 Harrison to Carnwath (Salé Roadstead, 29 September/9 October 1631), PRO, SP 71/12, fol. 196, also in SIHMA, III, p. 160.

63 The answer to Bradshaws peticion (n.p., 4/14 December 1635), PRO, SP 71/12, fol. 248, also in SIHMA, III, p. 219. See also SIHMA, III, pp. 219, n.3 and 258.

64 Rélation de Capitaine Pallot (n.p., early September 1630) in SIHMFl, III, p. 290; and Pierre-Priam du Chalard to Louis XIII (Salé Roadstead, 13 October 1635) in SIHMFl, III, p. 504.

65 Rélation d'Antoine Cabiron (Paris, 9 July 1634) in SIHMFl, III, p. 440. Cabiron never actually visited Rabat-Salé.

66 Edmond Bradshaw to the Privy Council (n.p., 17/27 November 1635), PRO, SP 71/12, fol. 227, also in SIHMA, III, p. 216; Edmond Bradshaw and Robert Pickford to the Privy Council (n.p., n.d. – between 14 December 1635 and 7 March 1636), PRO, SP 71/12, fol. 252, also in SIHMA, III, p. 325; Edmond Bradshaw to John Coke (Marrakesh, 30 September/10 October 1636), PRO, SP 71/12, fol. 262, also in SIHMA, III, p. 250; William Rainsborough to E. Coke (Salé Roadstead, 8/18 August 1637), PRO, SP 71/13, fol. 19, and William Rainsborough to the Lords of the Admiralty (Salé Roadstead, 8/18 August 1637), PRO, SP 71/13, fol. 23, also in SIHMA, III, p. 325; ʿAbd Allah bin ʿAli al-Qasari and Muhammad bin Amar to the States General (Qasba of Salé, 14 October 1635) in SIHMPB, IV, pp. 381–2; and Rélation d'Henri d'Escoubleau de Sourdis (Strait of Gibraltar, 12 July 1636) in SIHMFl, III, pp. 530–1.

67 William Rainsborough to the Lords of the Admiralty (Salé Roadstead, 20/30 May 1637), PRO, SP 71/13, fol. 8, also in SIHMA, III, p. 310.

68 Giles Penn to the Lords of the Admiralty (n.p., December 1636), PRO, SP 16/338, no. 51, also in SIHMA, III, p. 267; and Rélation de Jean Marges (n.p., end of 1637) in SIHMFl, III, pp. 539–40.

69 Treaty between Charles I and Sidi Mahammad al-ʿAyyāshī, PRO, SP 103/1 (English translation) also in SIHMA, III, pp. 292–4. Arabic text (Salé, 18 Dhu al-Hijja 1046/13 May 1637) in SIHMA, III, pp. 284–7; and William Rainsborough to Sir Henry Vane (Salé Roadstead, 9/19 May 1637), PRO, SP 16/360, no. 161.

70 William Rainsborough to the Lords of the Admiralty (Salé Roadstead, 20/30 May 1637), PRO, SP 71/13, fol. 8, also in SIHMA, III, p. 310; George Carteret to Sir Edward Nicholas (Salé Roadstead, 20/30 May 1637), PRO, SP 71/13, fol. 10, also in SIHMA, III, p. 316; Rélation de Jean Marges (n.p., end of 1637) in SIHMFl, III, pp. 540–2; and William Rainsborough to the Lords of the Admiralty (Salé Roadstead, 8/18 August 1637), PRO, SP 71/13, fol. 23, also in SIHMA, III, p. 324.

71 William Rainsborough to the Lords of the Admiralty (Salé Roadstead, 8/18 August 1637), PRO, SP 71/13, fol 23, also in SIHMA, III, pp. 324–5; and Rélation de Jean Marges (n.p., end of 1637) in SIHMFl, III, pp. 542–4.

72 William Rainsborough to the Lords of the Admiralty (Salé Roadstead, 8/18 August 1637), PRO, SP 71/13, fol 23, also in SIHMA, III, pp. 324–5; and Rélation de Jean Marges (n.p., end of 1637) in SIHMFl, III, pp. 542–4.

73 George Carteret's Journal in SIHMA, p. 447.

74 George Carteret's Journal in SIHMA, III, pp. 455–9; Letter from George Carteret (Safi Roadstead) PRO, SP 71/13, fol. 63; and Robert Blake's Journal (11/21 June 1638), PRO, SP 71/13, fol. 72, also in SIHMA, III, pp. 494–5.

75 Gaspard de Rastin to Cardinal Richelieu (Salé, 16 July 1639) in SIHMFl, III, p. 587.

76 al-Ifrani, F: p. 449, p. 270, Fez: pp. 231–2.

77 Robert Blake to the House of Lords (n.p., 26 August/5 September 1641) in SIHMA, III, pp. 548–9.

78 Qaids of the Qasba to the States General (Qasba, 18 Rajab 1053/2 October 1643) in SIHMPB, V, pp. 45–8; Journal of the Salamander (Salé Roadstead, 15 April 1644) in SIHMPB, V, p. 587; SIHMPB, V, p. xxv; and *Newes from Sally of a strange delivery of four English captives from the slavery of the Turkes* (n.p., 1642), also in SIHMA, III, pp. 556–8.

79 Resolution of the Admiralty of Amsterdam (Amsterdam, 2 July 1648) in SIHMPB, V, pp. 139–40; and Instructions of Johan van Gaelen *et al.* (Amsterdam, February 1650) in SIHMPB, V, pp. 180–6.

80 David de Vries to States General (Salé, 4 June 1652) in SIHMPB, V, pp. 330–2; same to same (Salé, 28 December 1651) in SIHMPB, V, p. 315; and Sa'id al-Janāwī and ʿAbd Allah al-Qasari to the States General (Salé, 24 May 1652) in SIHMPB, V, p. 327.

81 SIHMPB, V, pp. xxv and 34, n.1; and Muhammad Hajji, *az-Zāwiya ad-Dila'iyya. wa dawruha ad-Dīnī wal-ʿ Ilmī was-Siyāsi* (Rabat, 1964), pp. 173–6.

82 SIHMPB, V, p. xxvi; and Roger Coindreau, *Les corsaires de Salé* (Paris, 1948), pp. 47 and 183. Neither offers any documentation to support the claim. Coindreau, as so often is the case, merely reworded Castries.

83 Hajji, *op. cit.*, p. 178.

84 Francois Lanier to Cardinal Mazarin (Lisbon, 30 December 1647) in SIHMFl, III, p. 639.

85 David de Vries to the States General (Salé, 2 March 1660) in SIHMPB, VI, pp. 613–14; and same to same (n.p., 15 June 1660) in SIHMPB, VI, pp. 616–17.

86 Hajji, *op. cit.*, p. 223.

87 SIHMPB, V, p. xxvi.

88 Dapper, *Description de l'Afrique*, translated from the Dutch (Amsterdam, 1686), pp. 142–3; Godefrois d'Estrades to Louis XIV (London, 6 February 1662) in SIHMF2, I, pp. 24–5; SIHMPB, V, p. xxvii; and Instructions to the Earl of Tevoit (n.p., 21/31 December 1663), PRO, Colonial Office Papers (CO) 279/2, fol. 183.

89 Letter from Captain Charles Harbord (Salé, 20/30 July 1668), PRO, CO 279/3, fol. 227; Colonel John Fitzgerald to Sir Henry Bennett (Tangier, 17/27 July 1668), PRO, CO 279/3, fol. 201; Letter to Colonel John Fitzgerald (Salé, 8/18 November 1668). PRO, SP 71/13, fols. 121–2;

and Dapper, *op. cit.*, p. 143.

90 Letter to Colonel John Fitzgerald (Salé, 8/18 November 1664), PRO, SP' 71/13, fol. 121.

91 Thomas Warren to Lord Arlington (Salé, 18/28 October 1669), PRO, CO 279/12, fol. 65; Lord Howard to Lord Arlington (Cadiz, 13/23 February 1669/70), PRO, SP 71/14, fol. 49; and same to same (Tangier, 20/30 November 1669), PRO, SP 71/13, fol. 267.

92 List of the corsair vessels of Salé (Salé, 1 August 1669) in SIHMF2, I, pp. 279–80; Francis Burghill to Lord Howard (Salé, 14/24 September 1669), PRO, SP 71/13, fol. 219; Jean d'Estrées to Colbert (Salé, 28 May 1670) in SIHMF2, I, p. 302; Rélation de Chateau-Renaud (Salé Roadstead, 2 September 1671) in SIHMF2, I, p. 379; Memoire of the corsair vessels of Salé (Lisbon, 25 January 1672) in SIHMF2, I, p. 406; and Letter from Salé (Salé, 3/13 February 1672/73), PRO, CO 279/16, fol. 294.

93 Letter from Jacques Gosse (Fez, 20 August 1670) in SIHMF2, pp. 324–5; Relation of Chateau-Renaud (Salé Roadstead, 2 September 1671) in SIHMF2, I, p. 379; Memoire of the corsair vessels of Salé (Lisbon, 25 January 1672) in SIHMF2, I, p. 406; and Extract of a letter from William Sedgwick (Salé, 16/26 April 1672), PRO, CO 279/15, fol. 113.

94 Lucette Valensi, *Le maghreb avant la prise d'Alger* (Paris, 1969).

95 See Daniel Panzac, 'Une activité en trompe l'oeil: la guerre de course à Tripoli de barbarie dans la seconde moite du XVIIIe siècle', in *Revue de l'occident musulman et de la méditerrannée*, no. 48 (1988), pp. 127–41; and Michel Fontenay, 'La place de la course dans l'économie portuaire: l'exemple de Malte et des ports barbaresques', in *Annales ESC*, vol. 43, vi (November–December 1988), pp. 1321–47, for recent discussions of these issues.

2 The impact of the French conquest of Algeria on Morocco (1830–1912)

Mohammed Kenbib

Unitarian expectations in North Africa seem to have reached an historical moment with the birth, last February, in Marrakesh of the 'Arab Maghreb Union'. The question of whether this new stage conveys any decisive change for the whole area or would remain, in the long term perspective, just an event is as conjectural as the types of unitarian precedents this experience could be related to. The challenge of the European Economic Community (EEC) was certainly one of the strongest considerations that hastened this step. But it would be interesting to know the model its architects had in mind when they signed the treaty of Marrakesh: did they think to the EEC experience, or to historical 'precedents' such as the German Zollverein? To what extent did they combine western 'models' with the old 'dream' of Arab unity, not to mention the 'ideal' of Islamic unity? What sort of assessment did they actually make of the common, historical legacy of the Maghreb? Given the lack of reliable data, it is, for the time being, almost impossible to answer these questions. Considered in a comparative perspective with some historical examples, however they may be helpful in so far as they reveal the extent and limits of slogans such as 'common heritage', 'common struggle against colonialism', 'sense of common destiny', 'Islamic solidarity', etc.

The most apposite examples come from the nineteenth century. Among the developments that North Africa witnessed during that century, we shall consider here how the relations between Morocco and Algeria evolved after France began the conquest of the former Ottoman Regency and turned it into a colony. Two main phrases are worth examining in this perspective:

1 The period from 1830 to 1844/5.
2 From the Moroccan defeat at the Battle of Isly to the establishment of the protectorate regime.

FROM THE FRENCH OCCUPATION OF ALGIERS TO THE BATTLE OF ISLY

When Moroccans heard that French troops had defeated the Dey of Algiers, a feeling that the collapse of the Regency not only meant the implementation of 'Christian' rule in an adjacent Muslim territory but also implied a direct threat to Moroccan independence spread throughout the country. Bound to their eastern neighbours by all sorts of ties, despite old territorial, political and spiritual rivalries opposing the Sharifian court to the Dey and his Ottoman suzerain, the Moroccans became directly involved in the struggle the Algerians were undertaking. Even if great caution is required when dealing with the *makhzan* official discourse of that time, given the high degree of religious impregnation and the difficulty of identifying the real meaning behind the words, the documents exchanged between Sultan Mulay ʿAbd ar-Rahman bin Hisham (1822–59), his son Sidi Mohammed who acted as co-ordinator of civilian and military assistance to Emir ʿAbd al-Qadir as well as commander-in-chief of the Moroccan forces gathered to face the French army, and other Moroccan officials, indicate the attitudes the Moroccans took to Algerian resistance.

A general atmosphere of what a French diplomat in Tangier described as 'la consternation des Maures', characterised what the sultan wrote, after the news of the French invasion reached him through his Jewish consul in Gibraltar, in the following letter to the governor of Tetouan who, after 1845, became the head of the first Moroccan embassy sent to Paris to 'normalise' Franco-Moroccan relations:

> We have learnt through Ben Oliel the catastrophy inflicted upon Islam and the Muslims. Great sorrow afflicted the Believers and all men of Faith [because of the invasion of Algiers] by the Enemy of God, the capture by the French invaders of treasures and [large quantities of] money, and the subscription of the Dey to the unprecedented humiliating conditions ... May God assist the Muslims in facing this disastrous calamity, help them to defeat the Infidel enemy and return this place to Islam ... With the help of the Prophet ...'[1]

A few days later the same governor received a second letter instructing him to provide assistance to the Algerian refugees who had fled to northern Morocco and more particularly to Tetouan (Titwan), a city long known as an outpost of Islam and whose population derived basically from descendants of Muslims – and Jews – expelled from Spain after 1492:

> We have received your letter informing us of the arrival [at Tetouan] of two ships carrying the people of Algiers, might God return it to Dar Islam, and what they said about the other inhabitants and those of Oran as well about what the Infidel enemy actually did may God thwart his hope. [Know] that you should welcome warmly everyone seeking refuge, assist them, show them hospitality and moral support. Helping their broken heart to recover is an imperative duty, especially if we keep in mind that they are our Muslim brothers defeated and driven out by the enemy who took their country and their properties. They fled to escape his rule and thus safeguard their religion, may God the Compassionate assist them ...'[2]

The population showed even more enthusiasm in supporting the refugees, while their countrymen who remained in Algeria prepared to resist the invaders. A sort of *jihād* mobilisation prevailed all over the country. This 'mobilisation' remained strong even after the withdrawal of the Moroccan force sent to Tlemcen – a city known for its close commercial and family links with Fez – whose inhabitants hurried to proclaim their allegiance to the Sultan of Morocco immediately after the collapse of the Dey. This withdrawal came as a result of the clashes between the Moroccan expeditionary force and the *Kourloughli-s.* These disturbances gave France an opportunity to submit Mulay ʿAbd ar-Rahman to great pressure to remain neutral. A special embassy was sent to Meknes to show him the dangers of any further Moroccan involvement in Algerian affairs.

Despite his preference for peace and stability – a preliminary condition for the development of the trade, the increase of custom revenues and, consequently, less fiscal pressure on the population and a decrease of tribal uprisings – Mulay ʿAbd ar-Rahman could not abide by the assurances given to the French ambassador De Mornay (whose attendants included Eugene Delacroix) that he would do his best not to alienate his peaceful relations with France. Several reasons stood behind the decision to become involved, which expressed the narrow limit that existed in politics at that time between internal and external affairs where religious solidarity was concerned. Being the 'Commander of the Faithful', bound to his subjects – who perceived themselves as a 'Community of Believers' – by a *bayʿa* explicitly imposing upon him the obligation to defend Islam, Mulay ʿAbd ar-Rahman could not remain passive in front of what he himself referred to as a 'disastrous calamity'. His personal experience before 1822, his contacts with Europeans in Essaouira (As-Sawira), and his awareness that Morocco could not face France militarily without serious risks, were of almost no weight compared to the necessity of preserving his legitimacy through assistance to the Algerian *mujāhidin*. And when ʿAbd al-Qadir sent a letter to the ʿulamāʾ of Fez asking them to issue a *fatwa* on the *jihād* and tried to sustain his own legitimacy by acting only as the 'Commander of the Faithful's' deputy, the Algerian chief knew that the sultan had almost no choice but to join the *mujāhidin*.

Makhzan circles were unanimous in their determination to assist the Algerian *mujāhidin*. The Khalifa Sidi Muhammad bin ʿAbd ar-Rahman (the crown prince) was known to be particularly supportive. He had to supervise civilian and military assistance to the *mujāhidin* and played an important role in conveying to them arms and ammunitions bought abroad, especially in Gibraltar.

The religious and merchant elite shared this enthusiasm. Even if some *fatwas* were voluntarily ambiguous in order to secure a certain political freedom of manoeuvre for the sultan, the ʿulamāʾ insisted on the religious obligation of *jihād* against the 'infidels', especially when they invaded part of '*Dar al Islam*'. Apart from the business aspect of their involvement and the profits made in the importation and sale of arms, the big merchants felt that it was their duty as Muslims to back the *mujāhidin*. Talib Binjillūn was particularly active in this respect: he worked side by side with the Khalifa, Sidi Muhammad, in order to provide Algerian resistance fighters with food and arms. In order to avoid diplomatic complications with the French, he explained to them that he acted as a merchant seizing an opportunity to make money. But they rejected what they called 'de prétendues opérations commerciales' and insisted that Moroccan merchants – except the Jewish element – were performing a 'pious duty' and involving themselves not commercially but politically.[3]

Common people, especially the tribes in the eastern part of Morocco and more particularly those who used to herd in the border region with almost no regard to the frontier, were even more willing to respond to appeals to *jihād*. French observers in Tangiers and elsewhere followed the impact of these exhortations carefully. They considered voluntary assistance to the *mujāhidin* as just another expression of what they called 'Moroccan fanaticism'. They reported on long caravans of thousands of camels and mules carrying money, food, clothes, tents, arms and ammunition from Fez eastwards.

Solidarity with the Algerians was also expressed through the facilities and privileges granted to the refugees who fled to Morocco to escape, as it was said at that time, Christian rule and preserve the Islamic way of life. According to *fatwa-s* still in force, even if they were issued several centuries earlier by *'ulamā'* who dealt with the problem of Andalusian Muslims facing the *Reconquista*, migration was an imperative obligation for believers whose territories come under the control of infidels. Considered as *muhājirīn* – with all the symbolic strength that migration conveyed in Islamic history, which started with the *hijra* of the Prophet Mohammed and his followers, the *anṣār*, from Mecca to Medina – the Algerian refugees were indeed provided with numerous advantages and progressively integrated into Moroccan society. This assimilation began immediately after the arrival of the first groups of refugees. The governor of Tetouan, for example, received the following instructions in a letter addressed to him by the sultan on October 20, 1830:

> We have learnt that the people who fled from Algeria, may God return it to Islam, have among them sailors, artillery men, 'technicians' familiar with the craft of bombs, bullets, mortars, and cannons.
>
> So, immediately after reading this letter, select them and make each group join their [Moroccan] fellows. Let us know about these appointments. If no care is taken of them and if they are neglected, they will remain exposed to waste. So, it is imperative you act the way you are instructed. May God provide you with success.[4]

Other groups were given land concessions. They settled in different parts of the country. Some of them became very wealthy in the second half of the nineteenth century and held high *makhzan* positions as governors. In the Gharb province, for instance, the Ben Aouda emerged as big landlords. In the same region refugees from Meliana (Māliana) occupied a whole district as their own in a strategic location between Tangier and Fez.

In these circumstances, Mulay 'Abd ar-Rahman could pay but little attention to the 'friendly advice' of Great Britain. Lord Palmerston instructed his minister in Tangier to call the attention of the sultan to the necessity of avoiding any difficulties with France:

> The British Government feel a sincere friendship for the Emperor, and is desirous of seeing [him] continue independent and powerful. That the best rule by which the Emperor can guide his conduct in regard to other Powers with a view to maintain his independence and to preserve peace, is to be extremely careful never to give any Foreign Power a just cause of complaint against him ...[5]

One year later, Lord Aberdeen was even more explicit: 'It appears to Her Majesty's Government, that the Emperor would act wisely if he were to endeavour as much as possible to restrain from taking any part in the contest between ʿAbd al-Qadir and the French ...'⁶ The British minister in Tangier undertook a mission to Meknes to convey this 'advice' to the sultan who actually granted him a private audience.⁷

Given the circumstances, Islamic solidarity seemed the natural and appropriate response to the French invaders. *Jihād* and the subsequent mobilisation of the believers appeared the best way to counterbalance French military superiority. Despite ʿAbd al-Qadir's short-lived victories between 1832 and 1837, the gap between his power and that of the French tended to increase, especially when the latter started to implement General Bugeaud's 'total war' strategy and made no distinction between civilian and military targets. Algerian fighters had no choice but to retreat behind the Moroccan frontier. But Morocco was not a sanctuary; claiming the 'droit de poursuite', the French 'Colonnes infernales' chased them inside Moroccan territory and also took reprisals against the Beni Snassen (Bann Snassan), Riffians and other Moroccan supporters.

Serious difficulties arose, in consequence, between Mulay ʿAbd ar-Rahman and the Emir ʿAbd al-Qadir. The sultan considered that the latter was endangering his country's independence. The Algerian emir felt, for his part, that the sultan was bending under French pressure and reducing the assistance he ought to give to *mujāhidin*. Relations worsened after the battle of Isly, for this defeat put an end to Morocco's military reputation and showed all colonial powers the extent of the country's weakness. France took advantage of her victory to impose two conventions (Tangier and Lalla Maghnia) on the sultan. Several provisions compelled Mulay ʿAbd ar-Rahman to stop assistance to the Algerian 'rebels' and even commit himself to send his own troops against ʿAbd al-Qadir. Other provisions stated that no definite or materialised limits would be traced between the Sharifian Empire and the French colony. The absence of clear geographic boundaries gave France the opportunity to consider several tribes as former subjects of the Regency and therefore prepare the annexation of their territory to the colony (Hamiyan, Walad Sidi Shaykh, etc.). Facing the internal rebellions that spread in different parts of the country immediately after the battle of Isly – some tribes did not hesitate to attack and pillage even the remnants of the defeated troops who were retreating in disorder behind the Moulaya river – Mulay ʿAbd ar-Rahman found himself caught between two fires and had no choice other than to make futile diplomatic protests. He tried to rely on the British, but the Foreign Office was ready to provide no more than 'good offices'. Moreover, John Drummond Hay urged the sultan to reward Great Britain for her attitude after the battle of Isly when she made it clear to the French that an open advance inside Moroccan territory would not be tolerated. These considerations let to the conclusion in March 1856 of two Anglo-Moroccan conventions of 'friendship, navigation and commerce'. Their provisions, especially the dramatic decrease of the custom duties (limited to 10 per cent *ad valorem*), the dismantlement of the royal monopolies, and the quasi-disappearance of the '*tujjar sultan*' system, weakened the country and its government even more. An unprecedented extension of capitulatory rights to natives paralleled the development of imports and exports.

After the Battle of Isly France used Algeria and the Algerian refugees in numerous ways to unify North Africa under a French flag. The colony served as a strong base for colonial penetration eastwards and westwards. After 1881 the 'Tunisification' of Morocco became one of the most important targets of the French government and the Governor-General of Algeria. Stronger pressures were put on Morocco's eastern territories. The so-called 'droit de poursuite' against pillaging tribes served as a practical pretext for frequent military incursions in Gourara, Touat, Tafilalet and other south-eastern districts.

The crystallisation of the role devoted to Algeria in the intended integration of Morocco into the French colonial empire was also demonstrated by the sponsorship given by the Governor-General to exploratory missions aiming at a rational and scientific conquest of the country. Figures such as Charles de Foucauld, Edmond Doutté, Augustin Bernard, Auguste Moulièras, William Marçais, as well as other 'scientists' of the famous Ecole des Lettres of Algiers, all took part in these 'Missions' and 'Reconnaissances'. Among the colonial lobby pressing the French government to adopt a more aggressive line in Moroccan affairs, special mention should be made of the representative of Oran to the French Parliament and central figure in the 'Comité du Maroc': Eugène Etienne.

The Algerian refugees settled in Morocco were under constant pressure: France tried to manipulate them through 'capitulatory privileges' and they were indeed claimed as 'French subjects'. Nevertheless, many of them remained, at least until the end of the nineteenth century, reluctant to accept such a status and did not respond to these manoeuvres. In one of his reports to the Quai d'Orsay, the French minister in Tangier, De Monbel, wrote in response to a note from his government instructing him to 'secure French protection for the Algerians established in Morocco', especially those settled in Fez and known to be enjoying a relatively high socio-economic position:

> Three thousand people from Tlemcen are living now in Fez but more people have left Algeria to escape our jurisdiction. They are nowadays Moroccan *de facto*. Many of them live in a state of dependency on the *makhzan* and have no interest to seek our protection since they enjoy special privileges such as tax exemption. Out of the above mentioned 3,000 at Fez only 40 registered as 'French protégés'.[8]

Even if they enjoyed no privileges, certain groups of refugees had no interest at all in being identified as Algerians. They wanted to 'disappear' amongst the Moroccans. French representatives regarded them as 'even more fanatical than the Moroccans themselves'. Under this category came groups such as:

1 Insurgents belonging to south-western and sub-Saharan tribes who fled to Morocco after their revolts were suppressed. France interfered in their settlement in Morocco and insisted that they should be established somewhere in the south-western provinces rather than in eastern Morocco or even the Gharb province. This was the case of the Walad Sidi Shaykh Shraja. Some of them fled to Morocco after their revolt of 1864 was suppressed. They were transferred among the Wadaya tribe in the Hawz. Other insurgents, such as those who joined Muqrani in his revolt in Kabylia (1871), also fled to Morocco.
2 Deserters of the French Army who sought the sultan's protection (this was also the case of Christian soldiers who deserted the Armée d'Afrique or the Spanish Tercio). Despite his protests on the grounds that 'religion had primacy over nationality' and the humiliation inherent to the extradition of Muslims, the *makhzan* had, however, to give from time to time some satisfaction to France and extradite some individuals.[9]
3 Several convicts ('political criminals' according to the French Legation in Tangier) who escaped from convict-prisons such as that of Cayenne. According to Edmond Doutté, 'These refugees were numerous. They used to consider Morocco as a secure shelter.'[10]

However, out of some 20,000 Algerians settled in Morocco by the end of the nineteenth century, the tiny minority who responded positively to the French approaches created a lot of trouble for the *makhzan*. At the head of this group, in Fez for instance, was the factotum of the French vice-consulate there. Doctor Linarès, physician and French special agent at the Sharifian Court, wrote in a report devoted to the negative implications for France of the misconduct of this factotum:

> The inexplicable attitude of Si Allal Abdi might alienate all the sympathies [we have here]. The Moroccans believe that we are seeking serious complications ... Si Allal is a half-civilised Algerian ... Arrogant with the Moroccans, he tries to take advantage of his situation to obtain big benefits ... By acting so, he cancels, if I may say so, the good effects we could expect upon the Algerians ... through the establishment of a vice-consulate here. In his relations with *makhzan* officials, Si Allal acts as if he was in a conquered country. He insults Moroccan functionaries in front of people under their administration.[11]

Some elements amongst the merchant groups showed similar behaviour. Mulay Hassan (1873–94) protested to the French legation about their 'fraudulent practices ... and refusal to obey the *muḥtassib*'s orders'. 'If no end is put to their practices,' said the sultan, 'others will act the same way and all the rules and regulations in Fez will be broken.'[12] Complications arose also with the Algerians settled as landowners in the countryside. Given the *makhzan*'s particular structure, and the type of relations the sultan used to have with tribal notables which permitted their intermittent mobilisation for the *harka-s* or military campaigns, this category of Algerian claimed the status of French subject in order to escape fiscal and military obligations and to extend these immunities to Moroccans themselves who pretended that they were their agricultural associates. This phenomenon was particularly corrosive and had a decisive impact on Morocco's traditional socio-economic and political structures.

No less corrosive in this regard was the extension of French protections and naturalisations to a considerable number of Moroccan Jewish subjects. The Algerian connection played a determining role in this respect. In a report where he warned the Quai d'Orsay against the 'troubles caused to the Consulate of Mogador by this category of Jews who seek French protection here as in other parts of Barbary and the Levant just to involve us in inextricable matters', the French consul at Essaouira described the abusive means some Jews adopted to obtain French naturalisation:

A great number of Jews travel to Oran. There they seek the assistance of two accommodative 'witnesses' who accept to testify that they are Algerian-born natives. Relying on notarial documents, they apply for French passports. Holding these passports, they come back to Morocco and rush to the nearest consulate to register as 'French subjects.[13]

This category of French subjects, known to have been illegally naturalised, extended their newly acquired privileges to their relatives, other co-religionists, and Muslims. The latter being declared as censals (*censaux*) or agriculture associates (*mukhalāts*). Given the increasing fiscal pressure on common people and the potential immunities inherent to the status of 'censal' or *mukhalāt*, the market for illegal but effective capitulatory privileges expanded impressively. Despite the risks inherent in false official documents especially during periods of drought and the failure of the supposed native partner to reimburse the imaginary cash advances he had received, increasing numbers of landlords and peasants became *mukhalāts*. Their dependence on naturalised Jews and the usury abuses they suffered from were among the main causes of an inexorable deterioration of Muslim–Jewish relations in Morocco. The promotion or mass naturalisation of the entire Jewish community of Algeria to the legal status of French citizens through the famous Décret Crémieux (1870) had a large echo among their Moroccan co-religionists and it increased French political influence in the country.

This influence increased also through Muslim religious figures such as the head of the *zāwiya* of Wazzan, Mulay ʿAbd as-Salam, whose French protection and scandalous marriage with a British nurse, Emily Keen – author of an autobiography, *My Life Story*, published in London, 1911 – expressed the deep cultural and political change nineteenth century Morocco had to face. The French government started paying attention to the *zāwiya* of Wazzan as part of a global strategy of penetration based on co-operation with religious figures.

Initially, however, their main concern was to use the *zāwiya*'s influence in Algeria to strengthen their moral control over the population there. In order to convince Mulay ʿAbd as-Salam to co-operate, the Governor-General submitted the periodical visits of the *zāwiya*'s agents in the colony to administrative authorisation: these agents of the Grand Chérif could not visit their Algerian supporters and collect their gifts and donations (*ziara-s*) without the approval of French authorities.

Mulay ʿAbd as-Salam accepted this and went even further, backing the French territorial encroachments into the Touat oases, to spread their propaganda among his followers and sub-Saharan tribes. Mulay Hassan sent several messages warning the population of Touat against Mulay ʿAbd as-Salam's pro-French activities:

> To our magnanimous servants ... *qāʾid-s, qadi-s, fuqaha-s* ... of Touat.
> Our Sharifian Majesty has been informed that Haj ʿAbd as-Salam of Wazzan intends to visit your country and press you to conclude an alliance with the enemy government [France] ... We know him as a man who had abjured his faith and committed acts in violation of the religious prescriptions ... You have among you *shurafa*, learned people, and men known for their goodness and piety ... So, if the Wazzani tries to push you out of the right path, do not listen to him ... Behave in such a manner he will find no way to succeed in his treachery'.[14]

Despite the Wazzani's efforts, the tribes went on supporting Algerian insurgents and thereby exposed themselves to French attacks. One of the Sultan's letters describes the heavy price they had to pay for this assistance:

> We have received a letter from Saharan tribes informing us that Christian troops went there intending to repress the [Moroccan] tribe of Ammor ... who fled to the mountains ... where the French besieged them. A war broke there ... The French killed a lot of people, raped their wives mistreated their children ... took their belongings ... and imposed their authority upon the remnants ... The French columns moved afterwards to the Figuig region ... attacked the population and burnt their palm-groves.'[15]

No less important was the political price the sultan himself had to pay for his passivity towards French aggressions in this part of his empire and the threatening letters sent to the tribes requesting them to stop giving shelter to agitators such as Slimane ben Kaddour, Kaddour ben Hamza, Bou Amama, or other rebels seeking 'disorder in the border area'.[16]

Some religious figures in the south-east, such as Shaykh Muhammad Larbi Mdaghri, head of the Darqawa *zāwiya*, exhorted their countrymen to *jihād* with no reference to the sultan – the 'Commander of the Faithful'. Even the governors in that area did not strictly follow the sultan's instructions. Some of them did nothing to stop the smuggling of arms and ammunitions from Melilla and elsewhere to the Algerian rebels. Others responded 'disrespectfully' to the French authorities of Oran or Tlemcen who threatened them with reprisals.[17]

Under these circumstances the sultan could do almost nothing to preserve what remained of his independence and sovereignty. The reforms undertaken, especially after the catastrophic 'War of Tetouan' (1859–60), faced numerous obstructions. They generated serious problems and finally appeared to be even more harmful to the country and its government than the *status quo ante*. The problems that arose as a consequence of the *makhzan*'s attempts at reform in the fiscal and military fields were significant in this regard:

1 The proposal for a new fiscal system based on the principle of general taxation and abolition of traditional as well as capitulatory exemptions faced strong opposition – the former 'Algerian refugees' who, for a long time, had considered themselves as Moroccans and resisted French advances, started claiming the status of French subjects. Given the diplomatic situation and French progress towards the eviction of diplomatic rivals on the Moroccan scene, such a behaviour provided new options for the future.

2 The attempts at military reforms and the creation of a regular army were an opportunity that France seized to appoint political agents to the Court and thereby gain additional influence. Headed by French officers (*capitaines* or *commandants*) generally belonging to the Algeria-based Armée d'Afrique and reporting directly to the Ministry of War (Paris), the French Military Mission established in 1878 also included Algerian-born instructors. Besides being arrogant, ostensibly disrespectful of Islamic moral values, and insolent towards Muslim religious authorities such as *muḥtassib-s* and *qadi-s* (cf. the scandal caused by the removal from office of the popular *qadi* of Rabat, Al Bribri, after his clash with an Algerian officer and the intervention of the French government), thus causing anger at this example of 'dissolute conduct of Muslims inside the Muslim world', these instructors also took part in *makhzan* military campaigns and in the suppression of tribal rebellions. (cf. the role of Ben Sedira in the expeditions undertaken against Jilali Zarhuni 'Bou Hmara'). Their presence in Morocco as French *harrabas* could only give the impression to the population that they were assisting the infidels to enlarge their influence in the country and help in establishing an army for the 'true believers'. Their contribution to the suppression of rural uprisings could easily

have been perceived as participation to the repression of legitimate opposition to abusive taxation and a threat to the way the *makhzan* dealt with European threats and the unjust claims of the *Ahl al-Himayat* (protégés) and the *'Ahl al-Basbur'* ('naturalised persons' or 'passport holders') – namely, an abnormal situation that *'ulamā'* condemned but that, exceptionally, a *fatwa* printed in Algiers tried to justify by arguing that this privileged category was right in so far as its members sought refuge against injustice.

'Moroccan Anarchy' developed as an unavoidable result of the multidimensional and intense pressures put on the country after 1844. The reform attempts had dramatic adverse effects and the 1904 deal that Great Britain concluded with France (the 'Entente Cordiale') paved the way for a French protectorate as did the Algesiras Conference two years later.

French propaganda took advantage of the expanding tribal rebellions to focus on the 'natural propensity of Moroccans for anarchy'. French agents underlined the stability brought to Algeria and the beneficial effects of the *Pax Gallica*. These slogans had actually been spread even earlier among the Moroccan elite. The chronicler Ahmad Naciri (d. 1897) had eagerly condemned this tendency. He stated in his *Istiqsa*:

> What sort of good benefits did the French bring to the people of Algiers or Tlemcen? Don't we see that they have lost their religion, that corruption has spread among them and that, with few exceptions, all their children are badly educated and grow amongst misbelieving and infidelity. May God help the Islamic millet and break the strength of the corrupted worshippers of idols.[18]

Despite his initial radical programme and his success in trying to resist the French troops that moved from Algeria to occupy Oujda in 1904 and those which landed in Casablanca and occupied the rich Chaouia (Shawira) province, Mulay Hafid (1907–12), proclaimed as the 'Sultan of *Jihād*' in Marrakech, failed to achieve his goals. The situation became even worse than it had been under his brother and predecessor, Mulay 'Abd al-Aziz (1894–1907). Mulay Hafidh finally had to submit to France and sign the treaty establishing the protectorate regime on 30 March 1912. The French legation interpreter, the Algerian, Kaddur Bin Ghabrit, played a decisive role as 'mediator' between the French 'negociator' François Régnault (who also benefited from the skills of his countryman and consul at Fez, Henri

Gaillard) and Mulay Hafidh. Later on Bin Ghabrit was granted the Légion d'honneur for his 'services signales' during the sensitive 'negociations' that led to the treaty of Fez. However, one year earlier, several families left Tlemcen and other Algerian cities and fled to Syria in order to avoid military conscription. They preferred exile rather than to have to take part in the forthcoming conquest of Morocco as French soldiers.[19]

It goes without saying that these facts were just part of the more general process that shaped the mutual perceptions of Algerians and Moroccans as well as their perceptions of their own specific identity. Emir ʿAbd al-Qadir and his followers' conviction that the sultan's 'defection' had hastened their final defeat was largely counterbalanced on the Moroccan side by the impression that the Algerian refugees, assisted in Morocco, granted privileges, and promoted to positions as high as that of Grand-Vizir such as Muqri, were ungrateful. After the proclamation of Mulay Hafidh, this vizir had the responsibility of raising a French loan and expressing to the French government that the new sultan had agreed to ratify the provisions of the Algeciras Act. Furthermore, the commitment to the Algerian *mujāhidin* had led to the collapse at Isly and all the long term territorial implications of this defeat. Although the issue was frozen during the colonial era, the question of Moroccan territories annexed to Algeria surfaced tragically in 1963 and led to the inconclusive 'guerre des sables'.

The tremendous complexity of the events that took place during the nineteenth century and at the beginning of the twentieth, such as the Moroccan tribal assistance to the Bu Amama revolt in south-western Algeria, the transit of *makhzan* soldiers fighting Bou Hmara through Algerian ports, the participation of a descendant of Emir ʿAbd al-Qadir, ʿAbd al-Malik, in the Riffian armed resistance against Spain and France, makes it difficult to assess their precise impact on the general perception that Algerians and Moroccans had of their respective national interests. It seems, however, that these facts have contributed to give them a stronger secular sense of solidarity and unity quite apart from any common sense of religious identity – a new basis, perhaps, for future co-operation through a common Maghrebi legacy.

NOTES

1 Ouataiq, vol. I, 10 Safar 1246.
2 Vol. I, 22 Rabi I 1246.
3 J. L. Miège, *Le Maroc et l'Europe*, T.II, p. 161, quoting a diplomatic

report dated 3 March 1840: 'Taleb Bengelloun prétendait ne suivre d'impératif autre que celui de ses intérets matériels.'

4   *Ouataiq*, vol. I, 3 Joumada I 1346.
5   Foreign Office (FO) 99, 7, 12 February 1841.
6   FO 99, 9, 6 May 1842.
7   J. D. Hay to the Foreign Office, 21 June 1842.
8   Quai d'Orsay, AEP, CP, 72, 10 April 1895.
9   Quai d'Orsay FB, 14 Moharram 1295/19 January 1878, 'French claims'; AMG, C11, Marrakech, 19 February 1899, 'Le Makhzen's s'efforce d'acclimater cette idée que la religion prime la nationalité'.
10 Quai d'Orsay, AEP, CP, 72, Tangier 29 March 1895, report on the case of Omar Kouchti, escaped from Cayenne in 1885 and established in Tangier.
11 Quai d'Orsay Fez 28 September 1894.
12 FB, 16 Moharram 1302/5 November 1884.
13 Quai d'Orsay, AEP, CC, Mogador, IV, 16 April 1861.
14 AGP, Martin *Quatre siècles d'Histoire marocaine* (Paris, 1923), pp. 252–3.
15 FB, 26 Rabi I 1299/15 February 1882.
16 FB, 4 Moharram 1299/26 November 1881.
17 *Ibid.*
18 *Istiqsa*, t. IX, pp. 90–1.
19 Slimane Chikh *L'Algérie en armes* (Paris, 1981); C. R. Ageron *Les Algériens musulmans et la France, 1871–1919* (Paris, 1968).

3 Problems of interpretation of North African history: The impact of information on the policies of Hammuda Pasha (1810–13)

Abdeljelil Temimi

This chapter deals with a specific issue of Tunisian history and is based essentially on new revelations found in Tunisian archives. It is also a reflection on some general questions of Maghrebi history which need re-evaluation in the light of political distortion of the historical record.

THE SPECIFIC ISSUE

The first question refers to the significance of the mass of information of all kinds which reached Tunisian authorities in the early nineteenth century and which determined the economic, commercial and military decisions made by the government of the Regency of Tunis. It specifically relates to the quality of the information received from Alexandria, Izmir, and especially from Malta, thanks to the *Oukala* set up in the Western and Eastern Mediterranean.

We already know of the important role played by the annual pilgrimage of the North Africans through the Maghreb and Mashriq to Mecca which led some pilgrims[1] to settle in Cairo, Damascus or Istanbul. This phenomenon helped to enrich the network of commercial exchanges and which was itself profitable to the local authorities. Moreover, we know of hundreds of Tunisian traders in Egypt[2] who provided economic, commercial, political and military information not only on Muhammad Ali's Egypt, but also on the whole of the Mashriq.[3]

This is the context in which shall examine the information contained in the letters addressed to Hammuda Pasha by Mahmud Jellouli,[4] his delegate in Malta from 1810 to 1813. His copious information was to influence the decisions, orders and directives taken by the government of the Regency of Tunis.

Ever since its capture by England at the start of the nineteenth century, Malta had become very important in Mediterranean and international trade. The blockade imposed on France by England in the Mediterranean meant that Malta became the most economically and commercially privileged site in the region,[5] where the vast number of foreign ships anchored there ensured the free circulation and exchange of all kinds of information, in addition to fostering commerce. Thus, Mahmud Jalluli, the representative of Bey Hammuda Pasha in Malta, was able to send to the Tunisian authorities an abundant and meticulous correspondence on this issue, in which the quality of military, political and, above all, commercial information was striking. While economic information merely reflected the general situation in the Mediterranean, military information was of crucial importance because of its direct impact on military decisions. One example of this concerned Algiers.

We already know of the uneasy relations between the Tunisian and the Algerian Regencies, which were characterised by confrontation during the reign of Hammuda Pasha. The Pasha kept acquiring warships,[6] gunpowder,[7] and various weapons[8] from Malta, despite opposition from the Algierian Regency.[9] The decision of Hammuda Pasha's government to obtain this equipment was based on information on prices and availability provided by Jalluli. Because of Tunisia's success, the same thing happened in Algiers,[10] but this unfortunate competition between the two North African states only benefited the British and Malta. It was for this reason that the Tunisian Regency government followed with attention and anxiety details of the recruitment of janissaries from Anatolia for Algiers,[11] making note of their number, grade and lengths of service. Indeed, the Hammuda government also sought to recruit janissaries[12] in order to be ready to face a possible resumption of hostilities between the two Ottoman regencies.

The importance of 'economic and commercial' information, on the other hand, can be illustrated by the wheat trade. Jalluli gave useful information on economic circumstances and price controls in the Mediterranean. He reported on the various prices according to the quality of the wheat available,[13] its scarcity or abundance in Malta, its high price in Europe and how the Bey's representative used the Beylik's money for the purchase of wheat from Alexandria to sell it in Messina;[14] Jalluli also provided some information on the origin of wheat from the Black Sea, Derna, and from Benghazi. It was on the basis of this accurate data sent by Jalluli that the government of the Regency of Tunis then made its decisions regarding the sale of Tunisian wheat, its price and its export destination. Jalluli's influence also influenced the Bey's decisions on the sale of wool and other Tunisian export products such as olive oil, and the purchase of cattle from Alexandria. All this shows the crucial role played by commercial information from Malta in the policies of the Tunisian Regency at the end of Hammuda Pasha's reign.

As far as political information was concerned, Mahmud Jalluli reported on the rich panorama of political events in the capital of the Ottoman Empire, the situation in Egypt and Egyptian relations with the Wahhabi movement in Saudi Arabia which controlled the holy places there[15] and their war, and on the situation in Morocco. He also gave information on North African caravans, and on banking and the functioning of tribunals in Malta.[16] The military, commercial and political information that reached the Tunisian authorities thus justified their subsequent decisions. Ironically enough, however, this kind of historical information is a field of research which is still completely ignored. Yet it is fundamental to the understanding and definition of the objectives and reasons for political, commercial, economic and military decisions, not only of the Regency of Tunis, but also of the whole of the Maghreb states in the modern era.

PROBLEMS OF INTERPRETATION

It is undeniable that today, a new school of North African historians, freed from post-colonial complexes, is actively participating in the development of historical studies using a rigorous methodology. The vast number of theses and new sources publicly available, the numerous specialised congresses, and the highly specialist dialogue now taking place between historians, have all created a new dynamism between academics and researchers in North Africa and elsewhere.

In spite of these positive developments there is still one area where this dialogue has virtually failed, and where distrust is still the rule – between historians, on the one hand, and those who hold political power and thus exploit a certain concept of history and its interpretation, on the other. A whole range of commissioned historical studies which did not respect the final judgement of historical research must now be consigned to total oblivion.

Many historical facts and events have been designated taboo because they have been wrongly interpreted. Indeed, even as newly discovered documents shed a different light on the past, their validity is rejected by those who fear their disclosure may affect them and their established interpretations of the past. Here are some typical examples of this deliberate distortion:

1   The fact, for example, that the Emir ʿAbd al-Qadir was a freemason is still denied, in spite of the many authentic documents that confirm his affiliation. The whole of this controversy denotes the ignorance and the deliberate misinterpretation of events and refuses to admit facts which have been related by the Emir himself.[17]

2   Another example is that of a historian who was unable to complete his study of the relationship between various tribes and the French authorities during the Muqrani revolt of 1870. Eventually he had to abandon them because they implicated renowned families.

3   Another historical researcher in Tunisia did not dare to publish compromising documents. He did not even dare to allude to the legitimacy (or illegitimacy) of regimes, persons, parties or movements of national liberation.

4   Another very significant example is that of those North African historians and, above all, politicians, who persist in an irrational assertion, which is scientifically groundless, that the Regencies of Algiers, Tunis and Tripolitania were national states during the Ottoman period. It is well known that the Deys and the Beys of these regencies were *all* Turko-Ottomans, who considered the Ottoman Regencies to be an integral part of the Muslim *umma*, under the aegis of a central Ottoman power. Why then distort interpretations and historical facts which are confirmed by all the documentation emanating from the governments of the Regencies?

The price paid for distorting history has already been heavy for the historians involved in this falsification. This is illustrated in Tunisia by the unfortunate experience of the movement of national liberation. Its history was moulded into an official version which prevailed for thirty years. Today, this version, together with those who wrote it and sustained it, is held in contempt.[18]

The reality of that period involved a rather wider experience which also affected neighbouring countries. This involved the notion of the North African nation as a part of the Arab nation. It is an idea which has only been evoked, defended and conceived through the activities of North African leaders within the Arab Maghreb Bureaux in Berlin, Cairo and Damascus. The *Revue d'Histoire Maghrebine* (RHM) was the first publication to have the honour of carefully relating and collating these facts in numerous contributions to its columns. These now constitute an essential and fundamental reference for the history of the period.

The purpose of this brief reflection, therefore, is to urge historians to try to convince North African leaders to look at history in an honest and unbiased manner. They must also be persuaded to open archives – *all* archives – so that we may gain a better and more objective knowledge of our past. Politicians must be made aware of the necessity of accepting and respecting all historical and scientific research, regardless of who the author may be. Above all, they must trust historians. Could we interpret the events which have affected the Maghreb in the last few years – with the formation of the Union Maghreb Arabe – as the sign of a fundamental and radical change leading to the emergence of a new and dynamic generation of leaders? We hope and believe so.

NOTES

1 See Rashad Limam's thesis on the annual pilgrimage published by the Faculté des Lettres de Tunis, 1980.
2 *Ibid.*, pp. 293–8.
3 See the large number of contributions by historians to *Revue d'Histoire Maghrebine* (RHM) on this subject, particularly those of Abdurrahim Abdurrahmam and Leila Sabbagh.
4 No biography has been compiled on this very important figure who played a crucial role in the Tunisian diplomacy of the title, but see Ibn Ibi Diaf, *Ibhaf*, vol. 8, p. 42.
5 Here is how Jalluli describes Malta: 'It is like France or London; one finds everything one wants ... one finds here fabrics from India, sugar, coffee, cotton ... with booty, one finds French products; moreover, should one express the desire for any product, the factory owner will give entire satisfaction', in *Archives Nationales de Tunisie* (ANT), Box 225, File 408, Doc. 48.
6 For a lot of information on the commerce of warships, their price and condition, especially when dealing with booty, see ANT, Box 225, File 407, Docs 81, 82, 83, 88, 89, 117; and File 408, Doc. 220.
7 The information on the quantities of powder purchased in Malta are quoted in many letters: the price, weight in Maltese measure, the transfer to Tunis via Sousse or Sfax; see ANT, Box 225, File 407, Docs 59, 75 and 83.
8 Malta was the best place for the purchase of weapons. Jalluli says he sent 72 rifles to Tunis. See ANT, Box 225, File 407, Doc. 99. He also mentions in another letter that Egypt's Muhammad Ali asked for 3,000 rifles; see *ibid.*, File 407, Doc. 75.
9 Jalluli mentions that the Dey of Algiers spread in Malta the 'rumour that the Bey of Tunis sent Jalluli to Malta in order to purchase ships, powder and other ammunitions; Jalluli sent him two ships, under the English flag which he equipped in Malta, one with 44 cannons and the other with 32; he has now acquired two more and wants to send them to Tunis, whereas the English and Algiers are friends; the purchase of these ships is against

us, and, if the English want to remain friends, they must not provide them with passports'. See ANT, File 407, Doc. 117.

Indeed, the Algerian request that the English prevent the ships bought on behalf of the Tunisian Regency from leaving, was granted. This led Hammuda Pasha to complain, noting that 'the English are our friends and we do not want to offend them; we too, should have objected to the quantity of weapons and ammunitions sent from Gibraltar and Malta to Algiers; in July 1811, an English ship loaded with war ammunitions left Portsmouth for Malta and from Malta took the direction of Algiers, on 28 September, this matter is more important than the one that concerns us, and the shipment of weapons to our enemy [sic] from our friends who even take them to their destination, is a more serious matter ...'. See ANT, File 408, Doc. 220, letter dated 13 May 1813.

10   See above, note 9.
11   Jalluli informed the Tunisian authorities that 70 janissaries were on their way to Algiers from Rhodes on a ship bearing the Algerian flag. See ANT, Box 225, File 407, Doc. 127, letter dated 17 Shaaban 1127/28 March 1812.
12   ANT, File 407, Doc. 101, letter dated 25 Rabia 1127/19 January 1811.
13   For example, he denounces the bad quality of Egyptian wheat, indicating that wheat from Alexandria was full of dust. We can also learn from him that wheat was rare in Malta and its price very high in Europe (see File 407, Doc. 58); that its price had risen everywhere; from Egypt 62 thalers from Tunis 75; he also gives some information on relations between the Egyptian fellahs and Muhammad Ali regarding the sale of wheat in Egypt (see File 407, Docs 88 and 89).
14   ANT, File 407, Doc. 92.
15   ANT, File 407, Doc. 99.
16   ANT, File 407, Docs 94 and 99.
17   See my study 'The Emir ʿAbd al-Qadir in Damascus 1855–1860', in RHM, no. 15–16, pp. 107–15 (Tunis, 1979), the relevant documents in Arabic, written by the Emir himself. See also my article 'Unpublished letters of the Emir Abdelkader': 1st part in RHM, no. 10–11, 1978, pp. 159–202 and 2nd part in RHM, no. 12, 1978, pp. 308–43. See also Yacono Xavier, 'Abdelkader as a freemason', in *Humanism*, special issue, no. 57, pp. 5–37.

It is undeniable, too, that the image and the very philosophy of Freemasonry have changed a lot since the second half of the nineteenth century. At that time, it was neither a mistake nor a sin for the Emir ʿAbd al-Qadir to have been prepared to become a freemason, in full knowledge of what that implied – in view of the humanist tradition which spread in the Middle East in the nineteenth century, and which involved many eminent Muslim figures of the time who were affiliated to Freemasonry.

18   The RHM is the only review in the Maghreb, not to say in the Arab world, which has respected the objective reality of historical research and has never interfered in its definition. Moreover, it has published all documents, studies and theses sent to it, whoever the author. This constituted a considerable risk to the publishers, since some of the documents and the information published were very embarrassing for the regime of the

time. But the RHMs honesty, the integrity of the nationalist vision expressed in it, and the esteem that all readers, regardless of their political opinions, have shown for the journal and our work as independent historians, have constituted the basis of the RHM's success.

Part II
The colonial period

4 Opposing aspects of colonial rule in this century to 1930: the unusual case of the Beni Mzab

Jon Marks

The anti-colonial movement which developed in Algeria after 1930 was, in many respects, 'national' in character, bringing together political activists from different regions of Algeria in the nationalist political parties organised by Messali Hadj, or leaders of religous inspiration from different groups who followed Sheikh Ben Badis and the *'ulamā'* movement. As French rule entered its second century, resistance to aspects of that rule – and growing calls for an 'Algerian' response – was taking on a 'national' character, even before supporters of the reformist assimilationist tendency, represented first by Emir Khaled and later by Ferhat Abbas, could accept that there was such a thing as an Algerian nation or, rather, an Algerian nation-state.

For much of the first century of French Algeria, however, resistance to European rule was rarely so 'national' in character; that is, capable of rallying the bulk of the Muslim population against the colonial occupier within the frontiers on what is now independent Algeria. Although some risings could be argued to have a proto-national character – for example, the resistance led by the Emir Abdelkader ('Abd al-Qadir) during the 1830s and 1840s, which found support from tribes throughout Algeria and beyond – after the 1871 rising at least, much opposition was localised and limited to regional or ethnic groups, or support for local causes and charismatic individuals.

In such cases as the conscription of Muslim Algerians into the French Army or changes in the taxation or personal status of individuals, resistance did not often adopt a nationalist persona. Rather, it focused on specific issues and was localised. In the majority of cases this resistance was ill-equipped in organisational, material and ideological terms to face the European challenge.

Leaders of resistance against France in the nineteenth century have

59

been lauded as early nationalist heroes in the period since independence. But this may say more for the modern ideological need to emphasise the *national* character of anti-colonial struggles (as Front de Libération Nationale (FLN) leaders have sought to do in the difficult years since 1962), rather than the nationalist aspirations of the majority of nineteenth-century resistance leaders themselves.

Certainly not all resistance felt it necessary to promote 'national' aims – and could, indeed, be more successful when based on more particularist values. Indeed, among the groups most successful at achieving their aims were those with (relatively) limited objectives. Included in this category are the Beni Mzab (Mozabites), who articulated their opposition to aspects of French rule in ethnic and religious terms specific to a well-defined group. Until the late 1920s their struggles ran parallel to those elsewhere in the wider Muslim world.

One reason why the Mozabites seem to have been unusually successful in their campaigns against aspects of colonial rule was their very distinctiveness, which was exploited to gain advantages denied to other groups. There are good reasons to consider Mozabites a case apart:

1 In religious terms they are followers of an Ibadite rite of Islam in a predominantly Malekite country.
2 They are traditionally Berber-speaking and organised in communities which were organised along 'Berber' lines: that is, a community (the *'arsh*) divided into fractions (each) called *saff* (plural *sfuf*) and regulated by a system of secular and religious councils (the *jamá'a-s* and *halgat*).[1] As such they fitted well into French perceptions of ethnicity. This the Mozabites tried to exploit to reinforce their apartness and independence from France as well as from other Algerian groups.
3 The Mozabite heartland is geographically distinct, based in the pentapolis of the Mzab (Ghardaïa and four other towns), plus Berriane and Guerrara, all situated in a desolate region of the Northern Sahara. Their settlement of this region started following the sacking of the Rustamide capital of Tahert, with the foundation of the first Mozabite town, El-Atteuf, in AD 1014. The nearest similar communities are on the Tunisian island of Djerba and in the Djebel Nefousa. In many respects Mozabite architecture,[2] styles of dress, and other facets of local life – such as pottery[3] – are unique, adding to the group's image of apartness.
4 They were also economically distinct: for long the best-known and most dispersed group of traders in the country (they were

sufficiently numerous and well-established to have their own *amīn* in Ottoman Algiers). Most Algerian (and many French) towns still have their share of 'Mozabite' shops. The Mozabite merchants integrated economically but tried where possible to remain socially distinct, marrying and leaving their families in the Mzab while they traded abroad. In 1927 a French writer, Andre Chevrillon, underlined this identity in the title of his book *Les puritans du desert*. The same title has been used to describe the Mozabites' cousins on Djerba.[4]

This distinctiveness was certainly noticed by the French. In his book *Le M'Zab et les Mozabites* (1888), Dr Charles Amat wrote of the Mozabite as 'un type particulier', living in a 'cosmopolitan population'. 'Mercier, charbonnier ou boucher, petit de taille, trapu, à face large, au teint mat, à l'oeil enfoncé ... apte au commerce, capable d'épargne et détesté par l'Arabe autant qu'il l'abhore à son tour, c'est le M'zabite.'[5]

During the colonial period the impetus towards social distinctiveness at times took on concrete political expression, reflecting the Beni Mzab's religious and social apartness. This apartness could be used to good effect against the colonial power. In economic and political terms the Mozabites can be seen as 'self-improvers' – a distinct group with its own identity which was able to promote its interests over other groups in the colonial polity. Thus, there was strong opposition to the French on communal grounds when they tried to conscript Mozabites into the army, but Mozabite traders also exploited French rule, taking advantage of the money economy and military protection to penetrate new markets such as Tamanrasset and the deep south, for example. In North Africa this has often been associated with trade, such as in the case of the Swasa in Morocco, another group which started to become 'bourgeois' under the French and then prospered after independence.[6]

Mozabite opposition to France took different forms at different times. In the period from 1853, when the French first occupied the Mzab valley, to 1882 when Mozabite 'lawlessness' provided a pretext for full military occupation, the conflict between coloniser and colonised took on a classic form of resistance to encroaching rule from outside.

The 1853 occupation itself was not a dramatic affair; it followed the taking of Laghouat on 4 December 1852 after Mohamed ben Abdallah's rising, and the start of the French penetration of the Sahara. According to Bernard and Lacroix, the Mozabites entered

into talks, fearing reprisals for having sheltered the *sherif.* To Bernard
and Lacroix the 24 January 1853 convention – 'décorée plus tard du
nom de traité' – was more of a capitulation than a treaty.[7] The
governor, Maréchal Randon, stipulated that the Mzab and France
could not have the commercial treaty the Mozabites wanted: rather
the Mzab must submit. The Mozabite towns would pay taxes (and
customs duties on trade with Morocco and Tunisia); in return France
would give protection to Mozabite traders.

France thus asserted its dominance over the Mzab: it would,
however, be a form of indirect rule. On his arrival in Guerarra,
Commandant Berrail accepted the town's submission and appointed
two *qā'id-s,* one for the *saff* Chergui, the other for *saff* Gharbi. The
promise of indirect rule was explicit in Randon's conditions, which
promised: 'Nous ne voulons en aucune façon nous mêler de vos
affaires intérieures: vous resterez à cet égard comme par le passé.'
Only if order was threatened, or the rights of French nationals and
subject tribes were threatened, would France act. From day one,
Randon – whose governorship marked an important phase in French
land-grabbing policies – had hit on the formula by which France was
to deal with the Sahara. This formula was accepted by the Mozabite
jama'a-s.

Despite this apparent acquiescence to the French colonial penetration, there were none the less some cases of overt resistance.
According to French reports from the time, some *sfuf* did not support
the decision to deal with France. In 1885 the Guerarra *qā'id-s* were
forced to call in Commandant Marguerite and his *spahi-s* to crush
opposition. And it was not until 1857 that Commandant Marguerite
entered Ghardaïa, which had previously wanted to keep the infidels
out.[8] In 1860 it was alleged that a Jewish informant had been killed
by agents of the Ghardaïa *jama'a,*[9] and troops were again called in.
In 1864 the Mzab supported the rising of the Ouled Sidi Cheikh
(Walad Sidi Shaykh). Occasional killings, and the dispatch of troops,
established a pattern – and in French eyes a pretext for occupation.

Annexation was in line with wider French efforts to extend their
rule in Algeria under pressure from an increasingly powerful settler
lobby. In the Mzab, resistance to this process was articulated by such
religious leaders as the influential scholar and cleric El Hadj
M'Hamed Ben Youcef Atfièche (1820–1914), whose politics were
virulently anti-French and pro-Ottoman. Often resistance to colonial
encroachment focused on localised religious issues. For example, in
1903/4 Ghardaïa organised itself to prevent the construction of two
mosques being built in the town by the Beni Merzoug and the

Meddabiha (non-Mozabite, 'Arab' groups). In 1914 there was fierce resistance to an even greater threat, when the Pères Blancs planned to set up a school at Beni Isguen, the holiest city of the Mozabite pentapolis.[10]

Again it was the religious leaders who articulated this resistance, most notably before the First World War Sheikh Atfièche who led the nineteenth-century Ibadite reform movement. Among his best known actions, during a visit by the Under-Secretary of State for the Interior, M. Morel, was that he ordered no bunting to be hung from mosques – except over the latrines. More serious for the coloniser, Atfièche's celebrated pupil, the Ottoman senator Slimane el-Barouni, was active in the Mzab – whose independence he at one stage championed – and caused great concern for the authorities.

Barouni was a Nafousi pupil of Atfièche (from 1895–8). He returned to collect funds in 1907 for an unsuccessful venture to establish a publishing house in Egypt: El Metabaa El Barounia. This would publish a newspaper *El Ased El Islam* ('The Lion of Islam'). He came again (by car) to Atfièche's funeral in 1914 where, according to French reports 'there were no *serious* incidents'. According to a French informant, a local teacher, Mohamed Ben Bailich,[11] Barouni also attended Atfièche's funeral 'pour se poser en protecteur des Mozabites'. By this stage Barouni was leading a previously dormant Mozabite cause by arguing that he would go to Paris to protect the 1853 and 1882 privileges. But he went further still – as far as to tell his Mozabite audience that he would ask for a date for independence. In response the Mozabite *tolba-s* collected F.Fr.70,000 for Barouni, who told them: 'Plus tard ... à une epoche que je ne puis encore fixer, le Mzab obtiendra une indépendence complète et formera grand royaume delivré de toute tutelle.'

Independence was an extreme view and it is unclear how much support it had. But it would be true to say that French rule was always opposed to it and this opposition helped reinforce the French decision to rule the region indirectly through the military command in Laghouat and by liaising with local notables. In the first 60 years of contacts it was a case of France imposing a form of indirect rule exerted over the north. At every turn the Mozabites emphasised their apartness, playing on French perceptions of ethnicity to good effect.

From the turn of the century through to the 1920s, Franco–Mozabite conflicts were often articulated in religious terms but they were to focus on apparently 'secular' issues (for the French at least) – for example, efforts by the metropolis to conscript Mozabites into French Algerian society (notably by promoting 'national' rather than Mozabite education). As Benyoucef notes, there was also an economic element in these conflicts as the local organisation mobilised against the exploitation of Mozabite waters by French companies.[12]

Like it or not, as the new century unfolded, the Mzab was becoming more closely integrated into colonial Algeria. In a French report of October 1913[13] it was noted that the same M. Morel, the Under-Secretary of State for the Interior so insulted by Atfièche, visited the region and was met with respect. 'Dans le M'zab, pour la première fois dépuis l'annexation de ce pays, le drapeau français a flotté sur les mosquées de Ghardaïa et Beni Isguen ... [this display] traduit sous une forme symbolique ... de la réconnaissance par tous de l'autorité française.'

However, this official report may represent an over-smug view of the Mzab on the eve of the First World War. The *jihād,* called in late 1914 as the Ottoman empire took on the western allies, was widely welcomed in the Mzab, which became a centre for moral opposition and diffusing information about the Sanusi rising in Cyrenaica and Ottoman victories in the east. The French were well aware of this.

Mozabite traders and *haji-s* were instrumental in spreading word of the Sanusi advance: there were even plans to strengthen the ramparts of Guerrara, following rumours later found to be erroneous, that Barouni was soon to arrive to organise resistance in the Mzab itself. Algeria was awash with such stories from 1914 to 1918 – and also with calls for Islamic solidarity under an Ottoman banner, often diffused through Mozabite trading routes via Tripoli. The Mozabite traders (but not their very conservative leaders) were early adepts at using motor transport. A French report of 5 November 1914 states that the Mozabites have 'agents' in Istanbul and correspond with their Ibadite cousins in Zanzibar, Tripoli and the Djebel Nefousa. This network was to bring news of the allies' disastrous Dardanelles campaign to Algeria.[14] However, this was much the limit to direct resistance. The Mzab followed the First World War with greater interest – and better information – than much of North Africa, but could ultimately do little to change the political situation.

Thus, in April 1917 a report states that the south is quiet – except for 'fantastic rumours' in the Mzab, where there was also 'sensation' when five planes flew over the pentapolis. The writer noted that the locals could see they were heavily armed. Resistance was not limited through lack of organisation, or even ideological failings, but through a recognition of who had the big guns. Europe's technological advantage was clear, even to the ultra-conservative *'azzaba* of Beni Isguen.

As a result, despite the temptation towards violent resistance (in the nineteenth century) and the appeal of those who violently resisted (such as the Sanusi), Mozabite resistance took more limited form. In part this response stemmed from an effort to limit the damage to Mozabite society that more violent forms of conflict might inflict. Its expression include the mobilisation of religious arguments for the community's apartness; the building of links with groups outside Algeria (and especially in what remained of the Ottoman Empire); and, occasionally, violent rejection of French efforts.

The focus of Mozabite resistance was the Mzab and to protect Mozabites trading in the Tell and great cities of the north. For many Mozabites, Ghardaïa was the centre and 'Algeria' the periphery. However, a by-product of their communal resistance was to inform Muslim Algeria and beyond of developments in the east, including Turkish defeats of France and its allies and the rising in Tripolitania. The preservation of Ibadite/Mozabite trading and information networks played a national role in informing and influencing Muslim Algerian opinion, which the colonial authorities were otherwise often able to insulate from outside news.

The centre of resistance for two decades was the continuing conscription debate, in which the Mozabites organised themselves into what seems to have been an unusually successful and articulate – even artful – pressure group, whose organised resistance stands in marked contrast to many of the groups around them. This resistance has not been widely documented in the bibliography of colonial Algeria but can be traced from the reports of French officers operating in the *Territoires du Sud*, from contemporary mémoires and from the highly literate and well-argued petitions of Mozambite communities against conscription and other aspects of colonial rule. It should be noted that Algeria was a major source of conscription into the French Army. It has been noted that in the First World War the colony provided some 173,000 troops, of whom 87,000 engaged in combat with 25,000 being killed.

The conscription debate stemmed from a law of 3 February 1912 which allowed the authorities in Laghouat to call on Mozabites to send conscripts. At first this was limited to Mozabite traders working in the Tell, the men living in the Mzab valley itself not being affected. However, the move was opposed with unprecedented vigour. Elsewhere in Algeria a variety of means to avoid conscription were used – including bribery (meaning the poorest were most often recruited) and even temporary disablement. In Tlemcen, the capital of the traditional bourgeois west, there were calls for a mass flight out of the country to avoid the call up, following a campaign organised by the local mosque. Throughout Algeria it has been calculated that some 4,000 men migrated during this period to avoid conscription. In the Mzab, initial resistance was organised into evasive action. Notwithstanding continued complaints that the measure was illegal, in 1918/19 a communal payment was arranged to avoid having to send any Mozabites to join the ranks. However, on 5 March 1921 the War Ministry extended the measure by decree to cover the southern territories – crystallising opposition in the Mzab. The *jama'a-s* refused to fill in lists and called on *halgats* (assemblies) to reject overtures. This opposition was reflected in the failure of colonial recruiting officers to fulfil their quotas of conscripts. In 1922, 150 were called: only three did military service; it was the same in 1923, the most spectacular case of a national phenomenon (especially in the west) of rejection. Mozabites were active in their protest in the north, as well as in their heartland.

Mozabite arguments against conscription were based on a reading of the terms agreed in 1853 and 1882, and the 1871 Cremieux decree (which did not include the Mzab). The community also argued that conscription was absolutely ruled out on *Ibadite* religious grounds. To promote their case to the greatest effect, the Mozabites studied these documents exhaustively and argued their case in a series of erudite petitions. In the 1912–21 period the case against conscription was often put by the fathers of conscripts, who remained in the Tell while their sons returned to Ghardaïa. This 'traditional' community was thus using modern means to oppose the French will.

The debate focused minds on opposition and gave rise to considerable French concern. For example, a 23 November 1912 dispatch reports 'une effervescence assez serieuse' in the Mzab due to the conscription decree. It is reported that 'quelques mauvaises têtes' were talking of getting away from French domination by seeking the protection of Germany. The writer, Rebillon, notes that as it was strong enough to mount a successful insurrection this group was even contemplating moving to another region (not an unprecedented step in Ibadi history and theology): 'ou ils seraient plus indépendents.'

However, this was only a minority of the community, and the French did not want to play ball with the Mozabites' demands, even if they were drawn up in such a way as to appeal to the theory of colonial rule. Thus, in July 1917 we have a report[15] which tells how the *jama'a-s* were asked to draw up lists and refused: this was then carried out by the Bureau des Affaires Indigènes in Ghardaïa. Senegalese troops were sent to find conscripts, and some were taken by force. In the face of such frustrating opposition, the French were not above moving the goalposts. In 1925 and 1926, decrees were issued ruling that the 1902 law creating the *Territoires du Sud* included the Mzab. Therefore, previous agreements (such as the 1853 convention and 1882 treaty) giving the region separate status did not apply. French files of the period are typified by reports of rumour and opposition focused on conscription from the conservative *tulba-s*. There are some successes for the French, but usually quotas are left unfulfilled. One reason for the relative success of the Mozabites' strategy is that it was apparently gathered around Mozabite institutions such as the *'azzaba* and *halgat*.

The French did find locals to act as informers and as *qā'id-s*. But even so, reports often note that few '*chefs indigènes*' have been supportive.[16] Being a *qā'id* was one way of consolidating one's position as a 'local notable' in colonial society, but it had its drawbacks. In July 1919 it was reported that Si Daoud, *qā id* of Ghardaïa, had been murdered. In that difficult year it was reported that recruiting in Ghardaïa was strong – but only among the local Jewish community.

In the 1912–24 period small victories were won in the battle against conscription. Some were significant: on 30 September 1919 the Governor-General in Algiers wrote to the War Ministry in Paris that the Mozabites were to be excluded from the conscripted groups.[17] A larger victory still was won with an eventual agreement giving the Mozabites special status and allowing them to hire replacements. The French had had enough. Thus in 1926, six Mozabites signed up voluntarily and 26 replacements were called up – including two Jews and nine Arabs from Beni Isguen.[18] That year, Algiers had wanted a total of 30 conscripts from the Mzab: if Mozabites in the Tell were also taken into account the Governor-General concluded, 'les Mozabites ... ont fait plus qu'il ne leur était demandé' – and a contingent of 50 should be demanded in 1927. The writer, Meynier, went on to note that when the Mozabites fully understood the mechanism, 'l'apaisement se fera complet dans tous les milieux mozabites au sujet de la conscription'.[19]

French reports talk of the growing detente from 1924 on. Henceforth the Mzab would become more introspective, with internal debates dominating political life. By 1930 French rule in Algeria was reaching its zenith and a genuinely Algerian nationalist movement was emerging which would include Mozabites as well as activists from other regions. From then on conventional views of Algeria focus on the main pillars of the nationalist movement and the Mzab is something of a backwater. This point is highlighted by the activities of Sheikh Brahim Bayoudh: one of the main issues of the later 1920s and 1930s in the Mzab was to what extent the population should stick by its traditional values or follow Bayoudh's reformist Ibadism, linked from 1931 to the national *'ulamā'* movement (whose comité directeur he joined that year). He was later a spokesman for the Mzab in the wider Algerian polity as member of the Assemblée Algérienne.[20]

Similarly, other leading Mozabites of the 1930s were mainstream nationalists, such as Abou el-Yakdan Hadj Brahim and Moufdi Zakaria. Zakaria was close to Messali Hadj, not the tradition of Atfièche and Barouni. Zakaria wrote the Algerian national anthem, *Qassamen.* El-Yakdan published Mozabite newspapers like *El-Ouma* in Algiers in the 1930s but these identified with the Etoile Nord-Africaine (ENA) and Parti du Peuple Algérien (PPA) and thus had nationalist, rather than particularist, tendencies. However, at one stage el-Yakdan had to defend the Mozabites against Ben Badis and al-Okbi for inactivity, arguing, 'we can only participate indirectly in your political movement'.[21] It thus seems there may be limits to the national leanings of a group apart, even among its most militant nationalists – at least if one can accept the veracity of French police reports.

In the fifty years to the high summer of French rule in 1930, the Mozabites deserve a more intensive examination for their resistance to French rule. They were not, as French writers insisted, a docile group whose only interest was money: their resistance occasionally took violent form, but more often was skilfully articulated, using French perceptions of group politics to underpin efforts to save the group.

In the century after Abdelkader and before the nationalist movement got into full swing, the Mozabite resistance was also different from the 'primitive revolts' which so often typify histories of the period before nationalism became the dominant trend in Algeria.

NOTES

1 This aspect of Mozabite society has been well recorded. See, for example, E. A. Alport, 'The M'Zab', in Gellner and Micaud (eds), *Arabs and Berbers* (London, Duckworth, 1972), and Belhadj Merghoub, *Le Développement politique en Algérie: étude des populations du M'Zab*, Paris: Armand Colin, 1972). On a modern example of group dynamics and religious debate, see Slimane Chikh, 'Ibadisme et société: la déliberation de Azzaba de Beni Isugen (27 Ramadhan 1399: 20 Août 1979)', in *Annuaire de L'Afrique du Nord* (Aix-en-Provence, 1979).

2 For examples of Mozabite architecture and irrigation techniques, see Manuelle Roche, *Le M'Zab: Architecture Ibadite en Algérie.* A study

looking at the region's urban development is Brahim Benyoucef, *Le M'Zab: Les practiques de l'espace* (Algiers: Enterprise nationale du livre, 1986).

3 Anne-Marie Abderrhim-Reichlen, *Contribution à l'étude de la vie sociale et économique de la communauté ibadite au Mzab, Algérie. La potérie comme expression technique et culturelle,* Doctorat 3ème cycle (Paris: Ecole des Hautes Etudes en Sciences Sociales, 1980).

4 Andre Chevrillon, *Les puritans du desert,* (Paris: Plon, 1927). See, for example, Russell A. Stone, 'Religious ethic and the spirit of capitalism in Tunisia', in the *International Journal of Middle East Studies,* vol. V, 1974. On trade, see Donald C. Holsinger, 'Migration, commerce and continuity: the Mizabis in eighteenth and nineteenth century Algeria', *Journal of African History,* vol. 21, 1980.

5 Docteur Charles Amat, *Le M'Zab et les m'zabites,* (Paris: Challamel et compagnie, 1888). Amat was among the earliest European students of Mozabite society. He described himself as an amateur sociologist and was responsible for organising medicine in the Mzab during the 1880s.

6 John Waterbury, 'Tribalism, trade and politics: the transformation of the Swasa of Morocco', in Gellner and Micaud *op. cit.,* and Waterbury, *North for the Trade: The Life and Times of a Berber Merchant,* (Berkeley: University of California Press, 1972).

7 Augustin Bernard and Commandant N. Lacroix, *La pénétration saharienne (1830–1906),* (Algiers: Imprimerie algérienne, 1906).

8 Amat, *op. cit.*

9 Amat, *op. cit.*

10 As was expressed in a note to the Governor-General contained in file no. 22H17 of the Archives de la France d'Outre Mer (AFOM), Aix-en-Provence, concerning 'Installation des pères blancs à Beni Isugen. Creation d'une école à Beni Isugen', April–November 1914. All AFOM files cited are reports from the military authorities in the *Territoires du Sud,* based at Laghouat but with representatives in Ghardaïa.

11 AFOM 22H17.

12 Benyoucef, *op. cit.*

13 AFOM 23H1.

14 AFOM 22H17; The Mozabite role in the First World War is discussed in Gilbert Meynier's *L'Algérie révélée: la guerre de 1914–18 et le premier quart du XXième: siècle,* (Paris and Geneva: Droz, 1981).

15 AFOM 22H21.

16 AFOM 22H21, *op. cit.,* where one of the few, the *qā'id* of Berriane Si Daghor Bahmed Ben el-Hadj Brahim was recommended for the Légion d'honneur.

17 AFOM 22H21.

18 AFOM 22H23.

19 See Meynier, *op. cit.,* p. 262.

20 See Merghoub, *op. cit.*

21 AFOM 9H24 of 11 February 1938.

5 The best aircraft carrier in Africa
Britain and Libya 1943–51

John Wright

The North African campaigns of the Second World War were fought not for the possession of territory as such, but for the strategic domination of the Central Mediterranean. Control of the Suez Canal and the Middle East oilfields, and the fate of Italian Libya, were all secondary to this prime objective. And the same objective was to dominate western, and particularly British, regional strategy for long after the war, and ultimately to influence the very structure of the Libyan state that gained independence in 1951.

By January 1943 Italian authority had been replaced by British Military Administrations in Tripolitania and Cyrenaica, and in Fezzan by the authority of French forces that had invaded across the Sahara from Chad. Britain and France remained in control not only, as originally envisaged, until the end of the world war,[1] but for several more years until the post-war international debate on the future of all Italian colonies had been resolved.

Many Libyans had welcomed the British as their 'liberators' from Italian Fascism, and British standing was particularly high among Cyrenaicans who had suffered more than other Libyans for their prolonged resistance to their colonisers. The Cyrenaicans' acknowledged leader, Sayyid Mohammad Idris, had been a friend of Britain since 1916 when he became head of the Sanusi revivalist movement that had organised Cyrenaican resistance to the Italians. When Italy declared war on Britain in 1910, Sanusi exiles in Egypt had given moderate help to the British war effort[2] and Britain's obligations were duly acknowledged by the Foreign Secretary, Anthony Eden, in a statement to the House of Commons in January 1942 to the effect that the Sanusi of Cyrenaica would in no circumstances again fall under Italian rule after the war.[3]

By the end of the war, Libya was in a pitiful state. The people were politically retarded, under-educated, untrained and impoverished;

there was little trade and much unemployment; Italian development funds had dried up; and the British and French Administrations could only rule on a 'care and maintenance' basis. Yet until Libya's future had been decided, and its stop-gap military administrations replaced by more permanent forms of government, there could be little post-war recovery or development.[4] The political, economic and social destitution of the country suggested to all observers that independence was out of the question for many years to come.

It was against this background of general wretchedness that Libya's future was considered by the four victorious Great Powers – Britain, the United States, France and the Soviet Union – at a long series of meetings at which they sought mutually acceptable solutions to the many outstanding issues left over from the war, among them the disposal of Italy's colonies. While both liberal and post-1922 Fascist Italy had perceived Italy largely as a settler-colony, its sole value to outside powers after 1945 was strategic. By 1943, armed forces of Britain, France and the US were stationed there and Libya – either wholly or in its three constituent parts – was to become to each of them an asset of value, according to their differing strategic perceptions and priorities.

The United States Air Force had taken over the airfield at Mellaha, just east of Tripoli, from the British in 1943, and during the next two years reportedly spent $100 million on its development.[5] This first permanent US air base in Africa marked the extension of American military interest into an area up to then dominated by Europe. Although by 1947 Wheelus Field had been practically demobilised,[6] its strategic value greatly increased as the Cold War intensified. With its 'phenomenally long runways capable of taking the largest bomber yet built',[7] it was extended and brought back into full use in 1948.[8] It in due course became an essential link in the chain of American bases and 'facilities' in southern Europe, North Africa and Turkey covering the southern flanks of the Soviet Union and Soviet expansion into the Mediterranean.

The southern province of Fezzan had special political and strategic importance to its French administrators. Under the close control of a purely French (and not Allied) adminstration, Fezzan became a buffer zone protecting the otherwise exposed flanks of French West, North and Equatorial Africa from hostile powers and insidious political influences. At the same time, it provided the quickest overland route between French North Africa on one side of the Sahara and Chad on the other, while the airstrips at Ghadames, Ghat, Sebha and Brak offered useful staging facilities on the French African air network in an era of slow, short-haul transport aircraft.[9] Indeed, such was Fezzan's strategic value to France in Africa that as early as August 1943 General Charles de Gaulle was claiming its annexation to France.[10]

While French concern for Fezzan reflected the need to preserve long-standing interests in the Mediterranean, North Africa, the central Sahara and sub-Saharan Africa, British concern for Libya in general and Cyrenaica in particular was prompted by the need to sustain widespread interests in the Mediterranean and the Middle East. By the war's end, the regional interests of France and Britain were facing rising hostility from the Soviet Union and Arab nationalism, as well as an often disapproving attitude from Washington.

It is important to remember the extent to which in 1945 Britain's world-wide political, economic and strategic interests were reflected in a dominating position in the Middle East, from Libya to Iraq and from Cyprus to southern Sudan, to the virtual exclusion of any other power. The Middle East was the 'principal pillar of Britain's position in the world'.[11] And, as the Cold War intensified, so the importance of the Middle East for the in-depth defence of Western Europe and in countering anticipated Soviet expansion came to be recognised by both Britain and the US. 'Whoever controls the Middle East controls the access to three continents. Whether or not this area is held will determine whether we have a "big free world" or a "little free world"'.[12]

Since the 1880s, Egypt and the Suez Canal had been central to Britain's position in the Middle East. But by 1945 – even though the 1936 Anglo-Egyptian Treaty still had over 10 years to run – bilateral relations were already difficult and Palestine, Kenya and Cyrenaica were already being seriously considered as alternative, if less satisfactory bases than the Canal Zone from which Britain could continue to protect imperial communications through the Mediterranean Sea and Indian Ocean. The South African prime minister and senior philosopher-statesman, General Smuts, believed that if the British Empire and Commonwealth was to hold the post-war balance of power between the United States and the Soviet Union, 'a strategic base in Cyrenaica capable of delivering atomic bombs would forestall Russian aggression or American retaliation and would help preserve the peace of the world'.[13]

In acquiring strategic rights in Cyrenaica, ('undoubtedly the best aircraft carrier in Africa – although admittedly the territory lacked the necessary manpower and other resources'[14]) Britain would dominate the Eastern Mediterranean, as well as the Western Desert, and would thus be able to counter any threat to Egypt such as had occurred in 1942.[15] The airfields of Cyrenaica (and to a lesser extent of Tripolitania) offered staging-posts on the air routes to East and West Africa, the Indian Ocean and the Far East. And Cyrenaica, under the intended benign leadership of Amir Idris, and with a small population still grateful to Britain for 'liberation' from the Italians, posed (as yet) none of the difficulties and complications of Arab nationalism such as bedevilled British relations with Egypt and with Iraq.

At the end of the war, Italy still held sovereignty over Libya, Somalia and Eritrea. Their future had been considered at the four-power Potsdam Conference in 1945 and at the meeting of the Council of Foreign Ministers in London in September that year. Because of disagreement, a settlement was postponed until the council's next session in Paris in the summer of 1946, when it was agreed that a decision would be taken within one year of the peace treaty with Italy taking effect on 15 September 1947. Under the treaty Italy renounced her rights and claims to Libya, Somalia and Eritrea. But the territories were to remain in their existing state until their future had been decided. These decisions were to be based on the findings of a Four-Power Commission which visited all of them, arriving in Libya early in 1948. Its report, which was considered at the Four-Power conference of deputy Foreign Ministers in London in the summer of 1948, put on record the almost unanimous Libyan desire for full independence, but considered the country to be politically, economically and socially unready for it.[16]

The international debate over Libya's future, lasting several years, threw up differing ideas for trusteeship by various prospective administering powers. Such proposals tended in due course to be modified in response to the shifting patterns of post-war tensions. Britain's attitude was consistently governed by the wartime pledge (repeated in 1944) that Cyrenaica would never again come under Italian rule, and by the need to keep bases in eastern Libya. France was interested only in maintaining a position in Fezzan, while democratic (republican) Italy made a strong case for the restoration of African colonies acquired before Fascism.

The United States, which was perhaps the most disinterested of all the powers 'interested' in Libya's fate, had originally suggested placing it under the 'collective trusteeship' of the United Nations, with independence granted ten years later. Britain was prepared to support this arrangement so long as British strategic interests in Cyrenaica were secured.[17] But then the Russians dropped a bombshell into the debate by demanding a trusteeship over Tripolitania. The prospect of the Soviet Union gaining a foothold in the Central Mediterranean and possible access to Central Africa (Moscow was believed to be interested in the uranium of the Belgian Congo)[18] caused grave misgivings in the Western camp. (The Russians may in fact have merely been using the demand as a ploy for concessions elsewhere; they dropped their claim in the summer of 1946.) But it was not until 1948 (when the USAF began to reactivate Wheelus) that Britain and the United States started to co-ordinate their policy towards Libya, with the Americans prepared to give 'full support to British strategic claims in Cyrenaica'.[19]

By 1948 there was clearly stalemate in the international debate on the future of Italian colonies, and the matter was referred to the General Assembly of the United Nations, in accordance with the provisions of the Italian peace treaty. But before the UNGA got down to business, Britain and Italy made one last attempt to settle Libya's future between them. The plan drawn up by the British Foreign Secretary, Ernest Bevin and the Italian Foreign Minister, Count Carlo Sforza, proposed the granting of trusteeships to Britain in Cyrenaica, to Italy in Tripolitania and to France in Fezzan; Libya was to become independent after ten years if the UNGA approved. The so-called Bevin–Sforza plan was intended to satisfy British, Italian and French interests in particular, and American and Western interests in general. Although opposed by the Soviet and Arab blocs in the UN, the plan still had wide support, particularly among Latin American states which favoured Italian ambitions and at that time represented about one-third of total UN membership of 58 nations. But strikes and demonstrations in Tripoli and elsewhere made quite clear the Libyans' opposition to the plan, and especially the prospect of Italy's return to Tripolitania. In the event, a resolution based on the Bevin–Sforza plan failed by one vote to gain the necessary two-thirds majority for its adoption in the UNGA and the plan was dropped.

Unexpectedly, this defeat led to the problem's quick solution. In the second half of 1949, British and other western thinking on the Libyan question moved quickly from trusteeship to independence. Within two weeks of the UN vote, Britain made known plans for Cyrenaican self-government under Amir Idris who, the British claimed, could no longer be patient with British assurances going back to 1940 about eventual independence. In September 1949 the Cyrenaican government duly became responsible for most internal matters; foreign affairs, defence and military bases (including the allocation of base sites)[20] remained under British control. But this at least 'gave satisfaction to [the British Foreign Secretary Ernest] Bevin who at last saw a way of securing British bases in Cyrenaica and keeping Britain's pledge to the Senussi at the same time ...'.[21]

Although the British government insisted that 'in taking these steps ... nothing will be done to prejudice the future of Libya as a whole', much had in fact already been done. For in transferring internal power to Amir Idris in the summer of 1949 while the future of Libya still awaited a UN decision, Britain in effect unilaterally decreed that if there was to be an independent Libyan state at all and later that year the UNGA decided that there was it would take the only form that Britain and Britain's allies wanted: a federal monarchy under the Sanusi crown. And since Cyrenaica had already achieved self-rule, the case for similar autonomous but nationally divisive arrangements for Tripolitania and Fezzan became that much stronger.[22]

Thus, when the UNGA in November 1949 voted for the independence of Libya ('comprising' Tripolitania, Cyrenaica and Fezzan) the essential separateness of the three provinces had already been decided by the two administering powers, largely as a means of protecting what they perceived to be their vital strategic interests. And in the two subsequent years of preparation for independence under UN supervision, there was nothing the UN, or the Libyans and their sympathisers, could do to change that basic *fait accompli*. As Dr Adrian Pelt, the UN Commissioner in Libya during 1950–1 himself later admitted, 'the strategic interests of the two Administering Powers tended to work against the unification and complete independence of Libya'.[23]

The vote for independence represented a striking volte-face by the Western powers that only a few months before had been trying to divide Libya into a series of ten-year trusteeships. Various explanations have been offered for this sharp change in attitude, when the British, US and Italian governments concluded that their interests would be better served by an independent state than one under UN trusteeships. It is not clear what part the future status of military bases played in this change of view, but the first US Ambassador to Libya, Henry S. Villard, offers perhaps the most convincing explanation:

It may be worth noting that if Libya had passed under any form of United Nations trusteeship, it would have been impossible for the territory to play a part in the defense arrangements of the free world. Under the United Nations trusteeship system, the administrator of a territory cannot establish military bases ... As an independent entity, Libya could freely enter into treaties or arrangements with the Western powers looking toward the defense of the Mediterranean and North Africa. This is exactly what the Soviet Union feared and what Libya did. The strategic sector of African sea coast which had proved so important in the mechanized war of the desert was coming into its own as a place of equal importance in the air age.[24]

Villard had been chairman of the sub-committee set up by the State Department to consider the future of the Italian colonies, and his assessment may well be the right one. Nevertheless, if this was indeed the case, it implies that the British, US and French governments were not fully aware that, had they been successful in placing Libya under a series of UN trusteeships, they would have frustrated their own basic objectives of maintaining their military bases there. Indeed, there seems to have been a certain confusion of policy that still needs clarification.

But the fact remains that Libya itself came to independence as a federal kingdom in December 1951 – considerably sooner than it might otherwise have done. And it duly achieved the full union of the three provinces during 1963 and 1964.

In 1953 Britain signed a twenty-year Treaty of Alliance with the United Kingdom of Libya, thereby obtaining formal rights to bases in Cyrenaica that had for so long been a British objective, as well as bases in Tripolitania. The following year the US reached an agreement under which it retained Wheelus base and associated facilities up to 1970. But the French failed to obtain a similar bases agreement in Fezzan, which they were obliged to evacuate in 1956. This allowed the province to become – just as they had feared it would – an open supply route for the Algerian rebellion.

As for British bases in Cyrenaica, so long a basic objective of London's Middle East policy, they proved worthless in the very first Middle East crisis in which they might have been expected to play a part: the Anglo-French-Israeli invasion of Egypt in October 1956. During that month Libya sought and obtained a guarantee from Britain that the bases would not be used against Egypt. After the crisis, the British government reviewed the value of bases that had been effectively neutralised by diplomatic action and in 1957 the rundown of British forces in Libya began.[25]

NOTES

1 Lord Rennell of Rodd, *British Military Administration of Occupied Territories during the Years 1941–47* (London, 1948), p. 250.
2 J. Wright, *Libya: A Modern History* (London, 1982), p. 46.
3 House of Commons Official Report, Parliamentary Debates (Hansard), London, vol. 377, cols 77–8, (8 January, 1942).
4 Wright, *op. cit.*, p. 48.
5 *New York Times*, 13 February 1945. See also British Military Administration (Tripolitania) *Annual Report* (1944) pp. 9–10.
6 W. Roger Louis, *The British Empire in the Middle East 1945–1951* (Oxford, 1984), p. 301.
7 Henry Serrano Villard, *Libya: The New Arab Kingdom of North Africa* (Ithaca, New York, 1956), p. 139.
8 *Ibid.*, pp. 138–9.
9 J. Wright, *Libya, Chad and Central Sahara* (London, 1989), p. 123.
10 J. Bessis, 'L'evolution des relations entre la Libye independante et la France', *The Maghreb Review*, vol. 12, nos 1–2, 1987.
11 Louis, *op. cit.*, p. 5.
12 Sir Oliver Franks at a meeting of British and US Chiefs of Staff, Washington, 26 October 1950, quoted in Alan Bullock, *Ernest Bevin, Foreign Secretary 1945–1951* (London 1983), p. 831.
13 Louis, *op. cit.*, p. 5.
14 Sir Orme Sargent, quoted in *ibid.*, p. 105.
15 Louis, *op. cit.*, p. 274.
16 Wright 1982, *op. cit.*, pp. 52–3.
17 Louis, *op. cit.*, p. 302.
18 *Ibid.*, p. 271. See also Bullock, *op. cit.*, p. 130.
19 See Bullock, *op. cit.*, pp. 133, 135, 263; also Louis, *op. cit.*, p. 302.
20 N. A. Arsharuni, *Innostranniy Kapital v Livii (1911–1967)* (Moscow, 1970), p. 60.
21 Bullock *op. cit.*, p. 678.
22 Wright 1982, *op. cit.*, p. 56.
23 A. Pelt, *Libyan Independence and the United Nations* (New Haven, 1970), p. 33.
24 Villard, *op. cit.*, pp. 33–4.
25 Wright 1982, *op. cit.*, p. 86. See also Majid Khadduri, *Modern Libya* (Baltimore, 1963), pp. 267ff.

6 France and Islam

The Haut Comité Méditerranéen and French North Africa

William A. Hoisington, Jun.

Despite the binding sense of the phrase, French North Africa, Morocco, Algeria, and Tunisia were governed as separate and distinct political entities throughout the colonial period. There were only rare moments of unity and co-operation. If this ran counter to the centripetal forces of language, religion, and ethnicity and even the physical geography of the region, it squared with the history and politics of the North African conquest. French since 1830, Algeria was ruled directly from Paris through the Ministry of the Interior, whereas Tunisia and Morocco were states under the nominal sovereignty of native rulers and governed indirectly through the Ministry of Foreign Affairs. These were not simple administrative fictions, but reflections of the changing nature of imperial expansion in the nineteenth century as well as of changes in French colonial theory and practice. Algeria was the classic case of assimilation, the effort to make Algerians French; while Tunisia and Morocco represented association, the attempt to link diverse peoples with France in a more culturally pluralistic imperial structure. All this tended to divide rather than to unify.

The French were not unaware of the unity of North Africa, but, given the colonial realities, they found it difficult to express. The language they used to denote the region was clumsy. *Afrique française du nord* (AFN) never had the ring of *Afrique occidentale française* (AOF) and was rarely used; the gallicized Maghreb (or Maghrib) was exotic, but vague; *Afrique du nord* was uninspired. In the mid-1930s the Federation of Scholarly Societies of North Africa (*Fédération des sociétiés savantes de l'Afrique du nord*) invented the word 'Altuma' (*Algerie, Tunisie, Maroc*), but it sounded neither French nor Arabic and was shunned. In the end Frenchmen preferred to speak of Algeria, Tunisia, and Morocco and to leave the regional nomenclature to the Christian theologians who had experience with the problem of 'unity in three persons'.[1]

There was never an overall French policy for North Africa. Premier Georges Leygués acknowledged this in 1911 as the French prepared to add Morocco to Algeria and Tunisia. 'We have no Muslim policy' he told the Chamber of Deputies, and Minister of Colonies Adolphe Messimy explained that to have one would first require 'breaking down the barriers' which all too often existed among the several metropolitan ministries. There were complaints about this situation and even Marshal Hubert Lyautey, the 'creator' of modern Morocco, who rarely encouraged co-operation with Algeria or Tunisia, thought that some 'formula' ought to be found to tighten the connections which bound the three countries together.[2]

The formulas were complicated and unsuccessful. In 1911 the French parliament established an Interministerial Parliamentary Commission on Muslim Affairs (*Commission interministerielle des affaires musulmanes*), an advisory body attached to the Ministry of foreign affairs which had little to do with policy formulation or even policy co-ordination. After the First World War there were sessions of what was called the North African Conference (*Conference nord-africaine*) – an occasional summit meeting of politicians, soldiers, and administrators from both sides of the Mediterranean but it was mostly talk and show, not action.[3]

The initiative for change came from Albert Sarraut during his first, brief tenure as premier in October–November 1933. Sarraut was empire-minded and worried about North Africa's security. He had served as governor-general of Indochina before and during the First World War and had twice been Minister of Colonies in post-war governments. His book, *La mise en valeur des colonies françaises* (Paris, 1923), a basic text of the 'developmental' school of French colonialism, advocated the economic improvement of the colonies as a way of strengthening France's overall economic position in the world. To identify and propose 'precise solutions' for the regional problems of North Africa Sarraut recommended the creation of a committee for North Africa, attached to the premier's office. Its permanent members would include the premier and the ministers of foreign affairs, the interior, war, and the colonies, the governor-general of Algeria, and the residents or resident-generals of Tunisia and Morocco. Given the decision-making authority of its members, Sarraut assumed that this committee would talk, then act.[4]

Fifteen months later, President of the Republic Albert Lebrun decreed the Haut Comité Méditerranéen et de l'Afrique du Nord into existence. By statute the committee was authorized to inform itself on 'all the issues common to Algeria, Tunisia, Morocco and the states of the Near East [the Levant] under French mandate as well as the issues which involve these territories with each other or with the Metropole'. Despite this expanded competence (which acknowledged France's need for a co-ordinated Muslim policy at both ends of the Mediterranean), North Africa was always the committee's chief focus. In his report to the president Premier Pierre-Etienne Flandin had emphasised the necessity of co-ordinating North African policy – and particularly 'native policy' (*la politique indigène*) – given the crisis of the moment, namely the vigour of the nationalist movements across the Muslim world and their connection with one another through Islam. 'Islam is not and without doubt will never be the basis for political unity,' he asserted, 'but it remains the basis for spiritual unity.' And the appeal to Islam, already so powerful in Syria, was part of the nationalist call in North Africa and had led to 'more or less serious' disorders in Constantine, Tunis, and Fez in 1934. Flandin underscored the 'danger' in all of this for France. It could have 'incalculable consequences' in the case of conflict in Europe and the need to mobilize. In sum, the Haut Comité Méditerranéen was intended as a 'common centre' where the 'decisive issues' which affected French policy in the Mediterranean might be discussed and evaluated. Hopefully it would provide a measure of protection for France's Mediterranean territories 'against attacks from without and uprisings from within'.[5]

The Haut Comité pursued its internal security mission with a vengeance. In 1935 it suggested measures:

1 to reorganise the surveillance of the native population in North Africa, to reinforce the surveillance of native and metropolitan agitators, and to institute the surveillance of native students in French universities;
2 to restrict the freedom of the press in Algeria and of trade unions in Tunisia;
3 to expel outside agitators from North Africa and to deport Tunisian agitators to French colonies;
4 to apply in a more rigorous manner the penal laws designed to repress political crimes and to strip French citizenship from any naturalized North African convicted of anti-French activities.

The leading colonial periodical, *L'Afrique française*, applauded all action against what might be called the 'Islamic peril,' arguing that Islam could and did combine with a variety of contemporary evils – socialism, communism, nationalism, pan-Islamism, and Hitlerism – to create nightmares for France.[6] On the other hand, many in France objected to the fact that the Haut Comité had become an instrument for repression rather than for creative action.

When Premier Pierre Laval met with the Haut Comité in July 1935, he began by repeating the accepted truth that the 'destinies of France and North Africa were intimately bound together' on both the economic and political levels, then spoke with some eloquence about Islam and France's dilemma:

> From Tripolitania's borders to the beaches of the Atlantic Islam presents us with the same problems. Islam itself is being affected by the pressure of new forces. Significant changes are taking place within Islam which are infinitely more important in my opinion than a political demonstration here or there, however dramatic it might be.

How to handle this new situation? How to integrate these new tendencies into 'the French order that we have established in North Africa and that we intend to maintain?' How to define and pursue a 'native policy' applicable to all three of the North African territories, yet flexible enough to deal with the special requirements of each one? These broad issues were far from the narrow confines of crime and punishment. And Laval apparently intended to make that point, for he steered the committee away from their long agenda of police matters, suggesting that it would be 'dangerous' to get embroiled in issues that were the proper concern of the 'qualified authorities' in Algeria, Tunisia, and Morocco.[7]

Laval's strictures may have kept the Haut Comité Méditerranéen from becoming the 'top-cop' in North Africa, but at the same time seemed to push it down the corridor of debate without great impact. For the next six months the Haut Comité was dormant. To rescue what he yet hoped would be 'the cornerstone of our North African and Muslim policy', Albert Sarraut (once again premier in February 1936) recommended a permanent secretariat-general to prepare for the meetings of the Haut Comité and to follow up on its decisions, to establish a North African and Muslim documentation centre in the library of the premier's office, and to function as a liaison with the variety of metropolitan offices interested in North African affairs. At the head of the secretariat he wanted a 'high civil servant', armed with the 'indispensable authority' to carry out this 'delicate mission' and to facilitate his contacts with the directors of the several ministries. The budget for such a venture, which included salaries and space for the secretary himself, two clerks, one assistant clerk, one stenographer-typist, two liaison officers and funds to procure and translate materials, was well beyond Sarraut's means. The plan to reshape the Haut Comité had to await socialist hands.[8]

With Léon Blum's Popular Front government came the changes in the Haut Comité that Sarraut trusted would make it a force in policy making. Stressing again the need to co-ordinate Mediterranean affairs and to employ the Haut Comité to 'its full capacity', Blum created a permanent secretariat attached to the secretariat-general of the premier's office. The new secretariat, an instrument of information and co-ordination, would be staffed by a secretary and his assistants, all named by the premier. This was a scaled-down version of Sarraut's more expensive proposal. Moreover, to ensure that the work of the Haut Comité would be constant and serious, Blum established a separate eleven-member 'study commission' (*commission d'études*), which would meet on a regular basis when the Haut Comité was not in session or whenever the premier thought it necessary. In this commission experts would play a key role. In addition to representatives of the ministries of foreign affairs, the interior, national defence and war, and the colonies, five commission members were to be selected solely because of 'their expertise in Islamic or colonial matters.' Other specialists could be called in as needed.[9]

Blum's socialist party newspaper, *Le Populaire*, called the renovated Haut Comité Méditerranéen 'a sort of grand council' of Muslim and Mediterranean affairs and pronounced the changes 'especially necessary' at a time when the 'Islamic renaissance' presented France with similar difficulties in North Africa and the Near East.[10] And *L'Afrique française*, usually hostile to all things socialist, also endorsed the alterations in the Haut Comité as the very reforms it had advocated for months. The importance of the members of the committee, their expertise, their energy and commitment, and the information at their disposal would 'facilitate' the making of policy, even though *L'Afrique française* conceded that this had not happened in the past. What it most feared was the tyranny of the metropolitan experts, now more numerous than ever in the study commission, who might be tempted to put politics, personal rivalries, and ambitions before common sense and act irresponsibly or, 'dare one say it, academically'.[11] Finally, sensitive to the fact that the Haut Comité was being animated by a socialist premier, *L'Afrique française* reminded the government that politics 'like anti-clericalism' should not be an item for export.[12]

Blum had the good fortune to find the right man for the job of secretary of the Haut Comité Méditerranéen. Charles-André Julien 1891–1991), 45 years old, was a *professeur agrégé* of history and geography, whose academic speciality was North Africa. Born in northern France, Julien had spent time in Algeria as a young man and served as a *conseiller général* for Oran between 1920 and 1923. From 1926 to 1936 he was the secretary-general of the most prestigious French historical journal, the *Revue historique*, and his own survey of North African history, *Histoire de l'Afrique du Nord: Tunisie, Algérie, Maroc*, appeared in 1931.[13] Julien was no stranger to the territory that he was being asked to oversee, and, although not a high civil servant, he had put in 'quality time' behind a desk. Besides, as a Protestant, an intellectual, and a socialist, he exemplified the sort of outsider that the Popular Front wanted to bring into government in France. An open and generous man of liberal ideas and sympathies, Julien was someone in whom Blum surely found a kindred spirit.[14]

In the study commission Julien oversaw the appointments of three distinguished academics: René Hoffherr (1893–1966), professor at the École Libre des Sciences Politiques and director of the Centre d'Etudes Juridiques of the Institut des Hautes Etudes of Rabat; Louis Massignon (1883–1962), professor at the Collège de France and director of studies at the Ecole Pratique des Hautes Etudes in Paris; and Robert Montagne (1893–1954), director of the Institut Français of Damascus.[15] Ten years older than the others, Massignon was the doyen of the group. An Orientalist, he edited the important *Revue des Etudes Islamiques*. His 1925 work on Moroccan merchant and artisan associations, *Enquête sur les corporations musulmanes d'artisans et de commerçants au Maroc* (Paris, 1925), had established him as the leading French social historian of Muslim North Africa. Hoffherr was trained as a legal scholar, but he made his reputation as an expert on overseas economic and social organisation with the publication of *L'Economie marocaine* (Paris, 1932), the first serious study of the Moroccan economy, followed by *Revenus et niveaux de vie indigènes au Maroc* (Paris, 1934), an investigation into the cost and standard of living of the Moroccan native population. Montagne was a naval officer and political sociologist who combined colonial staff assignments with research. His work on the Berber tribes of southern Morocco, *Les Berbères et le Makhzan dans le sud du Maroc: Essai sur la transformation politique des Berbères sèdentaires (groupe Chleuh)* (Paris, 1930), explained how seemingly isolated and independent Berber communities allied with one another for self-protection and war-making. This made the book a sort of political Bible for inter-war French administrators in North Africa.[16]

In addition to these three academics, each of whom had somewhat coincidentally done research on Morocco, Blum named René

Gazagne and Jean Gout to the study commission. Gazagne had begun his career in Algeria and was currently the secretary-general of the Préfecture du Nord. He had preceded Julien as secretary of the Haut Comité Méditerranéen. Gout was a senior foreign service officer at the rank of *ministre plénipotentiaire.* For years he had presided over the Interministerial Parliamentary Commission for Muslim Affairs which was dissolved by Blum's legislation reorganising the Haut Comité.[17]

The new, improved Haut Comité Méditerranéen failed to impress Moroccan nationalists who were convinced that it remained 'an instrument of co-ordination and surveillance' and thus inadequate to solve the problems of the Maghreb.[18] By spring 1937 they had already had a chance to evaluate Blum's colonial initiatives and were not encouraged. General Charles Noguès, Blum's appointee as resident-general in Rabat, had authorised the use of force to contain the nationalists' meetings and marches in November 1936 and had imprisoned nationalist leaders; in March 1937 he had ordered the disbanding of the nationalist association. The nationalists professed surprise at his harsh methods and disappointment that a Popular Front government committed to 'the eternal principles of democracy and liberalism' could have acted in such a manner'.[19] Noguès countered that he had been compelled to take the action he had, but promised that, once order was restored, he would press ahead with measures for economic, political, and social progress within the framework of the protectorate treaty. All this was designed to leave the nationalists in history's dustbin.[20]

Nationalists in Algeria and Tunisia had the same negative reaction to the Haut Comité Méditerranéen. This prompted *L'Afrique fran-çaise* to suggest that the real reason for their discontent was that by centralising information and co-ordinating decision-making the Haut Comité would put an end to the compartmentalisation of North African policy which they had worked to their advantage for so long. Henceforth they would be confronted by an institution capable of blocking their 'cunning intrigues' by proposing effective reforms. This would strip their complaints of any 'semblance of legitimacy'. Face to face with the experts of the Haut Comité, the nationalists would be forced to give up their extravagant demands which until now, claimed *L'Afrique française,* had been the chief reason for their public notoriety.[21]

It was impossible for the Haut Comité to live up to such advance billing. It did make a start, however, on recommending social and economic measures which it believed would contribute to the political appeasement of North Africa. For example, in 1937 committee members discussed the 'diverse problems posed by the endless increase in the influx of North Africans into France and specifically the problem of the labour force'.[22] The study commission advocated extending all the benefits of French social legislation (which Algerians already enjoyed) to Moroccans and Tunisians residing in France. It recommended closer co-operation between North African and metropolitan labour bureaux for job placement as well as the creation of a North African employment office in France. It set an annual quota for Moroccan workers authorised to come to France (renewable in case of need) as a first act towards organising emigration.[23] The following year the Haut Comité pronounced in favour of plans for training programmes in agriculture and industry for North African emigrants and for the organisation of this labour force on a national scale. In addition, the committee urged pulling down the slum dwellings that had grown up on the outskirts of many French cities and replacing them with suitable working-class housing.[24] This was the first time that the topic of North Africans in France had been discussed as a whole rather than as a series of separate and unconnected issues.[25] As the director of political affairs in Morocco later noted, Morocco was above all 'an exporter of men'.[26] To recognise that basic fact was a step towards understanding the connection between employment in France and peace in the Maghreb.

In 1938 and 1939 the Haut Comité endorsed programmes to supply emergency financial aid to North Africa (particularly Morocco) because of the drought which had devastated the region and also to provide credit to native artisan corporations.[27] It also began a comprehensive study of the difficulties of the peasantry which *L'Afrique française* correctly recognised as one of the causes of '*la malaise nord-africaine*' about which the Metropole had little information. At its heart was the use and ownership of land, a problem which every colonial power had to tackle and which each handled in its own way. Wherever Europeans settled in large numbers, however, the result was always the same, the introduction of land laws which favoured the newcomers at the expense of the native population. This was the most serious consequence of the 'colonial situation', the introduction of an outside population of 'a certain density' into 'a circumscribed geographical space' already peopled by an indigenous population. Here, however, the committee made no dramatic proposals for change. It noted only that it favoured the development of the land and the construction of housing for the native population.[28]

The most important question facing the Haut Comité Méditerranéen was the need for a response to what was called the 'Islamic renaissance' in the Near East and North Africa. Charles-André Julien described the political manifestation of that rebirth in an article for the American journal, *Foreign Affairs*, published in 1940.

During the last two decades the Arab world, from the Persian Gulf to the Atlantic, has become growingly conscious of the unity of its faith and culture, and of the need for solidarity *vis-à-vis* Europe. At the same time each Arab country has sought with increasing ardour to attain its own national liberation. Pan-Arabism and nationalism, apparently incompatible, thus have developed simultaneously as a twofold expression of the East's resistance to the West.'[29]

Replying to the Islamic challenge required an appreciation of its development and its significance. In a report to the Haut Comité in March 1937 Julien analysed the 'regional nationalisms' of Algeria, Tunisia, and Morocco, then the larger 'Maghreb nationalism' (*nationalisme maghrébin*).[30]

He explained that in Morocco national sentiment was centred in the young and educated Arab middle class who were in contact with the 'modern ideas' of the west and yet because of 'the vast movement of the Islamic renaissance' were also in touch with the east. The mix had produced a western-style nationalism with a religious foundation. According to Julien, the 'decisive event' which roused Moroccan national sentiment was the revolt of Abd-el Krim in 1925 which brought a rebel army within 'a few kilometres' of Fez. Moroccans concluded that his defeat was due to the modern weapons of the French, nothing more, and that that alone had prevented their country from achieving independence. This heightened sense of what was politically possible was joined to a resurgent concern over the threat to Islam, made tangible by French patronage of the 1930 'Berber decree'. By transferring legal matters from Koranic courts in some Berber tribes to tribunals where Berber customary law was enforced, 'it deprived the faithful of Allah's justice'.[31]

Moroccan nationalism achieved concrete expression through the creation of a political association, Moroccan Action (*Action marocaine*), whose first public statement of demands was the 1934 'Plan for Moroccan Reforms' (*Plan de réformes marocaines*).[32] Brushed aside by the French government, the nationalists took their message to the streets and were at the heart of the protest demonstrations which shook Casablanca and Fez in November 1936. Moroccan

Action was organized, active, and filled with the energetic spirit of youth, and Julien believed it had the potential for becoming 'the centre of a more and more extended opposition'.[33]

Beyond Morocco, Moroccan Action linked itself with the nationalist associations in Algeria, the North African Star (*Etoile nord-africaine*), and Tunisia, the New-Destour (*Neo-Destour*), through the formation of a committee for concerted action. Although tenuous, these connections were important and coincided with Maghreb ideals. 'Pan-Maghrebism' – which Julien defined as the nationalist stage on the road to pan-Arabism – had first found voice in student groups in Paris, such as the North African Muslim Students' Association (*Association des Etudiants musulmans nord-africains*).[34] It was strengthened by annual student congresses. In 1935 the students urged that instruction in the schools be used 'to give birth to the consciousness of our unity in North Africa, a unity founded on a unified intellectual outlook, a single religion and common sentiments'. This was not some trumped up union they insisted, but the resurrection of 'an ancient unity which history is here to witness and to guarantee'.[35] Julien also reported that a Tunisian student had designed a membership card for a group he called 'Young North Africa' (*La jeunesse nord-africaine*) which showed a female representation of North Africa embracing young men from Algeria, Tunisia, and Morocco. On the reverse was an oath with phrases reminiscent of the French Constitution of 1793:

> I swear on the honour of North Africa that throughout my life I will work to raise high its standard and to unify its countries.
> North Africa is one and indivisible.
> North Africa is a single nation (*une seule et même nation*) and must remain so forever.
> North Africa is one people whose language, education, customs, and traditions must remain the same.
> North Africa is a single homeland (*patrie*) whose children must form a single front (*un front unique*) to defend it'.[36]

Julien concluded that for many Algerian, Tunisian, and Moroccan nationalists 'the national question no longer tends to be placed on the regional level, but on the Maghreb level'. This was as much a question of deep-seated beliefs as of the need to find a set of ideals capable of 'stirring up' (*soulever*) the masses against the colonial regimes.[37]

A united Maghreb called for a unified French response. This the Haut Comité Méditerranéen failed to provide. One reason was the disagreement over the seriousness of the nationalist challenge. Julien believed that it was of significance and required the thought, co-ordination, and action that only the Haut Comité could provide. But Montagne considered North African nationalism a teapot tempest, blown into gale-force winds only in the minds of sympathetic or frightened observers. For Montagne the acts of local authorities sufficed.[38] Another was the continued reliance on separate strategies for Algeria, Tunisia, and Morocco whether in matters of reform or repression. Here history and established interests determined the path and the pace of change. After five years of the Haut Comité (three of them with the Blum improvements), Julien admitted that France still had 'neither a colonial administration nor a body of doctrine suffi-ciently well developed to enable her to co-ordinate her Moslem policy effectively'.[39] A third reason was that domestic and European political crises (and ultimately the Second World War) constantly disrupted the committee's work. 'Political events' in the capital post-poned the October 1937 meeting; and the March 1938 session was held amidst a 'governmental crisis'. The March 1939 meeting was rescheduled because foreign 'circumstances' prevented the colonial administrators from leaving their posts, then cancelled when 'foreign threats' forced them to leave Paris sooner than they had planned.[40] Finally, there was the French inability to understand how North Afri-cans could prefer the 'darker' forces of language, race, and history when France continued to proclaim the brightness of liberty, equality, and fraternity.[41] Why had nationalism triumphed over liberalism in North Africa? Politics, like anticlericalism, *L'Afrique française* insisted, was not an item of export to the colonies. Neither apparently was the Declaration of the Rights of Man and of the Citizen.[42]

NOTES

1   Centre des Hautes Etudes pour l'Afrique et l'Asie modernes (CHEAM), Fonds Charles-André Julien, Haut Comité Méditerranéen et de l'Afrique du Nord (HCM), Carton 1937, session de mars 1937, rapport no. 1: *Le Haut Comité Méditerranéen et les organismes d'information musulmane*, pp. 1–4.

2   *Le Haut Comité Méditerranéen et les organismes d'information musul-mane*, pp. 5, 37.

3   *Le Haut Comité Méditerranéen et les organismes d'information musul-mane*, pp. 4–5.

4   *Le Haut Comité Méditerranéen et les organismes d'information musul-mane*, pp. 5.

5   Décret du 23 février 1935 [Haut Comité Méditerranéen et de l'Afrique du Nord], in *Le Haut Comité Méditerranéen et les organismes d'informa-*

tion musulmane, Annexe A. The committee was scheduled to meet only once a year (the second Tuesday in March), but it could be called into session at any time by the premier or any of the cabinet ministers who were committee members. In 1935 and 1936 only one of its meetings was 'statutory', the other four were 'extraordinary sessions'.

6   *Le Haut Comité Méditerranéen et les organismes d'information musulmane,* pp. 14–15.

7   'Extraits du discours prononcé par M. Laval, président du conseil, devant le Haut Comité Méditerranéen, le 9 juillet 1935', in *Le Haut Comité Méditerranéen et les organismes d'information musulmane,* Annexe B.

8   *Le Haut Comité Méditerranéen et les organismes d'information musulmane,* pp. 19–21.

9   *L'Afrique français,* 47, no. 4 (April 1937), pp. 230–1. As minister of state in the Popular Front cabinets of Camille Chautemps and Lyon Blum, Sarraut continued to play a co-ordinating role in North African affairs.

10   *L'Afrique française,* 47, no. 3 (March 1937), p. 129.

11   *L'Afrique française,* 47, no. 3 (March 1937), pp. 129–30.

12   *L'Afrique française,* 47, no. 4 (April 1937), p. 231.

13   Julien's classic *L'Afrique du nord en marche: nationalismes musulmans et souveraineté française* (Paris, 1952) was influenced by his tenure at the Haut Comité Méditerranéen.

14   Blum appointed Julien secretary of the Haut Comité Méditerranéen in 1936, then reappointed him secretary of the remodelled committee on 27 April 1937. *L'Afrique française,* 47, no. 5 (May 1937); p. 287. (At the secretariat Julien was assisted by Christian Courtois, professor of history, and Jean Loubet, a secondary-school teacher. Courtois's principal thesis for the *doctorat és lettres* was *Les Vandales et l'Afrique* (Paris, 1955)

15   *L'Afrique française,* 47, no. 5 (May 1937), p. 287.

16   Charles-André Julien, *Le Maroc face aux impérialismes, 1415–1956* (Paris, 1978), pp. 166–7. Montagne's lectures on the Berber tribes at the University of Paris in November–December 1930 were published as *La Vie sociale et la vie politique des Berbères* (Paris, 1931) and later translated as *The Berbers, Their Social and Political Organization* (London, 1973).

17   *L'Afrique française,* 47, no. 4 (April 1937), pp. 230, 232; 47, no. 4 (May 1937); p. 287.

18   *L'Afrique française,* 47, no. 5 (May 1937), p. 287.

19   *L'Afrique française,* 47, no. 5 (May 1937), p. 288.

20   On Noguès and French policy in Morocco, see my *The Casablanca Connection: French Colonial Policy, 1936–1943* (Chapel Hill, 1984), especially chapter 2.

21   *L'Afrique française,* 47, no. 5 (May 1937), pp. 288–9.

22   *L'Afrique française,* no. 3 (March 1937), p. 128.

23   *L'Afrique française,* 47, no. 12 (December 1937), p. 592.

24   *L'Afrique française,* 48, no. 4 (April 1938), p. 189.

25   *L'Afrique française,* 47, no. 12 (December 1937), p. 592.

26   CHEAM, Haut Comité Méditerranéen, Procès-verbaux des séances, séance du 9 mars 1938, p. 7.

27   *L'Afrique française,* 48, no. 4 (April 1938), pp. 188–9; 49, no. 4 (April 1939), 118–19.

28 *L'Afrique française*, 48, no. 4 (April 1938), pp. 189–90.

29 Charles-André Julien, 'France and Islam', *Foreign Affairs*, vol. 18, no. 4 (July 1940), p. 684.

30 CHEAM, Fonds Charles-André Julien, HCM. Carton 1937, session de mars 1937, rapport no. 2: *Les grands courants d'opinion dans l'Islam nord-africain*, p. 19.

31 *Les grands courants d'opinion dans l'Islam nord-africain*, pp. 72–74; Julien, 'France and Islam', p. 693.

32 *Les grands courants d'opinion dans l'Islam nord-africain*, p. 75.

33 *Les grands courants d'opinion dans l'Islam nord-africain*, p. 80.

34 *Les grands courants d'opinion dans l'Islam nord-africain*, pp. 20–1; Julien, 'France and Islam', p. 686.

35 *Les grands courants d'opinion dans l'Islam nord-africain*, p. 20; Julien, 'France and Islam', pp. 685–6.

36 *Les grands courants d'opinion dans l'Islam nord-africain*, p. 22.

37 *Les grands courants d'opinion dans l'Islam nord-africain*, pp. 21, 23. According to John P. Halstead, Julien overemphasized the importance of the Pan-Maghreb or Pan-Arab element in Moroccan nationalism. Halstead, *Rebirth of a Nation: The Origins and Rise of Moroccan Nationalism, 1912–1944* (Cambridge, Mass., 1969), pp. 127–8.

38 Robert Montagne, 'La crise nationaliste au Maroc', *Politique étrangère*, vol. 2, no. 6 (December 1937), pp. 535–62.

39 Julien, 'France and Islam', p. 680.

40 *L'Afrique française*, 48, no. 4 (April 1938), p. 188; 49, no. 4 (April 1939), pp. 118–19.

41 Julien believed that Islam was 'the only common denominator' among the Maghreb countries. Julien, *L'Afrique du nord en marche*, p. 400.

42 The Haut Comité Méditerranéen disappeared in 1940. Blum tried to resurrect it after the war, but was unsuccessful. See Julien, *L'Afrique du nord en marche*, p. 401.

7 The Spanish Protectorate and the occupation of Tangier in 1940

Claire Spencer

THE ROLE OF SPAIN IN MOROCCO

Much of the consideration of the protectorate period in Morocco concentrates on the French administered zone, with only passing reference to the smaller, northern zone under Spanish administration.[1] In many ways this bias is understandable: France occupied about three-quarters of the territory of what was still considered to be the sovereign Sharifian Empire of Morocco; the French Résidence Générale at Rabat undertook the most far-reaching reforms of the Moroccan economy and administration, and, arguably, indulged in the most far-reaching abuses of the Moroccan Sultan's sovereign powers. Moroccan foreign policy, moreover, was entirely in French hands.

In a strictly legal sense, France was also the sole protecting power over Morocco, since it was the French government which signed the Treaty of Fez in 1912 with Sultan Moulay Hafid. It was only later in the same year that a subsidiary treaty was signed between Spain and France, through which some of the widespread powers delegated by the Sultan to France were entrusted to a parallel Spanish administration based at Tetouan.[2] This fact was a constant bone of contention between the two powers, since many Spaniards claimed that their rights to participate in the protection of Morocco preceded those of France. Not only had Spain been in sovereign possession of a number of enclaves on the northern coast of Morocco – most notably Ceuta and Melilla since the late fifteenth and early sixteenth centuries[3] – but more importantly as the Spaniards often pointed out, France could not have established a protectorate at all if Spain had been excluded.

This second argument stemmed from specific provisions in the Entente Cordiale signed between France and Britain in 1904, when the British agreed to desist from claims to influence in Morocco in return for a similar undertaking on the part of the French in Egypt. One of the terms for this agreement, as far as the British were concerned, was the inclusion of Spain in any enterprise on the northern coast of Morocco.[4] This stipulation arose from the strategic importance of the Straits of Gibraltar in British trade routes to India and the East via the Suez Canal. The underlying imperative in British policy towards the region, both at the time of the Entente and later, was that no strong power (namely, France) should hold the southern shores of the Straits opposite Gibraltar.

The main effect of this was that from the very beginning of what became known as 'the Moroccan question' in the late nineteenth century, Spain could make no moves in the region without taking both French and British reactions into consideration. Despite justified concerns about the geographical proximity of Morocco, and the protection of the hinterland of the main enclaves, the policies of successive Spanish governments towards Morocco were reactive rather than assertive, evolved on an *ad hoc* rather than on a consistent basis.

An example of this came shortly after the Fashoda incident in 1898, when relations between France and Britain were particularly strained. On French instigation, secret bilateral negotiations were held with Spain with the aim of dividing Morocco into two spheres of influence which could, later, be presented to Britain as a *fait accompli.* A provisional agreement was reached in 1902, through which Spain would have gained a substantial portion of Northern Morocco, including Fez and the fertile plains later occupied by France. At the last minute, however, the Spanish government hesitated, and refused to sign for fear of the British response to this division of spoils. When the agreement became public knowledge ten years later, there were to be widespread recriminations directed against the the Liberal government which had lost this advantage for Spain irretrievably.[5]

In the event, time was on the side of the French, who went on to sign the Entente Cordiale two years later and consolidated their commercial and trading position in Morocco in the period up to 1912. Only Germany presented a passing challenge to French hegemony over Morocco from 1905, and even this was resolved – despite the drama of the Panther incident off Agadir – with relative ease by 1911.[6] Spanish inertia, meanwhile, meant that by the time of the 1912 division, Spain was left with what was ironically termed '*el hueso de la chuleta*' – or the bone of the chop.[7] In other words, Spain's sphere of influence was reduced to the mountainous and almost impenetrable north of Morocco, while France took the 'meatier' arable lands to the south. Subsequently, while French occupation of the central region, main urban centres and ports of the larger zone was relatively swift, Spain was constantly engaged in subduing uprisings and countering alternative centres of power in the period 1912–27. No sooner had the fiefdom of the first local contender, al-Raisuni, been reduced, than the Spanish military was faced with the more formidable Rif Republic, set up in the mountains of that name by ʿAbd al-Karim. That these campaigns involved both a humiliating defeat at the hands of the Moroccan Berbers at Anual in 1921 and, almost worse, the need to call on French help to defeat ʿAbd al-Karim in 1926 did nothing to popularize the occupation of Morocco in Peninsular Spain.

Despite these setbacks, Spain remained in Morocco with a tenacity which belied the expense of maintaining a military establishment which rivalled that of the French forces in the neighbouring zone, and the lack of immediate and persuasive economic gains. The temptation to leave was expressed on more than one occasion by both leaderships and opposition groups, even when the Rif War had been effectively won.[8] In practice, the reasons why Spain remained, just like the reasons for Spanish involvement in the first place, had as much to do with relations between European powers as to any direct benefits to be gained. Seen in this context, the question of why Spain ever embarked on what amounted to a precarious colonial venture for which she was both ill-suited and ill-prepared takes on a different and more intricate significance.

THE RISE OF SPANISH INTEREST IN MOROCCO

Since the eighteenth century and less noticeably before, Spain had been in a long and slow decline from the days of her global empire. In a dramatic fashion, the last parts of this empire had been lost in 1898 – subsequently known as the 'Year of the Disaster' – when both Cuba and the Philippines fell to the United States. With the military establishment in disarray, it was hardly the moment to be embarking on new, expansionary campaigns overseas. It is true that Spain, like Great Britain, was concerned with preventing France from occupying the northern coast of Morocco. However, another, less costly, solution might have been found through establishing a minimal Spanish presence on the littoral and in the immediate hinterlands of the enclaves. The occupation of the Rif highlands was an operation of an entirely different order, with few obvious commercial benefits beyond exploring the potential for iron ore mining.[9]

Nevertheless, by the time the fate of Morocco had become an international issue at the turn of the century, there were several forces at play in Spanish political and intellectual circles which favoured participation. While not all of these led in the same direction – namely, the inexorable occupation of Morocco – it was a period when external factors had most influence on Spain's own national self-perception. From the mid-nineteenth century, one of the dominant trends in the search for a new national identity was the growth of what was termed *Africanismo*, and which the historian Victor Morales Lezcano has depicted as an offshoot of the wider European interest in the 'Orient', or Orientalism.[10] There were several strains of this movement or ideology, but they arose from the same three factors – namely, the search for an external role for Spain which had been lacking since the secession of the last of the Latin American republics in 1826, a means of escaping from internal disorder and decadence, and a possible solution to the international isolation of Spain, particularly evident during the period of European alliance-making at the end of the nineteenth century.

The first and third of these factors were linked in that for the majority of the nineteenth century, Spain had existed apart from the mainstream of European politics. The last encounter with the outside world had been the Peninsular Wars – or War of Independence from the Spanish perspective – when after a long drawn-out campaign and with the help of the British army, Napoleonic troops had been driven out of the Peninsula in 1814. In Spanish national mythology, the first symbolic day of this uprising against foreign invasion: the *dos de mayo*, or 2 May 1808, was for a long time the only immediate source of national pride and dignity. After the French retreat, Spain was once more left to her previous internal divisions, further aggravated by the upheaval of war. A weak king was followed in 1833 by a succession crisis and the rise of the Carlist movement supporting a different branch of the royal family; the scandalous reign of the eventual victor, Isabel II, gave way to the First Republic in 1873, which in turn swiftly gave way to the restoration of the monarchy in 1874. Meanwhile, regionalism merely complicated the attempts of weak and short-lived governments to implement much-needed economic reforms.

In this state of fragile unity, it was not surprising that some means of restoring national dignity was looked for overseas. The frustrated military devised a small, but successful campaign to subdue tribal incursions into Ceuta and Melilla in 1859. This minor 'African War' or '*Guerra de Africa*' as it was called, was both a product of and stimulant for the growing Africanist schools of thought. It was ultimately futile, in that the Spaniards had no means of consolidating their position in Morocco, having been expressly warned not to proceed further by Britain, and fearful of what France would do from Algeria, in French hands since 1830. Nevertheless, in the absence of other events of positive, rather than negative significance, the symbolic victory of the *Guerra de Africa* entered both the national mythology and consciousness in a way which served to enhance the image of Morocco as a potential arena for future victories.

Other solutions to the national dilemma, focused on Morocco, were more cultural than military. A number of prominent thinkers and politicians began to talk of Morocco and Spain as natural and historic partners. They made allusions to a past of close cultural links, placing special emphasis on the richness of the long period of Muslim rule of southern Spain. The 1860s saw the flowering of the most pacific period of Africanismo, reflected in paintings and literature which expressed an attraction to the 'exotic' which Morocco then represented. Even the military were involved in relatively peaceful scientific missions to Morocco to discover more about Spain's close, but long-neglected neighbour.[11]

While at first there was no explicitly political content in this exploratory interest, there was an almost natural progression in the discourse of some of the *Africanistas* from a largely descriptive tendency to one of prescriptive action. One form of the argument was that just as the Arabs and Berbers of Morocco had once conquered and brought much of current Andalusian culture to Spain, so it now fell upon Spain to bring modern civilization to the declining Sharifian Empire across the Mediterranean.

The international Conference of Madrid held in 1880 was in part a reflection of the success of Spain's claims to historic links with Morocco in the eyes of other European powers. However, the international discussions which began here and culminated in the Act of Algeciras of 1906 only confirmed Spain's secondary position in deciding the fate of Morocco.[12] While the Spanish settler population in Morocco increased over other European communities during the nineteenth century (particularly in Tangier), Morocco's strongest trading partner was Great Britain, until the latter's interest concentrated on Egypt. Meanwhile, the officially-sponsored mobilisation of French commercial and business interests in Morocco swiftly outpaced the hesitant translation into practice of Spanish aspirations. As Victor Morales Lezcano has pointed out, the 'expansionist capital' of Spain was significantly less developed than its equivalent in France. Spanish capitalists, moreover, were considerably less willing to take risks, in reflection of the uncertain atmosphere for investment in the domestic economy of Spain.[13]

Only in 1904 were a number of commercial centres established in Morocco, and the interest of financiers from Catalonia and the Basque country awakened to the possibilities presented across the Mediterranean. The flourishing of a movement in favour of commercial rather than ill-defined cultural goals was echoed in a series of *Africanista* congresses held between 1907 and 1910, and the publication of an *Africanista* magazine, *España en Africa*, heralding a new and glorious – commercial – era for Spain in Morocco. However, just as Spanish diplomatic initiatives came on the heels of the strategies of her European neighbours, so this conversion to economic goals in Morocco was a reaction to what the French had promoted, and achieved, in a remarkably short space of time.[14]

THE EUROPEAN CONTEXT OF SPAIN'S MOROCCAN POLICY

The transition from commercial to political interest in Morocco was not divorced from a series of overall foreign policy perceptions which held true over the first half of the twentieth century despite changes in both governments and regimes. The Spanish historian José Maria Jover has identified three main strands to these perceptions which governed Spain's relations with other European states – in particular, with France and Great Britain.[15] The first was the growing realisation, then acceptance, of the translation of Spain's past greatness into a present of secondarity. By the turn of the twentieth century, Spain began to assume the role of 'small' or 'medium' power alongside the 'great powers', which even if not fully realised in the immediate aftermath of 1898, was confirmed in the failed accords of 1902. In practical terms, this involved attempts to use the influence of one power against the other as a means of creating an area in which Spain could exert leverage – particularly over France, as Spain's nearest neighbour both in Europe and Morocco. It also meant linking policy moves in one sphere to desired benefits in another, and the advancing of excessive demands in the hope, and expectation, of gaining at least half of what was sought. This type of approach was necessarily opportunistic and reactive, since it meant adapting to the overriding concerns of one or other of the powers in order to create the impression that Spain's support or obstruction could be decisive to their outcome.

The second underlying perception was the notion of the Iberian peninsula as a world apart from the mainstream of European events, supported by a conviction dating from the War of Independence that Spanish territory was impenetrable to outside attack. The impermeability of the Pyrenees, separating Spain from the rest of the European continent, served as a symbol of this. A third and related perception or tendency was to polarise in the south the concept of 'frontier', not as a fixed line, but as 'a zone characterised by the eventuality of danger and by a possibility for expansion' in the words of Jover.[16] In other words, Spain's window on the outside world was situated to the south, not the north, and it was to the south that Spain focused her arena for international action.

The combination of these three strands meant that Spain's most immediate relations with the major European powers were concentrated in Morocco. Outside factors also contributed to this, given that France had to accommodate Spain in Morocco on the insistence of Britain, while Britain needed to accommodate Spain as a buffer against French pretensions in the Straits of Gibraltar. Through involvement in Morocco and Moroccan issues, Spain found her role in European affairs in a way which had become inconceivable in any other sphere. Without Morocco, the great powers were neither obliged nor inclined to take Spain into consideration. As a result of the limitations imposed both by themselves and international settlements, however, Spain could not be overlooked whenever Morocco was concerned.

THE REFLECTION OF SPAIN'S EUROPEAN POLICY IN MOROCCO

The Tangier question

The translation into practice of these perceptions is best seen through a number of examples which illustrate the nature of Spain's involvement in Moroccan affairs. The most salient and long-lasting of these was the vexed question of the status of Tangier, which as Christopher Andrew and A.S. Kanya-Forstner comment, 'generat[ed] more paper and acrimony in proportion to the interests at stake than almost any other issue in modern diplomacy.'[17] At the heart of the problem was the fact that the city of Tangier had been left ambiguously to one side in the agreements which settled the fate of the rest of Morocco. For historical reasons, Tangier had acquired a special importance as both the centre of foreign diplomatic representatives to the Moroccan

Sultan and as the home of the largest European trading communities in Morocco. It was also the closest point of Morocco across the Straits from both Spain and Gibraltar. From 1906 onwards, all European treaties concerning Morocco included some reference – direct or otherwise – to the elaboration of a special statute for the city, inspired particularly by British concerns over the control of the north coast.[18]

The question was left pending at the time of the 1912 protectorate treaties, but became a condition for British acceptance of the Treaty of Fez, and, by implication of the Franco-Spanish treaty of November 1912. After a series of negotiations involving only France, Spain and Britain, a provisional statute was drawn up in 1913 which conferred both a regime of neutrality and international administration on a zone consisting of Tangier and its immediate hinterland. The dubious legality of excluding from the discussions the other nine signatories (besides Morocco) of the Act of Algeciras was overshadowed by greater world events. The outbreak of the First World War delayed the signing of the provisional tripartite agreement (again, mostly through Spanish hesitation, in the hope of gaining some advantage during the war), which was then left in abeyance in the changed circumstances of post-war European relations. From a position of relative strength, France avoided British overtures to renew contacts over Tangier, arguing instead that since the city had been specifically left out of the 1912 treaty with Spain, it automatically formed part of the French protectorate.[19] The Spanish government countered this argument by claiming that Tangier had been implicitly included in the Spanish zone of protection since the Entente Cordiale, when it was agreed that Spain was to control the whole of the Moroccan coastline on which Tangier was situated. The subsidiary 'special status' to be conferred on the city, therefore, did not necessarily mean its exclusion from the broader Spanish zone.[20]

Without entering into the details of a debate which lasted five years initially and continued in a different form for many years thereafter, it is interesting to note how the public campaign orchestrated in Spain in favour of 'Spanish Tangier' was out of all proportion to the city's value in other than symbolic terms. From the beginning of the 1920s in particular, a whole series of public meetings were held, and pamphlets issued, with the almost universal title: '*Tánger ha de ser español*' (Tangier has to be Spanish); the most prominent members of the ailing political establishment were drawn into a debate which galvanized opinion (for once) in the same direction to the exclusion of almost all other foreign policy issues beyond Morocco.[21] Underlying this national frenzy was that by 1920, the reality of the 'miser-

able' portion of Morocco allocated to Spain was becoming all too
obvious. The ignominious defeat of the Spanish Army by ʿAbd al-
Karim at Anual in 1921 merely accentuated the claims to Tangier.
More to the point in the European context was the high-handedness
of the French administrators of Morocco in their dealings with their
Spanish counterparts, which on more than one occasion touched on a
raw nerve of Spanish pride. In the balancing of relations between
France and Great Britain, it had become evident that France was the
immediate 'enemy' – if the term can be used – just as she had been
over a century before. The spirit of *'dos de mayo'* thus found its echo
in the public outcry over Tangier, serving both as a focus for an
increasingly fragile national unity and as a means of attracting European attention to Spain.

What the Spanish government did not count on, however, was the
ultimate collusion between France and Britain in the decision to make
the Tangier administration international. The French only ceded to
British insistence on an international (that is, tripartite) solution when
the atmosphere between the two states had soured over other post-
war settlements.[22] Under these circumstances, and with a severely
reduced margin for manoeuvre, the Spaniards had little choice but to
acquiesce. Their secondary status was even more closely felt, moreover, when the negotiations which culminated in the Tangier Statute
of 1923 coincided with yet more domestic instability and the imposition of the Directorate – or dictatorship – of Primo de Rivera in the
governmental crisis of September 1923. In the confusion of the
ultimate crisis of the liberal government which was removed with
King Alfonso XIII's blessing, incoherent instructions were sent to the
principal Spanish negotiator in London, who finished by adopting the
British position almost single-handedly.[23] Having surrendered claims
to Tangier so early on with nothing in exchange, the Spanish delegation at the final talks in Paris could only fine-tune the details of the
international administration drawn up by France and Britain.

Political capital was nevertheless gained from the intervening
change of regime. In January 1924, Primo de Rivera refused to ratify
the December 1923 agreement until a number of subsidiary concessions had been gained – most notably from France. While these were
of small material importance, they were preceded by the more
dramatic threat to leave Morocco entirely if the principle of inter-
nationalisation were not rescinded. The British, who were keen
neither to let this second Tangier settlement go the way of the first
nor to escalate it into a broader crisis, supported the Spanish position
against the French.

From the Spanish point of view, however, the discussions which continued into February were designed to embarrass both France and Britain in the wake of Italian claims to a role in deciding the fate of Tangier.[24] While France argued that Italy had unconditionally withdrawn all interest in Morocco through an exchange of letters between 1900 and 1902,[25] Mussolini countered that the clear relevance of Tangier as a question affecting all states with interests in the Mediterranean basin (and especially Italy) meant that it could not be decided behind the backs of the other Algeciras signatories. Both France and Britain were united in rejecting Mussolini's advances, but Spain's signature of the draft statute became crucial to the need to present Italy with a *fait accompli*. Additional fears that Primo de Rivera and Mussolini were planning some kind of Mediterranean pact against the northern powers only heightened the centrality of Primo de Rivera's role. In the event, this was short-lived, as Mussolini distanced himself from Primo de Rivera's Mediterranean designs. In March, and with sufficient gains from France to satisfy his domestic audience, Primo de Rivera ratified the Tangier Statute.

The application of the Statute, which was delayed until 1925 to gain the adhesion of the majority of Algeciras powers, presented Primo de Rivera with other opportunities to assert himself on the European stage. Spanish officials made numerous complaints over the alleged French domination of the administration, and disagreements arose over individual articles of the Statute. One of these was the allocation of customs dues between the three zones of Morocco according to the place of consumption or utilisation of imported goods.[26] In April 1926, Primo de Rivera played on the ambiguities of the Statute to impose a customs barrier between the Tangier and Spanish zones, which was only lifted when the issue was taken beyond the immediate institutions of the Statute to negotiations at European foreign ministry level. This wider recognition of Spanish demands was in the end of more importance than the financial compensation gained.

Soon after, in the summer of 1926, Primo de Rivera launched an initiative which linked Spanish claims to a permanent seat at the League of Nations with the question of Tangier.[27] He requested a meeting between European foreign ministers at Geneva to coincide with the League's discussions over admitting Germany, positing as a counter-demand Spanish control over Tangier should the request for a permanent seat be refused.[28] While the British Foreign Minister Austen Chamberlain was sympathetic to Spanish demands for a permanent seat, neither he nor the French Foreign Minister, Briand, was prepared to accept the linkage with Tangier, and the proposed meeting was, politely, rejected. In the face of this united Franco-British front, and following Germany's acquisition of a permanent seat, Primo de Rivera responded by withdrawing Spain from the League.

The timing and import of these initiatives, however, were not unconnected to the participation of France in the final defeat of ʿAbd al-Karim in northern Morocco, to which Spain had been obliged to make recourse in an agreement of July 1925. In the process, part of the border region of the Spanish zone was occupied by French troops, which even after the surrender of ʿAbd al-Karim, the French zone authorities refused to remove, citing reasons of security. By drawing attention to Tangier (and indirectly Morocco) at the League of Nations, Primo de Rivera was exerting pressure on France in a broader arena, given that his remonstrances had borne no fruit in Morocco itself. At the same time, this leverage was also aimed at Britain, in that the so-called 'international' statute had gained neither universal international support nor full participation beyond its initial signatories. Both Italy and the USA remained outside, in a way which plagued the effectiveness of the administration on the ground.[29] Austen Chamberlain responded to these attempts to discredit the Statute by sponsoring new discussions on its revision, with a view both to satisfying Spanish demands and gaining the adhesion of Italy, and possibly the USA. A protocol to this effect was eventually signed in July 1928, and Italy, but not the USA, adhered to the Statute.

The Moroccan arena

With the Tangier question settled, at least until the original Statute was due to expire in 1935, Primo de Rivera turned his attention to the mounting domestic opposition to his regime in the late 1920s. It was in keeping with the need for an external focus for national unity that the very 'pacification' of northern Morocco – described by Gerald Brenan as 'the most successful of the achievements of the Dictatorship'[30] – should have precipitated domestic instability. Once Spanish control extended over the Rif and the interior of the zone, the growth of private commercial and mining interests acted as a counterweight to Primo de Rivera's previous threats to withdraw completely from Morocco. Despite the cost of maintaining a military presence, a lobby of 'Moroccan' concerns grew up to parallel those of the *Africanista* lobby of the Peninsula, a factor which contributed to de Rivera's downfall in 1930. However, the movement away from large-scale investment projects to agriculture and small commercial and industrial enterprises was a poor shadow of developments in the neighbouring French protectorate. The French press, both locally and nationally, constantly made unfavourable comparisons between their own and Spanish achievements. This acted almost as an invitation to the Spaniards to launch another attempt to undermine France's much-vaunted hegemony of Morocco.

The replacement of both the Directorate and the Spanish monarchy by the Second Republic in 1931 coincided with the rise of another element which played into Spanish hands. While one of the first actions of the new regime was to reduce the number, and thus the cost, of Spanish troops stationed in Morocco,[31] the advent of Moroccan nationalism allowed for a more nuanced approach to the debate which resurfaced over Spanish withdrawal. The Moroccan nationalists in the Spanish zone were at first independent of, then linked to similar groups in the French protectorate, but as conditions in the two zones changed in the early 1930s they moved apart. This was partly because, in contradistinction to the repressive stance adopted by the French, the Spanish authorities chose to take a more benign approach to the movement, even integrating one of the nationalist leaders into the protectorate administration in 1936.[32] The inefficiency of the Spanish administration was also partly responsible; however, the opportunity to exert pressure on France was soon seized, by allowing a nationalist press to criticize the shortcomings of the French zone, on condition that no negative comment was passed on the Spaniards. The only recourse that the French had – besides official complaints – was to prohibit the newspapers' circulation in the French zone.

It remained the case during the Republic, nevertheless, that the Spanish enterprise in Morocco was far from being a universally popular cause. A number of changes were made to the military and civilian establishments in Morocco, but the instability of Peninsular governments was merely reflected in the lack of continuity in the Spanish zone administration. Over a period of ten years, for example, there were seven different High Commissioners overseeing the zone.[33] Little official encouragement was given to prospective settlers, in the form of agricultural credits, for example, until 1936, and as the Republic began to disintegrate towards the Spanish Civil War, there were as many good arguments for cutting Spain's losses in Morocco as there were for staying.

In the event, and as is well-known, the Civil War began from the Spanish zone of Morocco, where Franco staged his first challenge to the Republic in July 1936. In an attempt to maintain a position of neutrality in the conflict, the French authorities prohibited the export of vehicles, petrol or other provisions to the Spanish zone that might be used for belligerent purposes, but in doing so aroused the wrath of Franco. The significance of Tangier in Spanish designs against France once again came to the fore, when almost immediately after forming a National government on 21 July 1936, Franco threatened to bombard the city if a number of Republican warships stationed in the port were not forced to leave. The European consuls at Tangier formed an emergency 'Council of War' to deal with the affair, before handing over responsibility for the defence of the port to a commission of other European naval commanders stationed at Tangier. French protests at this violation of the provisions of the Statute went unheeded until the Republican warships were eventually withdrawn, and Franco's war proceeded to the Peninsula.[34] Once victorious, Franco did not forget the thorn in Spanish flesh represented by Tangier, particularly since the Civil War had been used as a pretext by France for reneging on a commitment over the distribution of appointments within the administration. In November 1935, when the Statute came up for renewal, Pierre Laval made a written undertaking to the Spanish ambassador in Paris that the French would support a Spanish nomination to the post of administrator in Tangier.[35] As the highest executive position in the international administration, this had previously always been occupied by a Frenchman, even though the original Statute limited French occupancy to six years. In exchange, the Spanish government had agreed to support a French nomination to the post of deputy Administrator, but even after the conclusion of the Civil War, this transaction had not taken place.

The occupation of Tangier

Shortly after the outbreak of the Second World War, Franco found his opportunity to wreak revenge on France. From a position of neutrality, which became one of non-belligerency after the Italian entry into the war, Franco sought to maintain Spain's freedom of action in Morocco. In proposals to the German Reich in June 1940, Spain's conditions for entering the war were almost entirely related to territorial gains in North Africa, including control over the French zone of Morocco.[36] However, even before the Hendaye meeting of October 1940, which effectively removed Spain from active participation in the conflict, Franco had achieved what many of his predecessors had only dreamed of: namely, the occupation of Tangier. In the spring of 1940, with the Italian declaration of war becoming increasingly inevitable, a weakened France opened negotiations with Spain to create a combined Franco-Spanish security force to defend Tangier. Italian activities in Tangier already looked set to threaten the neutrality of the zone, yet Franco delayed coming to an agreement with the French. Instead, taking advantage of the German advance on Paris, and acting on little more than the verbal assent of the French Ambassador in Madrid, forces from the Spanish zone of Morocco entered Tangier on the same day in June that Paris fell.[37] While the French authorities in Morocco were keen to show their approval of this action – not only to save face, but also to prevent Spain joining forces with the Italians – their control over events was minimal. From Algiers, the Moroccan Resident-General tried to organise the despatch of a company of French troops to Tangier, in order to appear to be participating in the 'provisional' defence of the city's neutrality, cited as the reason for the occupation.[38] In the aftermath of France's defeat, this company failed to materialise; the Foreign Office, meanwhile, engaged in weightier affairs, merely accepted the *status quo*. Franco, however, had other ideas, and over the next few months set about the progressive dismantling of the international administration. On 16 November 1940, Spanish officials announced the unilateral annexation of Tangier to the Spanish Zone, and against no effective resistance the Tangier zone came under the Spanish protectorate until the end of the war.

After years of playing second fiddle to France in Morocco, Spain had at last been able to act with impunity. As if to rub salt in the wound, Franco also proposed to move Spanish-led troops to occupy the territories to the south as far as the River Sebu which were originally to be Spain's at the time of the 1902 treaty.[39] Even though the Spanish successes were reversed in 1945 and the international administration of Tangier reinstated, the important symbolic victory had been won; the economic and strategic worth of Tangier paled in comparison when put alongside Spain's European coup.

NOTES

1   Apart from works published during the Spanish occupation of northern Morocco (1912–56) the Spanish historian Victor Morales Lezcano is one of the few to have assessed Spain's role in Morocco independently of France. See Victor Morales Lezcano *España y el norte de Marruecos* (Madrid: UNED, 1984).

2   For both 1912 treaties see Résidence Générale de la France au Maroc *Recueil des actes internationaux et à incidence internationale concernant le Maroc* (Rabat, 1941), pp. 73 and 91.

3   See Tomás Garcia Figueras *Marruecos – La acción de España en el norte de Marruecos* (Ediciones Fe, 1939), Chapters IV and V.

4   Article 8 of the public treaty included an acknowledgement of the interest of Spain in Morocco; article 3 of the additional secret treaty was more specific in conferring the control of the coast from Melilla to the right bank of the river Sebu to Spain. See *Recueil des actes, op. cit.*, p. 36.

5   See especially Victor Ruiz Albeniz, 'Tangier and Franco-Spanish co-operation' (Madrid, 1927), p. 6, where the author writes of the 'pusilla-nimity' of the Spanish leadership in 1902.

6   German diplomacy was behind the Moroccan Sultan's request for an international conference to be held on the future of Morocco, which led to the Act of Algeciras of 1906 signed by 12 powers in addition to Morocco (France, Britain, Spain, Germany, Austro-Hungary, Italy, The Netherlands, Belgium, Portugal, Sweden, the USA and Russia). Rather than preventing French ascendancy in Morocco, however, the Act of Algeciras authorised France and Spain to reorganise the police and finances of the Sharifian Empire. In February 1909, France and Germany signed a subsidiary joint declaration in which the political inter-ests of France in Morocco were recognised by Germany in exchange for assurances over her economic interests there. Economic competition, however, continued between the two powers, leading to a further German challenge to the incremental French occupation of Morocco, symbolised in the stationing of the warship 'Panther' off Agadir in 1911. The Franco-German Accord of November 1911 revealed the real nature of Germany's aims, when the French ceded almost half of the French Congo to Germany in return for a free hand in Morocco. See Graham H. Stuart, *The International City of Tangier*, (Standford, Calif.: Stanford University Press, 1931), pp. 68–75.

7   In practice, the division which 'deprived' Spain of territories including Fez had been drawn up in a secret Franco-Spanish agreement of October 1904, six months after the Entente Cordiale. See *Recueil des actes, op. cit.*, p. 37: 'Convention secrète approuvant l'accord franco-anglais du 8 avril ...'.

8   See Genoveva Garcia Queipo de Llano 'El problema de Tánger y la mediación de Gran Bretana durante la dictatura de Primo de Rivera', p. 470 in *Actas del Congreso International; 'El Estrecho de Gibraltar', Ceuta, 1987*, vol. III, (Madrid: UNED, 1988).

9   See Chapter 3 on Spanish mining interests in Victor Morales Lezcano *El Colonialismo Hispanofrancés en Marruecos (1898–1927)* (Ediciones Siglo Veintiúno, 1976), pp. 69–87.

10 See Victor Morales Lezcano, *Africanismo y Orientalismo español en el siglo XIX* (Madrid: UNED, 1988), p. 22.

11 *Ibid.*, p. 82.

12 The Madrid Conference addressed the question of limiting the foreign protection extended to Moroccan subjects; the Act of Algeciras guaran-teed the sovereignty and independence of the Moroccan Sultan, together with the 'integrity of his dominions'. See the preamble to the General Act

and additional Protocol of the International Conference on Morocco at Algeciras (7 April 1906) in J. Hurewitz, *The Middle East and North Africa in World Politics* (2nd edn), vol. I, (New Haven, Conn.: Yale University Press, 1975), p. 518.

13 See Victor Morales Lezcano, *Espana y el norte de Marruecos, op. cit.,* p. 148.

14 See Chapter II of Charles-André Julien's, '*Le Maroc face aux impérialismes (1415–1956)*', (Paris: Editions Jeune Afrique, 1978), for details of French economic control over Morocco.

15 José Maria Jover, 'La percepcion española de los conflictos europeos: noras históricas para su enrendimiento', in *Revista del Occidente,* February 1986, pp. 5–42.

16 *Ibid.,* p. 11.

17 Christopher Andrew and A. S. Kanya-Forstner, *France Overseas: The Great War and the Climax of French Imperial Expansion,* (London: Thames & Hudson, 1981), p. 31.

18 These concerns were also exploited by Germany in attempts to internationalise the Moroccan question; the French were later to present British insistence on the internationalization of Tangier as an entirely German-derived condition, which was no longer binding after Germany's defeat in the First World War.

19 For the Foreign Office's exasperated response to both this and other French arguments, see Public Record Office (PRO) FO 371 8344 W2207/197/28 'Memorandum on Tangier' (G. H. Villiers) of 10 March 1922.

20 In 1919, however, the Spanish premier, Romanones 'offered to sell France all Spanish rights in Tangier and the Spanish zone of Morocco for one milliard francs, keeping only Ceuta and Tetouan for a possible exchange with Gibraltar' (Andrews and Kanya-Forstner, *op. cit.,* p. 174). While the French did not take this seriously, it was indicative of the 'brokerage' role attributed to Morocco by Spain.

21 See, for example, the speech of Carlos Garcia Alonso at a conference held on 11 May 1920: 'Tánger para España', (Reus, Madrid, 1920); the anonymous pamphlet 'Tánger ha de ser español', (Ediciones Ibero-Africano, Americano, 1920); the interviews with prominent national figures collected by Antonio Cases in *Tánger, dignidad nationál,* (Madrid, 1922), etc.

22 See Andrews and Kanya-Forstner, *op. cit.,* p. 232, on the emotional scenes over the Turkish crisis of September 1922. The British Foreign Secretary's impatience with both the French and Spaniards by early 1923 led him to comment: '[I] wish there were no Latin races in the world' (Lord Curzon, autographed minute, PRO FO 371 9458 W2153-4/1/28, 21 March 1923).

23 See PRO FO 371 9459 W5533/1/28: Robertson (British negotiator) to Lord Curzon, 10 July 1923.

24 See PRO FO 371 10577: letter of the Italian Ambassador to London, the Marquis della Torretta to Lord Curzon, 1 January 1924.

25 See J. Hurewitz, *op. cit.,* vol. I, p. 477: Entente on Morocco and Tripoli, Franco-Italian exchange of letters: 14 December 1900, 1 November 1902.

26 See article 20 of the Tangier Statute of 1923, in G. H. Stuart, *op. cit.*, p. 244.

27 See David Armstrong, *The Rise of the International Organization – A Short History* (London: Macmillan, 1982), p. 44; E. H. Carr, *International Relations between the Two World Wars* (London: Macmillan, reprinted 1986), pp. 100–1.

28 See archives of Ministerio de Asuntos Exteriores, Spain, Legajo R 952, Ex. 7, Quinones (Spanish Ambassador to Paris) to Briand, 24 August 1926.

29 See Stuart *op. cit.*, pp. 131–3. Unbound by the provisions of the Statute, Italian residents were free to set up gambling dens, specifically forbidden to Moroccans and the communities of the signatory powers. All the other Algeciras signatories – except for Germany and Austro-Hungary, excluded from Morocco under the Treaty of Versailles – had adhered to the statute without actively participating in it. Only Belgium appointed a gendarmerie captain who never took up his post.

30 Gerald Brenan, *The Spanish Labyrinth* (Cambridge: Cambridge University Press, 1943), p. 80.

31 Victor Morales Lezcano, *España y el norte de Marruecos, op. cit.*, p. 92.

32 See J. Halstead, *Rebirth of a Nation: the Origins and Rise of Moroccan Nationalism* (Harvard Middle Eastern Monograph Series, 1969), p. 237.

33 Victor Morales Lezcano, *España y el norte de Marruecos, op. cit.*, p. 158.

34 For correspondence on this affair, see archives of the Ministère des Affaires Etrangères (MAE), Paris, Série Maroc 1918–40, 606: Laforcade (French consul at Tangier) to MAE, telegrammes nos 109–13, 22 July 1936, et. ff.

35 See MAE (Paris), Maroc Guerre Vichy 1939–45 – 121 – Copy of letter from Pierre Laval to Juan de Cadenas, 13 November 1935.

36 See Katherine Duff, 'Spain between the Allies and the Axis', in Arnold Toynbee and Veronica M. Toynbee (eds), *Survey of International Affairs, 1939–1946, The War and the Neutrals* (Oxford: Oxford University Press, 1956), p.273. Spanish demands also included possession of Gibraltar.

37 See detailed correspondence in MAE (Paris), Guerre Vichy 1939–40 Maroc 121: Noguès (Resident General of Morocco) to MAE, tel. nos 356–8, 7 June 1940, et. ff.

38 See MAE (Paris), Guerre Vichy 1939–40 Maroc 121: Noguès to MAE (Paris), tel. nos 49–50, 15 June 1940. Rumours of a pending Italian invasion of Tangier was another reason given.

39 Katharine Duff, 'Note on Franco-Spanish relations with regard to Morocco during the Second World War', in Toynbee and Toynbee, *op. cit.*, p. 311.

Part III
Independent states

8 The FLN

French conceptions, Algerian realities

Hugh Roberts

Do not, above all, confound me with what I am not!
(Friedrich Wilhelm Nietzsche, *Ecce Homo*)[1]

Since the dramatic riots in Algeria in October 1988, it has been a commonplace of media commentary on the country to suggest that the Front de Libération Nationale (FLN) is in irremediable decline. A stereotype of the decadent single-party socialist state has been repeatedly passed off as a serious analysis of the situation: the ruling parties of such states have been in decline virtually everywhere else, and why should Algeria escape this general rule? In particular, media coverage during the first twelve months after the riots concentrated almost exclusively upon the conflict between President Chadli Ben Jedid and elements of the FLN, and suggested that not only was this conflict substantially analogous to the struggle between 'liberal reformers' and 'Marxist hardliners' in the Soviet Union, with President Chadli in the role of the Algerian Gorbachev, but that it was the central aspect of the Algerian drama.

I tried to explain shortly after the riots that this was a misconception of the situation.[2] I suggested that what was at issue in the arguments taking place within the Algerian political elite was the basis upon which the good government of Algerians was to be secured, and that within the elite a consensus was in the process of being organised upon a new formula of both men and measures which would obtain a new lease of life for the state which the FLN had founded, and for the FLN itself as the necessary guarantor of this state. This view of the matter, which was very much a minority one, eventually appeared to have been vindicated by the extraordinary congress of the Party of the FLN held in November 1989, for this congress marked the return to politics of major figures from the past representing a wide variety of viewpoints and appeared to launch the FLN on a new phase as the

111

natural party of government, with a correspondingly rich inner life, within the new multiparty system.[3]

No sooner had this second perspective begun to achieve currency, however, than it was apparently refuted in the most devastating manner by the humiliating defeat of the FLN in the local and regional elections of 12 June 1990 at the hands of the recently formed Islamic Salvation Front (Front Islamique du Salut, FIS). But the spectacular rise of the FIS was also a massive complication from the point of view of Soviet and East European analogies. Suddenly, the duel between the Algerian Gorbachev and the Algerian Brezhnevites had been relegated to the background by this new and disconcerting development. The 'hardliners' had been disavowed by the electors, perhaps, but the 'reformers', far from inheriting the earth, had been entirely outflanked by something else altogether. On the other hand, the central tenet of the Soviet analogy, that the FLN, like the Communist Party of the Soviet Union (CPSU), was at the end of its tether, appeared to have been vindicated in the most thorough-going way.

This interpretation left two fundamental facts out of the account. First, whereas the Communist Party in the USSR and the East European countries had unequivocally been the centre of political power, to which other apparatuses and, in particular, the armed forces, were subordinate, the Party of the FLN (Hizb al Jabhat at-Tahrir al-Wataniyya) has never been more than a secondary apparatus, performing public relations, mobilisational and parallel diplomatic functions on behalf of a state machine which it has never even remotely controlled, and in which the armed forces have held unquestioned hegemony. Because of this, the humiliation of the *party* in Algeria could not be taken to be the moment of truth for the *state*. And the state which the FLN created, the armed forces, the civil service, the diplomatic corps and the intelligence and security organs, are all still very much in place and apparently unperturbed by the party's discomfiture.

Second, whereas the collapse of the Communist regimes has followed ineluctably from the collapse of Marxism–Leninism as their guiding and legitimating ideology, there has been no comparable collapse in Algerian society of the ideology which actually produced the FLN. The FLN was not the product of a secular or a socialist vision, still less a Marxist one, but of a vigorous nationalism in which populist, Islamic and pan-Arab elements have co-existed without difficulty. In this perspective, the success of the FIS can be seen to be a development of a central aspect of the FLN's ideology, the Islamic aspect, not a repudiation of this ideology overall. Moreover, there is a strong populist strain in the rhetoric of the FIS, nationalist strain: immediately after the results of the 12 June elections had been announced, the second most prominent spokesman of the FIS, Ali Belhadj, launched into a violent diatribe against France and demanded reparations for the French massacres of Algerian Muslims after the abortive uprising of 8 May 1945.[4] And the continuing vitality of pan-Arab sympathies has been made clear since 2 August 1990 by the massive support which Algerian public opinion has demonstrated for Iraq's defiance of the American-led intervention in the Gulf,[5] despite the long-standing hostility of the Islamist movement towards Iraqi Ba'athism and the ties which Algerian Islamists have had with Saudi Arabia.[6]

In short, the analogy with the USSR and other Communist states breaks down at crucial points. The substantial elements of the FLN, the state machine it constructed and the nationalist ideology it incarnated, are still intact and as vigorous as ever. The defeat of the *Party* of the FLN on 12 June was not a defeat of the *substance* of the FLN at all. Whether the Party has a future remains to be seen, but for the substance of the FLN, unlike the substance of Communism, the end is not nigh.

Forms of politics often, if not invariably, have their end in their beginning. And, if the substance of the FLN is still far from its end, this is undoubtedly due in part to the particular character of its beginning. One of the several interesting aspects of this complex character was the unmistakeably Nietzschean spirit which presided over the events of 1 November 1954. The extraordinary audacity of the political enterprise begun on that day has tended to go unremarked. The Algerian Revolution was, in its beginning, an affair of a small, determined, and, above all, adventurous band of free spirits intent on surpassing themselves and on impelling the Algerian people as a whole to surpass themselves. It is therefore appropriate to ask, in respect of the observer himself: *has it been understood?*

FRENCH CONCEPTIONS

French political conceptions abound in the contemporary discussion of Algerian politics, in the academic literature, in media commentary and in the animated debates of Algerians themselves. The radical Islamist movement which has now given birth to the FIS, for example, has regularly been referred to as *les intègristes*, by analogy with the traditionalist tendency within the Roman Catholic Church, especially in France, which has been at odds with Vatican orthodoxy.[7] Another example is furnished by the tendency within Algerian public opinion, articulated most uninhibitedly by the Rally for Culture and Démocracy (Rassemblement pour la Culture et la Démocratie, RCD), which is most hostile to the Islamist movement and alarmed by it, and which has been calling openly for *la laicité d'Etat* – that is, the radical separation of religion from politics in an explicitly secular state, a political conception whose French pedigree is incontrovertible.[8] And the Berberist movement which has developed in Algeria since the mid-1970s has been portrayed as analogous in essential respects to the Breton and Occitan movements in France.[9]

As for the FLN itself, three conceptions of French origin have been deployed, *inter alia*, in the discussion of its singular history. Algerian nationalism in general has often been characterised as 'Jacobin' and this epithet has frequently been applied to the FLN in particular. The conception of 'Bonapartism', derived partly from the experience of the First Empire but perhaps primarily from Marx's analysis of the form of government of France under the Second Empire,[10] has been employed by certain – especially *marxisant* – writers to characterise the form of government of the Algerian state, especially in the Boumedienne period.[11] And, finally, we may note a third conception of the FLN, in respect of the period of the war of national liberation – namely, that contained in the analogy with the French Resistance to German occupation during the Second World War. This is not merely a matter of the use of the term *maquis* to refer to the guerrilla forces of the Armée de Libération Nationale (ALN), nor has it been confined (any more than the other examples cited) to French commentators; the Algerian writer Mohamed Lebjaoui, a member of the wartime FLN, found it natural as well as apposite to describe his former chief Abane Ramdane as 'le Jean Moulin algerien'.[12]

Many other examples could be cited of the use, in the diverse literature on Algerian politics, of political conceptions drawn from the rich historical experience and political culture of France. But I shall take it that the point has been made.

I shall not pursue here the question of whether it is helpful to employ the term '*intègristes*' with reference to the radical Islamist movement; I have already argued elsewhere that it is not,[13] a point which other writers have also made.[14] As for the Berberist movement, I have already discussed the way in which this was misconceived in the widespread media coverage of the 'Tizi Ouzou Spring' in 1980 [15] and shall deal with the particular question of the Breton and Occitan analogies in a forthcoming book.[16] Both the radical Islamist and the

Berberist movements are important and impressive but none the less secondary factors in Algerian politics. The FLN is fundamental and central to Algerian politics. To misconceive the one is to misconceive the other. I wish to suggest that to describe and explain the FLN by means of a framework of interpretation constructed out of French political conceptions is to misconceive the FLN, and that the FLN has been repeatedly misconceived in the existing literature on Algeria. In fairness to the latter, there has been an element of inevitability about this state of affairs.

A COLLECTIVE RESPONSIBILITY

Every observer of politics in foreign parts brings his native political conceptions to bear upon the object of his study. The fact that Algeria was a French colony has ensured that the works of French authors have dominated the literature on the country. And the indisputable fact that French political conceptions have acquired a virtually universal status in the world of modern states as a consequence of the international impact of the French Revolution has made it particularly difficult for French observers to free themselves from their native presuppositions in their efforts to make sense of Algerian politics. After all, it can truly be said that most people these days, outside the ranks of the radical Islamist movements, tend to think about politics in French terms, for the simple reason that the French invented most of the vocabulary of modern politics.

Yet there is nothing fatal about a tendency and, while an agreed alternative way of conceiving Algerian politics has yet to be established, there is no lack of French scholars who have successfully avoided the mistake of misconceiving Algerian politics in French terms. It should be clearly understood that it is not French scholarship as such (to which I, like every other student of Algeria, am enormously indebted) which is the object of my criticism here, but the use of French political conceptions in the analysis of Algerian politics *by whoever may have employed them*. The mistake which I am criticising is a mistake which I have made myself, and American and not a few Algerian writers on Algerian politics have also succumbed to the same powerful temptation.

Finally, it should also be said that, by one of those huge ironies which make up so much of the actual history of ideas, if French political conceptions have tended to determine, with negative results, the study of Algerian politics, part of the responsibility for this state of affairs is not to be laid at the door of French observers of Algeria

at all but at the door of what is loosely called Anglo-Saxon anthropology, a point to which I shall return.

IMPLICATIONS OF A POLITICAL RUPTURE

Algerian politics are not French in character or pedigree. They have
in common with English politics since 1688 the fact that they are an
exception to a rule. The case which I am making is the case for
Algerian exceptionalism, that this exists and needs to be taken
account of in thought. Algerian politics have been developed by the
FLN, and the FLN has been a far more original and specifically
Algerian political phenomenon than has been recognised.

The FLN was formed in a political rupture with the part of popular
and explicitly separatist nationalism, the Parti du Peuple Algerien
(PPA) of Messali Hadj. This rupture was a protracted and very
complex event, and it was a political, not an ideological, break; there
was plainly a good deal of continuity between the FLN and its
precursor in respect of ideology, but politics is not at all the same
thing as ideology, and in respect of its politics the FLN was from the
outset a very different proposition from the PPA.[17]

The PPA was the successor of the Etoile Nord-Africaine[18] (ENA)
and its fundamental conceptions were those of the ENA. A number
of native Algerian ingredients went into the ideology of the ENA[19]
but as an organised movement it had been formed on the social basis
of the Algerian migrant community in France and under the political
aegis of the French Communist Party (Parti Communiste Français –
PCF). The PCF has been well described by R. W. Johnson, following
the late G. Lavau, as having the character of a 'tribune party' – that
is, a party of radical protest against the political order which is based
upon a section of the population which is effectively excluded from
this order, but which is obliged to presuppose this order as the actual
framework of its own activity.[20] Although Messali's ENA freed itself
from the Communist connection in the early 1930s, moderating the
social radicalism of its programme and placing fresh emphasis on
Islam in the process,[21] it retained the character of a tribune party:
while vigorously proclaiming the separatist objective of Algerian
independence, it canvassed this cause within the framework of the
one and indivisible French Republic of which colonial Algeria was
constitutionally a part, and its modus operandi presupposed the
framework of the French state, the PPA differing in no way from its
predecessor in this respect. Messalism as a form of politics was accordingly incapable of realistically conceiving how the separation of

Algeria from this framework might actually be effected. And the failure of the PPA as a whole to address this problem effectively led to the party being rent by doctrinal disputes and factional feuds from 1945 onwards, and paralysed by them from about 1950 onwards.[22]

The FLN was formed by veterans of the PPA's short-lived paramilitary arm, the Organisation Spéciale (1947–50) – that is, by that element of the PPA which had thought about this problem and had conceived a realistic answer to it: to go to war with the French state without further ado. In breaking with Messalism, the founders of the FLN were breaking with all other forms of Algerian Muslim politics simultaneously, for all of them – the Association des Oulema Reformistes, the Union Démocratique du Manifeste Algerien of Ferhat Abbas and the Parti Communiste Algérien as well as the PPA – had presupposed the French political framework and had shrunk from the unthinkable business of ceasing to do so.

Operating within the French political framework had of itself supplied Muslim anti-colonialism before 1954 with the political models and norms by means of which its several variants could naturally organise their respective internal affairs. In breaking with this framework, the FLN was breaking with the source of these models and norms and withdrawing from the ground upon which these models and norms were functional. It was therefore immediately confronted with a fundamental problem: that of the basis on which and the manner in which it was to organise its own internal political life.

PARTY? ARMY? FRONT?

From the moment of its foundation until the extraordinary congress of November 1989, the FLN was never a political party in the proper sense of the word. And if, as is by no means certain, future developments should enable us to take the 1989 congress as the moment when the FLN successfully reconstituted itself into a political party *à peu près comme les autres*, they will also, I believe, oblige us to recognise that the FLN did so without immediately or completely ceasing to be what it had been up until then, which is something else altogether. It is with what the FLN has been from 1954 to 1989 that I am concerned here.

The wartime misconception of the FLN as a party was exposed as a misconception by the crisis which erupted within it in July 1962, a crisis which was promptly misunderstood by many observers as the disintegration of the FLN. Parties do disintegrate from time to time, of course, but they are least likely to do so when they are on the verge of taking power. The fact that the FLN was apparently disintegrating in its moment of triumph brought home to certain observers at the time that it was not really a party in the first place. What has been less clearly understood is that the FLN did not really disintegrate in the summer of 1962 either: it sorted itself out and successfully constituted itself into the Algerian state. The fact that it managed not to disintegrate while giving a powerful impression of doing so, and that, despite not being a party, it was able to handle its bitter internal divisions without splitting[23] and so avoid civil war when civil war was very much on the cards, was undoubtedly connected with what the FLN actually was.

But, if the FLN was not a political party, what was it? Some observers have suggested that it was, in reality and in the first place, an army. In a sense this is obviously true, since its first act was to launch a war. But, if the FLN had been an army in the normal sense of the word, the business of organising its internal affairs would have been a relatively simple matter. And, in fact, the formal organisation of the purely military aspect of the FLN was done comparatively quickly and painlessly, when the first congress of the FLN in August 1956 agreed to generalise the system of ranks and the command structure already in use in Kabylia (*wilāya* III) to the rest of the ALN.

It was in part because the FLN was neither a political party nor an ordinary army that the business of organising its internal life was such an extraordinarily difficult, controversial and bitterly painful affair. Moreover, the FLN was not even what its name proclaimed. The term 'front' is normally applied to a movement grouping several parties in which each party preserves its separate identity, membership and organisation (the Front Populaire in France in 1936, Unidad Popular in Chile 1970–73, etc.). The FLN was nothing of the kind. It was a political movement fighting a revolutionary war for nationalist purposes which from the outset was at odds with all pre-existing political organisations in Algeria and determined to outflank and eliminate them. It eliminated them by absorbing them (except for the irredeemable disciples of Messali, whom it set about eliminating physically) and it absorbed them by dissolving them inside itself, by atomising their memberships, and restructuring this human material in a new way.

THE TRADITIONS OF THE *QBAIL*
The war the FLN launched was based in the Algerian countryside,

and it was the social realities and political traditions of the society of the Algerian countryside which relentlessly impinged upon the thinking of the FLN's leaders and provided them with their main political headaches and also the means of coping with them. These traditions informed the organisation of the FLN on the ground from early on; where the FLN got off to a firm start in November 1954, in the Aures and Kabylia, they informed its organisation from the outset; where they did not do so, the insurrectionary movement collapsed almost at once (the Algerois, the Nord-Constantinois and the Oranie) and drastic expedients were required to re-start it in the course of 1955. These expedients were successful precisely because they took account of local traditions, unlike their ineffectual precursors. In other words, notwithstanding the FLN's entirely modern objectives, its internal life was, as a matter of necessity, increasingly governed by traditional political norms.

There is a diversity of political traditions within the Algerian countryside. The principal tradition is that of the dominant element of non-urban Algeria, the sedentary tribesmen of the hills, whom the townsfolk of pre-colonial Algeria were accustomed to refer to as *al qbail* (literally 'the tribes'), unlike the nomadic or transhumant pastoralists of the high plateaux and the Sahara, whom they called bedouin (*al badawiyyīn*). The society of the *qbail*, by which is meant not only the Berber-speaking *qbail* of Greater and Lesser Kabylia and the Chenoua, but also the Arabic-speaking *qbail* of eastern Kabylia, the Collo and the Ferdjioua, the Medjerda mountains, the Blida Atlas, the Titteri, the Bouzegza, the Ouarsenis, the Dahra, the Tlemcen hills, the Trara and several other lesser ranges, was for the most part a society of self-governing tribes and villages. The characteristic institution of these societies was the *jam'a*, the assembly of heads of families or spokesmen of lineages or, in some cases, of all adult males.

The tradition of democratic self-government by the *jam'a* is not confined by any means to the wholly sedentary populations: the semi-transhumant populations of the Aures massif and the Nemencha mountains also governed themselves by such assemblies to a considerable extent, as no doubt did many of the wholly pastoral bedouin tribes. But it was amongst the sedentary *qbail* that this tradition was most firmly rooted and had undergone its most elaborate development.

The other political traditions and models were very different, and several of them might appear at first glance to have been more appropriate to the FLN's purpose. These were:

1   The aristocratic tradition of the nobles, of which there were two kinds, the warrior nobility, *ajwad* (singular *jawād*), which obtained in various parts of the country, where the absence or breakdown of egalitarian traditions had permitted the dynastic principle to establish itself as the determinant of local political leadership, and the religious nobility, *shurfā'* (singular *sharīf*), who claimed descent from the Prophet Mohammed and mediated between illiterate tribesmen and the divine, and between opposed clans, villages and tribes whenever they were asked, as they often were, to intercede in disputes.

2   The authoritarian tradition of the *qā'id, āghā* and *bachāghā,* local power-holders appointed (often, but not always, from the *ajwad* or the *shurfā'*) by the central (Turkish, then French) authorities and exercising a (theoretically) unambiguous right of command over the populations under their supervision.

3   The charismatic tradition and model of the religious brotherhood, *ṭarīqa* (plural *ṭuruq*) with its simple but clearly hierarchical organisation, from the *shaykh* at the apex, his assistants, *muqaddamīn,* and the adepts, *ikhwān* (literally 'brothers'), at the base.

4   The exceptional or revolutionary tradition and model of the *jihād,* with the *amir al mujahīdin* (commander of the fighters for the faith) at the summit exercising his authority through the agency of lieutenants, *khulafā'* (singular *khalīfa*).

5   The millenarian and prophetic tradition of the *mahdī,* the 'rightly guided one', who will return at the end of time to establish the reign of social justice on earth and purify the faith.

All of these traditions and models of politics, of decision-making, of legitimate authority and its exercise, were alive in the Algerian countryside in 1954. The colonial destruction of Algerian tribal society, the allusion to which has become a cliché without being a valid generalisation, was very far from complete, and even in those regions where it had gone furthest it certainly had not succeeded in erasing from the collective memory the most important political traditions the people had ever known.

But the very nature of the war which the FLN was waging meant that the Revolution's principal bases were in the mountains, among the sedentary *qbail* of the Tell Atlas[24] and the semi-sedentary Shawiyya of the Aures. And it was accordingly the model of the village or tribal *jama'a* which exercised the most influence upon the FLN's internal political organisation.

THE LOGIC OF THE *JAMA'A*

The most developed version of the *jama'a* was that which had been evolved by the sedentary hillsmen of Greater Kabylia, and especially by the Igawawen tribes of the central Jurjura, and it is this version which was most fully investigated by the nineteenth-century French ethnographers. Within the Kabyle *jama'a*, a crucial role is that of the *tamen* (plural *tamman*). This role and function was by no means unique to the *jama'a-s* of Kabylia, however. There is ample reason to believe that it was a characteristic and essential feature of the *jama'as* throughout the Algerian countryside, although perhaps given other names outside Kabylia.

In some of the contemporary literature on Kabyle society, the word *tamen* has been translated as '*mandataire*' ('proxy') or '*delegué*' ('delegate')[25] or even '*les leaders des lignées*' ('lineage leaders').[26] This is a mistake. Nor is it adequate to render *tamen* as 'representative'. The root meaning of the word is 'guarantor',[27] and the *tamen* is the man who answers for his group (lineage, clan, village, etc.), who vouches for it by giving his word on its behalf that it accepts and will abide by the decision of the *jama'a* as a whole. The function of the tamen is indeed a representative one, but the conception of representation involved is significantly different from that of the democratic tradition of Europe and North America. The *tamen* does not so much represent the interest of his lineage within the *jama'a* and report back from the *jama'a* to his lineage as the opposite, representing the *jama'a* to his lineage and answering for his lineage to the *jama'a*. He thus faces both ways, but he is first and foremost an officer of the *jama'a* rather than a spokesman for a particular interest.

The logic of the functioning of the *jama'a* is that each decision reflects the consensus of opinion of those present, but that a decision is valid only if all relevant groups are answered for by their respective *tamman* at the meeting in question. All groups must thereafter accept and abide by the decision if their point of view has been heard and taken into account. But, by the same logic, a group which has not been answered for, because its *tamen* was not present at the meeting, will not feel bound by the decision at all (unless the *tamen*'s absence was simply a matter of an individual's dereliction of duty). And a group whose *tamen* has not been invited to the meeting will feel obliged by the logic of its situation to reject and contest the decisions taken, irrespective of the content of these decisions, because to abide by them would be to acknowledge the authority of a body which denies to the group in question the right to have a say in the decisions it takes; it would therefore be to accept its own disfranchisement and its reduction to a dependent status in relation to one or another of the groups properly represented within the *jama'a*. And that would never do; no group possessing a respectable number of adult males could honourably resign itself to such a demotion in the political system.[28]

A second major feature of the Kabyle *jama'a* is the *saff* (plural *sfuf*). *Saff* means party. In any one *jama'a*, differences of opinion and alignment may be fluid over time and vary with the point at issue, but where a number of *jama'as-s* are in a regular relationship with one another, as for example in a tribe of several villages, where each village not only has its own *jama'a* but also is represented within the tribal *jama'a*, there is a strong tendency for the divisions and alignments within the *jama'a* of the tribe to have ramifications within the *jama'a-s* of the constituent villages, such that a stable party division develops and spans the tribe as a whole. This is what happened in the tribes of Greater Kabylia, where each tribe was invariably divided into two *sfuf*. Such party divisions did not stop at the ceiling of the tribe; where a number of tribes were linked in a supra-tribal confederation (as was often, although by no means always, the case), the *saff* division would appear at this higher level, and when, in exceptional circumstances, the villages and tribes of the region as a whole were obliged to take a stand on an issue or an event which affected them all – such as a major new decision or move by the Turkish authorities, or the French conquest, or El Moqrani's rebellion in 1871, etc. – a region-wide division would appear which would tend to dovetail with and galvanise the more permanent staff divisions at the local (tribal, village) level. Thus, political controversy, whether over routine and strictly parochial questions or exceptional issues and historic choices, was invariably mediated by the system of *saff* – that is, party, politics.

This, in the barest possible outline, is the political logic with which the FLN was obliged to come to terms in the Algerian countryside. But coming to terms with this placed enormous strains upon the FLN. As it expanded from its initial bases and established its nominal authority over more and more tribes and villages, it was confronted with the problem of accommodating all these discrete and stubbornly independent political entities within its own decision-making procedures and chains of command. This situation generated two diametrically opposed tendencies: a tendency towards ever-increasing complexity with the FLN's organisation and internal political life at *wilāya*, zone and sector level, and a tendency to resort to drastic measures in a desperate endeavour to reduce this complexity to manageable porportions; that is, a tendency to political simplification by authoritarian and frequently ruthless methods in a context of incessant political intrigue and conflict.

In this demanding political environment, the typical FLN commander in the field, whether at *wilāya* level or at junior levels in the chain of command, was necessarily obliged to be a kind of political Janus: vigorously claiming the status of *tamen* in the *jamaʿa* which existed at the next level up (the Conseil de Secteur, the Conseil de Zone, the Conseil de la Wilaya, the Conseil Nationale de la Révolution Algérienne), while unceasingly trying to pre-empt precisely the same demands from his subordinates by reducing as many of them as possible to the status of dependents; obliged, whether he liked it or not, to belong to a *saff*[29] within the FLN hierarchy, to have allies in other *wilāyat*, zones, and sectors and to make common cause with them on occasion, while trying to suppress the emergence of *saff* divisions within his own command or, at any rate, to remain personally above such divisions by acting as the authoritative arbiter of the disputes which they expressed.

In this way, several of the political traditions of the Algerian countryside which were mentioned above came to interfere with each other, and the FLN became their point of contact and interaction. While the egalitarian tradition of the *jamaʿa*, the *tamen* and the *saff* was omnipresent, the other face of the political Janus that was the FLN field commander would assume various shapes, depending on local circumstances and the temperament and background of the individual concerned.

In relating to their subordinates, some commanders would take the authoritarian tradition of the *qāʾid* as their model, others the charismatic model of the *shaykh of a ṭarīqa*. It is probable that the sheer presence or absence of political ability was a major factor here; a politically able commander would know how to lead his men and run his district by political means, winning enthusiastic obedience and support by persuasion and cunning and the force of example, and resorting to terror only against irredeemably refractory groups and when all other means had failed. Such men would evoke enormous loyalty and acquire a genuine personal charisma, and their style of leadership would not only approximate to that of the *shaykh* of a *ṭarīqa*, this approximation would be explicitly acknowledged by the attribution to them of the honorific title '*shaykh*' by their own troops.[30]

Other commanders, less endowed with political skills or aptitudes, would tend to the more authoritarian style of the *qāʿid*, which would as often as not provoke resentment in both troops and local population wherever the egalitarian traditions were strong, because the model of the *qāʾid* was unequivocally at odds with these traditions. The model of the *shaykh* of a *ṭarīqa* provoked no such resentment, however. This model had always coexisted with the traditions of the *jamaʿa* without difficulty, because it belonged to the religious rather than the political sphere; the relation between the two was accordingly one of complementarity rather than rivalry or conflict and, in the context of a revolution which was popularly conceptualised as a *jihād*, it was readily admitted that a religious model of charismatic leadership should take precedence over the secular tradition of democratic decision-making – at least where the local demonstrators of this charismatic model carried conviction.[31]

The *qāʾid* and the *shaykh* of the *ṭarīqa* were arguably the two main models of authoritative leadership available to the FLN commanders, but the aristocratic model of *jawād* and *sharīf* was also a constant reference. Although no doubt only a minority of the FLN's commanders were of bona fide aristocratic backgrounds, the general attraction of the model was clearly attested to by the pervasive practice of assuming *noms de guerre* prefixed by the aristocratic title '*Sī*', short for '*Sīdī*', 'My Lord', the expression of traditional deference par excellence.

The two tendencies – to increasing complication by parochial democracy and to increasing simplification by expeditious authoritarianism – were operating all over the place all of the time. Neither the numerous assassinations of FLN commanders by rivals within the FLN, nor the purges in Kabylia and the Algérois which are so frequently alluded to in the literature but never seriously explained, nor the notorious massacres of certain villages, can be understood if these fundamental features of the FLN's political predicament in the countryside are not taken into account.

It was these dramatic and infernal circumstances, arising out of the ineluctable political realities of the Algerian countryside, which forced the FLN as a coherent and original and quite extraordinary political phenomenon. Instead of succumbing to these realities, it learned to cope with them, and in this process the irrelevance of French political conceptions was established in the minds of its leaders empirically – that is, the hard way in the wake of Abane Ramdane's failure to organise the FLN's internal life in the French manner.

ABANE'S SUCCESS AND FAILURE

As is well known, the FLN's first congress at Ifri in the Soummam valley of Kabylia in August 1956 was organised and largely dominated by Abane Ramdane, whose purpose was precisely to organise the FLN's internal political life by endowing the Front with a functional political structure. The second part of this purpose he largely realised, and together with his prior achievement in securing the rallying to the FLN of all the other tendencies in Algerian politics (bar the Messalists) and in supervising the development of the FLN's civilian apparatuses (the FFFLN, the UGTA, the UGCA, the UGEMA, etc.),[32] it is his main and undeniable claim to an enduring and honoured place in Algerian history. But, while his actions succeeded in formally unifying the FLN in a coherent organisational structure, they also provoked a series of bitter conflicts within the FLN which eventually led to his own downfall.

Abane Ramdane, although a Kabyle, did not grow up in Kabylia. His formative experience was as a pupil at the College Duveyrier (now the Lycée Ibn Rochd) in Blida, which he entered in October 1933 at the age of 13 and left with a baccalaureate in mathematics in 1942,[33] and he received his political education in Messali's PPA from November 1946 onwards, as a regional organiser in eastern Algeria up until 1950 and thereafter in prison.[34] His political conceptions were entirely French in origin and were not tempered by an appreciation of the political realities of even his native Kabylia, because he had no personal experience of these realities beyond that offered by his agitational work in the Soummam Valley district of Lesser Kabylia, of which he was able to acquire only a very superficial acquaintance as a PPA organiser.[35] It was partly for these reasons that, when he joined the FLN upon his release from prison in early 1955, he quickly found that he could not function politically in Kabylia and made Algiers his centre of operations. I believe that it was also for these reasons that he made at least three crucial miscalculations in 1956 and 1957.

The first mistake was to enshrine a controversial conception of the character of the Algerian Revolution, which played down the Islamic aspect of this revolution and gave it a narrowly Algerian, as opposed to a wider Arab, perspective in the political platform of the Souumam Congress at which by no means all relevant sections of the FLN were fully answered for by their spokesmen. In the case of the guerrilla forces of *wilāya* I (Aurès-Nemenchas), this was almost certainly not Abane's fault, since *wilāya* I was in a state of anarchy at the time in the wake of the death of its first commander, Mostefa Ben Boulaid. But the available evidence suggests that the absence of the External Delegation of the FLN as a whole, and of its leading figure Ahmed Ben Bella in particular, was deliberately contrived by Abane.[36] There can be little doubt that Ben Bella considered that he had been intentionally prevented from attending the Congress and his reaction was not long in coming. It took the form of a critique of the Souumam platform for its departure from the FLN's original position on the place of Islam within its doctrine and for its implicit dissociation of the Algerian Revolution from the wider Arab nationalist movement, together with a most vigorous rebuttal of Abane's criticisms of the External Delegation's failure to obtain arms for the guerrilla forces of the interior.[37] But Ben Bella's reaction did not stop there, for his followers (notably Ali Mahsas) promptly began fomenting opposition to the new leadership appointed by the Congress (the Comité de Coordination et d'Exécution, CCE) among the guerrilla forces of *wilāya* I stationed in Tunisia, and Ben Bella himself, in prison from October 1956 onwards, began a discreet correspondence with the leaders of *wilāya* V (the Oranie), notably Abdelhafid Boussouf who had succeeded Larbi Ben M'Hidi as commander of the *wilāya* on the latter's elevation to the CCE, and whose point of view had been only nominally represented by Ben MˈHidi at the Congress.

Ben Bella's reaction, and that of the ALN chiefs in south-eastern and western Algeria, was the predictable response of someone whose political reflexes were the product of Algerian political traditions. Abane appears to have been genuinely unaware of the continuing vitality of these traditions and of the fact that he could not violate them with impunity. He did not violate them by eliminating Ben Bella; the elimination of a rival from the political leadership is not an un-Algerian thing to do by any means. And since the decision was taken before Abane was aware that *wilāya* I would not be properly represented at the Congress, he cannot be accused of miscalculating on that account. He was merely unlucky that unforeseen circumstances furnished Ben Bella with potential allies in *wilāya* I. The mistake was to insist on a controversial political platform in these circumstances, when by doing so he was giving Ben Bella two major cards to play, the Islamic card and the pan-Arab card, and thus powerful arguments with which to rouse the forces of *wilāya* I to contest the legitimacy of the Congress and of Abane's leadership.

The second mistake arose out of his attachment to, and particular interpretation of, another principle which he made a point of asserting at the Soummam Congress: that of the primacy of the political over the military. This principle was accepted by the Congress, in part because in one sense its validity was self-evident: the military struggle was quite obviously political in character as well as in purpose in that the political allegiance of the Algerian population was the immediate issue at stake, such that political considerations quite naturally took precedence over everything else. But thereafter Abane began to interpret this principle in a quite specific and highly controversial way, as implying the subordination of the 'military' commanders to the 'political' – that is, civilian – leadership. This interpretation presupposed that the military commanders had neither political functions nor political aptitudes. It rested upon a conception of the relationship of the political and military spheres which has been fundamental to both the liberal and the revolutionary traditions in modern Europe, but which was totally at odds with the realities of the wartime FLN. The guerrilla commanders were performing political functions continuously, as a necessary part of their role (a fact which was even formally recognised at the level of the *wilāya*, where each commander bore the official title of '*Chef politico-militaire*') and many of them were unquestionably men of enormous political ability. In claiming the right, as the leading civilian politician, to direct and supervise the military chiefs much as St. Just supervised the Army of the North on behalf of the Jacobin dictatorship in 1793 and 1794, Abane re-interpreted the principle established at the Soummam Congress in a manner which amounted to a doctrinaire deduction from a French conception in contempt of Algerian realities.

The third mistake which Abane made was to believe, as by all accounts he genuinely appears to have done,[38] that the FLN as a whole (as distinct from this or that sub-section of it) could be led in an authoritarian and '*dirigiste*' manner. His early achievements in Algiers had perhaps encouraged him in this belief, because in the very specific and untypical conditions of the city his personal leadership had been extremely effective and uncontested, and his remarkable achievements in this period had given him a considerable authority with the *wilāya* commanders of the countryside. But this personal ascendancy was to prove short-lived, as his later miscalculations came home to roost and his authoritarian manner became intolerable to his colleagues.

JACOBINS?

A bo ben, bid bont. – 'He who would be chief, let him be a bridge.'
(Welsh proverb)

Perhaps if Abane had been present at the creation of the FLN in the summer and autumn of 1954 he would have known better. For a crucial aspect of the FLN's beginning was the fact that it was a revolt against the personal leadership of Messali Hadj and expressed a visceral rejection of the cult of the individual.

It is a striking fact that the FLN has never endured any of its individual leaders for long. Its history and development has been punctuated by successful rebellions against individual leaders: Messali in 1954, Abane in 1957, Benyoucef Ben Khedda and Belkacem Krim in 1962, Ben Bella in 1965. One might even say that rebellion against successive leaders has been an intrinsic feature of the FLN's mode of development. It is also striking that, while the traditional political models of *jamaʿa, tamen, saff, qāʾid, jawād* and *sharīf* were widely employed in the FLN, there are no recorded instances of commanders taking either the *amir al mujahīdin* or the *mahdī* as their role model, despite the fact that the vocabulary of the *jihād* was extensively employed in other respects – the guerrillas were *al mujahīdin*, the non-combatant liaison agents were *al mussebilīn* and the urban terrorists were *al fidaʿiyyīn* – and the fact, for which there is ample evidence, that the Revolution was experienced by many Algerians as a *jihād* and was even conceived, in some areas, in overtly millenarian terms.[39] The point, of course, is that the roles of *amir al mujahīdin* and *mahdī* could be filled only at the apex of the FLN's hierarchy of command, and it was precisely at this level that the rejection of individual leadership and the insistence on collective leadership after the manner of the *jamaʿa* was most emphatic.

It is for this reason that attempts to explain Algerian politics in terms of *oriental* political traditions are as wide of the mark as attempts predicated upon French conceptions. P. J. Vatikiotis's suggestion that the Middle Eastern conception of political leadership, *zaʿama*, was a key to understanding the political approach of the FLN during Ben Bella's period as president from 1962 to 1965 was no sooner mooted than it was refuted by the abrupt overthrow of Ben Bella and the return to collective leadership by a Council of the Revolution in 1965.[40] It is certainly true that the role of *zaim* was the implicit model for Ben Bella's leadership, as it had been for Messali Hadj before him. But the FLN could no more endure Ben Bella in this role than it could endure Messali. It is a striking index of Ben

Bella's ignorance of the FLN as it actually evolved on the ground that he should have supposed that he could get away with a style of political leadership that the FLN had repudiated in the very act of its birth.[41]

There can be little doubt that the immensely reflective person that was Houari Boumedienne was aware of this aspect of the FLN and that he sought to ward off the danger that it represented for him from June 1965 onwards by avoiding as far as possible the adoption of an authoritarian manner towards his colleagues in the Algerian leadership, and by finding other ways of skinning the cat. And the survival to date of President Chadli Ben Jedid suggests that he has been guided by a comparable understanding of the FLN throughout his twelve years as Head of State.

The reason why I have discussed the political actions and style of Abane Ramdane is this. Of all the major leaders of the wartime FLN, he was the one most thoroughly saturated with French political conceptions and assumptions, and the one who was most detached from the realities and traditions of the Algerian countryside. The FLN appeared to outside observers at its most modern and its most Jacobin during the period of his personal ascendancy (mid-1955 to mid-1957), and it is not without reason that Abane's personality and role have been compared to those of St. Just and Robespierre.[42]

But the FLN was a very different animal from the network of Jacobin Clubs which Robespierre organised and directed. The Jacobin aspect of the FLN resided essentially in its determination to unify the nation in a highly centralising manner and to give short shrift to political and cultural diversity in the process, a determination it bequeathed to the state it constituted. But most nationalisms tend to be Jacobin in this sense, at any rate initially. Abane came to grief because the FLN could not be led in the way the Jacobins were led. It could not endure for long a leader whose model was Robespierre, and who was consequently unable to come to terms with the real nature of the movement he aspired to lead. And so it got rid of him.

It may be objected that the surviving Jacobins came to find Robespierre intolerable after a while, and promptly got rid of him when they did so. But to advance this as an objection here is to overlook the fact that the fall of Robespierre and St. Just very rapidly led to the overthrow of Jacobinism as a whole; Robespierre was the supreme leader of the Jacobins and of their most decisive and resolute wing, the Mountain, and the Mountain, which was the last faction of the Jacobins to come to power, could not survive the death of its creator. But Abane was not the creator of the FLN, the politics of the FLN were not thrown into terminal confusion by his fall, and the FLN has already survived this event by thirty-three years. There has been no Algerian Thermidor.

Far from Abane's fall precipitating the disruption of the FLN's politics, it was a condition of the survival of these politics. It was Abane's style of leadership which threatened the cohesion of the FLN, not his removal from the leadership. The FLN could not be led by the high-handed instructions and injunctions of one man, let alone of one inclined to the kind of indiscriminate and unmeasured criticism and moralistic denunciation of his colleagues in which Abane increasingly indulged himself in the manner of 'the seagreen incorruptible'. There had been a great deal more to Abane's leadership than this in 1955 and 1956 but, following the flight of the CCE to Tunis in retreat from the Battle of Algiers, these items appeared to be virtually all that he had to offer by August 1957, the moment of his fall.

There can be little doubt that these were the main considerations which actually motivated Abane's colleagues, and that the personal ambitions of Krim, Bentobbal and Boussouf furnish an entirely inadequate explanation of Abane's overthrow.[43] All political movements are led by ambitious men. The FLN could be effectively led only in a manner which took proper account of the political traditions which actually informed it and the impulses which actually animated it. Being essentially an elaborate pyramid of hierarchically related *jama'a-s*, it had to be led in the way every Algerian *jama'a* is led, by the force of argument backed by solid alliances and combined with careful consideration for the character and susceptibilities of others (something which Abane palpably lacked) – in short, by the ability to mobilise a genuine consensus in support of every major decision.

It is, I believe, no accident that the men who eventually won out in the power struggle within the wartime FLN should have emerged from *wilāya* V, the power base of Abane's most resolute and most principled enemy, Boussouf, and that these men should have functioned for so long as a collective. I am referring, of course, to the Oujda Group, the men who worked with Boussouf's protégé Houari Boumedienne and came to power with him. In much of the French-language literature on Algeria, the Oujda Group is referred to as '*le clan d'Oujda*'. But the Algerians do not employ any of the numerous words for 'clan', such as *farqa*, *kharruba*, *adhrum*, etc., to refer to it. In their own language they know it as *jama'a Oujda*.

One of the characteristic features of an Algerian *jama'a* is precisely the fact that it is an egalitarian assembly with no individual leader overall. The *sfuf* within it each have their own leaders, but the man who presides over its meetings, *al amīn*, does not direct it or impose his own point of view, he merely presides. This is how Boumedienne ran the Oujda Group from 1957 to 1971 and it is substantially how Chadli has conducted the affairs of state since 1979. Boumedienne eventually began to depart from this role model from late 1971 onwards,[44] and increasingly came to dominate his government as the principal architect of an increasingly controversial policy. This departure led to major strains in the Algerian body politic, which were resolved only with his sudden illness and death in late 1978. Chadli has not departed from the role model of the flexible and conciliatory *amīn*, and is still alive and in business. And the system of state which the FLN created, and over which Chadli has presided for the last twelve years, is still intact.

CONSENSUS VS IDEOLOGY

An implicit criticism of the Algerian FLN that is frequently encountered in the academic literature on Algerian politics concerns its lack of ideology, its congenital failure to elaborate a coherent and rigorous social project properly grounded in an internally consistent social doctrine. In sharp contrast to this perception, virtually all of the media coverage of Algerian politics since October 1988 has tended to suggest that the Party of the FLN has been opposed to President Chadli's reform proposals out of a doctrinaire attachment to some sort of socialist orthodoxy. There can be no doubt that the media picture is mistaken (or should one say misguided?) and that the academic view is factually correct. The FLN throughout its history has never committed itself to a sharply defined social vision derived from a prior attachment to a specific ideology. But the criticism which has invariably been implicit in (when it has not been a wholly explicit rider to) the observation of this fact has been entirely misplaced.

Algeria since the development of modern anti-colonialism in the early years of this century has been torn between conflicting ideologies. But it is not the clash of opposed social philosophies which has been subversive of national unity. The really divisive question has been the conflict between opposed cultural orientations, because of the mutually exclusive conceptions of the state which they have implied. The French model of the modern state has exercised an enormous power of attraction on the minds of many Algerians, very understandably, but so too have the movements which have developed and the political models which have been demonstrated in the

Mashreq, the Salafiyya movement and the Young Turks in the first decades of the century, and, since the Second World War, Nasserism, Ba'athism and Islamism.

These ideological differences could not be resolved by a political movement whose purpose was to unite the nation, mobilise all its energies in a bitter struggle for national liberation and endow it with a state of its own. The leaders of the FLN clearly took the view that it was not their business to make an ideological choice between these mutually exclusive models and impose this choice on the people, but to see off the French and establish an effective system of state within which an at last enfranchised people might eventually thrash out these disagreements for itself.

It should not be forgotten that the state established by the FLN is the first ever Algerian state. The state tradition in Algeria is a tradition of alien (Turkish, French) states imposed upon the Algerian population; the indigenous tradition is one of eternal resistance of such states by a fragmented population of self-governing tribes. Having mobilised this tradition against the French state, the FLN had then to canalise the popular energies it had tapped into participation in a project which was entirely at odds with this same tradition of resistance of the state. This ambitious and complex manoeuvre could not have been sustained had the FLN, by decisively opting for one viewpoint at the expense of the others, given ideological hostages to fortune which might have served to legitimate popular resistance of the new-born nation-state on a large scale. It was necessary to implicate the people as a whole in the construction of the state, and it was correspondingly necessary to evade the issue of hard and fast ideological choices, by a strategy of deliberate and sustained ambiguity, leaving options open for as long as possible.

The arduous business of establishing and consolidating this system of state during the thirty years since the formation of the Provisional Government of the Algerian Republic in September 1958, together with the complex and awkward consequences of the protracted mobilisation of national unity for this purpose, therefore precluded any immediate resolution of these differences by democratic process. But as these differences have crystallised since 1978 in distinct movements of public opinion canvassing alternative visions of the state rather than expressing the old-time hostility to the state as such, the FLN-state has tacitly evinced an increased willingness to accommodate this development, and since October 1988 it has been explicitly resolved to undertake the thoroughgoing democratisation of the state's institutions to this end.

Far from displaying a deplorable inability to cope with ideological issues, the principal leaders of the FLN appear rather to have displayed an extremely lucid understanding of these issues and of their actual relationship to the FLN's own project. They clearly came to realise early on what many of their intellectual critics still appear not to have learned: that ideological conflicts, at any rate among people who take their ideological commitments in earnest, cannot be resolved on the ground of ideology. It was accordingly an intrinsic and necessary aspect of the FLN from its inception that all the principle decisions within it were taken on non-ideological grounds, while programmatic declarations of an ideological character were made as rarely as possible and couched in the vaguest possible terms. Not the least of the FLN's achievements was its success in inducing its ideologically heterogeneous elements to agree to disagree about ideological matters while learning how to agree on questions of *policy*.

This achievement also is connected with the way in which the FLN has been animated by the traditions of the *jamaʿa*. For, whatever the arguments within a traditional Algerian *jamaʿa* may have been about they were never about ideology, and the serious debates (as distinct from disputes between particular individuals or families) were always about matters of policy: should the *Beni X* (or the *Ait Y*) ally with this tribe or that tribe? Should they react to a provocation from a neighbouring village or affect to ignore it? Should the *jamaʿa* promulgate a new article of its *qānūn* (code of local by-laws) to regulate its relations with its migrant community in France? Do the existing articles of the *qānūn* concerning dowry payments or sharecropping arrangements (or what have you) need to be modified to take account of changed circumstances? And so on and so forth. As the *amīn* reminds his hearers, in Mouloud Feraoun's humorous account of a village *jamaʿa* in Kabylia in the 1930s or 1940s (which, moreover, beautifully illustrates the way in which, in the countryside at least, modern ideological differences were often merely the superficial clothing of traditional *saff* divisions), *'notre politique, c'est le pain'*.[45]

TRADITION AND MODERNITY

In 1973/4 I spent a year in Algeria teaching English to teenagers at the Lycée Mixte at Bouira, a small but growing town on the edge of Kabylia 80 miles south-east of Algiers. The vast majority of the pupils at the Lycée were boys, but there were a number of classes for girls in the upper levels of the school. I soon noticed that a large vehicle of the *Sûreté Nationale* was stationed at the school gates every morning and evening and learned that the two policemen inside it had the job of watching the pupils on their way to and from school in order to see to it that the boys did not walk with the girls or vice versa. This state of affairs was viewed with high-minded indignation by the French *coopérants* who made up over half of the teaching staff. But it was explained to me by my Algerian friends that the girls would not be at school at all if this arrangement was not made. It was the price which had to be paid for their parents' consent to their having a secondary education, and the state was a party to this *quid pro quo* and organised the various elements of the transaction to the long-term benefit of female emancipation.

A few years later I returned to Bouira and discovered that the Lycée was no longer mixed, but had only male pupils. This departure from mixed schooling might be thought to have been an ideological regression, but it was explained by the fact that Bouira now had a second Lycée, for girls. Mixed schooling had been abandoned but there were now far more girls in secondary education than before. And in retrospect it could be seen that mixed schooling had simply been an expedient to get at least some girls into secondary school for as long as Bouira had only one Lycée for them to go to, and that the mixed character of the first Lycée in its early years had never been a matter of ideological principle for its character had been deliberately and strictly limited in various ways – by the fact of segregated classes for one thing, and by the policemen at the gate for another. In other words, there had been no real change, let alone a regression, in the substantive ideology which underlay Bouira's educational arrangements, and by the yardstick of the number of girls in secondary education there had been an undeniable advance within the framework of a new arrangement which was more acceptable than its predecessor to local parents.

Algerian politics can be fully understood only if account is taken of the extent to which they are informed by Algerian traditions and if it is realised that this state of affairs is not inimical to social progress but is inherent to its condition.

In the doctrinaire political conceptions which have been forged in France in the turbulent historical experience of the last 200 years, tradition and modernity appear as diametrically and totally opposed. It is entirely understandable, given this particular experience, that this should be so. But the French (and, these days, American) dichotomy between tradition and modernity is not universally valid. Burke's *Reflections on the Revolution in France* were predicated upon his rejection of this dichotomy, which had no application to the English experience. And it only acquired an application to French conditions once an extensive and irreversible piece of surgery had been performed on traditional French society during 1793 and 1794 in the Mountain's desperate response to the political disintegration of 1789–92, a disintegration which Burke, alone among his contemporaries, understood and explained in 1790.[46]

The absolute dichotomy between tradition and modernity has no application to the Algerian experience. The politics of the FLN have been the empirical politics of organising necessary change by innovating within the medium of tradition.

BACK TO THE FUTURE

It remains to be said that all this might have been better understood long ago had the insights of the main French ethnographers of nineteenth-century Algeria continued to inform Algerian studies in the twentieth-century. But the superb descriptions of the Algerian *jama'a* and its functioning which were produced by Hanoteau and Letourneux and by Emile Masqueray[47] were neglected and forgotten by their successors.

Louis Milliot's rejection[48] of the earlier view in the 1930s may have been prompted by other factors, but there can be little doubt that, since the 1950s, one cause of the continuing neglect of Algeria's real political traditions has been the influence of the segmentarity theory of tribal political organisation as developed within British social anthropology.[49] The irony in this state of affairs is thus that, by contributing, if only indirectly, to the obfuscation of Algerian realities, British anthropology has facilitated the misapprehension of these realities by means of French conceptions.

I have no wish to dispute the theory of segmentarity in general. I am not an anthropologist and have no axe to grind in this matter, and I do not doubt that the theory has contributed very considerably to the understanding of nomadic or transhumant populations in Cyrenaica and Morocco as well as in the southern Sudan. Whether it has much to offer to the understanding of entirely sedentary populations is another matter, however. Ernest Gellner's powerful explanation of the political organisation of the Berbers of the Central High Atlas in Morocco in terms of the segmentarity theory was explicitly predicated, at least in part, upon what he called 'the politics of transhumancy',[50] and the application of this theory to the sedentary Berbers of the Rif by David Hart in his splendid study of the Aith Waryaghar[51] has recently been subjected to cogent criticism by Henry Munson,[52] criticism which Hart has at least partially admitted.[53]

Whatever the truth about Moroccan Berbers, having lived and worked in Kabylia and having observed local political life in villages of the central Jurjura where the *jama‘a*, the *temman* and the *sfuf* have survived to the present day,[54] I have no hesitation in saying that Hanoteau and Letourneux and Masqueray were substantially right about Kabyle political organisation, and that those more recent observers of the region who have taken their cue from the segmentarity theory, which of necessity denies any real significance to the *jama‘a* and the *sfuf*, [55] have been seriously mistaken.

In defence of British anthropology, however, it should be said that the original mistake was not of its making. For there is a second irony *within* the first, which is the fact that the theory of segmentarity was developed by British social anthropology out of the concept of segmental social organisation first put forward by the French sociologist Emile Durkheim,[56] and that Durkheim had derived this concept, at least in part, from his reading of the works of Hanoteau and Letourneux and of Masqueray, *whose descriptions of Kabyle society he crucially misunderstood.*[57] But that is a story for another day.

Since the traditional political organisation of Kabyle society has owed little or nothing to the fact that the Kabyles happen to speak a dialect of Berber as their mother tongue, and since in many other respects the culture of the Berber-speaking hillsmen of Algeria has been substantially identical to that of their Arabic-speaking fellow-countrymen, I have no doubt that, notwithstanding regional variations in matters of detail, the fundamental principles of the political organisation of the *qbail* of Algeria have also been broadly the same, and that the tradition in question spans the country, like the FLN itself.

Whatever may happen in the party-political arena, I expect this tradition to inform Algerian politics for some time to come, and to continue to make possible all sorts of adventurous innovations within its medium.

NOTES

1 F. W. Nietzsche, *Ecce Homo* (translated by R. J. Hollingdale, Penguin, 1979), pp. 333ff.
2 In an article in *The Guardian*, 13 October 1988, and in several interviews on the BBC World Service in the weeks following the riots.
3 The extraordinary congress of the FLN was held from 28 November to 30 November 1989. This chapter is a revised version of a paper which

was first given, under the title 'The FLN and the mobilisation of consensus in Algeria', to a conference on 'North Africa and the Nation-State' held under the aegis is of the Centre of Near and Middle Eastern Studies at the School of Oriental and African Studies at the University of London on 9–10 November 1989. A second, more developed, version of this paper was subsequently delivered, under the present title, to a conference on 'France and Algeria: Identities in Interaction' at the University of Loughborough on 15 December 1989. For a fuller account of the extraordinary FLN congress, see H. Roberts 'A new face for the FLN' in *Africa Report*, vol. XXXV, no. 1, New York, March–April 1990.

4 Reuters, 15 June 1990.

5 Witness the massive demonstrations in Algiers on 18 January 1991, when an estimated 400,000 people marched in protest against the war; by this stage the FIS had adopted a position of unequivocal support for Iraq, a clear index of the shift which had occurred in public opinion. By January, pictures of Saddam Hussein were to be seen throughout the country, and there is no doubt that public opinion in Algeria was fully in support of Baghdad's defiance of the US-led coalition. For a full discussion of this, see H. Roberts, 'Algerian Islamism and the Gulf crisis' in *Islamic Fundamentalism and the Gulf War*, The Fundamentalist Project, American Academy of Arts and Sciences, University of Chicago Press, 1991.

6 Hugh Roberts, 1991, *op. cit.*

7 See my article 'The embattled Arians of Algiers: radical Islamism and the dilemma of Algerian nationalism', *Third World Quarterly*, vol. X, 2, April–June 1988, pp. 556–89.

8 See the Resolutions of the First Congress of the RCD, 15–16 December 1989, published in the RCD's monthly journal *L-Avenir*, no. 4, January 1990.

9 Camille Lacoste-Dujardin and Yves Lacoste, 'La revendication culturelle des Berbères de Grande Kabylie', *Le Monde Diplomatique*, December 1980, pp. 34–5.

10 Karl Marx, *The 18th Brumaire of Louis Bonaparte*, in Karl Marx and Friedrich Engels, *Selected Works In One Volume* (London: Lawrence & Wishart, 1970).

11 Kader Ammour, Christian Leucate and Jean-Jacques Moulin, *La Voie Algerienne*, (Paris: Francois Maspero, 1974), pp. 156ff. it should be noted that this view has been contested on a variety of grounds by other *marxisant* writers on Algeria, although not on the grounds adduced here.

12 Mohamed Lebjaoui, *Verités sur la Révolution Algérienne* (Paris: Gallimard, 1970), p. 151.

13 Hugh Roberts 1988, *op. cit.*

14 Notably Bruno Etienne, *L'Islamisme Radicale* (Paris: Hachette, 1987).

15 Hugh Roberts, 'Towards an understanding of the Kabyle question in contemporary Algeria', *The Maghreb Review*, vol. V, no. 5–6, pp. 115–24.

16 Hugh Roberts, *Revolution and Resistance: Algerian Politics and the Kabyle Question* (London: I. B. Tauris) forthcoming.

17 On this point I am in disagreement with Mohammed Harbi's *Le FLN: Mirage et Réalité* (Paris: Editions J.A., 1980), p. 171, while being greatly

indebted to Harbi's work in many respects.

18   Strictly speaking there were two organisations, the Etoile Nord-Africaine (1926–9), which was dissolved by the French authorities, and its successor, La Glorieuse Etoile Nord-Africaine (1933–7). These were substantially the same organisation, however.

19   Notably the social radicalism and refractory populism of the Derqawa religious brotherhood, to which Messali's father belonged and by which Messali himself had been profoundly influenced; see Harbi, *op. cit.*, p. 19, and especially Benjamin Stora, *Messali Hadj (1898–1974), Pionnier du Nationalisme Algerien* (Paris: L'Harmattan, 1986), pp. 24 and 108ff.

20   R. W. Johnson, The Long March of the French Left (London: Macmillan, 1981).

21   See Benjamin Stora, *op. cit.*, Chapters 3 and 4.

22   Harbi, *op. cit.*, Chapters 6–8; see his earlier work, *Aux Origins du FLN: Le Populisme Révolutionnaire en Algérie* (Paris: Christian Bourgois, 1975).

23   Individuals and splinter movements broke away from the FLN from 1962 to 1964, but the FLN did not split in the substantial sense of falling apart and giving way to rival organisations, as Sinn Fein did in Ireland in 1922.

24   The mountains of northern Algeria, which span the country in a series of ranges and massifs from west to east and are separated from the Saharan Atlas to the south by the broad belt of the High Plateaux.

25   Mohand Khellil, *L'Exil Kabyle* (Paris: L'Harmattan, 1979), p. 192; *La Kabylie ou l'Ancêtre Sacrifié* (Paris: L'Harmattan, 1984), p. 173.

26   Jeanne Favret, 'Relations de dependence et manipulation de la violence en Kabylie', *L'Homme*, vol. VII, no. 4, October–December 1968, pp. 18–43, reference from p. 23.

27   From the Arabic *dhaman*, 'responsible, liable, answerable for; bondsman, guarantor, surety'. Both Masqueray and Hanoteau and Letourneux rightly translate *tamen* by '*répondant*', as do Pierre Bourdieu (*Sociologie de l'Algérie*, Paris, PUF, 3rd edn 1963, p. 12) and Ramon Basagana and Ali Sayad (*Habitat Traditionnel et Structures Familiales en Kabylie*, Algiers, Memories du CRAPE, no. XXIII, 1974, p. 51).

28   Cases where a given lineage will agree to be answered for by the *tamen* of another lineage occur when the lineage is small and lacks adult males either because it is biologically speaking on the way out, i.e. heading for extinction, or because of a purely temporary lack of adult males in the village, a lack which all concerned can see is temporary because of the visible presence of a younger generation or because of the known existence of males away from home (in France, elsewhere in Algeria, etc.). In the first case, the failing lineage will be answered for by the *tamen* of the lineage to which it is most closely related and will in effect be absorbed by the latter; in the second case, the temporarily embarrassed lineage may pointedly choose to be answered for by the *tamen* of a lineage to which it is *not* closely related, in order to signal its refusal to be absorbed by its near relatives and thus its confidence in its own future recovery.

29   Virtually all the literature on the FLN and Algerian politics since 1954 speaks of the conflicts between 'clans', 'clannishness', etc. This is quite misleading; *saff* means party, not clan, and the *sfuf* were not kinship

groupings at all; the factional conflicts within the FLN have obeyed the logic of *saff* rivalry, not the logic of clan hostility (i.e. the blood feud).

30 See for instance the fictional portrait of an ALN commander in eastern Algerian in Taham Ouettar's magnificent novel *L'As* (French translation, Messidor/Temps Actuel, 1983), and especially the war memoir of one of the ALN's greatest field commanders, Commandant Azzeddine, *On Nous Appelait Fellaghas* (Paris: Stock, 1976).

31 The central Jurjura is the *locus classicus* of the democratic tradition of the *jamáa*, and in none of its numerous tribes is this tradition more fiercely alive to this day than the Illilten. Yet the first commander of the ALN in the central Jurjura in 1954 was Cheikh Amar, from the Illilten village of Tizit. In the literature (notably Harbi, 1980 *op. cit.*, pp. 65–405) it is implied that Cheikh was his surname; Yves Courriere refers to him, quite wrongly, as Amar Ait Cheikh, elaborating an honorific title into a full-blooded family name (*La Guerre d'Algerie, II, Le Temps des Leopards*, Paris, Fayard, 1969, p. 183). In fact, his name was Amar Oumohand, and Cheikh (i.e. Shaykh) was a title of respect attributed to him by his followers in the days of the Organisation Spéciale in the late 1940s. It is illustrative of the extreme difficulty which hampers the historiography of the Algerian Revolution that I had to go to Cheikh Amar's tribe to discover for certain the truth about his identity. A great deal of vital information about the wartime FLN is still scattered around the Algerian countryside. Even within the political and intellectual elite, knowledge is fragmentary.

32 Federation de France du FLN; Union Générale des Travailleurs Algériens; Union Generale des Commerçants Algériens; Union Générale des Etudiants Musulmans Algériens, all four founded in the course of 1955/6. For a detailed description of Abane's role in this period, see Khalfa Mameri, *Abane Ramdane, Heros de la Guerre d'Algérie* (Paris: L'Harmattan, 1988).

33 Mameri, *op. cit.*, pp. 28–30.

34 Mameri, *op. cit.*, pp. 55–70.

35 Abane was appointed to head the *wilāya* (region) of Setif for the PPA-MTLD in 1948 and appears to have been a member of its paramilitary arm, the OS. The *wilāya* of Setif included the Soummam valley but also the districts of Bordj Bou Arreridj, Bougaa, Jijel, Kherrata, M'Sila and Setif itself. Mameri discusses Abane's activities in this period (*op. cit.*, pp. 55–64) but cites only rare instances of Abane actually spending time on the ground in the Soummam valley region.

36 Harbi, 1980, *op. cit.*, p. 175.

37 See the texts of Ben Bella's letters to the CCE in the autumn of 1956 and early 1957, reproduced as Documents 34 and 35 in Mohammed Harbi's invaluable collection, *Les Archives de la Revolution Algerienne* (Paris: Les Editions Jeune Afrique, 1981), pp. 168–71.

38 Yves Courriere, *La Guerre d'Algerie, III, L'Heure des Colonels* (Paris: Fayard, 1970), pp. 104–7; Mameri, *op. cit.*, pp. 286–90.

39 *Al Mujahidin* literally means 'those who fight the holy struggle' and was applied to the guerrilla forces of the ALN in the countryside. *Al mussabilīn* literally means 'those who have dedicated themselves'; during the Revolution the term was used to refer to the members of the civilian

underground networks of the FLN (l'Organisation Clandestin du FLN, OCFLN), who worked as intelligence and liaison agents, couriers, guides, providers of safe houses, etc. *Al Fida'yyīn* literally means 'those who sacrifice themselves', and was used to refer to the urban commandos of the FLN. For evidence of the religious and millenarian terms in which the Revolution was experienced in the Algerian countryside, see in particular Mouloud Feraoun, *Journal 1955–1962* (Paris: Editions du Seuil, 1962); *Récits de Feu: temoignages sur la guerre de libération nationale*, presented by Mahfoud Kaddache (Algiers: SNED, 1977); Commandant Azzeddine, *op. cit.*; Mohammed Benyahia, *La Conjuration au Pouvoir: récit d'un maquisard de l'ALN* (Paris: Arcantere, 1988); and Slimane Chikh, *L'Algérie en Armes, ou le temps des certitudes* (Algiers: Office des Publications Universitaires, 1981), pp. 323–34.

40   P. J. Vatikiotis, 'Tradition and political leadership: the example of Algeria', *Middle Eastern Studies*, vol. II, no. 4, July 1966; reprinted in I. W. Zartman (ed.), *Man, State and Society in the Contemporary Maghrib* (London: Pall, Mall, 1973), pp. 309–29.

41   As Harbi, for long a supporter of Ben Bella, admits 'Boumedienne, avec le cynisme qui le caracterise, a eu raison de dire que Ben Bella ne connaissait la "révolution", c'est-à-dire la vie interieure du FLN' (1980, *op. cit.*, p. 297), although why this should be regarded as an expression of cynicism as opposed to simple lucidity Harbi, an inveterate enemy of Boumedienne, does not explain.

42   Alistair Horne, *A Savage War of Peace* (London: Macmillan, 1977), p. 132; Courriere, *op. cit.*, II, *Le Temps des Leopards*, p. 147; *op. cit.*, III, *L'Heure des Colonels*, p. 175.

43   As does an article in the Algerian weekly *Algerié-Actualité*, 24–30 August 1989 ('La Fin d'Abane'), without actually naming the three men in this context, but the implication is unmistakeable. Harbi also attributes Krim's attitude explicitly, and Boussouf's attitude by implication, to personal ambition (1980, *op. cit.*, pp. 200, 205).

44   The long-standing alliance that was the Oujda Group began to come under serious strain in late 1971, and broke up thereafter, and Boumedienne's style of leadership became increasingly emphatic and commanding from that time onwards.

45   Mouloud Feraoun, *Jours de Kabylie* (Paris: Le Seuil, 1968), p. 64.

46   Brendan Clifford, *Belfast in the French Revolution* (Belfast: Historical and Educational Association, 1989), and '1789: France's Glorious Revolution Manque', *Labour & Trade Union Review*, vol. I, 12, July–August 1989, pp. 15–18.

47   A. Hanoteau and A. Letourneux, *La Kabylie et les Coutûmes Kabyles* (Algiers, 1872–3, 3 vols); Emile Masqueray, *La Formation des Cités chez les Populations Sedentaires de l'Algérie* (Paris: Ernest Leroux, 1886; reprinted with an Introduction by Fanny Colonna, Aix-en-Provence, Centre de Recherches et d'Etudes sur les Sociétés Méditerranéenes, CNRS, 1983).

48   Louis Milliot, 'Le Qanoun des M'atqa', *Revue des Etudes Islamiques*, 1933, vol. IV, pp. 193–204.

49   This influence is especially clear in Pierre Bourdieu's account of Kabyle social and political organisation *Sociologie de l'Algérie* (Paris: PUF 1958,

1963), which was revised and extended in English translation as *The Algerians* (Boston: Beacon Press, 1962); and in the writings of Jeanne Favret (notably *op. cit.*), although neither Bourdieu nor Favret offer interpretations in terms of a pure segmentary model; it also informs Tassadit Yacine's interesting study of a poet from the Biban region of Lesser Kabylia, *Poesie Berbère et Identité* (Paris: Editions de la Maison des Sciences de l'Homme, 1987).

50 Ernest Gellner, *Saints of the Atlas* (London: Weidenfeld & Nicolson, 1969), p. 169ff.

51 David Hart, *The Aith Waryaghar of the Moroccan Rif: an Ethnography and History* (Tucson: University of Arizona Press, 1976).

52 Henry Munson Jun., 'On the irrelevance of the Segmentary Lineage Model in the Moroccan Rif', *American Anthropologist*, vol. 91, no. 2, June 1989, pp. 386–400.

53 David Hart, 'Rejoinder to Henry Munson Jr., 'On the irrelevance of the Segmentary Lineage Model in the Moroccan Rif', *American Anthropologist*, vol. 91, no. 3, September 1989, pp. 765–9.

54 I provide a detailed account of the interaction of *jamáa, teman* and *sfuf* in the local political life of the central Jurjura in the mid-1970s in my doctoral thesis, 'Political development in Algeria: the region of Greater Kabylia', Oxford, 1980, pp. 307–32.

55 Gellner, *op. cit.*, 65–7 and 89–90. The earlier passage discusses Robert Montagne's *liff* theory; *liff* (plural: *lfuf*) means alliance and is (roughly) equivalent to the Algerian term *saff*.

56 Emile Durkheim, *The Division of Labour in Society*, translated by George Simpson (New York: The Free Press/London: Collier-Macmillan, 1964), pp. 174–81.

57 Notably in his jumping to the conclusion that 'among the Kabyles, the political unity is the clan, constituted in the form of a village (*djemmaa* or *thaddart*) ...' (*ibid.*, page 178). This statement is quite mistaken, as I explain in some detail in my forthcoming book (see note 16).

9 *Glasnost* the Algerian way

The role of Berber nationalists in political reform

Salem Mezhoud[1]

Anda tqewwiden ccifan.

(Si Muh w Mhend. Isefra.)

La seule minorité c'est le pouvoir.

(H.H. on Radio Monte Carlo, April 1980)

INTRODUCTION

The riots which shook Algeria between 4 and 12 October 1988 have opened the way to a tremendous wave of change in the country. This unprecedented change, however, is not unique in the Maghreb. In Tunisia, since November 1987 when President Zine Abidine Ben Ali seized power constitutionally from former president Habib Bourguiba, a process towards relative democracy has been set in motion. If the Western Sahara issue has not yet been solved, in spite of contacts between King Hassan II and Polisario Front leaders, Morocco and Algeria, hitherto bitter rivals, are seemingly working together towards a regional union to which Libya too seems committed. But it is undeniable that the most radical changes have taken place in Algeria. There, the remaining pillars of dogmatic socialism are being swayed by a wave of *glasnost* which is sweeping the political landscape.

GLASNOST AND ITS ORIGINS

Historic though they may be, the changes in Algeria do not guarantee a safe passage for the country to democracy. The riots which sparked them off were a culmination of nearly three decades of frustration and the developments which have taken place since 1988 represent only a portion of the changes needed. It is therefore astonishing to realise that the riots came as a surprise to some. To the well-informed observer they were indeed bound to happen; in fact, the surprise was that they did not take place much earlier. To the author they were ten years overdue.

However, nearly ten years before the 'October Riots', an event of great significance occurred which began a new era of opposition to the Algerian regime. Indeed, the October 1988 riots, the ensuing reforms and the *glasnost* which have taken place in Algeria, might not have happened at all had it not been for one important event and one important force which stood out in the Algerian political landscape during the three decades after independence. These are:

1 The April 1980 insurrection in the Kabylia region;
2 The 'Berber Cultural Movement' (MCB), often dubbed 'Berber Nationalist Movement' (mainly by English-speaking analysts) which was responsible for that uprising.

The 1980 insurrection (also known as 'the Kabyle or the Berber Spring'), much too quickly forgotten, was by far the most important, perhaps most revolutionary event to take place in Algeria since 11 December 1960 when the population of Algiers took to the streets to demonstrate its massive opposition to colonial rule. This event was of historic importance in spite of a subsequent return to a degree of *status quo* engineered by the government.

THE 'KABYLE SPRING'

On 10 March 1980, following the banning by the authorities of a conference on Ancient Berber Poetry by the well-known writer and anthropologist Mouloud Mammeri, the students of the University of Tizi Ouzou, the capital city of Kabylia[2] staged demonstrations to protest 'cultural repression' directed against the Berbers. During the following days demonstrations were organised in Algiers and throughout Kabylia to call for democracy, freedom of expression and respect of Berber language and culture. A visit by President Chadli to Tizi Ouzou, scheduled for 15 March, was cancelled. In Algiers two student demonstrations on 16 March and 7 April were violently dispersed by the police and a number of students were arrested. In Tizi Ouzou, students voted in favour of a strike and occupied the university. After 9 April strikes and demonstrations were organised throughout Kabylia.

On 20 April, at 1 a.m., a brutal police operation[3] was launched on all the occupied institutions of the Tizi Ouzou area (the university, the hospital, and industrial plants), and students and workers alike were the victims of savage repression. Amid rumours that 32 people were killed a general strike was spontaneously declared in Tizi Ouzou and then in the entire region. The authorities in Algiers cut off all supplies and cordoned off Kabylia. Between 21 and 24 April populations of surrounding villages converged on Tizi Ouzou, barricades were erected and violent clashes took place between demonstrators and the police aided by dogs.

Following those four days of rioting, the regime in Algiers took a number of measures to alleviate some of the hardship in Kabylia and, in the following days, in the hope of putting an end to the protests, made promises in favour of Berber culture, including the creation of university chairs of Berber studies. Under sustained pressure from a very highly mobilised Berber community, all the students, workers and activists arrested during the unrest – some of whom had already been tried and sentenced – were released by the government.

A one month 'seminar' was organised in Kabylia[4] in August, under the aegis of the government, to take stock of the situation of Berber culture in the country. An elaborate project for the advancement of all aspects of that culture was drawn during this, the first democratic experience known to Algerians since independence and was sent to the Front de Liberation National (FLN) Central Committee whose annual meeting was scheduled for September. However, once official contacts took place between representatives of the government (under the leadership of the Minister of Universities, Abdelhak Brerhi) and of the Cultural Movement, the government progressively regained control by using its immense resources, and by 1981 the *status quo* was virtually re-established and none of the numerous promises were kept.[5] The political importance of the Kabyle Spring and its impact on the Algerian population will be discussed below.

THE BERBER CULTURAL MOVEMENT

The force behind the insurrection – namely, the Berber Cultural Movement – had been the most important opposition force in the country since about 1968,[6] with considerable popular support,[7] until the tremendous, almost overnight, inflation of the Islamic movement in the aftermath of the Iranian revolution. Until the early 1980s the Islamists[8] had good organisation, while the Berberists[9] had popular support, although in the Kabylia region and chiefly in Algiers, the capital. At the end of the 1980s the Islamists saw their membership and the population's support for them decline sharply (as the image of the Iranian regime became more negative), then soar again, especially after the 1988 riots. Their determination, however, never diminished: what had changed, rather, was the attitude of the regime towards them. After backing them in the 1970s, the Algerian government found itself threatened by them and in attempting to manipulate them, allowed them to acquire considerable strength.

The Berberists for their part, have, over the years, and especially after 1980, gained considerable (and now irrevocable) support from the population in the Berber areas. During the 1980s they also succeeded in inspiring resistance to the regime and even rebellion in other parts of the country. The 1988 riots would not have happened without the 1980 precedent and without the inspiration of the Berberists.

THE ALGERIAN POLITICAL SYSTEM

To say, as virtually every reporter did, that the riots of October 1988 were caused by a harsh economic situation, is similar to saying that an AIDS victim has died of pneumonia. The symptoms are, indeed, real; they had become more and more obvious in recent years. But the virus had been present for much longer. Most of the ingredients for the economic catastrophe faced by the Chadli government are well known; from the total neglect of the country's agriculture (in a land which was once the breadbasket of both Rome and France) to the squandering of enormous oil revenues and, later, the sharp fall of oil prices. However, the failure of Algeria's economy and the acuteness of the crisis are due to the nature of the political system in a country not short on resources.

The two main problems of the Algerian political system are the lack of accountability and legitimacy. Since 1962 Algerian leaders have had two preoccupations:

1   efficient control over the land and the population and,
2   legitimacy of the regime and of the positions of the individuals who represent it.

This, to a large extent, distinguishes the Algerian regime from those of neighbouring countries.

In Morocco, King Hassan II has been able to claim dynastic as well as 'spiritual' legitimacy, which stems from his official role as the "Commander of the Faithful". Former President Habib Bourguiba, for his part, was the recognised leader of the Tunisian struggle for independence, the Father of the Nation (as his nickname of "Combattant Suprême" reminded everyone). As such, he enjoyed, initially, the respect of Tunisians. His successor, Zine Abidine Ben Ali, seized power constitutionally and therefore enjoys constitutional legitimacy, while reinforcing, by the same token, the country's institutions. But when Colonel Mohammed Boukharouba (Houari Boumedienne) seized power in a coup on 19 June 1965, he was perhaps the most feared and despised personage in the entire Algerian political spectrum. Both as president Ben Bella's defence minister – in which post he had shown himself to be a master of intrigue – and as the commander of the FLN's wartime Frontier Army, he was unpopular with the majority of the population. As head of state, Boumedienne was, from the beginning, confronted with the problem of remaining in power, and he had to do so by gaining firm control and/or by winning popular support. The former he did with the use of a very efficient (and ruthless) secret police, and the latter by making his regime appear legitimate to the eyes of the Algerian nation.[10]

LEGITIMACY OF THE REGIME

Colonel Boumedienne sought to establish the legitimacy of his regime by performing two tasks. First, he drew on the symbolic value of the 'Revolution' by inflating the part he played in it (short of claiming to be its sole leader) and by making his partners in the ruling Council of Revolution the heroes of the independence struggle at the expense of the majority of the 'historic leaders' most of whom were killed, exiled, or otherwise neutralised.[11] The reference to the Revolution would recur incessantly during the thirteen years of Boumedienne's term. And, second, after three years of near inaction, he decided to tackle the economic problems of the country by declaring development the top national priority. The first four-year development plan was launched in 1968 with one of the most lavish advertising campaigns in the Third World. Ultimately, this approach proved extremely successful in a nation tired of fighting and eager for social peace and economic prosperity.[12]

Boumedienne's regime was composed partly of the military junta which helped him to seize power in 1965 and partly of party bureaucrats who used the ruling party, the FLN, as an instrument for the advancement and promotion of their own careers and fortunes. One attractive aspect of party membership is worth noting: party members enjoyed an almost total immunity which went far beyond that granted parliamentarians in many other countries. And as the party grew in size and power – and, conversely, lost all credibility with the general public – it became a pole of attraction to an ever-growing class of bureaucrats and other ambitious entrepreneurs who considered, and ultimately treated, public assets as their own property. This virtual private ownership of public resources – and, by the same token, of state institutions – put the party bureaucrats beyond any public accountability and, to a great extent, above the law. This was indeed simplified by the long absence of a legislative body in Algeria.[13] Officially the single party, the FLN, provided the nation with political leadership and an ideological framework for its economy and social organisation. In reality, the Cabinet (and the Council of Revolution whose members did not, most of the time, have a clear role) governed by decree, thus allowing all manner of excess, abuse and repressive measures with an added propensity for bureaucratic chaos. This also helped develop corruption – a hitherto limited, if not rare, phenomenon in Algeria. It is safe to say that in contrast to its neighbours, Algeria has never known the rule of law.

PROSPERITY AND POPULARITY

Faced with such a system of government, it is difficult to assume that the fate of the Algerian population was ever the prime concern of the ruling elite. In spite of the official pro-development policies, this conclusion is supported to a great extent by evidence. And while it is not necessary here to refer to the numerous instances of squandering of public funds which translated into rapidly created individual fortunes (and Swiss bank accounts), one example stands out for its more ideological nature.

While, since 1962, every government adviser, economist, ideologue, observer or concerned citizen agreed on the absolute necessity of an agrarian reform for the country's economy to perform well, and everybody, throughout the 1960s expected such a reform to take place (many official statements and declarations were made to that effect), it was none the less completely neglected for years. One possible and oft-cited reason for this neglect was that the head of the FLN throughout that period, Kaid Ahmed, was also one of the most important landowners in the country and, logically, a prime target for expropriation under any serious reform. He, therefore, allegedly opposed it, and the path to Algerian development was to take the shape of industrialisation. And when, ultimately, an 'Agrarian Revolution' was launched in the early 1970s, it was clear that its main objectives were highly political. The first four-year plan had come to an end and the results were not positive; in fact it was deemed a failure. A second plan was launched immediately afterwards, but by that time the population was disillusioned. In addition, a very large number of students and unemployed youths were growing restless and needed to be controlled.[14] They were therefore recruited to be 'volunteers' of the Agrarian Revolution in a vast indoctrination campaign.[15] In order to successfully launch a highly demagogic enterprise, Kaid Ahmed, a long-term Boumedienne associate, was, therefore, sacrificed and replaced as head of the FLN.

From 1968 till about 1974, the regime on the whole enjoyed relative popular support thanks to its economic policies[16] enhanced by a very vocal militant stance in world affairs. The consequent growth in importance of Algeria on the world scene was welcomed as a source of pride by a shattered nation. By advocating development and, seemingly, defending the rights of weak and subjected peoples in the international arena, Boumedienne's regime during those years succeeded in partly acquiring, in the eyes of a section of the Algerian population at least, the legitimacy to which it badly aspired. Development and militancy through international activism constituted the much publicised 'revolutionary legitimacy'.

DISSATISFACTION AND DEMAGOGUERY

In the mid-1970s the tide began to turn. A deteriorating economy, intense dissatisfaction with, among other things, chronic shortages of nearly every commodity, growing corruption, a total lack of liberties, together with internal conflicts within the Council of Revolution, began to wear on the government. Incapable of dealing successfully with the economy, Boumedienne resorted to political devices to quash any opposition to his regime. Between 1975 and 1977 a National Charter and a new Constitution were drawn and adopted by referendum, a National Assembly as well as a new 'President of the Republic' were elected amid so-called public debates[17] – a series of very organised and very controlled public meetings in which the population was supposed to express its opinions. Those 'debates', whose purpose was really to give vent to popular frustrations and which were not taken into account in the decision-making process, ultimately only underlined the size of the popular opposition to the regime. By 1978, tension was so acute that major unrest was expected, but Boumedienne died suddenly of a rare disease.[18]

Boumedienne's death in December 1978 did much to diffuse the tension. The novelty of the situation and the ensuing expectations brought about calm, if not order. To many people, the first few months of Chadli Ben Jedid's presidency brought hope of improvement of the situation. But soon discontent began to surface again, with Algerians showing impatience towards, amongst other things, what appeared to be the incompetence of the new president. At the end of 1979, severe strikes paralysed some of the country's universities, in particular the University of Tizi Ouzou. In addition to dissatisfaction with chronic problems of living and working conditions on university campuses the quarrel between the students and the authorities also reflected a much more profound division on the more fundamental issue of the country's identity. Facing the regime were two main groups of actors: students educated in the Arabic language (*'arabisants'*) and those educated in French (*'francisants'*).

ARABISATION AND THE BERBER HERITAGE

The *francisants* were opposed to the fast pace of the nation's programme of 'Arabisation'[19] which they considered an impediment to academic and research careers. For, in addition to studying their chosen disciplines, they were also required to learn, within a short time, enough literary Arabic to be able to teach in that language. They also claimed that limitation on the use of European languages was putting the country more and more out of touch with modern science and technology.

The main complaint of the *arabisants* was that while the authorities encouraged them to study and receive professional training in Arabic, they were ultimately faced with the harsh reality of a job market dominated by French-speaking executives and managers. They demanded, as a result, immediate and total Arabisation of the country's entire administrative and educational systems. It was a policy which, to them, was in accordance with official ideology and should not be subject to delays.

Among those Algerians who opposed rapid Arabisation (which many still consider as the main cause of the dramatic deterioration in the quality of the country's educational system) were the Berberists. Their reasons were of two kinds: political and sociological. To them:

1   Algeria was not a democratic country and all political, social and economic life in the country was determined by the state without popular consent. There never was a free democratic consultation on the issue of the country's identity and all important decisions such as the choice of a national language had been forced upon the Algerian people by the regime.[20]

2   The Algerian population is composed of Berbers and of people

of Arab or Berber origin who are now Arabised. The Algerian government ignored this reality and did not even acknowledge the existence of the Berbers. Moreover, it implemented a systematic policy of 'de-Berberisation' by slowly suppressing all remaining institutional reminders of non-Arab culture and by accelerating Arabisation. To the Berberists, this amounted to ethnocide and should be stopped. While recognising the dual character of North Africa's people and culture, the Berberists still reject Arabisation on the grounds that it is based on false premises. To them, two languages are spoken in Algeria: Berber and Algerian Arabic, the latter being a very different idiom from what was made the official language of the country, this being a mixture of Classical and Modern Standard Arabic. The Berberists advocate, therefore, the abolition of this official language and its replacement, on equal terms, by the two truly national languages of Algeria: Berber and Algerian Arabic.

As a result of the 1979 and 1980 strikes, the government, entirely ignoring Berber grievances, gave in to the Islamists and decided to accelerate Arabisation. In January 1980 the authorities launched what was seen as an all-out effort to suppress Berber culture. A series of anti-Berber measures had been implemented throughout the 1970s[21] and the last tolerated symbol of Berber culture was a radio programme in Kabyle Berber on the government-owned station. Since the 1960s its duration, quality and watt-power had been gradually reduced and the presenters had been under instruction to introduce Arabic terminology in the language they used. Early in 1980, a rumour circulated of the impending disappearance of the programme. On 10 March, Mouloud Mammeri was banned from delivering his scheduled lecture on Berber poetry, sparking off the Kabyle, or Barber, Spring.

THE LEGACY OF THE BERBER SPRING

The importance of those four days of rioting was manifold. The sheer fact of such an event happening was in itself remarkable. Since 1968, Boumedienne had succeeded in suppressing not only all major political opposition on the ground, but even opposition at the psychological level. Gradually, for over a decade, the Algerian people had come to see the government in a purely Orwellian fashion: as an invincible monster, ubiquitous and capable of crushing the slightest manifestation of disagreement with officialdom. To use violence against the government or government symbols was unthinkable. The regime had given the Algerian people a few opportunities to exercise 'legal' – controlled – disagreement, especially in the form of so-called national debates organised during the campaigns for the amendment of the National Charter and the Constitution or during the presidential election. Although these opportunities were seized with avidity by a people eager for any sign of freedom of expression, the results were insignificant. Not only were these debates used for the sole purpose of diffusing tension, but particularly articulate speakers were allegedly arrested afterwards and punished. Although this did not entirely deter people from speaking out, it reinforced the belief in the invulnerability and omniscience of the regime. This, in turn, emphasised the immense importance of the Kabyle insurrection.

In spite of its importance, the Berber Spring was overshadowed internationally by the coincidental occurrence of another social protest whose global importance was considerable: namely, the Polish labour movement and the birth of *Solidarnosz*. The two contemporary movements had a lot in common. They were both the expression of the people's search for freedom and democracy and their respective adversaries were very similar. However, the ethnic nature of the Berber Spring recalls the nationalist movements which, subsequently, were to shake Yugoslavia and later, the Soviet Union.

The extent and violence of the revolt took the regime by surprise and showed both its weakness and its determination to remain in power. Not only were hitherto unknown special riot squads[22] sent to Tizi Ouzou with instructions to crush the rebellion, but the entire region was cut off from the rest of the country and troops everywhere were put on alert. The isolation of Kabylia from the rest of the country enhanced both the region's internal unity and its prestige outside. First, the Berberist movement, which for many years, was mostly an intellectual phenomenon, mainly among students and teachers, now had the total support of at least one entire geographical area. Second, the success of the rebellion – if only by defying the state unpunished – restored pride and courage to older generations such as the frustrated veterans of the liberation war who had become disillusioned and pessimistic. More important, at the psychological level it destroyed the myth of the regime's invincibility.[23]

The Berber Spring had two important consequences for Algerian politics: it destroyed the dominant fear of the state, and it opened a whole new process of non-violent confrontation with the regime[24] which, in turn, created an environment for popular resistance and subsequently, helped bring about social and political reforms.

THE MOBILISATION OF THE BERBERISTS

The remarkable atmosphere of solidarity and unity which reigned in Kabylia during those days of rebellion – reminiscent of wartime – convinced most of the people involved of the necessity to pursue the confrontation by other means. Many realised that in the past, similar uprisings failed because of an absence of follow-up. In other words, once the flare-up died down, the authorities were free to exercise reprisals as they pleased. The most serious and pressing problem the population had to face after the rebellion was the fate of the great number of young people, students, factory workers, doctors, and other professionals arrested in Kabylia and Algiers during and after the riots. In order to obtain their liberation, the Berberists organised a series of demonstrations in various places, including outside the prisons where some of them were detained. Anti-Repression Committees were created in Algeria and in France and, for the first time in Algeria, petitions signed by hundreds of people were sent to the President.[25]

For the first time also, repression and oppression in Algeria were denounced both at home and abroad and direct criticism of the regime was openly voiced. Twenty-four persons detained during the riots were finally freed under popular pressure, the first instance of the kind in the country.[26] The government showed signs of weakness which the protesters were quick to use, especially to obtain freedom for remaining detainees.

Later, when the government started to regain control of the situation, a favourite tactic was continuous harassment of Berber activists individually. Passports were taken away from their owners, employees were fired or transferred, travel abroad was denied, individuals were subjected to short-term detention and interrogations and were freed as soon as news of their arrest reached the public.[27] This led the Berberists to organise various associations, among which the most active were the Committees of the Children of Martyrs (Comité des Enfants de Chouhada) and the Berber Cultural Association, none of which were recognised officially. The main achievement, however, was the founding, in July 1985, of the Algerian League for the Defence of Human Rights, known as the Human Rights League (LADDH, subsequently LADH and then again LADDH). The statutes of the League conformed to the Algerian Constitution and to Algerian law. Nevertheless, the government refused to give it official status and its president, lawyer Abdennour Ali Yahia, was immediately arrested. It was to be the first of a series of measures to be taken against him and other Berber activists over the next three years.

BERBER CULTURAL MOVEMENT AND DEMOCRACY

The Berberists chose to call their movement a 'Cultural Movement' in the early 1970s for a very simple reason. It was impossible at the time to openly question the legitimacy or otherwise criticise the activities of the regime. As mentioned above, by 1970 Boumedienne had accomplished two major goals. He did away, aided by very efficient secret police, of any opposition to his rule and he succeeded in gaining support for his development policies. For an unorganised, unstructured, undefined 'movement', whose members were mostly students originating from only one of the country's Berber areas, to challenge the rule of such a determined dictator was very hazardous. Young people frequently 'disappeared' after school, and reprisals struck whole families of suspected opponents. The coining of the term 'cultural movement' was more than sheer expediency, it was a tactical decision which proved successful in the long run. Many a staunch adversary of the totalitarian way in which Boumedienne ran the nation in the early 1970s would have disclaimed any suggestion that they opposed official economic policies or the socialist character of the Algerian nation; all they wanted, the Berberists would have claimed, was to obtain respect for, and recognition of, Berber culture. Fundamentally however, the main concern for the members of the 'movement' was democracy. For obvious, logical, reasons the Berberists considered democracy the only tool for cultural liberation and, conversely, the absence of democracy was the main cause of the cultural genocide the Berbers of North Africa were experiencing. There were a few opposition parties in exile, but their audience was insignificant. The MCB had the advantage of a strong representation inside Algeria as well as outside (mainly in France with small pockets in Canada, Germany, and elsewhere in Europe). To keep that internal base it was therefore necessary to publicly limit the scope of its platform to ethnic 'cultural' claims. This had the added advantage of being attractive to Berbers across the political, ideological, and social class spectrum. It allowed Berberists to gain support for their platform even at the height of Boumedienne's popularity. Although it was never spelled out that way, the goal of the Berberists from the inception of their movement was, therefore, intrinsically and extrinsically to restore democracy in Algeria.[28]

This step-by-step tactic was to prove relatively efficient. It needed impetus, however, and the government provided it in 1980 at the height of the Berber outrage and, paradoxically, at a point when morale was very low in Kabylia. Exhibiting immense arrogance and overconfidence for over a decade, the regime also implemented policies which were humiliating to Berbers, especially in Kabylia and the Aures regions whose populations had suffered a very heavy toll during the war of liberation. Eventually its own stubbornness brought it to the verge of collapse.

THE IMPACT OF THE INSURRECTION

The Algerian government was not alone in feeling the threat of the MCB and the tremendous psychological effect of the Berber Spring. The impact was felt elsewhere at home and in neighbouring countries, especially Morocco. In Algeria, the population's reaction was far from unanimous. It consisted largely of two types: support, if only for the sheer fact that the Kabyles defied the regime; or anger and even hatred.[29] The latter was partly due to a total ignorance of the Berberists' claims by the rest of the Algerian population, stemming, among other things, from complete control of the national media by the government and partly to Islamic agitation.

The supporters of rapid and total Arabisation and especially the Islamic movement felt particularly threatened by the Berberists because they represented the most articulate, the most determined, and the most fundamental opposition to their own claims and ideology. Until then, the Islamists had been virtually unopposed, feared, and helped at different times and to varying degrees by the government and by part of the population. In the late 1960s and early 1970s, when the 'Frères Musulmans' were only small in number, they often violently assaulted those who, in their eyes, did not respect their standards of Islamic behaviour.[30] The Boumedienne regime gave them tacit support for at least two reasons: first, an alliance with the Islamists was part of the move towards the religious legitimacy sought by the regime and, second, Boumedienne manipulated the fundamentalists into doing his 'dirty work' – in other words, unpopular acts with which the government did not want to be directly associated. This had two advantages: it served as a barometer of the population's feelings towards Arabo-Islamism, showing at what point saturation was reached; and it allowed Boumedienne to punish the Islamists if and when he judged that they had gone beyond the permitted limits which were determined, among other things, by the same barometer. The latter motivation itself also served two purposes: on the one hand, by publicly punishing or appearing to punish the fundamentalists the regime told the Algerian people that it was not responsible for any excesses and, moreover, was prepared to chastise when necessary; and, on the other hand, it sent a message to the Islamists themselves, signalling to them that although they were being tolerated Boumedienne was 'still the boss'. The combination of Boumedienne's own anti-Berber feelings and the Islamists' implacable opposition to the MCB could only stimulate ignorance of, and negative propaganda about, Berber claims.

Abroad, the repercussions were diverse. The most significant reactions were those which occurred in Morocco, the country most concerned with possible Berber unrest.[31] King Hassan chose to keep ahead of events and while the Kabyles in Algeria were asking for the introduction of Berber language courses in the country's universities, the monarch announced the creation in Morocco of an Institute for Berber Studies and he authorised the publication of a Berber language magazine. This had the effect of diffusing tension before any agitation could start. A decade later, however, the magazine has stopped publication while the Institute is not even at the blueprint stage.

RETURN TO THE *STATUS QUO*

In Algeria, soon after the Berber Spring, the government prepared its recovery. The Yakouren Seminar Report was considered far too radical for any FLN *apparatchik* to stomach. Following a 'national debate on culture', the FLN Central Committee met in the summer of 1981 and rejected everything remotely connected with the Yakouren Seminar. The hardline 'Arab-Islamists' of the party prevailed and the Arab and Muslim identity of Algeria was emphatically reaffirmed. As it slowly regained control of the situation, the government began to feel confident enough to bargain and change or reinterpret various previous decisions.[32] A campaign for the 'de-Kabylisation' of the Algerian administration was discreetly launched and numerous changes in personnel took place. Civil servants and staff members in the nationalised industries who hailed from Kabylia, were removed from key posts and were given unimportant positions. The university of Tizi Ouzou itself was forced to open its doors to an obligatory quota of students from other regions.

After the initial stage of total panic and disorganisation the regime had pulled itself together and, as was often the case later on, President Chadli himself was the main beneficiary of the crisis. After a year of indecision and interfactional strife, the new president finally managed to hold the reins and assert himself as a ruler.

Confidence – stemming from the feeling that as early as October 1980 it had regained control of the situation, together with the

Berberists' seeming willingness to 'play the institutional game',[13] – persuaded the government to show firmness and not be seen to back away
from established principles. In fact, it had already made its choice and
a series of direct and indirect confrontations which culminated in
1985 were to take place between the state and the Berber opposition.

CHALLENGING THE INSTITUTIONS

Between 1981 and 1985, a hitherto unknown phenomenon in Algeria
– free association – was to be used by the Berberists as their main
tactic. The Berber Spring had succeeded in almost permanently
ridding the region of the tight control exercised everywhere else by
the regime.[34] In Tizi Ouzou, associations and organisations not affiliated with the FLN (and normally prohibited) mushroomed and
Berber language publications proliferated, the authorities being both
powerless and unwilling to act. The Berberists wanted, therefore, to
extend this relative freedom of expression to the rest of the country
and – as they put it – to avoid being confined to a 'regional ghetto'.

A particularly significant move was the founding of the committees
of the Children of Martyrs (CM). The shield of a sacred institution,
the Revolution, was thus used to promote ideas which were in total
opposition with those of the regime. This was, in effect, the first
attempt at denying the state the monopoly it had always enjoyed over
national institutions, including the Revolution. If the very founding of
the committees of the CM was in itself a challenge to this government
monopoly, their action was to confirm and strengthen this challenge.
From its first meeting in November[35] 1980 in Tizi Ouzou to the publication of an official 'dossier' in November 1984,[36] the CM movement
organised peaceful marches and meetings and wrote open letters and
letters of protest to local authorities as well as to the government and
to President Chadli Ben Jedid. Its main strategy consisted in lobbying
and in making use, among other things, of the proposed 'associations'. The Tizi Ouzou committee, on 14 April 1984, requested legal
status for an association whose purpose, according to its statutes, was
to:

• contribute to the writing (...) of a history of national liberation
  movements (...);
• contribute to [the nation's] cultural life; (...)
• commemorate important events in the history of the nation.[37]

These objectives are clearly a statement of rejection of the official
view of the country's history[38] and a statement of a desire to promote

human rights in the country.[39] The project was turned down by the local authorities and an appeal to President Chadli Ben Jedid did not result in his overriding the decision.

One of the main symbolic acts carried out on 1 November and/or 5 July (Independence Day) every year by the CM, wherever one of their committees was in operation, was to lay a wreath at the local memorial to the 'martyrs' of the Revolution (by definition the parents of the CM) outside of, and independently from, the official ceremonies. Everywhere the local authorities opposed this parallel, alternative, ceremony and arrested some of the actors. In letters of protest to Chadli the CM called on him to respect the 'ideals of November' including: 'democratic freedom, human rights and cultural and linguistic diversity'.[40]

In February 1985, the Tizi Ouzou committee staged a protest outside a conference room where a 'seminar for the re-writing of Algeria's history' [sic] was taking place under the aegis of the FLN,[41] and on the following 5 July they organised an alternative observance of the National Holiday by laying a wreath on the tomb of martyrs, independently from the official ceremonies. This constituted a serious challenge to the authorities and a number of Committee members were arrested and tried by the special State Security Court. When the newly created League for the Defence of Human Rights lodged a protest – its first important act as a human rights watchdog – its president, Abdennour Ali Yahia was himself arrested. The following month, he and a dozen others, amid international protest, organised a hunger strike in order to obtain special status as political prisoners.[42]

HUMAN RIGHTS AS A WEAPON

The creation of the LADH was a blow to the Algerian authorities. To discredit it, the government resorted to the usual cliché of 'foreign manipulation' of the founding members.[43] According to one of the latter, Vice-President Mokrane Ait Larbi, discussions on the creation of a committee for the defence of human rights started in Tizi Ouzou in December 1984 during the celebrations of International Human Rights Day. During several months, contacts had been established with various groups 'including those close to the regime'.[44] However, some 'irreconcilable differences' appeared right at the beginning. 'One Algiers-based lawyer'[45] was the spokesman of a group in favour of a conditional seal of approval by the FLN 'for all activities in defence of human rights' whereas the Ali Yahia-Ait Larbi group supported the ideas of total independence[46] and of seeking international solidarity which, to them, were not negotiable. The question of the League's affiliation with the International Human Rights Federation was, however, responsible for the final split. According to Ait Larbi,[47] 'a former politician' justified non-affiliation with the International organisation by the fact that the latter was 'under the control of a Zionist lobby'.

The arrests and condemnation of Ali Yahia and, a few weeks later, of Ait Larbi, prompted the International Human Rights Federation to give its seal of approval and to accept the affiliation of the LADH[48] although the latter had still not been recognised by the Algerian authorities. The government then responded by a wave of repression which struck all the leading members of the League and of the MCB. A number of them were arrested, sentenced and imprisoned over the following three years. But by that time, the Berberists had acquired tremendous popular support and were determined to ignore or defy punishment, convinced that unlike previous activists[49] they were not isolated. Accordingly, the government, in handing down sentences,[50] was caught between applying harsh punishment to make examples of the 'guilty' and fear of the popular unrest which might result from it.[51] After the trial, however, in contrast with the situation before 1980, agitation in favour of the prisoners continued unabated in Kabylia, Algiers, and Paris.

In spite, or perhaps because, of repression the notion of human rights was now fairly established and was becoming more and more a household word in Algeria. Challenged in its claims to be the sole champion of human rights, the Algerian regime tried to overcome the pressure by manipulating the concept. In 1987, while still denying legal status to the LADH, the government sponsored a new Human Rights League (with the same name as the earlier one), presided over by another lawyer (Miloud Brahimi) and immediately granted it official recognition. The very creation of this second league was, in itself, a victory for the MCB. It constituted the regime's capitulation and its acceptance of the need for a human rights organisation, a serious blow to previous government monopoly on political life, as well as a recognition of the existence of abuses in the country. An independent human rights organisation was hitherto considered a virtual contradiction in terms, for, according to official propaganda, the Algerian state was by definition the guarantor of human rights.[52] The creation, shortly thereafter, of a third league contributed to giving the issue of human rights an unprecedented status in the country and it greatly helped increase awareness of abuse. For better or for worse, the defence of human rights, both as a philosophical concept and as a reality to aim at, had definitively found a place in the Algerian consciousness.

LEST KABYLIA SHOULD SNEEZE

With the creation of the second league the regime was attempting to improve its external image at a time when the country's economy was being restructured. With the worsening of the economic situation, discontent grew proportionately throughout the country and the lessons of the Berber resistance to the regime were being learnt. Violent riots had taken place in Constantine in November 1986, almost a replica of those at Tizi Ouzou six years previously. But, apart from the Islamists, there was no other popular 'movement' or structured organisation, as determined in its opposition to the regime and as steadfast in its struggle as the MCB, and none other could have any pretension to inspire and provoke agitation and unrest among the Algerian population.

When riots spontaneously broke out in October 1988, the Islamists did try to jump onto the bandwagon and some foreign media were quick to point to them as the source of the trouble. But it soon became clear that they had no direct role in the revolt. If those riots ultimately led to the most comprehensive and most substantial changes in the political system since Algeria's independence, the initial intention of the government, however, was to repress them very harshly, as indeed was the case during the unrest.[53] The government was once again taken by surprise and was profoundly shaken. What it had in store, however, as a response, was also the answer to a question many journalists and scholars abroad asked: why did Kabylia not join in?

One indication is furnished by the very measures taken by President Chadli Ben Jedid himself. Shortly after the riots, he made a number of changes in the political structure. A referendum on the amendment of the Constitution took place in November, but that was only a form of stalling; the decision was announced in Ben Jedid's address to the nation at the height of the riots. More significant was the reshuffling of the cabinet and the appointment of a new prime minister. Kasdi Merbah[54] had powers none of his predecessors possessed.[55] He had been for many years head of the Military Security, the Algerian secret police, and as such was one of the most powerful men in the land. Known as 'l'homme des dossiers' ('the man with the files'), he was supposed to possess information on every politician in the country and was therefore feared by many – but, more importantly, he was a Kabyle.

During the riots – 'the earthquake' as they were called in Algeria – the regime had one nightmare: if Kabylia were to 'move'[56] there was no telling how bad the situation could become. Kabyle interests (Berber claims) were now established and represented throughout the country, and a response to unrest in that region would create a chain reaction that would be extremely difficult to control. The appointment of Kasdi Merbah indeed took place after the riots, but it was none the less symptomatic of that underlying fear. One of the few Kabyles to be part and parcel of the Boumedienne regime,[57] he was asked by allies to take power at the latter's death. He felt, however, unprepared, preferring the backstage of secret services, and he was allegedly instrumental in imposing the Army's choice, Ben Jedid, as president over the two serious contenders, Foreign Minister Abdelaziz Bouteflika and party head Mohammed Salah Yahiaoui.

The government's perpetual fear of a Kabyle uprising did, nevertheless, not diminish its resolve. If the regime did not foresee the likelihood nor the extent of the 1988 riots, it had been, on the other hand, prepared since 1980 for the idea that Kabyle unrest could occur at any time. A decision was made that in the event of its occurrence the government should act with particular swiftness and brutality in order, once and for all, to get rid of the problem. A plan allegedly existed to that purpose and was ready for use during the first days of the riots.

LESSONS OF A STRUGGLE

In Kabylia, meanwhile, after nearly a decade of political mobilisation and activism, both the population and the leadership had also learnt a few lessons. Knowing the regime to be implacable in its desire to suppress opposition, particularly Berber opposition, and its intent to maintain the supremacy of the official Arab-Islamic ideology, many leaders of the movement sought to widen their sphere of influence and gain support from non-Kabyles as well as trying to carry their message outside their region. They wanted to avoid confinement in a 'regional ghetto' and, at the same time, prevent the threat of further repression in Kabylia which they were certain was being plotted in government circles in Algiers. Berberist leaders had been aware for some time of the desire of some factions in government to 'teach the Kabyles a lesson'. They had, indeed, received a warning during the first few hours of the riots in Algiers that a brutal operation was ready to be put into action in Kabylia by the government.

Leaders of the movement in recent years had been concerned with two major issues: to avoid repression in Kabylia and to get the rest of the country to adopt their claims for democracy.[58] Having already paid a heavy price for their activism they did not wish to attract more hardship on their region unnecessarily[59] and they tried hard to avoid any act likely to provoke harsh government reaction. Second, Berber-ists saw their claims and their fight for democracy as the struggle of the entire nation and many were concerned that they did not receive the support they deserved, for the majority of Algerians would fall victim to the regime's powerful propaganda machine.[60] They were eager to see other regions emulate Kabylia and share its burden in the anti-government struggle.

When the revolt flared up in Algiers in October 1988, tension was already high throughout the country. Strikes had taken place almost everywhere and a confrontation with the authorities seemed inevit-able. The government resorted to preventive action and attempted, as it had done in the past, to deter any serious agitation.[61] Leaders of the MCB decided to limit unrest in Kabylia and prevent any pretext for government action there. The warnings they received at the inception of the riots on 5 October only confirmed their fear of repression. They consequently called on the population of the region to refrain from rioting[62] in order to avoid a massacre.[63] The operation was, on the whole, successful; only a few incidents of unrest took place in Kabylia.[64]

If the government feared a Kabyle revolt most of all, the extent of the riots in Algiers and elsewhere was none the less unexpected and did shake the regime. The riots led to reforms but they first of all allowed Algerians, for the first time since independence, to denounce an element of repression which, common though it was, was a strictly taboo subject: torture.

THE ROAD TO DEMOCRACY

With its president convicted two days previously,[65] and no access to the media, the original LADH did not make its voice heard success-fully during the unrest. Ultimately, however, the entire Algerian spec-trum was completely overtaken by the events and, ironically, it could be considered a victory for the LADH that its government-sponsored rival became the chief critic of human rights abuses throughout that period. Although hesitant at first, and conforming to a long-established practice[66] of paying homage to the leaders, the so-called Brahimi League nevertheless acquired respectability by strongly denouncing harsh repression and systematic use of torture by the authorities. It later became a fairly credible, if somewhat limited, watchdog of human rights practices.

After the announcement of constitutional changes, and the prospect of a multi-party system in Algeria, the first significant reaction to the new situation came from the MCB. Nearly two weeks before the referendum on a new constitution (which took place on 23 February 1989), the MCB held a general meeting (hailed by the Algerian press as a model of democracy) in Tizi Ouzou, and on 11 February announced the creation of a Rally for Culture and Democracy (RCD),[67] a 'semi-political' association designed to become a full political party[68] with the implementation of the new Constitution. It was the first such move in the country and it showed the already high level of mobilisation and preparedness of the Berberists.

Dissensions quickly appeared among the Berberists, however, many of them not being altogether certain that one political party should be the sole guardian and legitimate spokesman of so-called 'cultural claims' – that is, Berber demands. A 'movement' has the special attraction of being a meeting place for a large spectrum of people from different social, economic or political backgrounds, united by their common commitment to the preservation of their ethnic identity. In contrast, a political party is limited to specific ideology which might not be that of the majority of Berberists. At that stage, therefore, although the RCD and, later, other political parties such as the FFS and the PAGS[69] included Berber claims in their platforms, many members of the MCB felt that 'Berberness' and Berber demands should not be the preserve of one or several political parties.

To them, dependence on a political party could lead to a confusion of issues and interests. In the new political context, issues of social justice, economic welfare, and even that of democracy, are each represented, expressed and defended by numerous parties, groups and organisations. Berber claims cut across social classes and could not be limited by ideology. Since October 1988 the issue of democracy has been on the agenda of Algerians of almost every possible belief and conviction, and perhaps as a result of this rediscovered concept the Berber Cultural Movement has really become what it purported to be in the early 1970's: a 'cultural movement'. Ideologically, it remains what it has always been: the main popular counterweight to the Islamic fundamentalists.

CONCLUSION

I have tried in this chapter to show that the Berber movement has been, since the early 1970s, the main source of popular opposition to the Algerian regime, first under Colonel Boumedienne and then under Colonel Chadli Ben Jedid. My aim was not to make a detailed study of the Algerian political system nor, for that matter, to provide an analysis of the inner structure of the Berber movement (this is the subject of ongoing research), but simply to show that the Berberists are, for a very large part, responsible for the political climate that has prevailed in Algeria since 1988. This is not to say that other opposition groups did not exist in Algeria and abroad; many did. But these were generally limited to a few dozen individuals at best and never had a serious, or at least effective, presence 'on the ground'. The Berber Cultural Movement was remarkable for at least two reasons: it mobilised a very large portion of the population (not just in Kabylia, but most Kabyles elsewhere in the country and abroad), and it led a *sustained* struggle for two entire decades.

NOTES

1 Part of the research for this article was done while the author was a guest scholar at the Woodrow Wilson International Center for Scholars, Washington, DC. I wish to express my thanks to the Center for their generous support and for allowing me access to their facilities long after the end of the guest scholarship.

2 Kaylia, about 50 miles east of Algiers, is a poor, mountainous region traditionally a source of emigration to industrial centres of Europe. Owing to the proximity of Algiers and the Mediterranean, its population, nearly 100 per cent Berber speakers, has long been exposed to outside influences. A significant emigrant element in the population brought back labour union traditions from Europe, and nationalistic feeling has always been very strong there. This tradition led to an extremely important Kabyle contribution to the anti-colonial struggle.

3 Allegedly by army commandos in riot police uniforms.

4 Known as the 'Yakouren Seminar' from the name of the summer resort where it was held.

5 For example, responding to one of the Berberists' main demands, i.e. that their language be taught in the country's schools and universities, the government promised the restoration of the Chair of Berber at the University of Algiers and the creation of a new chair at the University of Tizi Ouzou. Later, the Ministry of Education announced that there were to be courses of Berber language and culture in six university centres around the country with the exception of that of Tizi Ouzou. Furthermore, these courses were to be taught in 'departments of popular culture' in the Arabic language – almost a contradiction in terms. The latter announcement was but a negation of the very meaning of the Berberists' struggle: that the Berber language and culture be given a recognised status as an integral part of Algerian identity, on equal terms with, and independently from, Arabic culture. In addition, the Berberists, who always proclaimed that 'Popular Arabic', i.e. Algerian Arabic, and not

Classical (or Modern or Literary) Arabic, is the language really spoken by the rest of the Algerian population (and is, therefore, with Berber, one of the 'national' languages), were doubly snubbed by the proposed measure. The Classical variety (considered as foreign and elitist) is maintained as the only officially recognised 'national' language, and Berber is again reduced to the level of a 'folklore product' to be taught only as a curiosity.

6   Severe riots and strikes that year resulted in the crushing by the Boumedienne regime of all students' and workers' unions and of all remaining fragments of underground political organisations. That year marked the end of the political structure inherited from independence and the beginning of Boumedienne's unchallenged dominance.

7   This support was massively Kabyle in origin but no other group, movement or cause, had at the time a comparable following in the country.

8   The word 'Islamists' has now become the accepted term to designate the Islamic movement. Both Islamic 'fundamentalist' and, in French, '*intégriste*' are considered controversial by specialists, especially scholars. In Algeria the most popular name given to the Islamists is 'Frères Musulmans' (or 'Soeurs Musulmanes' for women) by analogy to the Egyptian Muslim Brotherhood movement, although only a section of the Algerian fundamentalists has actual links with the latter.

9   For a long time, the term 'Berberist' was considered subversive in Algeria. Anyone identified as such could be arbitrarily arrested and put in prison. 'Berber nationalist' is a term used by foreign scholars and media, mainly Anglo-Saxon, to describe the Berberists. It is not improper in so far as the ideology of many Berberists incorporates some form of 'Berber nationalism', or, more precisely, the concept of a Berber nation which crosses the borders of present-day nation-states. However, Berberists both call themselves and are called by other Algerians – including the government – Berberists. This term is given a pejorative meaning by their rivals (the regime, the Islamists, and some sections of the Algerian population) and is either neutral or a source of nationalist pride when used by Berberists themselves.

10 Especially as several attempts on his life were made during the first three years after his accession to power.

11 Two of the original leaders ('*chefs historiques*') of the independent struggle, Mohammed Khider and Belkacem Krim, were assassinated under Boumedienne's rule (and allegedly on his orders): the former in Madrid, Spain, in 1967, and the latter in Frankfurt, West Germany, in 1972. One, Ahmed Ben Bella, was jailed after the coup and released only when Chadli Bendjedid became president and two, Hocine Aït Ahmed and Mohammed Boudiaf, were in exile.

12 Until the mid-1970s, when the failure of the development plans became apparent.

13 And, later, the first National Assembly created under Boumedienne was to be a rubber stamp for the regime's decisions.

14 A 'National (military) Service' was created to that effect in the late 1960s. The period of service lasted 24 months, but once returned to civilian life the young conscripts often joined the ranks of the unemployed.

15 The ludicrous character of some forms of the 'volunteer' programme was frequently illustrated by the sight of young urban humanities students, on their first-ever visit to a farm, teaching jaded peasants how to get the most out of their lands. However, the campaign had a certain amount of success from another point of view as it allowed thousands of frustrated young people to travel and discover their country cost-free and in 'mixed' surroundings in a society where the two sexes were being drawn farther and farther apart.

16 The oil boom provided immense resources for the industrialisation endeavours of the government, and big spending eventually trickled down in terms of revenues and provided employment.

17 The debates were merely staged opportunities to release popular tensions and were, even so, very carefully monitored.

18 Extreme measures had to be taken during his funeral to avert any disturbances. Mob scenes nearly turned to riots and it was clear that the crowds which filled the streets of Algiers were not made up only of the late leader's supporters.

19 The ultimate objective of the Algerian authorities is, officially, total Arabisation of the country, its institutions and its people. Algeria, when this process is completed, would be transformed into a 'pure' Arab country adhering to all the principles of Arab-Islamic ideology. To achieve this goal, the country must go through a process of Arabicisation, a progressive implementation of the Arabic language as a vehicle for all social, political and cultural life in Algeria. Needless to say, this ideology not only ignores the entire Berber heritage of North Africa which concerns an overwhelming majority of its people, but, moreover, plans its progressive disappearance through a forced Arabisation of the remaining speakers of the Berber language.

20 On 14 April 1962, a newly liberated Ben Bella celebrated his first few moments of freedom on Tunisian soil by declaring to a welcoming President Bourguiba: 'We are Arabs. We are Arabs. We are Arabs.' Such a statement by someone who, contrary to common belief, was never the leader of the Algerian revolution, infuriated the FLN leadership who found it unjustified and inappropriate. Besides being politically unsound, as it could alarm the Europeans who might have wanted to remain in Algeria, Ben Bella's statement was particularly unwelcome to the Berbers who took a very heavy toll during the war and were *de facto* excluded by that remark. See Mohammed Harbi, *Le FLN, mirage et réalité* (Paris: Editions Jeune Afrique, 1980), p. 329.

   Subsequently, Ben Bella, a fervent admirer of Egypt's President Nasser, seized power and imposed a policy of Arabicisation later reinforced by Boumedienne who, although himself of Berber origin, was a product of the Islamic University of El Azhar, Egypt, and a staunch supporter of the Arab-Islamic ideology.

21 Some examples: Berber singers were barred from taking part in cultural events during the Cherry Festival at Larbaa Nath Iraten, in the heart of Kabylia, in 1974; the Fichier de Documentation Berbères, a research operation run by a Franco-Algerian Christian group was closed down in 1976; and the same year the government decreed that all personal names of new-born babies would be Arabised.

22 Nicknamed 'gladiators' by the rioters.
23 Months later when students and other youths rioted for the first time in Oran, they taunted the police by challenging them to go and display their strength in Kabylia!
24 Although the regime's response was not peaceful. This process, begun in 1980, culminated in 1985 but continued until 1988.
25 Including an 'Open Letter to President Chadli' on 25 May which gathered some 3,522 signatures.
26 On 26 June, a motorcade left Tizi Ouzou for the infamous prison of Berrouaghia, near Algiers, and brought back the 24 detainees who were welcomed as heroes in Kabylia.
27 This proved relatively efficient. The tactic consisted in releasing a detainee as soon as international human rights organisations had received information on him/her, and then to arrest another activist. The advantages of the tactic were manifold and the psychological effect very strong.
28 In 1977, during a football game attended by President Boumedienne and at which JSK, the Kabylia team, was a finalist, several thousand supporters brandishing Berberist banners chanted anti-Boumedienne slogans (the first time that this was done) and denounced his dictatorship in very plain terms. Then they marched in the streets of Algiers demanding democracy. Shortly thereafter, Boumedienne took a number of political measures which were clearly anti-Berber in nature. In addition, the name of the team was changed from Jeunesse Sportive de la Kayblie to Jeunesse Electronique [sic] de Tizi Ouzou (JET).
29 Late in 1980 a violent earthquake destroyed the town of El Asnam, south-west of Algiers (thereafter renamed Chelif), and caused several hundred casualties. One of the first medical teams to arrive on the spot came from the Tizi Ouzou hospital (it included Dr Said Sadi one of the principal leaders of the Berber movement) and it brought with it blood for transfusions. According to reliable sources, one hundred containers of this blood were thrown away by another rescue team whose members allegedly said they had no use for Kabyle blood!
30 Young women with short skirts were often bullied in the streets of Algiers and the parts of their legs not covered with clothing were smeared with paint. Young men with long hair were equally roughed up and given an unsolicited haircut. The police seldom intervened in those situations.
31 The foiled coups of 1971 and 1972 were largely led by Berber elements of the Royal Armed Forces and, had they succeeded, many maintain that a mainly Berber or a strongly pro-Berber regime would have been established in Morocco.
32 See note 5.
33 A favourite call by the Algerian government is for problems not to be debated in the streets but 'within the framework of the country's institutions'.
34 In an article on 20 July 1985, titled: 'L'Algérie ou la sérénité difficile', outgoing *Le Monde* correspondent in Algiers, Jean de la Guérivière, wrote: 'For the time being, Tizi Ouzou University is the only "area of freedom" in Algeria. The authorities allow protest to be expressed there, provided that it does not cross the narrow boundaries of the campus' [translation mine]. In fact, the mountainous Kabylia largely escapes

central control when it comes to freedom of expression. One repercussion of the Berber Spring there, is that police informers were no longer feared and coercion was discouraged.

35 The date of the official beginning of the war of independence, 1 November, is symbolically used by the Children of Martyrs for most of their activities.

36 For the 30th anniversary of the Revolution.

37 'Statuts de l'Association "Tighri"', in *Dossier Réalisé par le Comité des Fils de Chouhada de Tizi Ouzou*, November–June 1984, p. 6.

38 Reference to pre-Islamic North Africa is all but banned in textbooks and one might surmise that among the 'commemorations' envisaged by the CM, would be included those of acts of resistance (in North Africa), not only to Roman occupation but also to the Arab invasion.

39 Article XXII of the proposed association stipulates that in case of dissolution the Association's assets would be donated to (1) any Algerian organisation whose objectives are the defence of Human Rights; (2) any Algerian organisation whose objective is [the promotion of] amnesty; (3) any Algerian organisation whose objective is to maintain peace.

40 See 'Déclaration du Comité des Fils de Chouhada de la Wilaya de Tizi Ouzou à l'occasion du 5 juillet 1984': letter of 28 August 1984 to President Chadli Bendjedid by the Comité des Fils de Chouhada de Tizi Ouzou, in *Dossier realisé par le Comité des Fils du Chouhada de Tizi Ouzou*, 1er Novembre 1984, p. 16 and p. 21.

41 The CM protested against the FLN's monopoly over Algeria's history and pointed out that they, the heirs of those who gave their lives during the liberation war, were entitled to contribute to its interpretation.

42 Algeria did not acknowledge the existence of political prisoners on its soil. Although arraigned, the detainees and their families were not informed of specific charges.

43 Algérie Actualité, no. 1031, 18–24 July 1985.

44 'Autonomie absolue', letter of 29 July 1985 to *Libération* (Paris), published 8 August 1985.

45 Although not named in the letter, he is suspected to be Miloud Brahimi who was to become the president of the 'official' League of Human Rights.

46 'Autonomie absolue', *op. cit., Libération* 8 August, 1985.

47 *Ibid.*

48 At a meeting of its Bureau in Paris, 2 November 1985.

49 In 1976, a group of young Berberists allegedly close to the Paris-based Berber Academy attempted to bomb the offices of the government daily *El Moudjahid.* Although there were only very light damages, the State Security Court handed down a very severe verdict. Most of the accused were given a death sentence or life imprisonment (the last of them, Mohand Haroun, was released in the aftermath of the 1988 riots). This case, dubbed 'l'affaire des poseurs de bombe' ('The Case of the Bomb Planters'), is still very unclear, but was manna from heaven for the Boumedienne regime. Capitalising on its propaganda value, the government tried to discredit the entire Berber movement by 'showing' how it was manipulated from abroad. Two years later, in December 1978, while Boumedienne was on his deathbed, his secret services devised their own operation for more or less the same purpose. According to Algerian press

accounts, weapons sent by the Moroccan government were dropped by parachute at Cap Sigli, a beach in Kabylia. Until the Berber Spring, all persons sentenced for this were virtually 'lost' as casualties of the anti-regime struggle.

50   Needless to say judges received direct instructions from the Ministry of Justice.

51   In addition, aware of the serious deterioration of its international image, the government allowed international observers to the trial.

52   *Algérie Actualité*, no. 1031, 18–24 July 1985: 'Algeria in its entirety is a League for the Dignity of Man'(!)

53   The official death toll was 176, but according to independent accounts between 600 and 2,000 people were killed with many more injured.

54   Like many Algerian politicians, Kasdi Merbah is known under the *nom de guerre* he assumed during the liberation war. His real name is Abdallah Khalef.

55   He was, however, responsible for his actions before Parliament, which somewhat limited his powers and protected the president.

56   'Si la Kabylie bouge'.

57   The so-called 'technical' ministries, Finance (Small Magroug), Commerce (Layachi Yaker), Industry (Belaid Abdeslam), etc., were held by Kabyles, but these were not represented in the Council of Revolution. Merbah is among the very few who had remained in, or close to, government since independence.

58   The decision to claim national language status for Algerian Arabic (as against Classical Arabic), on a par with Berber, was denounced by some critics. At a meeting attended by the present author in 1978, the late French political scientist and Breton nationalist Yves Person, himself a sympathiser of Berber claims, advised Berberists to concentrate on 'their own cause' and not become champions of other people's causes. 'Let them [Arabic-speaking Algerians] defend their language and you defend yours,' he said to a group of young Berberists. However, it was clear in the late 1970s that most Berberists considered theirs to be a struggle against an oppressive elite and for the 'democratic rights' of all Algerians. They therefore pressed demands based on their definition of the country's cultural identity as a bilingual state.

59   A favourite saying among Berberists was: 'we've had more than our share of martyrs'.

60   All the media were government or FLN-owned.

61   On 3 October, Abdennour Ali Yahia, the president of the LADH, was charged with 'contempt of constituent bodies' (outrages à corps constitués) following statements he made in Paris. This decision seemed to foreshadow a crackdown on dissidence and an escalation in the repression of Berberists.

62   Lounes Matoub, a famous Kabyle singer, was shot by gendarmes while touring Kabyle villages in his car and distributing leaflets calling on the population not to riot.

63   See note 53. Repression in Kabylia would have led to much higher figures. Calls for calm were criticised by some as being government manipulation designed to neutralise Kabylia by preventing it from giving support to 'ungrateful Arabs'.

64 Some of them happened mainly as a response to decisions by local authorities to organise 'demonstrations of support' to President Ben Jedid. These were considered provocations by the population who then organised 'counter-demonstrations' in support of the rioters.

65 See note 61.

66 In its first statements the government-sponsored LADH, while denouncing torture and abuses by the authorities, also called for punishment of the rioters guilty of vandalism (!)

67 *Rassemblement pour la Culture et la Démocratie.*

68 It became a recognised party later in the year together with over twenty other groups.

69 *Front des Forces Socialistes* of historic leader Hocine Aït Ahmed; *Parti de l'Avant-Garde Socialiste*, an off-shoot of the Communist Party and the only one tolerated under Boumedienne, although with a semi-clandestine status.

10 Algerian theatre and protest

Youssef Selmane

The history and nature of Algerian theatre are closely linked to a tradition of struggle and protest. If one takes the example of the *maddah* – story-teller – as a major component of traditional performing arts, one can trace this tradition back to the *quṣṣaṣ* – the ancient story-tellers – particularly in Arabia and Iraq.

The *quṣṣaṣ* appeared and developed alongside the spread of Islam. They were intended to operate within a religious context, presenting to their audiences epic religious stories. However they tended to glorify the life of the Prophet Muhammad and exaggerate his deeds and exploits. The reason for this tendency was both social and religious. On the one hand, disseminating knowledge about Islam and persuading their audiences of the value of strict adherence to Islamic precept was their primary function, and the embodiment of such values within a historical figure was a simple way of making the message accessible to an audience conditioned by oral tradition. On the other hand, the *quṣṣaṣ* had also to face competition which no doubt, led to distortion of the inherent message in a desire to capture audience attention.

With the economic and political evolution of Arab society occurring as a result of Islam and the conquest that followed the Prophet's early ministry, the *muqallid* (traditional bedouin and tribal story-tellers) accompanied their tribal clienteles as they were originally Arabic. As a result, many of them settled in Iraq in Basra and Kufa: two towns which came to dominate the social, economic and cultural life of the early Islamic empire. They added new elements drawn from Islam to their traditional tribal repertoire, as well as new events associated with Islam. They would perform in public squares in the mosques and in the main market place. They were very popular and highly appreciated in Iraq. The *quṣṣaṣ* were originally largely a response to this success and, as the new Islamic world developed, two types of *quṣṣaṣ* appeared – one official, used as an instrument of propaganda and drawing only on Islamic sources, and the other using the same material but adding to it new material and imagination. The second type of *quṣṣaṣ* actually appeared after the Prophet had died, while the first type had already developed during the Prophet's lifetime. The second type, however, rapidly gained importance as the *muqallid-s* developed their art and repertoire. Although their function was primarily religious, they would use the Quran freely as a source for their own independent literary inspiration. Their material consisted of anecdotes, stories, myths and legends often, but not exclusively, derived from religious sources with the primary purpose of stimulating audience interest.

Because of the religious material used by the *quṣṣaṣ* they often acquired a prophetic persona in the popular mind. They therefore also acquired considerable influence which irritated the religious authorities, particularly the orthodox leadership. The Caliph ʿAlī, for instance, expelled the *quṣṣaṣ* from the mosques because of the danger he considered them to represent. Indeed, after the death of ʿUmar and under the caliphates of ʿUthmān and ʿAlī, there was a period of extended disruption. In the confused atmosphere, the *quṣṣaṣ* were very active and influential. They were also an easy target for officialdom to blame for the disturbances because of their role in popular culture. As a result, they were soon accused of fomenting trouble by encouraging the emergence of different religious sects. The process has been admirably described by Youssef Rachid Haddad:

In fact, the *gussas* become dangerous when they used besides words, other artistic means to express their ideas. The word, sacred and respected in Arab-Islamic society, seemed to be threatened by the '*gussas*' who ignored the 'law of God'. As the *gussas* developed their art in this sense, they integrated it into the domain of the spectacle and thus began to stray onto dangerous ground. Yet, although Islam may have rejected figurative arts because of the *ḥadīth*, religious doctrine of Islamic tradition, they did not cease to exist in Arab society at a popular level, despite constant official harassment. The fact that there is little comment about them in doctrinal studies merely reflects religious and political power. We find the same attitude in the Church (particularly when it is integrated into the state) towards actors and the theatre. The attitude of St. Augustine (4th–5th century AD) and that of the Byzantine Church towards actors, representation and theatre contrasts with the attitudes of the pre-Islamic Era (4th century AD) and compares well with attitudes adopted towards story-tellers after the first Islamic period, particularly those groups which acquired increasing popularity and distinctiveness because of their innovations in presentation. They moved closer to the notion of spectacle as they failed to respect the strict letter of the transmitted texts and experimented beyond the limits of Koranic interpretation. They added in other stories, tales, legends and events of the day, largely using imagination and techniques to attract the listener-spectators. They resorted to the world of fairies, myth and legend and mingled scenes from the life of the Prophet and other religious figures from Judeo-Christian traditions as well as Islam.[1]

The *quṣṣaṣ* developed their art further in the eleventh and twelfth centuries (during the Abbasid period) when there was a tremendous development in science, humanities, literature, translations from Greek and religious works. In succeeding centuries, however, the *quṣṣaṣ* were banned from mosques and condemned as heretics as religious orthodox, was enforced. The result was that the two separate art forms *muqallid* and *quṣṣaṣ* eventually merged. The two techniques have, therefore, achieved the same mode of expression by running different historical paths, and today there is a single popular tradition that extends from Morocco to Iraq, although the artist himself is known under a variety of names – *muqallid, maddah, rāwī, qawwāl, ḥākiya* – depending on the country or region concerned.

This art form was to suffer harassment and restrictions once western domination had come to the Arab world, particularly in Algeria. The *maddah* and the *haraquz* or theatre of shadows were among the major performing acts in pre-colonial Algeria. The *maddah* also used religious stories and fairy tales, irony, satire and farce to ridicule religious, administrative or political authorities.

The 'Theatre of Shadows' or *haraquz* arrived in Algeria from Turkey via Sicily and was one of the main sources of leisure in large towns throughout North Africa, such as Fez, Tangier, Oran, Algiers, Constantine and Tunis. It consisted of the projection onto a screen of the shadow of puppets manipulated by one man, who also spoke the dialogue. The stories were based on the adventures of the hero Karaguz and became political after the invasion of Algeria by France in 1830 with Karaguz changing from his role as virile hero to that of victor over the French. These anti-French overtones led to the prohibition of the Theatre of Shadows in 1843, although it survived as an underground activity in Algiers and Blida. The *maddah* also changed the nature of his art, moving from traditional material to condemnation and virulent attacks against the French occupation. The performers were consequently harassed and often arrested.

MODERN ALGERIAN THEATRE

The period after the First World War was one of political and social unrest due mainly to the fact that Algerians were still denied the most basic human rights and refused any kind of reward for their contribution to the war effort in the French Army. This led to a general sense of discontent and stronger nationalist sentiments, especially amongst young Algerians whose political awareness developed as they became more involved in the creation of cultural and social societies. At the same time, the emergence and development of modern Algerian theatre was rooted in opposition to colonialism and western values and also in the condemnation of negative, indigenous customs and values.

The cultural life of the time was mainly dominated by poetry, pamphlets, and short stories. The need for the assertion of an Algerian personality led most Algerians to turn to the Arabic language which had its own cultural and historical expressions. Their motto reflected the feelings: 'them and us', 'their religion and ours', 'their culture and ours'. This cultural revival was to a certain extent associated with the birth of three cultural groups:

1 *L'Association des Etudiants Musulmans Algériens*: mainly composed of young students from Arabic and Koranic taught schools.
2 *Al-Muhadhiba*: a cultural society founded by Tahar Ali Chérif which concentrated on the production of plays in literary Arabic.
3 *Al-Mutribyia*: a music society founded by an Algerian Jew, Edmond Yafil, it later incorporated sketches and plays.

An Egyptian theatre company led by George Abiad visited Algeria in 1921 and performed its plays in literary Arabic; the small Algerian elite who were educated in this language took pride in its use and urged the newly born groups to use it as well. However, this resulted in a total failure and the *Al-Muhadhiba* company was to disappear soon after its creation. The other two groups survived, but their experience in literary Arabic was ephemeral for they realised that:

We were faced with the major problem of literary Arabic. It was agreed that it was the only noble language for the stage. So be it – but the halls were empty or full with guests, which commercially was the same. The very noble literary Arabic was useful for great evenings where the pundits, who came to honour us, paid for their seats with warm compliments. And that same elite had not only free access to the theatre but it could not even help us to start [a theatre] or to use their presence as good publicity; the reason was ... *The audience could not understand the texts we performed.*[2]

Indeed, the problem of language was very important since the vast majority of Algerians were denied access to education, and the very few who were educated fell into two categories:

1   those who attended French schools and who usually did not go beyond the third or the fourth form at the *lycée*;
2   those who attended Arabic schools or *médersas*[3] which were very limited in number, under strict French control, and whose syllabuses had a strong emphasis on Islamic teachings.

The latter produced a cultural minority which was very conservative, very narrow-minded as regards religion, and claimed Arab-Muslim culture as their unchallengeable prerogative. This minority regarded itself as the *'ulamā'*, or the learned men of Islamic culture and belief, people of wisdom and knowledge, and hence the guardians of Arabic and Islamic culture. They developed an arrogant and often scornful attitude towards ordinary people. The illiterate masses were therefore rejected by the French, looked down upon by the Muslim elite, and even cut off from it. Social relationships within Algerian society in terms of culture and ideology were those of the dominant/dominated and educated/illiterate and were reflected in French rejection of and contempt for Algerians which was matched by Algerian rejection and utter disdain for the French. Alongside this divide was the Algerian elite which considered itself the spiritual guide and leader of the ordinary people, whilst in part tacitly accepting the French presence. For its part the vast majority of the population equated the Arabic educated elite with those religious men endowed with a knowledge of the Koran – the Word of God – and wisdom. The one small faction which dismissed both the French presence and the Algerian elite elements was composed of young Algerians who were politically and socially conscious. Their main concern was the plight of the ordinary people which led them to struggle against religious and social taboos, ignorance, superstition and illiteracy.

It was the social and cultural divide, coupled with this new politically aware group, which led to the use of colloquial Arabic or Algerian Arabic rather than 'Classical' or 'Literary Arabic' and thereby to the growth of a popular theatre. The use of literary Arabic in drama had an audience of philistines and pseudo-intellectual pedants 'who paid for their seats with warm compliments'. The question was then: what would serve the Algerian theatre best – applause from 150 intellectuals (of which 149 were guests), or 1,200 spectators who would come to see a play they understood.[4] The switch to Algerian Arabic was the obvious and necessary requirement for survival, and the experience of the first two years after 1921 was vital because it set the path for the young theatre.

On the political side everything had gone smoothly up to then: 'The old rigorous Muslims looked at us with disdain, but their disdain was silent. The French administration did not pay attention to a student pastime.'[5]

But from 1932, the developing Algerian theatre started to experience problems from fundamentalist Muslims and from the French authorities. During Ramadan in that year the Algerian stage saw the production of six plays by Ksentini which drew 8,000 spectators but it also upset conservative Muslims, a good number of whom started to petition the French administration: 'We had a perfidious enemy: the clan of the Muslim charlatans could not get over the fact that our fellow citizens filled up the Opera six times in a month.'[6]

Additional problems with the French administration were generated by *Faqo* (*They Are Aware or You Can't Fool Them*), a play by Ksentini, adapted and rewritten by Bachetarzi. The play was in fact a mild attack on *marabouts*, Muslim fundamentalists, and French rule. Bachetarzi tends to exaggerate the political and educational impact of the play as well as the penalties it engendered. Nevertheless, the production subsequently prevented the Algerian theatre from appearing at the Opera d'Alger more than once a year. From then on all plays were scrutinised by the authorities and special permission had to be sought before plays could be performed. The Algerian theatre had now become a common enemy of both the administration and the Muslim elite. Although *Faqo* brought problems and drew more enemies, it enhanced Algerian theatre and enlarged its audiences. The new theatre and the hostile official approach was crucial: 'But our enemies did not realise that they were developing our image in the eyes of the Algerian people and strengthening our moral prestige.'[7] This phenomenon was not new: under French rule any prohibition brought about greater solidarity among Algerians.

The year 1939 was another turning point: a new generation of young talent appeared on the stage and a contract was signed with the management of the local radio station for the presentation of music and drama. The same year showed more maturity in skills, but it also saw three major setbacks: Bachetarzi went bankrupt in his theatrical activities and had to turn to his singing in order to survive; the French authorities exerted more pressure putting the company under strict control, severely limiting its freedom of expression; and the Second World War broke out, bringing the company to a temporary halt.

However, in 1946 Mustapha Kateb obtained permission to establish the first 'Troupe Municipale Arabe' at the Opera d'Alger. The directorship was given to Bachetarzi, the 'troupe' was financially supported by the Opera, and all its members received monthly wages. In short, the Algerian theatre had become an institution, falling into the lap of the colonial authorities and becoming totally tied down to its dictates. Nevertheless, the young generation – with actors like Mustapha Kateb, Mohamed Touri, Mustapha Badie and Abderrahim Rais – gave a new impetus to the Algerian theatre in that they had a better knowledge of the intricacies of the stage and the techniques of acting than their predecessors. Being permanent residents at the Opera d'Alger brought two advantages: first, they had adequate economic and technical conditions and second, since the Opera used to host many European artists (mainly from France), they had the opportunity for better training and the improvement of their skills. They had intensive training in the art of theatre, and later, in 1953, a Department of Arabic Diction and Elocution was created at the Conservatoire of Algiers.

With the start of the Algerian revolution in 1954, the Troupe Municipale lost most of its members as some joined the *maquis* and others went to Paris where they produced plays for the North African community which denounced French colonialism. This led the French administration to put an end to their activities in 1955. This meant that they would have to engage in underground activity or exile. As a result Mustapha Kateb and other actors were asked to create the 'Troupe Artistique du FLN' in March, 1958, in Tunis.

The new company performed its first work a month later in Tunisia then travelled to Libya and Yugoslavia. The work was essentially a review entitled *Algeria and its Regions* presenting the different regions of the country through various costumes and music. The purpose was mainly to inform people that Algeria, contrary to French propaganda, was not part of France but had its own history and culture.

Abderrahim Rais, who produced the first show, also wrote a play – *The Children of the Casbah*, which the FLN company also produced. From 1961, tours included the USSR, China, Morocco, Egypt and

Syria, with the last performance taking place in Iraq in 1962 when the independence of Algeria was finally declared.

The original founders of the FLN theatre were not concerned with stage techniques and aesthetics. They were more concerned with informing their foreign audiences about the Algerian struggle against colonialism and saw the theatre as the mouthpiece of the revolution abroad.

Nevertheless, it was mainly the people involved in the 'Troupe Artistique du FLN' who were to start the TNA ('Théâtre National Algérien') after independence. It is this that explains the strong influence they exerted on the TNA and the prevailing aspects of struggle, revolution and socialism.

THE PERIOD AFTER NATIONAL INDEPENDENCE

Independence led to the taking over of all theatres left by the French and which were mainly located in the North. The TNA was created as a public institution in 1963 under the Ministry of Information and Culture. Its administrative structure is considered to be the best in the Arab world and Africa – a general manager, a secretary general, an arts committee, a technical department, a department of public relations and a secretariat – but this has also meant that the TNA has had the monopoly of all professional theatre activity in the country except in radio and television. Unfortunately the encouraging and impressive name of the TNA was not (and still is not) reflected in the quality of the product. The contradiction lies within the organisation itself – namely, in the inability and impracticability of the organisation to achieve desired aims and standards, particularly in problems of centralisation. These had led to many management problems and problems in productions of plays for large audiences in different parts of the country. The lack of playwrights led to the translation and adaptation of plays from the general theatrical repertoire, especially plays reflecting the political guidelines of the government – broadly socialism and struggle against imperialism – and thus names like Brecht or O'Casey topped the repertoire list. Productions were well spaced out and in order to fill the gap foreign groups were invited, mainly from France, Morocco and Tunisia. In order to tackle some of these problems the TNA was decentralised in 1970 and regional theatres were created: TNA – 'Théâtre National Algérien', based in Algiers; TRO – 'Théâtre Regional d'Oran'; TRAC – 'Théâtre Regional d'Annaba et de Constantine'. The TNA gathered together most of the people in the 'Troup Municipale d'Alger' and the

'Theatre du FLN' – six directors (Alloula, Hachemi Noureddine, Allal Mouhib, Hadj Omar, Mustafa Kateb and Rouiched) and eight actors in 1963. Up to 1978 there was only one director, Hadj Omar, and thirty-five actors. After a good start and in spite of big efforts to publicise its plays through radio, the press and even television, the TNA failed to attract large audiences except for concerts of Andalusian music or folk music. The irony was that a *maddah* performing in Port Said Square right opposite the Opera d'Alger would gather more than 200 people – a larger audience than the TNA could achieve.

The experience of the TNA was very important in that it provided a paradigm against which the trends of the Algerian theatre as a national art form after Independence (namely the amateur theatre, the theatre of Kateb Yacine, Abdelkader Alloula and Slimane, Benaissa) could be measured and assessed. There are several reasons why this major institution should have failed where the theatre of the generation before 1946 succeeded. The most prominent and pertinent include the fact that, as discussed earlier, Algerian audiences especially in Algiers, could not conceive of going to the theatre if the bill did not include music and dance as well as the play. Bachetarzi and his friends had to adapt to this situation throughout their careers: 'This prejudice prevailed for a long time and it did not encourage the performance of major plays. It had certainly harmed the Algerian theatre and it took many years to eradicate it – in fact, it has still not completely disappeared.'[8]

The previous generation had created a large theatre public responding to its demands and catering for its taste – so why should the Opera d'Alger in the hands of the Algerians have failed to attract large audiences? A full answer to this problem would require a complete sociological study of theatregoers in Algeria, but there are some obvious reasons that can be easily identified. A large section of the new generation was not acquainted with the theatre and the TNA failed to reach them, or even hang on to those who had a first taste of drama. On the other hand, there was a myth surrounding the Opera d'Alger – people used to see in it (and to a certain extent still do) the exclusive place of culture and entertainment for the French and the elite. The TNA has not tried to demystify this social label attached to the Opera d'Alger nor to transform the other theatres left by the French. It stubbornly uses techniques and the proscenium arch which are still alien to the majority of Algerians. Most productions revolve around adaptations of foreign plays, the theme being the struggle against imperialism and the socialist revolution, while the few Algerian plays fell into sterile moralising about the revolution or some social taboo. Furthermore, it wraps itself up in the obstinate idea that there is a lack of playwrights or a lack of interest in the drama of potential writers. Yet the publication of plays both in French and literary Arabic never stopped – indeed, both famous and interesting writers, including Assia Djebbar, Mohamed Dib, Tahar Owettar, Noureddine Abba, Djamal Amrani and Mustapha Haciene, never had their plays performed on the Algerian stage. A factor which was outside the responsibility of the TNA was, and still is, censorship, which the Tunisian critic Mohamed Aziza, speaking about the Arab Theatre, described in extremely precise terms:

> The [Arab] dramatist finds himself in a situation where he is faced with a stronger political authority, and with a unique omnipotent party which has become the norm in most Arab countries. There-fore, he seems to have only two attitudes to adopt: either keep out of the way and practise self-censorship or follow the 'movement', that is the official guide-line.[9]

In view of this the TNA had no other choice but to be totally committed to party politics. However, any evaluation of the TNA cannot be totally negative for even if it failed in certain areas it certainly made a big step forward in acting techniques and brought interesting works to the Algerian stage such as *Don Juan* (Molière), *The Taming of the Shrew* (Shakespeare), *The Plough and the Stars* and *Red Roses for Me* (O'Casey), *Mother Courage and her Children, The Exception and the Rule, The Caucasian Chalk Circle* (Brecht). Another achievement to be praised is the creation, in 1965, of the 'Institut National d'Art Dramatique et de Choréographie', which is the fruit of the prolonged efforts of Mustapha Kateb, who strongly believed in the Algerian theatre. He believed in the young generation and saw in it the best potential for the development of drama in the country – hence his idea to create an institute for that purpose. Unfortunately his dream did not materialise for in 1974 the drama section of the Institut was closed for undisclosed and mysterious reasons.

After decentralisation in 1970, the regional theatres of Oran and Constantine were more successful than their counterpart in Algiers. While the TNA stagnated or even declined, they turned away from the translation and adaptation of foreign plays to collective writing. Alloula in Oran and, later others in Constantine introduced new methods and techniques of production. They put an end to the proscenium and the traditional European stage, and geared their theatre towards more flexible productions which enabled them to perform anywhere – in cafés, schools, factories, cinemas. Their enterprise was slow to take off, but proved to be successful to a certain extent. In other words, the success or failure of the TNA, or the Algerian theatre as a whole, is linked with the concept of drama and theatre and its intrinsic dynamics and mechanisms as much as with its social and artistic rapport with society. Present-day theatre activity shows that there is a definite shift in audiences from the TNA to the more successful new trends of the three kinds described below. Has the TNA become alien to the Algerians? Are we back to square one, to the situation of the 1920s, with the French theatre and the pioneers of the Algerian theatre? The answer is clearly positive and the comparison evidently true.

THE AMATEUR THEATRE – LABORATORY AND PULSE OF ALGERIAN SOCIETY

The main focus here is the amateur theatre after Independence, although a few groups did exist before 1962. The two main youth organisations took the lead: 'Jeuness du Front de Libération Nationale' (JFLN), and 'Scouts Musulmans Algériens' (SMA). Their theatrical activity was limited to sketches, short plays and sometimes to plays based on the armed struggle or the 'glorious' Arab-Muslim past. From 1964 many amateur groups were created throughout the country; they emerged in a period of almost total cultural stagnation when the TNA was unable to cover the whole country. However, the main reason for the emergence and the quick expansion of the amateur theatre is more socio-political in nature – new social, cultural and political problems arose and people saw in the TNA a cheap purveyor of entertainment and leisure rather than a catalyst to translate and express the preoccupations of a developing country. The result was that new forms of expression were sought to cater for the latter concerns. Many young Algerians (generally under 25) from different walks of life took the initiative to create theatre groups to express their views on stage. There are now more than 100 groups throughout the country and none of them has benefited from any financial or material help from the government until very recently. Exclusively based on the initiative, enthusiasm and charisma of young individuals, the experience of the amateur theatre was to give a new and important dimension to the Algerian theatre; it has widened its scope and, to some extent, changed its course.

This amateur theatre is totally committed to the struggle for socialism. Its aim is to identify with the workers and peasants and to educate them; all the themes tackled by the different groups are entirely based on social, cultural and economic problems, as well as on the struggle of the Third World and colonised countries. The overall picture which emerges from the various plays is the emphasis on the struggle for socialism which is seen as the only answer to the problem of Algeria and, in particular, to those of the poor classes; and on the international scene, the continuous struggle against imperialism and international capitalism which are shown as the main causes of problems and backwardness of the Third World. The amateur theatre gave a fresh impetus to the Algerian stage and in twenty-five years of existence the groups have held four conferences and eighteen festivals.

Collective creation helped the amateur theatre deal with most social, political and cultural problems: all burning issues were approached without prejudice. No political speech, newspaper or magazine, TV or radio programme had ever tackled openly and objectively the situation of Algerian women, juvenile delinquence, corruption, or abuse of power, but the amateur theatre movement has done so. The way these problems were analysed and presented made the amateur theatre the pulse of Algerian society. However, this was only true of the period before 1971–2 because new major political events were to affect the amateur theatre and give it a new dimension. Indeed, the introduction of the 'Agrarian Revolution', the 'Charte Socialiste des Entreprises' and free health care, redirected the whole of the theatrical activity towards these three issues; most plays were henceforth based on the new division and distribution of land, involvement of workers in the management of factories, and the issue of free health care. The result of this was disastrous, for the amateur theatre fell into propaganda and declamation of slogans. These new areas of interest gradually put an end to the outstanding groups which were outspoken in their choice of social issues, and of a high standard. Harassment by the party – the FLN – finally put paid to all their efforts to survive in these adverse circumstances.

Furthermore, it has partly solved the problem of the lack of playwrights through collective creation and paved the way for a new and dynamic type of theatre. It has even influenced professional theatre, particularly the regional professional theatres of Oran, Sidi Bel Abbes and Constantine which started to write and produce plays collectively. So far, the 'Théâtre de Constantine' is the most outstanding and the most prolific. Success here is assessed mainly on the ground of audience appeal and attendance because collective creation does seem to have its limitations. This, in fact, led two experienced men of the theatre, Abdelkader Alloula and Slimane Benaissa, to give up collective creation and respond to their own creative talent which has proved highly innovative and successful. However, the number of successful productions is limited and the audiences are growing larger and more demanding, thus there is short supply despite high levels of demand. Slimane Benaissa stated that Kateb Yacine, Abdelkader Alloula, the 'Théâtre de Constantine', and himself cannot meet the demand, 'what can we do? We are just four drops in a desert.'[10]

Indeed, four theatres based in different cities, which travel throughout the country when the material and financial support is available can in no way meet the increasing demand. They always play to full houses whenever and wherever they appear. Despite all the efforts it is making and the material and the financial support it is getting, the TNA is still trapped in the same problems and is unable to reach or attract a large public.

To promote professional theatre, and the TNA in particular, the Ministry of Culture introduced a theatre festival – 'The National Festival of Professional Theatre' in 1985, which was to be held every year and organised and administered by the TNA. The first three festivals attracted large audiences and each performance played to full houses. These events are exceptional in the cultural desert prevailing in the capital city and in the country in general and have proved that there is a big demand for drama. They have also proved that the TNA still fails to meet people's expectations; the TNA productions did not get a favourable response from either the audience or the press. Abdelkader Alloula with the TRO ('Théâtre Regional d'Oran') was the exception: his *Al-Ajwād* (*The Story of the Generous People*) won most prizes in the first festival and was restaged for the second festival; *Al-Khubza* (*Loaf of Bread*), which was first produced in 1972, won the first prize at the third festival. Kateb Yacine was invited to the first festival only and was excluded from the other two events; a new version of *Palestine Betrayed* was presented. Slimane Benaissa was totally ignored, yet the irony is that on the fringe of the third festival his play *Babūr Ghraq* (*A Ship Sank*) which was programmed for one week, was performed for five weeks by popular request.

In the works of Kateb Yacine, Slimane Benaissa and Abdelkader Alloula, successful contemporary Algerian theatre is formed through the exploration and integration of cultural and social factors relevant to a popular audience. It is in this respect that the theatre exemplified by these three playwrights and other amateur movements has succeeded and the operations of the establishment (TNA), by comparison, have failed.

CONCLUSION

The three major plays these writers have produced share two major aspects in common: comedy through irony and satire together with denunciation and protest. In *Palestine Betrayed*, Kateb Yacine aims to show that originally Arabs and Jews lived together in peace as good neighbours and friends and that the conflict in Palestine was generated first by the two main religions involved – Islam and Judaism – and then developed and increased by Zionism, western powers such as Britain, France and the United States, and the betrayal of Palestine by some Arab leaders. These factors are criticised and denounced through satire in a series of tableaux. The play tackles a problem of international importance and breaks through national boundaries to acquire a universal dimension by calling on all exploited people to unite and continue the struggle against injustice and imperialism.

The Story of the Generous People is a bitter attack and protest against the abuses and the injustices of a corrupt system. The title of the play refers to the generosity and the good nature of Alloula's characters who – despite their poverty and the problems they encounter in their daily life because of the aberrations of a system ruled by incompetence and corruption – care about their work and about society as a whole. In this play too, irony and satire are major supports of the different tableaux and alternate with the songs which function as comment. The overall tone is optimistic and the message seems to be one of hope and faith to the 'generous people', to the ordinary Algerian worker not to give up because there are still ways to beat the system. The kind of problems portrayed in this play are in many ways similar to those in other developing countries and it seems that *The Story of the Generous People* would appeal to audiences in those countries as it does in Algeria. It would be even more successful in developed countries because of its original form and humour.

Slimane Benaissa has opted for a kind of theatre with a minimum of characters and props, thus *Carry on Bū'lām* involves only two protagonists, a push-cart and a few other accessories. Benaissa's theatre is different from the other two because he not only protests against wrongs in Algerian society but he also challenges a wide spectrum of values and received ideas and brings to the surface the malaise and anxiety of society through an approach based on ideology. The conclusions to be drawn are that the problems and the contradictions which exist in contemporary Algerian society are of an ideological nature and if there is progress to be made it is only by doing away with taboos, hypocrisy and conservatism and by assuming one's true national identity, history, and culture in order to move towards socialism. Here again irony and humour prevail.

It is no coincidence that these three plays – as samples of the three major trends in contemporary Algerian theatre – belong to the 'theatre of protest' genre. It is a long-standing tradition which goes back to the French occupation of Algeria in the nineteenth century when the *maddah* and the *haraquz* (Theatre of Shadows) changed the nature of their material to criticize, condemn or protest against the French occupation and the injustices it brought. It was a tradition that lasted until independence.

Throughout its history, Algerian theatre has already developed essentially through comedy which is a form which seems to be favoured by Algerian audiences. The first major play in Algerian Arabic was *Joha*, a comedy written by Allalou and produced in 1926. The comic folk hero still finds echo in contemporary Algerian theatre, mainly with Kateb Yacine who makes extensive use of the facetious. The traditional 'Joha' always plays tricks on notables or rulers and ridicules them. When confronted by the rulers or when in trouble he always finds a solution and comes out on top. Joha, like many other folk heroes in other cultures, is a means by which dominated people take revenge on the ruling class, a means to release their frustrations, and also a weapon of defence against those who exploit them. If the social function of humour, irony, satire and laughter is to ridicule, take revenge, demystify or release frustrations, as a shared experience, for instance, and also as a shared and hidden agreement as Bergson suggests, it seems that this is precisely the aim of the three playwrights in this study and indeed of most contemporary Algerian theatre.

Modern Algerian theatre developed through different stages. It started with improvised sketches by young enthusiasts who had no training in the art of the theatre. It then developed through the creation of full-length plays until the 1940s. Later, a new generation with more training took over and produced plays which were mainly adaptations of the world repertoire at the 'Opera d'Alger' from the mid 1940s until 1954 when the war of Independence started. During the armed struggle the FLN theatre group in exile was not very productive despite its best efforts. After independence in 1962 the 'Théâtre National Algérien, which was very active, produced a large number of plays (mainly political) from the world repertoire and very few national plays. In the 1960s and 1970s plays were produced through collective writing in the regional theatres, essentially through the amateur theatre. With the exception of Ould Abderrahmane Kaki who started his own experiments in Mostaganem much earlier, it was only during that period that experimental work took place in search of new forms. So far the performing arts which exist in the cultural heritage, particularly in the oral tradition, have been ignored while western theatrical forms have been used or adapted.

The three playwrights in this study have benefited a great deal from the previous experiences of Algerian theatre as a whole. They have, each in his own way, drawn extensively from the Algerian traditional cultural heritage to develop theatre forms which are original and highly successful as they also seem to suit public taste and identify with audience expectations. The art of the *maddah*, in particular, has been and still is being thoroughly studied and adapted to the requirements of the modern stage. The revival and development of some traditional performing arts and certain aspects of traditional culture such as folk tales and rhymed verse into new forms of theatre, has proved to be successful and viable not only in Algeria or North Africa but also in the Middle East where similar attempts are just as successful or even more so – for example, the Palestinian 'Hakawati' theatre group which seems to win more and more acclaim among European audiences.

Kateb Yacine apparently does not wish to modify his approach, whereas Slimane Benaissa and particularly Abdelkader Alloula still pursue research and experimentation. One major area where Kateb Yacine differs from the other two playwrights is language which, in his case, is not elaborate enough and rather limited for the ordinary Algerian or North African audiences. Benaissa and Alloula, on the other hand, use a language which corresponds to the changes and evolution of Algerian society. If, as Benaissa says, 'language acquires the standards of those who speak it'[11] then the language spoken nowadays by the average Algerian is certainly richer and of a higher standard than the language spoken ten or twenty years ago. The influence of French is still felt but people are more exposed to modern Arabic through the media, some public services and administration, and the environment itself – names of streets, different signs, posters. This takes place alongside the education system which operates in Arabic. Benaissa and Alloula have adapted their language to this change, which helps towards a better expression of ideas in their plays because, 'colloquial Arabic as we know it is unable to carry a discourse which aims at expressing the complexity of society as it exists. One must exploit language through all its registers.'[12]

This Alloula and Benaissa certainly do and their language is developing towards standard Arabic, the language beyond regional and colloquial boundaries and understood by all, thus making their plays accessible to Arab audiences outside North Africa. The forms developed by the three playwrights are well established and Alloula and Benaissa are still exploring new material from the cultural heritage.

NOTES

1 Youssef Rachid Haddad, *Art du Conteur, Art de l'Acteur* (Louvain: Cahiers Theatre Louvain, 1982).
2 Mahieddine Bachetarzi, *Memoires (1919–1939)* (Algiser: SNED, 1968), p. 60. The emphasis is the same in the original text.
3 *médersa* – transliteration of the Arabic *madrassa* (school).
4 Bachetarzi, *op. cit.*, p. 26.
5 *Ibid.*, p. 141.
6 *Ibid.*, p. 146.
7 *Ibid.*, p. 230.
8 *Ibid.*, p. 47.
9 Mohamed Aziza, *Regards sur le Théâtre Arabe Contemporain* (Tunis: Maison Tunisienne de l'Edition, 1970), p. 20.
10 Interview with Benaissa on 12 January, 1988.
11 *Ibid.*
12 *Ibid.*

11 The political role of Islam in Morocco (1970–90)

Henry Munson, Jun.

Morocco has a number of Islamic movements that demand the establishment of a truly Islamic society. We can classify these groups into
three types: traditionalistic, as represented by al-Fqih al-Zamzami;
moderate, as represented by Abd al-Slam Yasin; and radical, as
represented by Abd al-Karim Muṭiʿ. This a rather crude typology, but
useful none the less. My discussion of these movements, especially
the first two, will be based on my conversations with Islamic activists
and primarily with ʿ*ulamā*ʾ in the summers of 1987 and 1988 and on
a number of texts, both published and unpublished, to which I did not
have access when I wrote my earlier papers on this topic (see Munson
1986a, 1986c, 1988b).[1] I'd like to begin by focusing on Abd al-Slam
Yasin – the best-known of Morocco's 'fundamentalists'. This term is
somewhat misleading with respect to the most radical of Morocco's
Islamic activists, but it fits Yasin quite well.

ABD AL-SLAM YASIN AND THE MAINSTREAM ISLAMIC OPPOSITION

Yasin was born in about 1928 (Munson 1986a: 277). In the 'open
letter' he sent to the king in 1974 he spoke of himself as an Idrissi
sharīf of Berber peasant origin (Yasin 1974: 8–9). Yasin studied at
the traditional Islamic al-Yusifiya University in Marrakesh and
became a teacher of Arabic and then an inspector in the Ministry of
Education (Burgat 1988: 21).[2] He held the latter position at the time
of what he calls Morocco's 'spurious independence' in 1956 (*al-
Jamaʿa*, no. 2, 1979: 22, 24–5). He remained a devout Muslim in the
1950s, praying the five daily prayers and fasting during Ramadan
(Burgat 1988: 21). But his way of life was highly westernised. He sent
his children to French schools (interview Nadia Yasin, June 1987).
Then, in 1965, at the age of 38, he had what he calls a 'spiritual crisis'

which some people who knew him could not distinguish from a nervous breakdown (interview, June 1987; Yasin 1974: 5). Yasin told the French political scientist Francois Burgat: 'You have no doubt read biographies of Christians, Muslims or Buddhists who, at about the age of forty, experienced this spiritual awakening' (Burgat 1988: 21).

After reading a wide range of mystical texts, Yasin joined the Sufi brotherhood of the Butshishiyya, becoming a follower of Sheikh al-Hajj al-ʿAbbās (interview, 26 June 1987). Six years later, al-Hajj al-ʿAbbās died. After his death, Yasin was dismayed by the materialism that prevailed in the brotherhood, and he left it (Yasin 1974: 7). At about this same time (the early 1970s), Yasin read the writings of Hasan al-Banna, which transformed his zeal into more political directions (Burgat 1988: 22). He decided to write an 'open letter' to King Hassan II explaining to him what he had to do to purify Morocco.

Yasin's 'open letter' of 1974 was entitled *al-Islam aw al-Tūfān: risāla maftūḥa ila malik al-Maghrib* ('Islam or the Deluge: an open letter to the king of Morocco.') This text is 114 pages long, 114 also being the number of chapters in the Qurʿān. Yasin had it privately printed in Marrakesh and sent copies to many prominent Moroccans before having it sent to the king (interview, June 1987). Yasin's epistle does not contain any ideas that have not been expressed before by Hasan al-Banna or Sayyid Qutb. But its originality lies in the incredibly violent and patronizing language Yasin uses to address Morocco's king. He begins by saying: 'My letter to you is not like all letters for it is a letter that demands an answer ... ' (Yasin 1974: 1). And he repeatedly addresses the king as 'O my brother' (*ya akhī*) or 'O my beloved one' (*ya habībī*), terms not usually employed by Moroccan functionaries in addressing their sovereign (Yasin 1974: 11, 16–17). When I interviewed Yasin in June of 1987 he told me that he had stressed his descent from the Prophet Muhammad in his letter to the king so that the latter would regard him as a spiritual equal entitled to speak to him frankly. But there are hundreds of thousands, if not millions, of Moroccans who claim to be descendants of the Prophet. Most of these people do not generally address the Commander of the Faithful as 'my brother' or 'my beloved one'.

In *al-Islam aw al-Tūfān*, Yasin declares:

> Shall I tell the *umma* what everyone knows, namely that after the incident of Skhirat [the attempted coup of 1971] the king added a palace in France to his other palaces and sent to it his most valuable possessions and furniture so that he would be prepared in the event of an emergency? Or shall I inform the people that the king

has sold and is selling his properties and lands that cover an important part of Morocco?

(Yasin 1974: 11)

Yasin goes on to discuss a speech of the king's in which he said that he did not like to see beggars:

Islam gives him who spends the night hungry the right to bear arms against him who has deprived him of the bounty of God (*ḥara-mahu rizqahu*) ... Your palaces, your properties, and the opulent class in the land all explain the presence of beggary and misery.

(Yasin 1974: 12)

Yasin notes that after the king had informed his subjects of his senti-ments regarding mendicants, the police removed Morocco's beggars from the streets so that 'our Lord (*mawlānā*) would not be vexed by a painful sight' (Yasin 1974: 12). After elaborating further on the lamentable state of Morocco's economy, which he says is dominated by foreigners and 'Zionist wealth' (p. 12), Yasin assures His Majesty that 'the solution to all these problems can be summed up in one word: "*Islam*"' (p. 13).

When I interviewed him in June of 1987, I asked Yasin how he felt about the king's status as *Amir al-mu'minīn*, or 'Commander of the Faithful'. He chuckled and said, 'Well, he is the *amir* [i.e., the head of state], and his subjects are *mu'minīn*, or "believers"'. In other words, Yasin does not accept the idea that the king's role is sacrosanct.

In *al-Islam aw al-Tūfān*, Yasin contends that the king simply camouflaged his western 'liberal' ideas with Islam when he realized that it was politically expedient to do so (p. 14). Yasin tells Hassan II that his 'playing with Islam' has convinced young Moroccans that religion is indeed 'the opium of the people and mere trickery by means of which hypocritical rulers exploit the gullibility of the masses and enslave them' (p. 18).

You do not realize that you are the ally of communism in our country and that your senseless and deranged actions are manifest proof of the accuracy of what is claimed by the enemies of God! How will you face God you so and so? (*Bi ayyi wajhin talqa Allah yā hādha?*) Tell me how you if you are [truly] a believer! (*Qul lī bi ayyi wajhin in kunta mu'minan!*).

(Yasin 1974: 18)

Yasin then urges the king to repent and mend his ways and seek refuge with God (p. 18).

This epistle appears to have displeased Hassan II, who asked 'Abdallah Guennun, the head of the league of Moroccan *'ulamā'*, how he should respond to it (interview with Guennun 27 August 1987). When I interviewed Guennun in August of 1987, he claimed that he had suggested that Yasin be put in a psychiatric hospital. He said only a lunatic could attack the king as harshly as Yasin had. So Yasin spent the next three and a half years in a psychiatric hospital. He notes that 'they did to me what the Communists do in Russia' (interview, June 1987). But he may well have suggested this strategy to the king and Guennun in *al-Islam aw al-Tūfān*, when he acknowledged that some people had mistaken his spiritual crisis of 1965 for a nervous breakdown (Yasin 1974: 5).

Once released from the psychiatric hospital, Yasin resumed his campaign for a strictly Islamic polity in Morocco, but his language was now somewhat more circumspect – he no longer criticized the king directly. In 1979, he began publishing an Islamic review entitled *al-Jama'a*, 'the group,' of which no more than 3,000 copies were ever published (Tozy 1984: 394). The government had obstructed the publication of this review for at least a year before the first issue was published (*al-Jama'a* 2, 1979: 123). The fifth and tenth issues were banned and confiscated in 1980 and 1983 (*al-Jama'a* 11, 1983: 4). An eleventh and apparently final issue was clandestinely published in May of 1983 (Tozy 1984: 394). The government also informed Yasin that he could no longer preach in mosques (Tozy 1984: 394).

Then, in December of 1983, Yasin tried to publish another newspaper entitled *al-Subḥ* ('the Dawn') (*Le Monde*, 15 Feb. 1984; Tozy 1984: 383). But this was immediately banned, as was another newspaper Yasin tried to publish, and he was imprisoned just before the riots of January 1984 (Tozy 1984: 383; *Sou'āl*, no. 5, 1985: 152). Yasin says he remained in prison from December 1983 until January 1986 (interview, June 1987).

In the July 1982 issue of *al-Jama'a*, Yasin had dismissed Moroccan elections as a farce (*al-Jama'a* 10: 29). But in the last clandestine issue of 1983, he stressed that he wanted to establish an Islamic party to participate in these very elections (*al-Jama'a* 11: inside back cover). He also stressed this point in talking with me in June of 1987, but he said he doubted that the government would allow the creation of such a party.

Since 1986, Yasin has lived at his home in Salé, with policemen constantly watching the house and everyone who enters and leaves it (interview, June 1987). But despite this *de facto* 'house arrest', and despite the fact that he cannot preach in mosques or publish his writings in Morocco, Yasin remains active. He contends that most Saturday nights large numbers of 'Islamists' (*Islamiyyin*) gather in his home to discuss their plans and aspirations. When I was with him, two young teachers from the Rif arrived wearing *jillāba-s*. They listened to every word he spoke with the utmost reverence. Yasin had a larger group of visitors when he was interviewed by Burgat in October of 1987 (Burgat 1988: 114).

In person, Yasin exudes a spirituality as well as a gentleness that comes as quite a surprise to anyone familiar with the harshness of his published polemics. He has a straggly beard and twinkling eyes that suggest a grandfather rather than a religious fanatic. He was about 60 years old when I saw him in 1987 and was rather emaciated – perhaps as a result of the years in prison.

Speaking with Yasin is disconcerting in that at times he sounds quite rational and well-read whereas at others he seems hopelessly out of touch with reality. He has taught himself English, just as he taught himself French. He has read Vincent Crapanzano's book *Tuhami* and asked me, 'How could anyone publish such a book?' He criticises Khomeini for antagonizing the United States – not for the pragmatic reasons one might expect but because he predicts it will become a Muslim country – through conversions – within the next 200 years. When I expressed some doubt as to the plausibility of this prediction, he smiled in the manner of a wise old man listening to a child.

Yasin has two children who are active in his movement: a daughter named Nadia and a younger son. A third son is a student in France and 'writes occasionally'. Nadia, with whom I spoke in June of 1987, attended French schools and wore T-shirts and jeans until the early 1980s. She now wears an all-enveloping *jillāba*. She got a degree in law at Muhammad V University and is married to a young man, 'Abdallah, who is also active in the movement.

As for Yasin's social base of support, as I have shown elsewhere, it consists primarily of students and the educated young (Munson 1986a; Wahbi 1987: 1, 8, 24, 40). Yasin insists that the movement 'is spreading to the working class' (interview, June 1987). But I have not seen much evidence to support this contention. In the summer of 1987 I asked dozens of people in several popular quarters of Tangier if they had heard of Yasin. The only one who had was a university student whose father was a factory worker in Belgium. When Burgat interviewed Yasin in October of 1987 his other visitors included an unemployed doctor, two civil servants, a data processor, a bookseller, 'cousins from the country and the whole range of students'

(Burgat 1988: 114). As already mentioned, when I spoke with him two young teachers from the Rif came to visit him – both obviously disciples. The educated young remain Yasin's principal supporters. I have heard five *'ulamā'* criticize him, although three tempered their criticism by saying that his intentions were good. I do not know of any *'ulamā'* who openly support him.

AL-FQIH AL-ZAMZAMI

Yasin and his followers represent the mainstream of the politicised Islamic movement in Morocco. But there is another more 'traditional' and less overtly political wing represented by al-Fqih al-Zamzami of Tangier and his sons 'Abd al-Bari', Shu'ayb, and Ubayy. When I spoke with al-Zamzami at his home in 1987, he was a frail old man in his late seventies. With a wispy white beard and his white *jillāba*, he had a prophetic aura about him. Unlike Yasin, who writes in French as well as Arabic, al-Zamzami and his sons know only Arabic. The Fqih's son Ubayy told me that his father deliberately prevented his children from learning infidel languages to keep them pure (interview, 16 July 1987). This concern for purity may be why al-Zamzami only spoke with me briefly before asking his son Ubayy to answer my questions. His failing health may have been another factor.[3]

Whereas Yasin is largely unknown in the popular quarters of Tangier, virtually all the Muslims of the city have heard of al-Fqih al-Zamzami. Many, including 'Abdallah Guennun and other 'ulamā', regard him as an ignorant rabble-rouser (interview with 'Abdallah Guennun, Aug. 27, 1987). I recall being asked by one *'ālim*, 'Would *you* want to be governed by al-Zamzami?' But in popular quarters such as Dradib and Ayn al-Hayyani, both young and old generally speak of al-Zamzami with awe. One young jeweller told me that people thought of the Fqih 'as a prophet'. However, some high school and university students from these quarters speak contemptuously of al-Zamzami, as do Yasin and his more militant followers.

Yasin and his daughter Nadia both laughed when I mentioned al-Zamzami to them. Nadia suggested that he was actually a government agent. Yasin himself said that regardless of his intentions, al-Zamzami was in fact helping the government by focusing attention on matters of ritual and dress rather than on the need for a fundamental transformation of the economic, social, and political orders (interviews, June 1987). Al-Zamzami himself would not discuss Yasin with me, but his son Ubayy condemned him as a wild-eyed revolutionary (brief interview with al-Zamzami 16 July 1987; long interviews with

Ubayy bin al-Zamzami, 17 July 1987 and 4 June 1988). Although Ubayy praised the Iranian revolution for having shown 'the true face of Islam' he observed that, unlike Yasin, he and his father wanted to change people rather than overthrow the government (interview, 16 July 1987). One must of course always be sceptical of such statements when said to Americans. However, it is certainly true that al-Zamzami has never openly advocated revolution in his writings or in his taped lectures and sermons.

But al-Zamzami and his sons are by no means docile sycophants of the government. While denying that he and his father seek to overthrow the king, Ubayy does contend that monarchical government is contrary to Islam (interview with Ubayy bin al-Siddiq, 16 July 1987). Al-Zamzami does not go quite this far in his booklet *Mawqif al-Islam min al-aghniyā' wa'l-fuqarā'*, but he does say in this work that among the worst crimes of the Umayyads was the transformation of the caliphate into a hereditary monarchy (al-Zamzami 1979–80: 37). He also states that the *Imām*, that is, the king, 'is like other people, he is no better than anyone else' (p. 39). These are of course thoroughly conventional views in most of the Islamic world, but expressing them openly in Morocco is somewhat more delicate than in Algeria or Tunisia.

The second edition of al-Zamzami's *Mawqif al-Islam min al-aghniyā' wa'l-fuqarā'* was published in 1979–80 (1400 AH) by the Maṭābi' al-Bughaz of Tangier. This 91-page opus is apparently banned in Morocco, since I was given my copy in great secrecy by one of al-Zamzami's sons in 1987.

The book begins by stressing that Islam does not allow the rich to possess wealth beyond what they need to live on (al-Zamzami 1979–80: 9). To support his critique of the rich, al-Zamzami cites a *ḥadīth* that says that 'I saw hell and most of the people in it were women and the rich' (*ittal'at fī al-nār fa ra'at akthar ahlahā al-nisā' wa'-l-aghniyā'*) (p. 18). The fact that al-Zamzami would cite such a *ḥadīth* illustrates his traditionalism *vis-à-vis* someone like Yasin, who would certainly stress the spiritual equality of men and women in Islam. Al-Zamzami goes on to say that the rulers and the rich of the present age squander vast sums on worldly goods even though this is forbidden by Islam (pp. 20–1). By referring to 'the rulers and the rich of the present age' (*al-ḥukkām wa'l-aghniyā' fī hādha'l-waqt*), al-Zamzami avoids direct criticism of King Hassan II – although it is obvious that his words are in fact aimed primarily at the Moroccan monarch. He continues, describing 'the rulers and the rich' as follows:

We find that they squander more than even the kings and the rich of the infidels!!

And their goal is eminence, and the display of fake greatness and pageantry!

They oppress 'the weak' and devour the rights of the poor in order to live in luxury and to increase their enjoyment of the pleasures of the world ...

(al-Zamzami 1979–80: 21)

Like Yasin, al-Zamzami says that the exploitation of the poor by the rulers and the wealthy of the present serves to strengthen and legitimate Communist attempts to overthrow them (al-Zamzami 1979–80: 21).

Al-Zamzami contends that the *imām-s* and *mu'izzin-s* of Morocco's mosques are paupers living on the crumbs from the tables of the wealthy bureaucrats in the Ministry of *al-awqāf*, or religious endowments (p. 22). He says that one room in the house of a former Minister of al-awqaf was so big that one could barely see who was sitting at the opposite end (p. 23).

One of al-Zamzami's favourite themes is corruption:

The aid provided to the poor by 'foreign countries' does not reach them and they know of it neither much nor little. For those in charge (*al-ru'asa'*) take from it what they please. If anything remains – and it is only flour – they distribute it to the poor by way of the government employees, whose wages for this consist of 'the flour of national co-operation' (*ṭāḥīn al-ta'āwun al-waṭanī*)!

As for sugar, oil, butter, chocolate, cheese, and similar wholesome foodstuffs (*al-mawadd al-ghidhā'iyya al-nāfi'a*), they are among what is selected by those in charge for themselves!

(al-Zamzami 1979–80: 25–6).

Another example of al-Zamzami's ability to condemn corruption by means of concrete and comical anecdotes goes as follows:

It is said that a king gave the prime minister a thousand dinars and told him to spend it on the illumination of the capital on a certain night. The prime minister took half the money for himself and gave the rest to the mayor (*muḥāfidh*) of the capital. The mayor kept half of this and gave the rest to the head of the *muqaddim-s* in charge of the city's neighbourhoods. The head of the *muqaddim-s* kept all of this money for himself and told the inhabitants of the city that the king had ordered them to illuminate the capital on such and such a date.

On the designated night, the king observed the city and saw that it was indeed illuminated as he had ordered by means of the money he had given to the prime thief. [al-Zamzami writes *ra'īs al-ṣurrāq* instead of *ra'īs al-wuzarā'* – that is, literally, 'the leader of the thieves' instead of 'the leader of the ministers'.]

(al-Zamzani 1979–80: 26–7)

Al-Zamzami and his sons have repeatedly protested against specific policies of the Moroccan government, but they have never tried to overthrow it. In the 1980s, al-Zamzami protested the fact that women were being forced to show their hair when photographed for a national identity card (*biṭāqa waṭaniyya*). According to his son Ubayy, the Fqih wrote to the Minister of the Interior demanding that this practice be terminated, and it was – at least in the province of Tangier (interview, 17 July 1987).

Also in the 1980s, al-Zamzami's sons led a campaign against the way the poor were treated at al-Qurtubi and other hospitals in Tangier. Ubayy cites the case of a woman who had been badly burned in an accident. At the hospital she went to her burned arm became stuck to her torso and she suffered terrible pain. Al-Zamzami himself condemns corruption at al-Qurtubi Hospital in *Mawqif al-Islam min al-aghniyā' wa'l-fuqarā'* (pp. 28–9). Because of this criticism by al-Zamzami and his sons, Ubayy contends that the director of al-Qurtubi was dismissed (interview, Ubayy bin al-Siddiq, 4 June 1988).

The governor of the province of Tangier once sent a representative to al-Zamzami's house in the old city asking him to give a speech for the celebration of the anniversary of Muhammad V's famous speech of 9 April 1947, in which the king stressed Morocco's ties to the Arab and Islamic world while deleting the sentence praising France that had been included in the text distributed to the press. Al-Zamzami refused. On another occasion, the governor invited al-Zamzami to have dinner with him and some other guests. Al-Zamzami refused. According to his son Ubayy, the Fqih 'does not eat the food of bureaucrats because it is derived from the sweat of the people' (interview, Ubayy bin al-Siddiq, 16 July 1987). Such acts are about as close as al-Zamzami has come to open defiance of the Moroccan government.

Al-Fqih al-Zamzami is a folk hero in Tangier but his influence is by no means restricted to this city. His books are distributed in all the cities of north-western Morocco (al-Zamzami 1979–80: 5). Cassette tapes of his sermons and lectures are sold in most Moroccan cities, including Casablanca (Tozy 1984: 296–7). Moreover, according to his son Ubayy, the Fqih travels throughout Morocco listening to the grievances of the poor and attempting to help them by speaking with government officials and landlords (interview, 4 June 1988). Ubayy contends that al-Zamzami attracts reverential crowds all over the country.

The most influential of al-Zamzami's sons is ʿAbd al-Bāriʿ bin al-Siddiq, who used to preach in the mosque of the popular quarter of Hasnuna in Tangier (interview, Ubayy bin al-Siddiq, 16 July 1987). In 1983, which Ubayy referred to as 'the year that Dlimi died' (a reference to the death of a famous Moroccan general), ʿAbd al-Bāriʿ delivered a sermon which provoked the local authorities to arrest him. The day after the sermon, policemen surrounded the al-Zamzami home in Tangier's old city. ʿAbd al-Bāriʿ was detained and spent, according to his brother Ubayy, one month blindfolded in a house in Casablanca. Soon after his release, ʿAbd al-Bāriʿ began preaching in Casablanca, where he has gained quite a following (Tozy 1984: 296, 300–2; al-Muwadawwir and al-ʿUthmānī 1987: 14–20). ʿAbd al-Bāriʿ now avoids direct criticism of the government.

Although al-Zamzami publishes his books under the name of 'Muhammad al-Zamzami', his family name is actually bin al-Siddiq. The bin al-Siddiq family has headed the principal *zāwiya* of the Darqawi Sufi order in Tangier since the beginning of the twentieth century.[4] Al-Zamzami was born in the home of the *muqaddim* of the *zāwiya* of the Darqawi Sufi order in Port Saʿid in 1911–12 (1330 AH) when his father Sidi Muhammad bin al-Siddiq was on his way to Mecca for the pilgrimage (interview, Sidi Ibrahim bin al-Siddiq, 25 August 1987). The Fqih and his seven brothers were all active in the Darqawi order when they grew up. Al-Zamzami himself preached in the Siddiqiyya *zāwiya* of the Darqawi order in the 1950s. In sermons he gave on 17 July and 24 July 1953, he denounced the Moroccan nationalists for protesting the deposition of Muhammad V (Rézette 1955: 26, al-Wazzani 1984: 342).

But al-Zamzami became disenchanted with the Darqawa and the Islamic mystical tradition. By the 1960s, he was openly condemning Sufism as a perversion of Islam – despite the fact that he continued to preach in the Sidiqqiyya *zāwiya* of Tangier until 1971–2 (1391 AH). Ubayy bin al-Siddiq contends that his father's transformation occurred from 1950 through 1956. (He only uses Islamic dates.) For over a decade, then, al-Zamzami condemned Sufism from the pulpit of a Sufi lodge – despite his brothers' strenuous efforts to remove him. The hostility between al-Zamzami and his brothers continues to this day. Although they all live in Tangier, al-Zamzami and his sons have severed all contact with the other members of the bin al-Siddiq family. They do not even attend their weddings or funerals. Al-Zamzami's son, Ubayy, attributes this to his father's view that his brothers are not true Muslims. Resentment of their campaign to oust him from the Siddiqiyya *zawiya* would appear to have something to do with it as well.

When al-Zamzami was finally forced out of the *zawiya* in 1971–2 (1391 A.H.), he began to preach to about fifty followers in his home. His *Sunni* movement, as it is generally referred to by his sons and by the residents of Tangier's popular quarters, was, in the words of Ubayy bin al-Siddiq, 'completely isolated from society'. But during the course of the 1970s, al-Zamzami's followers raised enough money to build a new mosque in the Hasnuna quarter. By the late 1970s, the Fqih's sermons at this new mosque were attracting huge crowds, and cassette tapes of these sermons were being sold in all of Morocco's cities.

Al-Zamzami and his *Sunni* movement do not appeal to the same audience as Yasin and his *Islami* movement. Al-Zamzami is venerated by pedlars, labourers, shopkeepers, and many blue-collar Moroccan workers who are employed in Europe and only return to Tangier for their summer vacations – until they retire. I have spoken with roughly a dozen such people, none of whom had heard of Yasin and all of whom stressed that al-Zamzami was simply trying to purify Moroccan society rather than overthrow the government. (I knew some of these people quite well and had heard them condemn the government in terms that could get them into a lot of trouble. So I don't think they were misrepresenting their perceptions of al-Zamzami.) Yasin's followers are more educated as well as more radical.

ABD AL-KARIM AL-MUTI' AND THE SHABIBA AL-ISLAMIYYA

Much as Yasin dismisses al-Zamzami as a simpleton who either intentionally or unintentionally helps the government, there is a more radical wing of Morocco's Islamic movement that condemns Yasin for his lack of revolutionary zeal. This is *al-Shabiba al-Islamiyya*, or 'The Islamic Youth'. This organization was founded in the early 1970s by 'Abd al-Karim Muṭi', who like Yasin was an inspector in the Ministry of Education (Tozy 1984: 346).[5] Al-Zamzami's son Ubayy sees no difference between Yasin and Muṭi'. (interview, July

16, 1987). But Yasin, while stressing that he feels no hostility toward Muṭīʿ, does note that the latter's methods differ from his own (interview, Yasin, 26 June 1987).

The following passage from an editorial in the first issue of al-Shabiba's review *al-Mujāhid* in 1981 illustrates its radical rhetoric:

> Our present and our future are caught between the hammer of American imperialism and the anvil of its agents represented by the corrupt monarchical regime and those who support it ...
>
> Your review appears in these circumstances to be, God willing, in the vanguard of an authentic Islamic revolution in Morocco; a revolution that enlightens the horizons of this country and liberates its people to bring them back to the Islam of Muhammad and those of his people who have known how to follow him – not the Islam of the merchants of oil and the agents of the Americans.
>
> (Dhaouadi and Ibrahim 1982: 57–8)

Abd al-Karim Muṭīʿ, who has remained the dominant figure in al-Shabiba since its founding, was at one time active in Morocco's teachers' union and in the socialist party, the Union Socialiste des Forces Populaires (Leveau 1983: 212). He is reported to have undergone his transformation into an Islamic activist while on pilgrimage to Mecca in the late 1960s when he was in his thirties (Munson 1988b: 133). Under his leadership, *al-Shabiba al-Islamiyya* began to attract supporters in Morocco's high schools and universities in the early 1970s and clashes with students of a secular leftist orientation were common (Munson 1988b: 134).

On 18 December '1975, ʿUmar Ben Jelloun, editor of the socialist party's newspaper *al-Muharrir* and one of the most prominent of Morocco's Marxist intellectuals was assassinated (*Souʾāl,* no. 5, 1985: 160). The government claimed that the murderers were members of *al-Shabiba al-Islamiyya*. But this is denied by Muṭīʿ himself, who claims that the government planned the murder to get rid of both Ben Jelloun and him at the same time (Burgat 1988: 189–90). Muṭīʿ left Morocco three days after Ben Jelloun's murder, to attend a conference in Cordoba according to some accounts, and he has not been back since (*Souʾāl,* no. 5, 1985: 161–2). There are rumours that he was involved in the seizure of the Great Mosque of Mecca in 1979 (Tozy 1984: 348; Burgat 1988: 141), and he is said to have visited Iran after the Islamic Revolution (Burgat 1988: 49). Some people say Muṭīʾ was in Libya for a while. Perhaps he is now in France, where *al-Shabiba*'s review *al-Mujāhid* is edited, or in Belgium, where it is printed (Burgat 1988: 107).

But wherever he has been since 1975, Muṭīʾ has tried to retain a high degree of control over *al-Shabiba*. Resentment of his authoritarian leadership was one of the causes of the fragmentation of *al-Shabiba* into a number of mutually antagonistic groups in the late 1970s and early 1980s (see *al-Jamaʿa*, no. 5, February–March 1980: 105–15 and no. 6, April–July 1980: 92–4; Burgat 1988: 194; Munson 1988b: 135). One rebellious faction of *al-Shabiba* rejected Muṭīʿ's advocacy of Muṭīʿʾs with regard to the use of force against 'those members of the community who have been led astray' (Tozy 1984: 351).

Other factors that have contributed to the fragmentation and decreasing influence of *al-Shabiba al-Islamiyya* have been repression and co-optation by the Moroccan government. In 1984, seventy-one members of *al-Shabiba* received sentences ranging from four years' imprisonment to death (Munson 1988b: 135). Even before this, a number of activists in the organization had decided that it was too dangerous to challenge the current regime. So some of them left *al-Shabiba* and established groups and publications that continued to advocate a strictly Islamic polity, but refrained from any direct criticism of the government (interview with Yasin, 16 June 1987). The magazine *al-Furqān* and the newspaper *al-Islah* are both published by such former militants (Burgat 1988: 108). Al-Zamzami's son ʿAbd al-Bāriʿ has close ties with some of these people, who, as Yasin observes rather sardonically, now serve the king's purposes (interview with Yasin, June 1987; al-Muwadawwir and al-ʿUthmānī 1987).

Al-Shabiba al-Islamiyya and its still militant offshoots remain significant in Morocco's high schools and universities. But even here, these groups do not have mass support.

CONCLUSION

The movements represented by al-Zamzami, Yasin, and Muṭīʿ, all challenge, in their very different ways, the present regime of King Hassan II.[6] But they have been unable to do so with much success. This inability is partially due the king's Islamic legitimacy as *Imām*, as *Amir al-muʾminīn*, and as a descendant of the Prophet Muhammad (Munson 1986b). I have heard an illiterate old woman telling a group of her relatives in Tangier that the king survived the coup attempts of the early 1970s because of his *baraka*, or 'sacredness'.

However, the argument that Morocco's Islamic opposition is weak because of the popular belief in the king's sanctity is not the whole story. The fact is that the 'fundamentalist' movements of the Sunni Islamic world have all been quite weak when compared with the Shī'ī movement that overthrew the Shah in Iran. Admittedly, the fundamentalist movements of Egypt and Tunisia appear to be stronger than those of Morocco but it is precisely the most moderate and least revolutionary elements of these movements that have attracted the most support in both of these countries (Burgat 1988; Munson 1988a: 77–83). A Sunni Islamic revolution does not appear imminent anywhere despite the major impact the 'fundamentalists' have had on public discourse.

A major reason for the relative weakness of Sunni 'fundamentalists' generally is that their ideologised version of Islam differs quite radically from the more strictly religious ways in which most Muslims understand their religion. Khomeini and the Shī'ī *'ulamā'* of Iran were able to overcome this problem, which they too faced, in part because of the tremendous authority of the Shī'ī *'ulamā'* even in every popular version of Shī'ism (see Munson 1988a). In the Sunni world, the *'ulamā'* lack this authority and do not have much impact on popular belief. Moreover, as has often been noted, *'ulamā'* have rarely led the Islamic movements of the twentieth-century Sunni world. In Morocco, as in most predominantly Sunni countries, the *'ulamā'* have generally shied away from challenging the reigning regime. And the middle-class intellectuals (using the word loosely) who have generally led the radical or revolutionary Sunni 'fundamentalist' movements have had a hard time mobilising large numbers of supporters outside the ranks of students and the educated middle class.

It is true that a man like al-Fqih al-Zamzami is closer to popular belief than are the more radical Islamic activists.[7] But al-Zamzami and his sons have never tried to mount a revolution. If they and their followers were to join forces with Yasin and Muṭī' and their more educated supporters in a serious attempt to overthrow the Moroccan government, they might well pose a serious threat to King Hassan II. But it is hard to imagine such a coalition taking place. And, for the time being at any rate, the king has effectively muzzled those who seek to overthrow him in the name of Islam.

NOTES

1   My research in Morocco in 1987 and 1988 was made possible by grants from the Social Science Research Council and the University of Maine's

Summer Faculty Research programme. I am grateful to Jean-François Clément, David Hart, and George Joffé for helping me to obtain some important texts. I thank Mohamed Tozy for sending me a copy of his dissertation. And I thank all those who allowed me to interview them in the summers of 1987 and 1988.

2 For a good discussion of the Yusufiya educational system, see Eickelman 1985.

3 Unlike Yasin, al-Zamzami sometimes praises non-Muslims in his writings. In *Mawqif al-Islam min al-aghniyā' wa'l-fuqarā'*, he says that prisons were much cleaner under French and Spanish rule than they are in independent Morocco – because of the corruption of the officials in charge of them (al-Zamzami 1979–80: 29–30). Al-Zamzami's son, Ubayy, told me that the Nahons, a Jewish family that used to own al-Zamzami's house in Tangier's old city, were 'a respected family' (*'ā'ila muḥtarama*) and were *al-shurfa diyalum* – that is, the Jewish equivalent of the partilineal descendants of the Prophet Muhammad among the Muslims.

4 I was able to gather considerable information about the Siddiqiyaa *zāwiya* from interviews with Sidi Ibraham bin al-Siddiq, Sidi'Abd al-'Aziz bin al-Siddiq (both brothers of al-Fqih al-Zamzami), 'Abdallah Guennun, and Mustafa 'Uthman in the summer of 1987. Further information was obtained from Ubayy bin al-Siddiq in the summers of 1987 and 1988. See also Michaux-Bellaire 1920.

5 Tozy contends that *al-Shabiba al-Islamiyya* was founded in 1972 (Tozy 1984: 346). An unsigned article in *Sou'āl*, no. 5, 1985, p. 162, gives a date of 1973. François Burgat says 1970 (Burgat 1988: 187).

6 For discussions of the various explanations that have been profferred to account for the emergence of these groups, see Clement 1980 and Munson 1988a.

7 See al-Hajj Muhammad, the peddlar's narrative in Munson 1984.

REFERENCES

Burgat, François (1988) *L'islamisme au Maghreb: La voix du Sud,* Paris: Editions Karthala.

Clément, Jean-François (1980) 'Pour une compréhension des mouvements islamistes', *Esprit,* no. 37 (January), 38–51.

Dhaouadi, Zouhaier and Amr Ibrahim (1982) 'Documents, Maroc', *Peuples méditerranéens,* no. 21 (October–December), 57–60.

Eickelman, Dale (1985) *Knowledge and Power in Morocco: The Education of a Twentieth-Century Notable,* Princeton: Princeton University Press.

Leveau, Rémy (1983) 'Réaction de l'Islam officiel au renouveau islamique au Maroc', in Christiane Souriau (ed.), *Le Maghreb musulman en 1979,* Paris: Editions du Centre National de la Recherche Scientifique, pp. 205–19.

Michaux-Bellaire, Edouard (1920) 'Les Derqaoua de Tanger', *Revue du Monde musulman* 39, 98–118.

al-Muwadawwir, Rashīd and Sa'ad al-Din al-'Uthmānī (1987) 'Al-ustādh

ʿAbd al-Bāriʾ bin al-Siddīq fi ḥiwār ḥawla al-ʿamal al-islāmī', *Al-Furqān* 3 (9), 14–20.

Munson, Henry, Jun. (1984) *The House of Si Abd Allah: The Oral History of a Moroccan Family*, New Haven: Yale University Press.

—— (1986a) 'The social base of Islamic militancy in Morocco', *The Middle East Journal* 40, 267–84.

—— (1986b) 'Geertz on religion: the theory and the practice', *Religion* 14, 19–32.

—— (1986c) 'Islamic revivalism in Morocco and Tunisia', *Muslim world* 76, 203–18.

—— (1988a) *Islam and Revolution in the Middle East*, New Haven: Yale University Press.

—— (1988b) 'Morocco', in Shireen T. Hunter (ed.), *The Politics of Islamic Revivalism*, Bloomington: Indiana University Press, pp. 133–47.

Rézette, Robert (1955) *Les Partis politiques marocains* (2nd edn), Paris: Librairie Armand Colin, Cahiers de la Fondation nationale des sciences politiques, partis et elections, no. 70.

Tozy, Mohamed (1984) 'Champ et contre champ politico-religieux au Maroc', Thèse pour le doctorat en science politique, Faculte de Droit et de Science politique d'Aix-Marseille.

Wahbi, Muhammad (1987) *Al-Uṣūl al-ijtimāʿiyya lil-ḥarakāt al-islāmawiyya: namūdhaj al-ṭalaba*, Baḥth li-nail al-ijāzā fī shi ʿbat al-falsafa takhassus ʿilm al-ijtimāʿ, Kulliyyat al-Adab waʾl-ʿUlūm al-insāniyya, Jāmi ʿat Sīdī Muḥammad bin ʿAbd Allah, Fas.

al-Wazzānī, Muhammad Hasan (1984) 'Mudhakkirat ḥayātī wa jihādī: Al-tārīkh al-siyāsī lil-ḥaraka al-waṭaniyya al-tahrīriyya al-maghribiyya', vol. 3, *Marḥalat al-inṭilāq waʾl-kifāh, 1930–1934*, Beirut: Muʾassasa Jawād lil-Tabʾa waʾl-taṣwīr for Muʾassasat Muḥammad Hasan al-Wazzānī.

Yasin, ʿAbd al-Slam (1974) *Al-Islām aw al-ṭūfān: risāla maftūḥa ila malik al-Maghrib*, Marrakesh: privately printed.

al-Zamzāmī [bin al-Siddīq], Muḥammad (1979–80) *Mawqif al-Islām min al-aghniyāʾ waʾl-fuqarāʾ* (2nd edn), Tangier: Naṭbaʿat al-Bughāz. (The date of publication is given only as 1400 AH, which corresponds to 1979–80.)

12 Libya and Morocco

Consensus on the past

Richard Pennell

INTRODUCTION

On and off for a very long time now, people have been predicting the imminent fall of both Colonel Qadhdhāfī and Hassan II. It does not seem to have happened yet. That is not to say that it will not, of course, but the longevity of these two regimes – which at first sight appear to be almost as different as it is possible to be and stay in the same political galaxy – needs explanation. This chapter will concentrate on only one aspect of the regimes' survival and only a very partial explanation. The explanation to be proposed is not in any way the whole story, or even a majority of it: it is *one* aspect and no more. There are numerous other considerations: economic questions, questions of the way in which political power is shared out between the elites of the political, civil and military wings of the regimes and the efficacy in both countries of the security services, for example.

The subject here, however, is an intriguing aspect of both countries' political life. Stated in outline it is this: that the 'ruling ethic' of both countries is based upon patterns of political thought which can have a wide degree of acceptance because they reflect patterns of political behaviour and understanding which are deeply rooted in the cultural life of both countries, and which predate the colonial regimes. In both cases, pre-colonial patterns and methods of political thought provide some sort of norms against which post-colonial political structures are formed and debated (the element open to debate is also important). Despite the opposition of both 'governments', there is a potential for common ground which both government and opposition can share.

THE LIBYAN CASE

The Libyan case is in many ways the simpler and aspects of it have been discussed in some detail in a book by John Davis.[1] The title of the book, *Libyan Politics, Tribe and Revolution, an account of the Zuwaya and their Government*, is both clear and confusing. Davis is writing about one area in Cyrenaica – although it is a very big one – and this does not represent the whole of the Libyan political system – yet he calls it *Libyan Politics*. He also refers to 'the Zuwaya and their government' – and the confusion between the different uses of the word 'government' is well known. The ambiguity is deliberate – the book is about both the Zuwaya's relationship with state authority and the way in which they govern themselves. However, Colonel Qadh-dhāfī claims there is no state in Libya, and that it is the 'people' who are the 'governor'. So in theory – or Third World Theory at least – the ambiguity does not exist. The 'statelessness' of Libya has been described and explained more than once – notably by Lisa Anderson, and she definitely *is* talking about Libya as a whole, rather than a single part of it.[2] Interestingly, Lisa Anderson also suggests that there is a historical continuity in the political organisation of Tunisia from pre-colonial to Bourguibist times.

In brief, the origins of Libyan 'statelessness' are to be found in the way in which Libya developed in the nineteenth and twentieth centuries. Ottoman rule on Libya was reimposed after 1835 after a long period when the authorities in Tripoli had been acting practically independently of Istanbul. During the period of independence the tribes of the interior, who made up the bulk of an extremely small population, were not really controlled directly from Tripoli, but worked with, or rejected, the authorities there on the basis of their perceived interests – one aspect of which was the extent to which Tripoli could bring force to bear. The Ottomans behaved in very much the same way, 'modernising' Tripoli and the coastal strip around it and around Benghazi (and a few other towns), but other-wise leaving local control in the hands of local leaders whom it co-opted to some extent, or in the hands of the Sanusiyya order, which was organised on a tribal basis and had considerable influence in Cyrenaica. In 1911, 'Libya' was occupied by the Italians, or at least parts of it were. It took twenty-odd years before the occupation was finally completed. Opposition came from a number of sources – tribal/Sanusi in the case of ʿUmar al-Mukhtar, from local leaders in Tripoli who formed a brief Tripoli republic which collapsed, at least partly because of personal rivalries between its leaders. Thus the initial resistance, like in the other Maghribi countries, was not organised nationally. The Italian occupation carried the process further – not only did it prevent the emergence of any formal Libyan nationalism, by removing the local leadership from any effective power at all and by maintaining education of extraordinarily low levels, but it disrupted all political patterns and networks. The Sanusiyya was deprived of its property, no local responsibility for political matters was permitted and in Anderson's words 'The traditional patrons and brokers for the Libyan people were long gone, and the acephalous equality of kinship was the only organisational structure still available.'[3] As a result the tribes became more important.

The process by which Libya became independent increased the tendency still further. Independence was achieved not because of the demand of a nationalist movement, but because it was the most convenient solution to the problems of the big powers and their rivalries after the Second World War. Leadership over a 'federal' state was given to the Sanusi family, but it was federal because that was the only way in which Tripoli and Fezzan in the southern region would accept the integration.

The subsequent royal regime did not do much to further the creation of a nation-state in Tripoli. It was very corrupt, too poor for much of the time to integrate large numbers of people, and then suddenly very rich. This has the effect, as Davis has pointed out, of allowing the government to act independently of the people since it did not rely on them for supply of wealth in the form of taxes. Finally, during this latter stage as opposition did build up, one of the currents of thought which attracted that opposition came from Nasserism – the idea of an Arab identity which overarched the Libyan identity. This was the strain of the people who made the coup of 1 September 1969 which brought Qadhdhāfī to power: his nationalism is an Arab one in which Libya would participate as a part of a fused Arab state – hence his unity plans ever since he came to power. So Libya is subsumed as a national identity into a wider Arab identity.

At the same time 'government' was to be placed in the hands of the people. This is not an easy thing to achieve, and Qadhdhāfī has shifted around trying to find workable ways of doing it. The way he has finally adopted is, in essence, that of delegatory democracy rather than representational democracy. Decisions are taken by 'the people' at local levels, who then mandate their affairs. I do not propose to enter into the question of the differences between delegation and representation in this system, because despite the apparent simplicity of the Libyan system it does not work in a very elegant way at all.

However, it did respond to some sort of perception about the way in which people wanted to live. That is not to say that Libyans as a whole had a coherent 'world view' or even as individuals that they had one. But there were a series of images which have continued to operate about the way in which the system should be run. Davis's Zuwaya talked about the concept of 'statelessness' of lack of government. In the past, the image was one of a society consisting of people who refused to submit to government, who refused to recognise that 'the law is embodied in a person or office'[4] and who took steps to make sure that their 'freedom' from government was maintained: either by fighting it or by moving further away from it into the desert; away from the Turks or from the Italians. They lived off their trade across the Sahara which crossed their territory, and by taxing others who passed through: this money was the collective property of the group as a whole and was distributed among themselves. Justice and peace were secured not by authority from outside but by mediation and by collective agreements to end fighting, or by collective balancing of forces.

Now things were never quite as pure as the image suggested: people *did* serve both the Turks and the Sanusis, and there were people who were more powerful in Zuwaya society: society was hierarchically ordered in families but outside them authority was based upon the idea of personal influence and personal respect.

Qadhdhāfī himself announced that the state was abolished, and his vision of society incorporates – or at least resembles – some of the elements of the tribal view of the past. He puts the family at the centre, and his view of the national (which? Arab or Libyan is not made entirely clear) is based upon descent. On the other hand, there are distinct differences – in practice (the theory does not mention it) the army does not allow most officers to serve in their home areas. But the concepts of political organisation outlined by Qadhdhāfī are based upon segmentary lines.

THE MOROCCAN CASE

The aspect of Moroccan political concepts that I want to deal with is concerned with the basis on which Moroccan political power is defined. This concerns the fundamental question of the *bay'a* and the concept of *siba* and *makhzan*. Both these concepts pre-date colonialism.

One of the extraordinary things about modern Moroccan political writing is its starting point. It is not independence, or even colonialism, but the direct relevance of much older practice and theory

A biography of Mohammad V published in 1980 begins with the Saʿdi dynasty in the sixteenth century, and the role played by the Sultan at the time.[5] A long treatise on the political history of Morocco goes back to the conceptions of politics at the time of the Prophet Muhammad, before examining the typically Moroccan political experience which dates to the Almohads.[6] The Moroccan arguments in the United Nations over the Moroccan claims to Mauritania in 1960 and to the Western Sahara since 1974/5 begin with the Almoravids, not as a general basis for comparison, but as a particular part of the argument. A work on the pre-colonial political system published at the time of independence and clearly referring to what sort of independent Morocco its author wanted, begins with al-Mawardi and again emphasises a peculiar Moroccan political tradition dating back to the Khajirites.[7] Everyone, therefore agrees that the past is immediately relevant as a focus for political debate.

The BayʿA

The nature of the *bayʿa* is one area of discussion. This refers to how, in pre-colonial Morocco, groups expressed their allegiance to the Sultan. There are two views as to what this *bayʿa* represented. For some it was a contract, we will obey you if you rule us justly and properly, and if not, not. For others – particularly supporters of the present king – it is a ritual act of allegiance:

> The modern practice of *bayʿa* in Morocco refers to a two-way acceptance of allegiance. It is ritual of submission which is celebrated annually, and a solemn act, which states and recognises the legitimacy of the Sultan (which exists quite apart from the *bayʿa*), and marks the adhesion to a new authority.[8]

Clearly, these two views are very different. But they represent two currents in Moroccan political thinking which greatly pre-date colonialism. If one examines the period of the Saʿdi sultans in the sixteenth and early seventeenth centuries one finds a repeated argument between those *ʿulamā* on the one hand who believed that there were certain functions the Sultan had to carry out if his rule was not to become invalid, and therefore liable to be overturned – not so much a legitimation of rebellion as a making of rebellion mandatory in certain circumstance – and the argument of some of the sultans and those *ʿulamā* who supported their view that there was an absolute right of rule which could not legitimately be challenged however the

Sultan behaved, and that all rebellion was rebellion against God.

The argument continued under the ʿAlawīs and came to a climax in 1908 with the removal of ʿAbd al-Aziz from the throne and his replacement by his brother ʿAbd al-Hafiz. This was accompanied by a declaration by the *qadi* of Fez that in the opinion of the *ʿulamāʾ*, 'This man [ʿAbd al-Aziz] must be deposed right away' and a new *bayʿa* given to his brother, which specified certain acts which he was expected to carry out in order for the *bayʿa* to be valid.[9] That was, so to speak, the triumph of the 'constitutionalist' cause. The attempt which was then made by some more radical Moroccans to set up a constitution was aborted.[10]

The concept of Protectorate

The attempt to reform the pre-colonial system failed, but the protectorate which followed came into being to preserve the Sultanate and at the same time to modernise it. What in fact had happened was that Morocco was economically modernised – mainly for the benefit of France – while the Sultanate was isolated from real influence, a 'decorative appendage of a modern and for the most part a non-Moroccan administration' as John Waterbury neatly puts it.[11] There was a paradoxical result of French rule. On the one hand, 'Morocco is unique in that so much of the traditional governmental and political system survived the half-century of direct French rule relatively intact.'[12] On the other hand 'The stimulative effect of France's material contribution to Morocco can hardly be overestimated ... [France] taught the Moroccan to appreciate effective government, sober justice, secular education and an expanding economy.'[13] King Hassan would agree with that. As he wrote in his autobiography:

> Those who assert that in the years between 1910 and 1935, France turned Morocco into an underdeveloped country know perfectly well that they are lying.[14]

But he also complained that Moroccan political traditions were traduced:

> When some historians talk of the 'absolute power of the Sultan' in the time of the Protectorate, they mean 'the absolute power of the Resident-General'.

There was no protectorate, according to him, only the maintenance of the formal framework of *makhzan* supremacy.[15]

One of the forms which the French did maintain was the *bayʿa*.

They tried to make it into a simple affirmation of loyalty. When Muhammad V was imposed as Sultan by the French in 1927, the *ʿulamāʾ* and notables in Fez gave him the *bayʿa* without making any real difficulties, although some of the *ʿulamāʾ* complained that they would have liked to have *seen* the new Sultan at least once before they signed. They were ignored.[16] In fact, when it came to the crunch, and the French needed to provide for the legitimacy of Ben Arafa, the *bayʿa* mechanism did not work[17] – it was empty of content.

Thus far, the royal point of view and the nationalist point of view would coincide: that real power was in the hands not of the Moroccans but of the French, that the protectorate was a sham, that the colonial regime was highly centralised and had a monopoly of force which no previous ruler of Morocco had possessed. On the other hand, the nationalists did not simply reject everything French. When they protested about the Berber Dahir it was on the grounds that it contravened the Protectorate treaty. In 1934, the Comité d'Action Marocaine, the main nationalist group in the French zone at the time put forward a 'reform plan' in which it demanded that the French should carry out the terms of the Treaty of Fez by abandoning direct rule and affirming the sovereignty of the Sultan, while at the same time bringing about democratic political reforms (separation of powers, an assembly, Moroccan participation in power).[18] For them, the Sultanate and a democratic system were inseparable.

So, while there was a lot of common ground, as well as practical political advantage to be had from an alliance between the monarchy and the nationalists, the nationalist cause contained the germs of an idea of constitutional monarchy.

The struggle for Morocco after independence

The protectorate period has been pictured as a historical parenthesis in Moroccan constitutional development. Agnouche comments that:

> This parenthesis supposes, therefore, the continuity of the same essence of power, that is to say of an absolute monarchy ... The unanimity of the nationalist elites was no more than a matter of circumstance. Once independence had been achieved, the contradictions which had been sublimated resurfaced openly.[19]

In fact the King was able to scoop the spoils of independence for himself. The leaders of the Istiqlal Party 'failed to realise ... that in successively building the image of the sultan as the most prominent symbol of independence, they were, at the same time, giving him the ability to act autonomously'.[20] Once independence came, it was soon clear who was to be in control. It would not be the modern nationalists, except as part of an elite which had been incorporated into the system, but the king, who exercised a monopoly of force which had not existed before the protectorate.

The point was made on the first occasion that Muhammad V reviewed the army which gave him that monopoly of force. In May 1956 he told his new army that the king was 'the trustee of Moroccan sovereignty'. In later speeches he insisted that there should be no wholesale importation of European institutions:

> In order to give the country solid and healthy institutions ... [we must] avoid any hurry or improvisation. The real danger is not that we do not have representative institutions, the real danger lies in setting up a purely formal parliamentary regime, which will become a factor of disorder and destruction, while a real democracy should be a factor for stability and construction.[21]

It would therefore be the King who decided what was authentic and what was not, and he would lay down the rules of the political life. This worried a great many of the Moroccan nationalists, and at the time of independence Mohammed Lahbabi wrote a book on precolonial government which expressed precisely this worry. Lahbabi opens his book with a clear enough hint of what he is about:

> In 1956 Morocco regained its sovereignty and independence. It now has, after a long interruption, a truly Moroccan government which exercises power. It is proper to ask by what means Morocco has regained its independence, since the Protectorate had as its official aim to introduce the Moroccan state to a modern government and modern institutions. This aim was to be attained by the reform of the old Moroccan government, a reform which would result in making it more effective. The history of these past fifty years, while rich in both plans for reforms and their completion, has not ended in the modernisation of the Moroccan government. Quite the reverse, these reforms have served to eradicate the national government and effectively replace it with the government of a foreign state.
>
> Thus the reforms of the Protectorate had a result quite the opposite of the official aims. They have served, in reality, as a screen for the liquidation of Moroccan institutions, a screen which has been convenient both because of its effectiveness and because of its hidden nature.[22]

The first part of Lahbabi's book is concerned to show that the institution of what he sees as an absolute monarchy is an introduction of French colonialism, that this is the result of the betrayal of the official objectives of the Protectorate, and that in order for Morocco to be truly independent – and truly Moroccan – the organisation of the state must be returned to its original bases. In essence this means that the position of the Sultan as the executive power must be recognised, while sovereignty resides in the community. Concealed, not very much, in all this was an appeal for a form of constitutional monarchy, in which sovereignty would once again reside with the people.

In the first few pages Lahbabi establishes a number of things: first, that the Caliphate was limited in its powers to carrying out a specific function, that a Caliph had to fulfil certain conditions – of which membership of the Prophet's family was one. If he did not fulfil them he could be deposed.

This is perhaps an extreme viewpoint – but it is eloquently expressed and the idea of the *bay'a* as contract 'is defended by the majority of the nationalist elite, salafist and modernist: the *bay'a* in the same way as the *sunna* reveals in itself the democratic essence of Islam,' as Muhammad Tozy puts it[23]. Tozy goes on to show that King Hassan has emphasised an entirely different approach to the *bay'a*, the version which presents itself as the acceptance of allegiance. As a consequence of his religious role as Commander of the Faithful, the King has a sacred personality which is inviolable and incontestable. Tozy quotes two speeches of Hassan and from them derives a political science-style schema of the Moroccan political system (it is important to note that the arrows lead downwards!)

Dieu

Le Prophète et son descendant

La Communauté

Les représentants

L'électorat

The King now holds not only executive power, but legislative 'He transcends completely the separation of powers' and the 'contractual' basis of legitimacy is discarded, and the *'ulamā'* are driven from the political landscape. Their place is taken by parliament whose job is to *rule* the people rather than represent them.

It must be said that things are not quite as simple as this. Neither Hassan nor his father Muhammad V rejected the concept of a constitutional monarchy entirely. When speaking to his new army Muhammad V said that his wish was 'to set up ... a constitutional monarchy based upon the separation of powers'. When warning about the dangers of a false democracy in 1958 he also said:

> We are going to build a constitutional monarchical regime which will take account of the higher interests of the country and will respond to its native characteristics. It will be a regime that allows an authentic democracy to emerge, which will simultaneously be inspired by the spirit of Islam and the evolution of our country, and will put into effect our wish to let our people participate progressively in the management and control of affairs of state.[24]

When Hassan came to the throne he proceeded to act in the role of an absolute monarch – it was his *dahir* in June 1961 which provided the fundamental law for Morocco while a Constitution was worked out – but that too talked of a 'constitutional monarchy ... [with] representative institutions'.[25] When the Constitution was produced in 1962 it placed considerable power in the hands of the King, who had made it. The King presented it to a referendum with the words:

> The Constitution which I have made with my own hands ... is above all the renewal of the sacred pact which has always united the people and the King ...[26]

Thus the new document was presented in traditional terms, with reference to traditional obligations on both sides: the people by voting 'yes' gave him their *bay'a*, in return the King would rule justly:

> It is necessary ... that your King, who is the guarantor of the Constitution and defends the liberties of everyone, should at every moment be able to control and follow the affairs of state.

The Constitution of 1972 which eventually replaced this 1962 Constitution also reserves enormous powers for the King, but at the same time it still declares that 'Morocco is a constitutional, democratic and social monarchy' and that 'Sovereignty belongs to the

Nation', and goes on to give, on paper, considerable political and civil rights – including a multiparty system.[27]

The King's politics are, of course, dynamic, the product of his own attempts to control events. It is not the intention of this chapter to discuss the historical process of this developement. That has been done many times before. What is important here is the weapons that are used in the struggle. On Hassan's side this is what Agnouche calls 'the mobilisation of tradition'. But it is mobilised in a different way. The *bay'a* is now repeated on numerous occasions, and is used as a way of letting people repeat their allegiance. There is no conditionality attached any more. Hassan is owed allegiance as *Amir al-Mu'minīn*.[28]

It looks as though the King has won the argument over constitutional issues for the moment at least. But the dialogue has taken place in terms which both sides have been using for a long time. The political field may no longer have the same participants, the *'ulamā'* having been driven from it (that was Lahbabi's intention as well), but the struggle continues in essence. And the King continues to use the language and institutions of constitutional monarchical systems. This may simply be, as Agnouche suggests to 'confer on the Moroccan regime the image of modernity which it needs'[29] but it may have another purpose: to allow both sides room to manoeuvre, and to give a place to the other great basis on which modern Moroccan nationalism is built.

Makhzan and Siba

What the *bay'a* means is the subject of political argument about the relationship between ruler and ruled. This is so central to the political argument about Morocco that it is not surprising that Agnouche and Lahbabi have taken so much care to examine its meaning. But in Moroccan historiography the political campus is defined in another way as well: by the concept of *Makhzan* and *siba*. The concept itself was first defined by French colonial historians and ethnographers who divided Morocco into two parts, respectively the *bilād al-makhzan* (the land of government), and the *bilād al-siba* (the land of dissidence).

'*Makhzan*' is the Arabic term for 'treasury', so the territory which the government controlled was one in which the tribes concerned paid taxes or provided military service. *Siba*, on the other hand, was a colloquial Arabic term meaning 'rebellion' or 'insolence' in which temporal authority of the Sultan was not recognised, although his religious leadership was. Thus Robin Bidwell, a British historian of French colonial administration in Morocco summed it up:

> It has long been the custom for writers to divide Morocco into two parts – the Bled *makhzan* which obeyed the Sultan and the Bled Siba which did not. In general the Bled *makhzan* consisted of the tribes between the Atlas and the Atlantic and was therefore the first to be encountered by the French who landed at Casablanca ... The Bled Siba consisted of those tribes which have been subject only to the strongest of sultans and some indeed claimed that they had never been conquered. Each of these tribes needed individual study and attention by the French.[30]

That is the traditional view painted with a very broad brush, and some Moroccan nationalist historians have provided revisionist versions – 'versions' in the plural because there is some disagreement.

Abdallah Laroui represents one point of view – and by far the most subtle. He explained that he had first had the idea for writing his book on the origins of Moroccan nationalism *before* colonialism in the period immediately *after* independence:

> In the context of an intensely political, not to say dramatic, political condition, social aspects had so overwhelmed the political and, even more, the religious aspects of groups' activities that nationalism, as it was understood between the two world wars, no longer had any precise meaning. It seems to have been relegated to a remote past and could therefore become the object of critical investigation.[31]

He went on to complain that the administration which had been erected by the Protectorate had been taken over by a 'nationalist' government, but that nothing much had changed: there was still the same emphasis on French as the language of culture and administration, with traditional forms still abandoned. So what did independence really mean?[32]

Laroui is a nationalist, that much is clear, but he is not necessarily a full-blooded supporter of the monarchy. When he turns to *siba*, he first turns the concept on its head to examine what it meant for the tribes. He points to a wide variety of rural revolts, of which those led by self-appointed *mahdī-s* worried the *makhzan* the most because they called the Sultan's legitimacy into question. Tribal revolts against unjust governors, and attempts by local 'grands caids' to extend their power at the expense of their neighbours did not call that legitimacy into question,[33] and could therefore by dealt with by political or military means. Such revolts were effectively tribal in nature and concerned the amount of autonomy that local structures would be allowed:

> Depending on the strength of either side, autonomy was either actual or remained potential: allegiance to the makhzan added nothing except an increase in burdens, financial or otherwise. It is not surprising that people tried to escape it.'[34]

The other side is that of the *makhzan*. What was its attitude towards the *siba* tribes. A good deal depended upon *which* tribes were in question. The *makhzan* seems to have been far less tolerant of the Berber-speaking tribes because of their attachment to customary law and tribal solidarity in solving disputes rather than relying on the *shar'*. This called into question both the political and the religious justification for the Sultanate.[35]

The other prominent reviser of the *makhzan–siba* theory is Germain Ayache. In an article entitled 'The makhzan's role as arbitrator', he has argued that the traditional view was constructed from a colonialist viewpoint. Ayache writes that every state has seen rebellions, but that in general the Sultan did not need to exercise direct control over the people in the outlying districts because local political systems among the tribes were able to maintain order. In a large country, with difficult communications and limited wealth, at least in the nineteenth century, it made sense for the Sultan to rely upon these local systems in the peripheral areas:

> The Sultan was not rich enough to set up a tax-collector, judge, and policeman in each town and hamlet of his empire. But why should he do it anyway, if the tribes already had institutions which allowed them to organise justice and keep their own internal order? We are dealing, in essence, with devolved systems of government, but ones in which the religious leadership of the King is accepted.[36]

The Ayache concept is not just a useful little historical argument in the long debate over 'decolonising' African history, it is part of a whole way of seeing the Moroccan state, and one which has its political uses. Ayache neatly skirts the question of law in this analysis: it is purely a matter of administrative convenience, and the Islamic basis of the sultanate is not affected. The argument had already been used by the monarchy. In its submission to the International Court of Justice in the Western Sahara case in 1975 the Moroccan government claimed that:

The two expressions, Bled *makhzan* and Bled Siba, merely described the two types of relationship between the Moroccan local authorities and the central power, not a territorial separation; and that the existence of these different types did not affect the unity of Morocco. Because of a common cultural heritage, the spiritual authority of the Sultan was always accepted.[37]

Jerome Weiner has shown that the timing of the King's interventions over the Western Sahara responded to immediate political demands in Morocco to prove that he was a *real* nationalist.[38] It was, in fact, the Istiqlal which first raised the issue of Moroccan sovereignty over the Sahara. To be precise it was ʿAllāl al-Fassi who raised the idea of reconstituting Greater Morocco and later boasted, 'Originally I was the only person to call for the liberation of the Sahara and I was greeted with laughter.[39] It was al-Fassi who prepared the famous map of Greater Morocco and distributed it in 1955 and 1956.[40] And it was another of Istiqlal's leaders, M. Babana, who stated in 1956 that Mauritania was part of Morocco 'because it had always conserved its Muslim religion'.[41] In 1958 al-Fassi criticised the then Crown Prince, Mawlay Hassan by saying:

Mauritania has no right to separate itself from the rest of Morocco. In such an event – which God forbid – the King and the people would have a duty to constrain the Mauritanians by force to preserve the unity of the homeland.[42]

And it was under prodding from the nationalists that the Moroccan government opposed the independence of Mauritania and that country's membership of the United Nations. When the argument came before the First Committee of the General Assembly in November 1960, the Moroccan delegate, Boucetta, described the bases on which Morocco claimed sovereignty over Mauritania:

The attributes of sovereignty were exercised in the ways typical of the period but, until 1912, the whole of the population unreservedly recognised the authority of the Sultan of Morocco. In the mosques, prayers were always said in the name of the King of Morocco and this is still the case in some mosques, despite many years of occupation. On the other hand, the Mauritanian tribes had always played an active part in the investiture of the sultans of Morocco. Each time this event occurred, educated men and tribal chiefs from Mauritania took part in the election of their monarch ... In short, Mauritanians have always contributed to the defence of the kingdom against attacks by the colonial powers ...[43]

That was only part of the argument, however. The other 'supplemen-
tary' (as Boucetta put it) proof, was that Moroccan sovereignty over
Mauritania had been accepted by European powers in treaties signed
before the imposition of the Protectorate.[44]

Much the same arguments were used in the course of the Western
Sahara case in the International Court of Justice. At the beginning of
its case, Morocco told the court that it would 'put together a bundle
of historical arguments which confirm the existence of legal ties' and
would seek 'to prove the ties which throughout history united
Morocco to Western Sahara. In order to do so we based ourselves in
particular on the work of recognised historians, specialists in these
ancient periods' and assured the Court that the Moroccan statement
was prepared 'with the greatest possible historical accuracy'.[45]

The evidence that was put forward had two main thrusts: that
there existed the traditional ties of allegiance, which were demonstrated using the Avache-type version of *makhzan–siba* already
referred to, and that this was recognised by other countries 'in
accordance with the conditions laid down by public international
law'.[46]

As far as domestic politics were concerned, to a considerable
extent the King was able to use the Sahara issue – or batten onto it to
outflank his opponents. The political parties all agreed with the
Saharan cause, and some even went further than the King – in 1981
Union Socialiste des Forces Populaires (USFP) leaders were jailed for
criticising the King's acceptance of the principle of a Saharan referendum.[47]

One thing should be noted, however. This is that the Ayache
explanation of *makhzan–siba* and the Laroui version are rather
different. The 'official' revised, anti-colonial version emphasised the
idea of *siba* as devolved government, but keeps rather quiet about
Laroui's description of it being, in the eyes of the *makhzan*, sometimes synonymous with irreligion.

For 'Morocco' was to be defined territorially in religious terms.
But if the *religious* authority of the Sultan is the issue, the political
argument over what was the religious authority of the Sultan cannot
be avoided. It ties in nicely with the argument over royal authority.
Since the nationalists accept this definition of the territorial integrity
of the old Moroccan state, a definition which is supplied by the
monarchy, it appears to be a tacit acceptance of the royalist arguments. In one sense, then, it is a gift for the King.

On the other hand, the acceptance of *makhzan–siba* as a way of
explaining Moroccan claims to the Sahara and other chunks of North

Africa, implies the acceptance, at least in part of the idea of contract, rather than submission – which is what the left are putting forward.[48]

The reference to the past is clearly a double-edged sword, and equally clearly muddies the waters nicely: because Hassan has never *clearly* formulated his notion of political power he has room for manoeuvre. That room for manoeuvre is expressed politically by emphasising not only the traditional bases of power, but also by using concepts like constitutional monarchy, and popular sovereignty. The edges are fudged, so that when political needs change the formulations can be altered without undermining their foundations.

The room for manoeuvre can also be extended to the Saharan war. For a while in 1989 it looked as though an end might be in sight. Although this seemed less likely at the year's end, the recourse to theories of traditional allegiance allows Hassan room to shift the ground: an 'autonomy' for the Western Sahara can be justified in *makhzan–siba* terms which Hassan accepts, just as the need which Hassan has expressed for an imitation of Spain as a model for a monarchical regime may be justified on traditional grounds as well.

The essence of all return to the past is that it is so very protean but it is also remarkably effective. Side by side with an extensive use of modern political theory of constitutionalism and public law, it gives the Moroccan monarchy great room for manoeuvre. It has survived – but, it should also be noted, so has the nationalist movement managed to hang on to a good deal of its intellectual coherence. They have accepted the past as well.

NOTES

1 John Davis, *Libyan Politics, Tribe and Revolution, an account of the Zuwaya and their Government* (London: I. B. Tauris, 1987).

2 Lisa Anderson, *The State and Social Transformation in Tunisia and Libya, 1830–1980* (Princeton: Princeton University Press, 1986).

3 *Ibid.*, p. 221.

4 Davis, *op. cit.*, p. 188.

5 Mohamed el Alami, *Mohammed V. Histoire de l'Indépendance du Maroc* (Salé, 1980), 11ff.

6 Abdelatif Agnouche, *Histoire Politique du Maroc, Pouvoir – Lègitimités – Institutions* (Casablanca: Afrique-Orient, 1987).

7 Mohamed Lahbabi, *Le Gouvernement Marocain à l'aube du vingtième siècle* (Casablanca: Les Editions maghrébines, 1975).

8 Mohamed Tozy, 'Le roi commandeur des croyants', in D. Basri, *et al.* (eds), *L'édification d'un état moderne, Le Maroc de Hassan II* (Paris: Albin Michel: 1986), 51–69; reference here to p. 57.

9 Edmund Burke, *Prelude to Protectorate in Morocco* (Chicago: University of Chicago Press, 1976), pp. 115–16.

10 *Ibid.*, p. 132.
11 John Waterbury, *The Commander of the Faithful, The Moroccan Political Elite, A Study in Segmented Politics* (London: Weidenfeld and Nicholson, 1970), p. 34.
12 *Ibid.*, p. 4.
13 John P. Halstead, *Rebirth of a Nation, the Origins and Rise of Moroccan Nationalism, 1912–1944* (Cambridge, Mass.: Harvard University Press, 1969), p. 114.
14 Hassan II, *The Challenge*, trans. A. Rhodes (London: Macmillan, 1978), p. 90.
15 *Ibid.*, p. 64.
16 El Alami, *op. cit.*, p. 51.
17 Agnouche, *op. cit.*, p. 266.
18 Charles-André Julien, *Le Maroc Face aux Imperialismes, 1415–1956* (Paris: Juene Afrique, 1978), p. 176.
19 Agnouche, *op. cit.*, p. 308.
20 Waterbury, *op. cit.*, p. 49.
21 Quoted by Agnouche, *op. cit.*, p. 311.
22 Lahbabi, *op. cit.*, p. 7.
23 Tozy, *op. cit.*
24 Agnouche, *op. cit.*, p. 310.
25 *Ibid.*, p. 360.
26 Quoted in *ibid.*, p. 316.
27 Quoted in Hassan II, *op. cit.*, pp. 226–38.
28 Agnouche, pp. 326–27.
29 *Ibid.*, p. 331.
30 Robin Bidwell, *Morocco under Colonial Rule: French Administration of Tribal Areas, 1912–1926* (London: Frank Cass, 1973), p. 33.
31 Abdallah Laroui, *Les origines sociales et culturelles du nationalisme marocain (1830–1912)* (Paris: Maspéro, 1977), p. 11.
32 Laroui, p. 12.
33 *Ibid.*, pp. 158–9.
34 *Ibid.*, p. 163.
35 *Ibid.*, p. 166.
36 Germain Ayache, 'La fonction d'arbitrage du Makhzen', in *idem, Etudes d'histoire marocaine* (Rabat: SMER, 1979), pp. 159–76; reference here to 167.
37 International Court of Justice, 'Advisory opinion on the Western Sahara, October 16 1975', *Reports of Judgments, Advisory Opinions and Orders* (The Hague, 1975), 44. The text of the advisory opinion is also contained in *International Legal Materials* 14, 1975, pp. 1355–1408; reference here to p. 1386.
38 Jerome B. Weiner, 'The green march in historical perspective', *Middle East Journal* 33, 1979, pp. 20–33.
39 Quoted in International Court of Justice, 'Advisory Opinion', sep. op. de Castro, pp. 118–19.
40 Weiner, *op. cit.*, p. 22.
41 Maurice Flory, 'La notion de territoire arabe et son application au problème du Sahara', *Annuaire Française de Droit Internationale*, 1957, pp. 73–91; reference here to p. 77.

42   International Court of Justice, sep. op. de Castro, pp. 127–8.
43   Nations Unies Assemblée Générale, 15è session, lère Commission, 15 November 1960, A/C, 1/SR.1109, pp. 143–4.
44   *Ibid.*, p. 144.
45   International Court of Justice, sep. op. de Castro, p. 131, quoting Moroccan submission of 25 July and 21 July.
46   International Court of Justice, sep. op. de Castro, p. 127, quoting Moroccan submission at UN General Assembly.
47   William I. Zartman, 'King Hassan's new Morocco', in *idem* (ed.), *The Political Economy of Morocco* (New York: Praeger, 1987), pp. 1–33; reference here to p. 10.
48   Alain Claisse, 'Makhzan traditions and administrative channels', in Zartman (ed.), *op. cit.*, pp. 34–58; reference here to p. 38.

13 The impact of the French colonial heritage on language policies in independent North Africa

Rachida Yacine

In this chapter I propose to discuss problems common to the three states of the Maghreb at independence in terms of their French colonial heritage, particularly its imprint on the linguistic orientations of their governments during the process of modernisation. Algeria, Morocco and Tunisia have common characteristics which bring them together and differentiate them from other nation-states in North Africa. They are located in the same geographical area, and have had a common historical experience as a result of invasion and European domination.

The French colonisation left an important heritage which was to play a relevant part in the making of the nation in the Maghreb. One of the major problems of the Maghreb at independence was the dilemma generated by the desire for modernisation as quickly as possible and, at the same time, for the development of an authentic national identity. Since independence, these problems have affected all aspects of communal life. They reflect the different historical and political stages that have developed since independence and which correspond to specific stages of social development as well. They also correspond to the linguistic controversies since independence in all the Maghrebi countries, which, in themselves, reflect the constraints that each country has experienced in its attempts at modernisation. In short, they have also had a strong impact on development, and have been a threat to national unity.

THE EFFECTS OF FRENCH COLONIALISM

The realities of decolonisation in each country demonstrated that colonialism had produced a decultured population, a dominant traditional economy and nascent industrial sector which lacked capital and

221

qualified manpower, against the background of political instability which resulted from the political changes created by independence.

Political instability

Morocco and Tunisia emerged as independent states in 1956 after 44 and 77 years of French colonisation respectively, while Algeria became independent in 1962 after 132 years of French control. The removal of such control inevitably generated political instability which was also stimulated by the internal political tensions that prevailed throughout the Maghreb at independence. The degree of instability varied, of course, from one Maghrebi country to another.

The transfer of power from colonial authorities to the newly independent administration in Tunisia was smooth but was marked by a political struggle for power in Morocco and suffered from factional conflict in Algeria. Whatever the circumstances, however, the transfer of power allowed political leaderships consisting of a leader and a party to engage as symbols of nationalism.

In Tunisia, Habib Bourguiba, at the head of the Neo-Destour Party, became the '*Interlocuteur valable*' in the negotiations with France for independence, which meant that Tunisia was characterised by continuity and stability of leadership in the transfer to independence – unlike Morocco and Algeria. In Morocco, King Mohammed V,[1] together with the Istiqlal Party, emerged as the most legitimate claimant for power, thus providing the country with effective political leadership.

The long period of colonisation in Algeria had a deep impact on the emerging Algerian political elites there, particularly over the creation of a central authority and over their access to political power. There was an innate division in the ranks of the nationalist movement that went back to the foundation of the FLN Party in 1954. This suppressed conflict was renewed in May 1962 at the Tripoli Congress which was devoted to establishing the future political orientation of the new Algerian nation, after the Evian Agreements had been signed with France, thus giving Algeria its independence.[2]

In short, whatever the type of transfer of power from colonised to newly independent state, political tensions appeared in all three Maghrebi countries – Algeria, Morocco and Tunisia. In Tunisia, political divisions existed within the Neo-Destour Party, and were typified by two political leaders, both influential but with different views of the future of their country – Habib Bourguiba and Mustafa Ben Youssef. Ben Youssef's opposition to Habib Bourguiba was focused on the Convention of Interdependence of 1955, which he described as a step backward, and on the Neo-Destour Party which he saw as pro-western and far removed from Arab-Islamic values. This opposition created a political crisis which only ended when Habib Bourguiba took control of the National Assembly, and when the Neo-Destour Party won 90 per cent of seats. The opposition was then forced outside the political arena.

In Morocco, the emergence of Istiqlal Party as the dominant party at independence led to a bitter controversy between it and the other political parties. The consequent crisis caused the collapse of the Moroccan government and ministerial resignations. There was even a division within the Istiqlal Party which resulted in the creation of the National Union of Progressive Forces (UNFP), four years after independence.

Politics in Morocco developed differently from its neighbours because it enjoyed a degree of political pluralism, while both Algeria and Tunisia had single political party systems. The presence of small political parties in Morocco was a consequence of the Royal desire to maintain a balance of power with the Istiqlal as the majority party.

In Algeria, the provisional government (GPRA)[3] was criticised, together with the Evian Agreements, as being neo-colonialist. Two major groups emerged from the Tripoli Congress in 1962 – one, considered to be radical under Ahmed Ben Bella[4] supported by the Army, and the other led by members of the provisional government who were mostly politicians and considered moderates. The contest for power between them threatened political stability in the first decade of independence, particularly when the radical group emerged as the leading contender for power and Ahmed Ben Bella became the exclusive candidate in the elections of 1962. In 1965, however, he was ousted from power by Colonel Houari Boumedienne, and 'Le Conseil de la Révolution' emerged as a new political institution and continued to be the central unit of decision-making between 1965 and 1979. Power was increasingly concentrated in the hands of Houari Boumedienne, who became president and remained so until his death in December 1978. In short, Maghrebi political instability has led to the concentration of power in the hands of a single individual in each of the three states.

The economic context

Political instability in the Maghreb was the result of an economic situation severely affected by political change. Indeed, whatever the differences in resources between the three states of the region, the economic problems and constraints were very similar.

The Maghrebi economy had originally been essentially agricultural in nature. During the colonial period industrialisation had begun but colonisation established and reinforced a dual economic system based on modern and traditional sectors. The modern sector, which belonged to the European community, was mechanised and specialised, while the traditional sector was by definition underdeveloped, with no opportunity to improve, and was the property of the Maghrebi peasantry. This colonial economic structure inevitably impoverished the indigenous population, an impoverishment which was the cause of the economic problems of the transitional and post-independence periods.[5]

Modernisation meant rapid economic development, but the socio-cultural and economic circumstances of the transitional period proved to be too weak to support such a process.[6] At the same time, this failure rendered change and improvement in the Maghrebi cultural context far more complex. All three states opted for rapid industrialisation and modernisation on gaining independence. This decision was a consequence of France's economic legacy to the Maghreb but it inevitably generated problems which obstructed development. The most important of these was the land tenure system which hindered development in agriculture, and the flight of foreign capital abroad as a result of domestic political change.

The socio-cultural situation

The populations of the Maghreb at independence were essentially rural and predominantly young, with most young people having enjoyed very limited educational opportunities. Underdevelopment of agriculture in the dominant traditional sector, and the very low standard of living of the peasantry, generated rural migration to the cities. The exodus caused problems of population pressure in cities and raised rates of unemployment. Literacy in the population was also very low and constituted a basic obstacle to development. In Algeria and Morocco, almost 90 per cent of the rural population were believed to be illiterate. In Tunisia, there was a significant imbalance between the rural and urban populations, with about 85 per cent of the overall population being illiterate.

THE LINGUISTIC SITUATION

In 1956, the linguistic situation appeared to be very poor. Classical Arabic had not been accessible to all Maghrebis during colonisation. Classical Arabic was highly academic and restricted to the learned elites educated in the universities of Karaouyn and Zitouna, and in the Middle East.

At independence, the French language has emerged as a modernising vector and as an instrument of social and political mobility. It was used by Maghrebi intellectuals, and by those who attended the French schools. Once again, this language was not accessible to all. The linguistic situation generated the birth of two groups called 'Arabophones' and 'Francophones' which were to complicate the Maghrebi social climate. The Maghrebi desire for rapid modernisation has increased dependence on France and the West. Consequently, the utilization of the language has been reinforced and French was considered as an instrument of development and modernisation. The important use of this language restricted the development and expansion of Arabic in the Maghreb. The linguistic problem became even more crucial with the existence of a colloquial spoken form and a more refined written form of Arabic, plus the borrowing of French words.

The medium of communication in the Maghreb has been spoken Arabic which differed from one area to another within the same country and within the Maghreb as a whole. The Berber was and is still spoken by 30 per cent of the Algerian, 5 per cent of the Tunisian, and 40 per cent of the Moroccan populations. This language has not complicated the linguistic situation in Tunisia, while it has worsened the socio-cultural context in Morocco and Algeria. Multilingualism has existed in the northern part of Morocco where Arabic, French and Spanish languages have been used – indeed, 10 per cent of the Moroccan population speak Spanish, a consequence of the earlier Spanish colonisation.

At independence, the national governments of Algeria, Morocco and Tunisia sought to encourage the use of Arabic as a means of asserting national identity. However, it was limited in use and development. The claim for Arabic as a national language, and the expansion of the French language to all the activities of life in the Maghreb, generated contradictions and often provoked conflicts. It is commonly assumed that the linguistic situation has been dramatic in the first decade of independence, and considering the political tensions of the transition there were no national debates on the linguistic issues. In that period, the language had become an instrument of social promotion, progress and power. It established conflicting social and political relationships in the Maghreb; at first it was an obstacle to national development and modernisation, then later a contradiction to the official claims for authenticity and national identity.

CASE FOR A LANGUAGE POLICY

In the three nation-states of the Maghreb, language is perceived as a powerful symbol and means of identification, unity and modernisation. Hence, it is an integral part of national planning.

The goal of the governments of the Maghreb was the recovery and affirmation of national identity. They assumed it to be the necessary condition for the assertion of their existence as independent sovereign states, national unity being closely linked and even dependent on the former and as a prerequisite for national integration. The emphasis was on social and ethnocultural identity, whereby language and culture in many cases play a central part in these developing nations. The specific policies, and the constraints faced by these countries contest the validity and utility of the 'western theories of modernisation', based primarily and essentially on the predominance of economic development and the universalism of 'the western model and culture'.

Since the Second World War, it has been proved inadequate, in the theoretical perspective of development, to consider economic growth as the main indicator of development and as a potent means to ensure an overall modernisation, of the developing nations. Economic growth has been asserted to be but one variable in the process of modernisation, and culture a dimension of development. This assertion has made development dependent on, and related to, the different components of society including the human factor.

For these emerging nations, the western model of development seemed to constitute a source of inspiration and a reference to modernisation. But, once again, the inadequacy of the transplant of the western model of development has been proved by the existence of specific characteristics, potentialities, needs and aspirations in the Maghreb. This transplant has had disruptive effects on the socio-cultural, economic and political structures of the Maghrebi societies. In these nation-states of the Maghreb embarking on modernisation, economic development is a means of achieving an important series of changes and transformations in different spheres, and at different levels of their socio-political and economic settings. In their process of modernisation and decolonisation, the cultural dimension holds a salient place. Cultural assertion, then, appears to be the key to the affirmation of sovereignty, and to the eradication of the colonial imprint. 'National culture' seems to be the means to achieve national unity, to ensure a conscious mobilisation, and to promote participation of the Maghrebi populations around national objectives.

It is commonly assumed that language is a fundamental element of culture, a component of national identity, and an indicator of authenticity. In the Maghreb, however, the language issue has raised bitter controversies and has disrupted national unity, with the existence of multilingualism in Algeria, Morocco and Tunisia making both the adoption of language policies and planning to overcome particularism and to foster unity necessary. Therefore national governments have adopted specific language policies. However, the imposition of a national language caused fragmentation at the political, and socio-economic levels, and created obstacles to development. So, in relation to the goal of national unity, the three nations of the Maghreb have had to face the problem of the choice of the national language as this would have a determinant effect, being either unifying or divisive of national unity and identity.

In all three countries, Algeria, Morocco and Tunisia, the issue of language is still one of the most 'explosive'. In these nations great hopes seem to be invested in both language and culture to achieve the ultimate objective of national identity and modernisation.

The effects of colonialism on the linguistic policy in the independent Maghreb

From what has been discussed above, it appears that all aspects of life in the Maghreb have submitted to the effects of colonialism and to the political changes brought about by independence. The different approaches to the language policy have also been strongly marked by the colonial imprint. The French colonial heritage appeared to have had an important influence on Maghrebi public reactions which either revealed a traditional attitude to the question of language or a modernist one fed on universalism and French culture.

The Maghrebi claim for Arab-Islamic characteristics, with the emphasis on a national language, has been used either as a political issue, as was the case in Algeria and Morocco, or as a means of political legitimacy as in Tunisia. As soon as independence occurred, these nations selected Arabic language as an official national language. Their preferences were found in official documents and speeches. For Algeria, this choice appears in the Tripoli programme of 1962 which underlines the process of Arabisation. In this programme which states the main political options of the Algerian nation, it is declared that the Algerian culture will be national and that its role will include that of the restoration of Arabic language (at first) to reflect the values of the nation and its dignity, and to make the language itself effective as a language of civilisation.[7] Articles of the Algerian Constitution of 1963 focused on Arabic as a national language.[8]

The National Constitution of 1976 described Arabic as an element of national identity.[9] Again, article 273 of the Second Constitution of 1976 stipulated that Islam is the religion of the state, Arabic is its national language, and that the government will work to generalise the use of the national language at the official level.[10] In Tunisia, the Constitution of 1959,[11] in article 1, stipulates that Arabic is the language of the state and that Islam is its religion. This option for Arabisation is found in Habib Bourguiba's speech of 1958. When speaking of the Tunisian[12] educational programmes he insisted that these programmes must reinforce the national character of Tunisia which is rooted in the Arab culture and Islamic religion. Also, the preamble of the Moroccan Constitution of 1962[13] defined Morocco as a sovereign Muslim state whose official language is Arabic. Mohamed V's speeches emphasised this official view and expressed the general guidelines for the irreversible adoption of Arabic as an official language. Nevertheless, decisions as to its implementation were left to the various ministries concerned.

Official documents and statements in the Maghreb have focused on speeding up the process of Arabisation to reinstate quickly the Arabo-Islamic characteristics of the nation. It appeared however, that the official position of each government remained theoretical and divorced from reality. Moreover, the gap between theory and practice has been pointed out in the national debates of the decade of independence between the claims for the urgency to use Arabic language, the establishment of an Arab-Islamic culture and the maintenance of French as a working language. Contradictions are also reflected in the implementation and fluctuation of Arabisation and culture according to different political trends, power and the influence of those involved in decision-making. The fluctuation changed from the *radical* positions of the nationalists and traditionalists to the moderate and cautious attitudes of the modernists.

The oscillations of the Arabisation policy in the Maghreb are revealed by the government's attitudes at one period of time or another. For instance, in Algeria, Arabisation has been among the most important priorities from 1965 to 1978. The late President, Boumedienne, was in favour of Arabisation and considered it as a 'revolutionary objective'. Under his leadership the process can be divided into two phases. The first phase, from 1965 to 1974, was characterised by an intensive implementation of Arabisation in the administration and the educational system, and the setting up of the Party's National Commission for Arabisation in 1973. The second phase, from 1974 to 1978, can be determined by President Boumedienne's declaration of 1975: 'When Arabic becomes the tool of work and communication in the petro-chemical plants of Skikda and the steel plant of el-Hadjar (Annaba) it will be the language of Iron and Steel.[14] This declaration marked the beginning of a more moderate approach towards Arabisation. It seemed to be dictated by Algeria's economic policies of that period. So, the French language was considered to be highly operational and the Arabic language inadequate in the process of modernisation.

In 1977, modernists such as Mostefa Lacheraf, then Minister of Higher Education, and Abderrahim Rahal, Minister of Primary and Secondary Education, marked a pause in the process of Arabisation and a return to French–Arab bilingualism. Mostefa Lacheraf ascertained that this pause was the result of a lack of a realistic and objective basis to the language policies, and that the Arabic language was a 'hostage of nationalism' because it was strongly ideologised.[15]

In Tunisia, the language issue appears to be far less passionate and radical, especially among the political elite. It never constituted an ideologised doctrine, just an instrument of legitimacy. Consequently, Tunisian language policy is more pragmatic, cautious and systematic than in Morocco and Algeria. However, it denotes similar contradictions between past (ancestral heritage) and future (modernisation), and between the gap which separates the *rhetoric* (in favour of Arabic language) and *practice* (supporting the French language as an instrument of development). Nevertheless, in Tunisia political options were much clearer than in Morocco and Algeria. In fact, it is commonly assumed that modernisation and openness to the West had been the main Tunisian principles of action.[16]

Language policy in Morocco, and the effectiveness of its implementation, has been highly influenced by different political tendencies and its position in terms of government approach has been changing. But the content remains constant in terms of the original language policy.

Morocco was the first of the three Maghrebi countries to launch a rapid and radical policy of Arabisation. This step has been marked by the presence of the Itstiqlal Party at the forefront of the political scene. The Istiqlal members were known for their traditional attitude and educational profile (*Quaraouyn*): impregnated with Arab-Islamic values and traditions. This rapid Arabisation has resulted in the quality of education being affected, and has led to confusion according to critics.

The objective of spreading Arabic throughout the educational system, together with the goal of the achievement of universal and compulsory education, was expressed in 1956/7 in Mohamed Al Fassi's plan for the schooling of Moroccan youth. The implementation of this ambitious policy met practical problems, such as lack of teaching materials and staff. It resulted in a wave of doubts, and in Arabisation being considered as inadequate. The resolution of Moroccan teachers, at the end of the 1957 school year, asked for the suspension of the current experimentation in Arabisation. This criticism came about when the Istiqlal Party began to lose prestige in the government. The modernists replaced the 'Istiqlalians' and centred their action on the immediate needs of the nation for economic and social development. They considered French to be the instrument of universal education and national industrialisation for the time being.

The position of the modernists exerted a strong pressure on the Moroccan government, with the modernists showing their dissatisfaction and criticising the initial language policy of a radical Arabisation. This resulted in a more moderate and cautious approach for a gradual Arabisation and then led to the setting up of a Commission of Educational Research. This commission was confronted with the dilemma of the twofold objective of the educational and economic needs being dependent on the French language and the nationalistic objective of establishing or re-establishing a complete Arabisation. The problem was the question of bridging the gap between idealistic principles and practical realities.

From 1958 to 1959, there was a flexible approach to Arabisation with Benjelloun as Minister of Education. Shortly after, in 1960, the approach to Arabisation became cautious and was based on pragmatism to complement the government's emphasis on social and economic development. It also marked the time when modernists began to be influential in decision-making.

In 1965, Dr Benhina expressed a cautious approach to Arabisation and a tendency towards Arab–French bilingualism – thus, bilingualism began to be advocated more and more in official statements and educational planning. Thirteen years later, in his speech of

April 1978, King Hassan II declared that 'he was in favour of Arabisation, but that bilingualism was a necessity'. The King expressed the feeling that bilingualism was an obligation. He stated:

> We must be bilingual, even better, we must acquire these languages because we have a mission which we assumed for a long time and which consists in defending the "Arabness" and Islam in this part of the world.[17]

This official declaration generated a strong reaction and criticism from the members of the public, and especially from the political parties in opposition.

The governments' attitudes towards the language policies in the Maghreb have revealed the strong influence of economic policies which imply Maghrebi dependence on the West – especially on France – and their stances have widened the gap between the need for decolonisation through the use of Arabic language and the will for modernisation in the Maghreb.[18]

CONCLUSION

It is now clear that the conflict-prone and complex linguistic situation in the Maghreb has prevailed, in spite of the efforts undertaken since independence to bring about a change in the situation inherited from the colonial period. It is a situation which seems to be characterised by a wish for the *status quo* in some of the aspects of Maghrebi life, in some values and institutions. This appears to be due to a lack of serious assessment in the Maghreb specific initial conditions when elaborating the language planning, and there seems to be a need for a reassessment of the policies adopted and for a different approach which will take into consideration the contextual features of the three countries.

Not accounting for contexts, and neglecting other language alternatives while planning language policy has generated consequences which, after a decade, have made the linguistic issue in the Maghreb as problematic as before and highly controversial.

NOTES

1 See *Annuaire d'Afrique du Nord,* 1962, for a description and analysis of the Moroccan Constituent Assembly. Also, King Mohamed V's speech of 12 September 1956, quoted in M. Camau, *La notion de démocratie, dans la pensée des dirigeants maghrébins* (Paris: CNRS, 1971), p. 272.
2 See 'Textes des Accords d'Evian', quoted in F. Perroux (ed.), *L'Algérie*

de demain, (Paris: PUF, 1962), p. 240.
3 GPRA. The Algerian Provisional Government was founded in 1958 in Tunisia. Ferhat Abbas, one of the nationalist leaders, was its president until 1961; he was then replaced by Mohamed Benkhedda.
4 Ahmed Ben Bella was one of the Revolutionary leaders. He was arrested by the French Army in 1956, and later became the first president of the Algerian Republic.
5 For the Tunisian economic situation at independence see M. Guen, *La Tunisie indépendante face à son économie: enseignements d'une expérience de développement*, (Paris: PUF, 1961), pp. 69, 93.
6 See also R. Gallisot, *L'économie de l'Afrique du Nord*, Que Sais-je? (Paris, PUF, 1962), p. 75.
7 See the Tripoli programme, 1962.
8 The Algerian Constitution, 1963. See *Annuaire d'Afrique du Nord* (Paris, 1964).
9 La Charte Nationale, (Alger: SNED, 1976).
10 La Constitution Algérienne de 1976 (SNED, 1976).
11 The Tunisian Constitution, 1959. See *Annuaire d'Afrique du Nord* (Paris, 1962), p. 51.
12 Habib Bourguiba's speech, 1958. See Publications du Secrétariat d'Etat à l'Information (Tunis, 1975).
13 The Moroccan Constitution of 1962.
14 President Boumedienne's speech published by *Révolution Africaine*, 12–22 May 1975, Alger.
15 Lacheraf Mostefa, *L'Algérie Nation et Société* (Paris: Maspéro, 1964), p. 323; also see Mostefa's 'Réflexions sociologiques sur le socialisme et la culture en Algérie', in *Temps modernes*, March 1964.
16 See A. Micaud, *Tunisia, The Politics of Modernization*, (London: Pall Mall Press, 1964), p. 89.
17 King Hassan II's speech of April 1978.
18 A. Moatassine in *Le bilinguisme sauvage: Blocage linguistique, sous-développement et coopération hypothéquée, l'exemple du Tiers-Monde* XV (59–60), p. 657; and Gilbert Granguillaume, *Arabisation et politique linguistique au Maghreb* (Paris: Maisonneuve et Larose, 1983), p. 31.

BIBLIOGRAPHY

Annuaire d'Afrique du Nord, 1962, 1965–1984.
Gallisot, R. (1962) *L'économie de l'Afrique du Nord, Que sais-je?* Paris: PUF.
Grandguillaume, Gilbert (1983) *Arabisation et politique linguistique au Maghreb*, Paris: Maisonneuve et Larose.
Micaud, A. (1964) *Tunisia, The Politics of Modernization*, London: Pall Mall Press.
Mostefa, Lacheraf *L'Algérie Nation et Société*, Paris: Maspéro.
Palazzoli, L. (1973) *Le Maroc politique de l'Indépendance à 1973*, Paris: Bibliothéque arabe Sinbad.
Souriau, Christiane (1975) *L'arabisation en Algérie, introduction à l'Afrique du Nord contemporaine*, Paris: CNRS.

Part IV
The region today

14 Morocco's argument to join the EEC

Ali Bahaijoub

HISTORICAL BACKGROUND TO EEC–MAGHREB RELATIONS

European states along the North Mediterranean shore have enjoyed a long-standing relationship with the Maghreb witnessed by over 1,000 years of history. Dictated by geo-political and strategic considerations, these links were either colonial, commercial or political. France appears to play a dominant role in trading with North African states but Spain, Portugal and Italy also have close ties with the Maghreb to varying degrees. Formal relations between the EEC and the three central Maghreb countries – that is, Morocco, Algeria and Tunisia have been marked by ups and downs and much ambiguity. When the Treaty of Rome came into effect at the beginning of 1958,[1] France was still in Algeria while Morocco and Tunisia had been independent for only two years.[2]

A 'Declaration of Intent' in the final act of the Treaty of Rome referred to 'the association of the independent countries of the Franc zone [that is, countries with currencies tied to the franc] with the EEC'. This declaration expressed without reservations the readiness of the six founding member states of the EEC to enter into negotiations with independent countries to conclude 'conventions for economic association with the Community'. It referred only to Morocco and Tunisia, as Algeria was not yet independent. A protocol annexed to the Treaty allowed France to maintain preferential trade arrangements with the Maghreb states by way of derogation from customs union rules.[3]

It was not until March 1969 that Morocco and Tunisia signed 'Association Agreements' with the EEC which related to trade only. These fell short of expectations as they did not provide for any real economic association. When the first enlargement of the EEC took place in 1972,[4] the Council of Ministers decided to promote a 'Global Mediterranean Policy' aimed at establishing a free trade zone of industrial goods for the community and the whole Mediterranean basin. This policy provided the basis for the bilateral 'Co-operation Agreements' concluded in 1976 with Algeria, Morocco and Tunisia. These replaced, in effect, the 1969 'Association Agreements' concluded between the EEC and the governments of Rabat and Tunis.

The 1976 Agreements were valid for an unlimited period and provided for bilateral trade, EEC development aid and some legislation governing immigration and labour. By the end of the first half of the 1980s the 'Global Mediterranean Policy' seemed to be working more to generate rhetorical statements than what it was originally designed for.[5] A Commission report submitted to the Council of Ministers on 30 March 1984 concluded that the objectives of the Mediterranean policy had been only partially achieved.[6]

The 1976 Agreements which entered into force on 1 November, 1978, were aimed at helping develop the complementary aspects of Maghrebi states and their interdependence. They were also meant to contribute towards the economic and social development of the Maghreb countries through trade, and economic, technical and financial co-operation.

In the eyes of the policy-makers in Brussels, Maghreb co-operation was set in the perspective necessary to enable longer-term development problems to be tackled. In other words, only if market access was guaranteed for an indefinite period could productive investment be stimulated to an extent far exceeding the Community's financial contribution to such investment. The industrial sector is a case in point. The question remains whether Maghrebi industry will ever be able to compete with that of the EEC. The 1973–4 oil shock was partly to blame for leading to a period of economic recession within the EEC. Consequently, protectionism became the order of the day and the Maghrebi partners bore the brunt.

In textiles, for instance, the free trade provisions of the '1976 Co-operation Agreements' were temporarily suspended. The agricultural sector was also affected when protectionist measures were tightened through the Common Agricultural Policy (CAP).[7] As a result, Morocco and Tunisia suffered most from the EEC's, newly adopted policy.

ALGERIA, LIBYA AND MAURITANIA

Unlike Morocco and Tunisia, Algeria has traditionally adopted a more reserved and ambivalent view of its relations with the EEC. In 1963, the Algerian authorities expressed the desire to enter into negotiations with the EEC officials for an overall agreement, but these negotiations were not to get off the ground until late in 1972.

Meanwhile, trade exchanges were conducted at random and Algerian products continued to enjoy duty-free access to French markets, with the exception of wine from 1971. It was not until 1 January, 1973 that Algeria was given the 'third country' treatment applied by the Community, thus doing away with any preferential treatment.

The Co-operation Agreement concluded with the EEC on 26 April, 1976 was to allow for 'the participation of the Community in the Algerian efforts to develop the production and the infrastructure of its economy'. The agreement provided for the setting up of a Co-operation Council (Article 16) to review annually the results of the financial and technical co-operation. The Council did not meet until 27 April, 1987[8] – that is until Algerian hydrocarbon exports suffered a severe setback caused by the 1985 oil price slump and also because the Algerian government considered that the agreement was not entirely satisfactory.[9] The April 1988 meeting resulted in an aid package to Algeria in the form of food supplies to offset the growing food import bill.[10]

Despite the economic downturn which has affected all OPEC countries since the oil price dive of 1985, Algeria's relationship with the Community is still strong. It remains an important market for a number of European companies and exports much of its hydrocarbon products to the Community. The potential will be even greater in the 1990s, especially when the planned gas pipeline via Morocco reaches Europe.[11]

The continuation of Algeria's traditional ambivalence towards the EEC is changing and so is its attitude to Paris which has been marked by a recent improvement in relations after years of acrimonious exchanges and low keyed trade links. President Chadli Ben Jedid has certainly shifted from the radical socialist policies of his predecessor, Houari Boumedienne, an indication perhaps that Algeria is about to adopt a liberal doctrine. The policy of a market economy is on the cards, a move that may lead to strengthening ties with the EEC even further.

Mauritania and Libya fall into a different category of partners of the EEC. Libya is the only Mediterranean country, with the exception of Albania, that has no conventional agreement with the Community. None the less, Libya's bilateral trade links with the EEC remain important and diversified in volume and value.

A net exporter of oil, which constitutes the backbone of the country's economy, Libya's trade links with the EEC tend to rely mostly on imports of basic foodstuff and manufactured consumer goods. Development projects to improve the country's infrastructure were mostly allocated to European companies and have been reduced in number following the oil price fall in 1985.[12] There is more scope for trade and the Arab Maghreb Union may provide the missing link to substantial commercial ties.

Mauritania, on the other hand, is linked to the EEC through the Lomé Convention.[13] It is economically part of West Africa although inter-Maghrebi relations allow it to become politically involved in the region's international affairs.

THE IMPACT OF EEC ENLARGEMENT

When Greece joined the EEC in January 1981, its membership had some repercussions on Moroccan and especially Tunisian olive oil exports, not to mention other agricultural products. It did not, however, have the same impact that Spain and Portugal's January 1986 accession to the Community had had on the two Maghrebi states, for this inflicted a damaging blow to Moroccan and Tunisian exports of leather goods, textiles, agricultural products, and olive oil.

The Community now has more olive oil than it can cope with while Moroccan and Tunisian exports of the product have been simply reduced to nil. The advent of Spain and Portugal to the EEC has clearly introduced a new and irreversible dimension to the EEC–Maghreb partnership with dire consequences for Morocco and Tunisia.

The protocols amending the 'Co-operation Agreements' with Tunisia and Algeria were ratified in May and June 1987 respectively. For Morocco, however, a fishing agreement was signed in May 1988 following lengthy negotiations. The four-year fishing agreement, with effect from March 1988 replaced an earlier Spanish–Moroccan accord concluded in 1983.[14] The agreement allows Morocco to receive licence fees for fishing in its Exclusive Economic Zone from which Spanish and Portuguese trawlers will be the main beneficiaries. The accord also provides for trade and is designed to encourage Moroccan industrial exports to Europe while restricting agricultural products. The latest agreement is important in the sense that it covers the transitional period during which Spain and Portugal will be fully integrated into the EEC.

Meanwhile, a number of constraints justify the looming apprehension in official circles in Tunis and Rabat. The introduction of the reference price system, compensatory taxation, and quota restrictions (to name but a few) have made the modalities agreed upon in the Additional Protocols limited in scope. For instance, the application of the reference price system may contravene the terms of the Additional Protocol meant to preserve trade links at traditional levels. This anomaly has already occurred in 1989 with regard to some agricultural and textile products.

When the single market is completed at the end of 1992, the European environment will undoubtedly change in terms of attitude, commercial patterns and economic interests. Morocco's apprehension about this change is reflected in King Hassan's application to join the EEC.

MOROCCO'S APPLICATION FOR EEC MEMBERSHIP

Morocco and Tunisia opted for closer association with the EEC from the outset. In 1987, 53.7 per cent of Morocco's imports and 59.6 per cent of exports were with the Community. Tunisia's trade volume is even greater and stood at 67.1 per cent and 78.8 per cent, respectively, for the same year.

While Spain and Portugal's entry to the EEC was pending, King Hassan, having sensed the consequences such a move would have on his country's exports to the Community, raised the possibility of Morocco's membership of the EEC with the french president, François Mitterand, as early as 1984. France was then assuming the presidency of the EEC Council of Ministers. The hypothetical question became reality when Morocco's formal application was delivered to the Council of Ministers in July 1987. Morocco's move was based on three criteria – namely, the development of a system of liberal market economy, the long-standing ties with Europe, and the implementation of democratic principles.

Indeed, with Portugal and Spain's entry into the EEC, Morocco became the Community's southern flank. Its strategic location, controlling the Strait's of Gibraltar, is of considerable importance to the defences of the Western hemisphere.

Morocco's argument to join the EEC reflects the need to allow equal competition in a market it has been associated with for two decades. None the less, the conceptions of Morocco's needs and status have not been reconciled in Brussels. The kingdom's request was deferred to the post-1992 period on the grounds that it was not a European state. The legal obstacle to Morocco's accession to the Community resides in article 237 of the Treaty of Rome which stipulates that 'any European state may apply to become a member of the community'. The Treaty does not, however, specifically state that membership of non-European states is to be ruled out.

EEC states bordering the Mediterranean are most sympathetic and traditionally have a close interest in the kingdom. This is partly because of colonial, cultural and trading links as well as political interests and labour migration. They also view Morocco as an important market, politically stable and with enormous untapped potentials.

In terms of trading ties, economic conceptions and political ideologies, the kingdom remains a close partner not easy to ignore. However, the further one goes from the Mediterranean basin, the less important it becomes. Whether Morocco's application is a success or a failure will be measured by the response from Brussels and the awareness of the importance of the country in the eyes of the EEC member states especially those north of France. Most important is the fact that EEC accords will be reviewed in 1995 and it remains to be seen what the outcome will be and how best the Community can deal with Morocco's application to join.

In whatever light Morocco is seen, it remains a neighbour that can not be displaced or ignored and should command the respect that neighbourliness entails.

FORTRESS EUROPE

EEC exports to the Maghreb have increased annually in real terms at a rate of 7.2 per cent over the past fifteen years. The Maghreb has not experienced the same growth rate nor is it likely to in the foreseeable future. There is a persistant trade deficit which has trebled for Tunisia in five years while for Morocco the trade deficit has increased from 304 million ECU in 1979 to 500 million ECU in 1987.

Profound apprehension looms over whether the Single European Market, scheduled to be completed in 1992, will create a more open and competitive market or simply turn into 'Fortress Europe'. European commissioners and European heads of state and government have given a flood of assurances that the Single Market does not imply increase in protectionist measures. Yet Maghrebis, and the rest of the world for that matter, remain sceptical as history alone is enough to justify the scepticism.

The EEC has always been protectionist. The question is whether protectionism will become worse as a result of the Single Market or whether it will ease. It is evident that protectionist factions will always exist within the EEC. What gives grounds for concern, however, is the impact 1992 will have on the alliances and coalitions the Single Market may enable protectionists to form.

The case for harmonisation and standardisation is important in the sense that decision-making provides large scope for experiment – an experiment that may be of benefit to all concerned. Nonetheless, it is not yet clear in which direction the Single Market is moving. Once this is established, it would at least help to dissipate the looming fear over the future of associate members of the EEC. One can also speculate on whether the 1992 market will remain open to Maghrebi goods and if it will continue to lower trade barriers through the forthcoming GATT agreement.[15]

The debate also concerns the existing preferential arrangements between the EEC and Maghreb states which may not necessarily be renewed when they expire or may be replaced by more general agreements within the GATT. There is, however, the argument that any protective measures that contravene GATT rules in a new or major way are unlikely to win approval. That is not due to any respect for, or interest in, the GATT rules or their function, it is due to a simple desire to avoid the debating disadvantage of having broken the rules. Unfortunately, the 'GATT rules leave a great deal of latitude for policies that are *de facto* protectionist'.[16] The major problem will be whether the EEC will follow in the footsteps of the Common Agricultural Policy characterised by protectionism or whether a policy of openness will be the order of the day.

Most important is the fact that in October 1989 the European Commission announced that its export guarantee programme for the 66 African, Caribbean, and Pacific countries was running out of money and that grants would have to be sharply reduced. The announcement fuelled Third World fears that the EEC is turning its attention and resources to Eastern Europe at the expense of developing nations, including the Maghreb.[17] The complaint is justified and is substantiated by figures published by the Organisation of Economic Co-operation and Development which groups 24 of the world's leading industrialised nations. The report revealed that in 1988 these countries invested 19 billion dollars of private funds in developing nations, a drop of one billion dollars on 1987. By contrast, it is the same group of industrialised states that came together in Paris to propose emergency economic aid for Poland. Hungary is also receiving the same treatment, a strong indication that EEC countries are indeed preoccupied with developments in Eastern Europe at the expense of heavily indebted developing nations.

A key element is what access post-1992 Europe will provide for manufactured and semi-manufactured goods from the Maghreb. Fortress Europe is already in motion in the textile sector in the form of the Multi-Fibre Arrangement (MFA). The MFA restrictions are only imposed on developing nations, while exports from industrialised countries such as the US and Japan are allowed in without any restrictions. The fourth MFA which expires in July 1991, was originally intended as a 'breathing space' but will have lasted seventeen years. It is highly unlikely that any change will occur beyond 1992. It is feasible to argue that the EEC is currently so preoccupied with the implementation of the 1992 initiative that there is no room to consider, let alone carry out, any new arrangements with the Maghreb states or the African and Caribbean countries for that matter.

UMA–EEC

The EEC is the world's largest trading bloc, with an internal market of 323 million people accounting for 19 per cent of world trade. The combined GDP of the Community was almost 4,000 billion dollars in 1989 while that of the Maghreb could hardly reach 100 billion dollars (which represents under 4 per cent of the EEC total). The three central North Africa States – that is, Morocco, Algeria and Tunisia – still look to the EEC as the main trading partner for over 65 per cent of their imports and just as much for their exports. Over half the Maghreb's exports valued at some 14 billion dollars went to France, Italy and Spain in 1987. This contrast indicates to a large extent the dependence of the Maghreb on the EEC. It also weighs heavily in favour of the Community.

The prevailing state of uncertainty over the benefits of 1992 for developing nations has undoubtedly contributed to the proclamation of the 'Union of the Arab Maghreb' (UMA) in Marrakesh in February 1989.[18] The event is considered a historical milestone in inter-Maghrebi relations and politics[19] and it set the seal on reconciliation, putting an end to years of suspicion and hostility which at times verged on open warfare between one state and another. The overwhelming argument is that economic sense has won the day over political bickering. The economic factor has indeed dictated the future course of action to such an extent that it prompted Maghrebi leaders to at least temporarily transcend political differences.

The vital economic benefits generated by the Union could eventually help improve a political climate that has, for years, been marred by Moroccan–Algerian differences over the Western Sahara issue.

The newly established Union is widely viewed more as an economic grouping than a political pact. Indeed, there is a clear economic complementarity between its member states which will undoubtedly improve their bargaining stand especially with the EEC. The Union is in many respects a response to the unpredictability arising from the 1992 programme and its impact on future relations with countries on the southern shore of the Mediterranean. EEC financial institutions hold some 70 per cent of the debt of Algeria, Morocco and Tunisia which amounts to some 47 million dollars.[20] This illustrates that the extent of relations in financial and commercial terms is considerable by any standard.

The Maghreb states are also confronted with a real demographic challenge. The population of the region is growing at the annual rate of 3 per cent, making it one of the highest growth areas in the world. The overall population may reach 100 million by the turn of the century. Some EEC members look upon this as a threat, especially those countries experiencing a drop in population growth. Skilled immigrants are viewed as an impediment to industrialisation in the Maghreb. Their scarcity reduces the attraction of the Maghreb to foreign investors when cheap migrant labour can be mustered in Europe. The demographic potential should be viewed as a large market for European consumer goods at the EEC's doorstep and not always as an exodus of the unemployed. Europeans have everything to gain from helping such a market to develop and prosper in order to guarantee the existence of the sought-after outlets for manufactured goods on which most European states depend heavily for their economic growth and prosperity.

The encouragement of a unified grouping on the southern shore of the Mediterranean can only benefit the EEC's own strategic and economic interests on a long-term basis. It will also contribute significantly to preserving security and stability in the region. The EEC has a lot to gain from closer ties with the Maghreb at a time when American and Japanese competition is sharpening.

Compared to other regions in Africa, the Maghreb has much to gain from a truly united group. The region is relatively wealthy in human and material terms. Indeed, Morocco and Tunisia's agricultural products, light industries and material, together with hydrocarbons in Algeria and

Libya, provide a considerable potential for complementarity.

Much of the rhetoric in favour of this, unfortunately, comes from those who are more interested in symbols of Maghrebi unity than in the implementation of its programme. The challenge to this attitude may come from Maghrebis in a quest for pragmatic policies. A Maghreb common market might, if the political will exists, present the five states with a degree of economic interdependence at a time of growing uncertainty and economic hardship. Whatever the political implications of the Union, the fact remains that economic necessities seem to dictate the future course of action the Maghreb's leaders must adopt. Economic integration looks to be the only viable option and there is much scope for improvement of co-operation on a bilateral or multilateral basis.

An economic community like the EEC could render the Maghreb substantially attractive to foreign investors and would significantly accelerate the pace of economic growth. Maghrebi leaders know that their commitment to the Arab Maghreb Union must be seen as a common voice if they are to carry weight in Brussels in anticipation of the Single Market. The very limited volume of business conducted among Maghrebi states, now 1.5 per cent of their total foreign trade, stands in sharp contrast to the importance of exchanges with the Community. Such a trend must change drastically to enhance the Maghreb market, restore confidence in the business sector and catch up with lost opportunities. How far such a process will go depends largely on decisions made in Maghrebi capitals.

On the other hand, the Union must not set in motion a process that will turn it into 'Fortress Maghreb' for the simple reason that the degree of the Maghreb's economic integration will invariably be drawn into the dynamic of the EEC. Any such controversial decision made in Brussels or a Maghrebi capital may prove an error of judgement on future relations between one group or the other. However, one must not rule out some new initiatives in the future that may offer a compromise solution to years of scepticism and ambiguity. As an observer rightly pointed out, 'a judicious mixture of vigilance and optimism, tempered by low expectations of reward, would seem to be the best prescription for developing countries as 1992 approaches'.[21]

STATISTICAL INFORMATION CONCERNING FOREIGN TRADE

Algeria, Morocco, Tunisia: percentage of foreign trade in 1987 with Maghreb countries (including Libya and Mauritania)

	Algeria	Morocco	Tunisia
Exports	1.1	3.7	4.2
Imports	1.1	1.8	2.7

Algeria, Morocco and Tunisia: percentage of foreign trade in 1987 with EC

	Algeria	Morocco	Tunisia
Exports	63.5	59.9	78.8
Imports	68.4	53.7	67.1

EC: percentage of foreign trade in 1987 with Algeria, Morocco and Tunisia

	Algeria	Morocco	Tunisia	Total
Exports	0.5	0.3	0.2	1.0
Imports	0.6	0.3	0.2	1.1

Source: IMF, *Direction of Trade Statistics*, and OECD, *Monthly Statistics of Foreign Trade*.

NOTES

1 The Treaty was signed on 25 March 1957 and came into force in January 1958.
2 See chapter on Algeria in Wilfrid Knapp, *North-West Africa, a Political and Economic Survey* (London: Oxford University Press, 1977).
3 *Co-operation Agreements between the EEC and the Maghreb Countries*, Commission of the European Communities (Brussels, February 1982), p. 1.
4 In 1972 the United Kingdom, Denmark and the Republic of Ireland joined the six founder-members of the EEC.
5 A commission report on ten years of Global Mediterranean Policy recognised that co-operation fell short of expectations. See *Bulletin of the*

European Communities, no. 6, Brussels, 1982, pp. 1.2.1–1.2.4.

6   *Bulletin of the European Communities*, no. 3, Brussels, 1984, p. 2.2.28.

7   The Common Agricultural Policy aims to rationalise agricultural production and establish a Community system of aids and import surveillance. It encompasses over 95 per cent of the community's agricultural production.

8   J. M. Portillo, *La Communidad Europea y Argelia, un Deceio de Cooperacion* (Madrid: INCI, 1988), p. 67.

9   *The Maghreb Review*, no. 2, London, August–September 1976, p. 12.

10 *Bulletin of the European Communities*, no. 4, Brussels, 1988, p. 2.2.24.

11 *Arab–British Commerce*, London, July 1989, p. 12.

12 *Libya Country Report*, no. 3 (London: The Economist Intelligence Unit, 1989), p. 9.

13 The Lomé Convention resulted in the association of the EEC with 66 African, Caribbean, and Pacific countries. A fourth Lomé Convention is expected to have been signed by the end of 1992.

14 *Le Matin du Sahara*, Casablanca, 25 May 1988, pp. 1, 5.

15 The General Agreement on Tariffs and Trade.

16 Brian Hindley, *Europe: Fortress or Freedom?*, Occasional Paper (London: The Bruges Group, 1989), p. 12.

17 *The Times*, London, 13 October 1989, p. 10.

18 *Le Monde*, Paris, 18 February 1989, p. 3.

19 See, *Maghreb-Unity or Disunity?*, presented by the author and published by the European Commission in Brussels.

20 *The Financial Times*, London, 14 February 1989, p. 4.

21 Dr Michael Hodges, 'Europe 1992: Fortress or Partner?', paper presented at the Conference on North Africa and the EEC convened in the University of London (SOAS), 10 February 1989.

15 Reflections on the state in the Maghreb

Remy Leveau

The debate on Islam and the state, revived by the Iranian experiment as a result of the Islamic Revolution there in 1979, has highlighted the discrepancy between what is seen by Islam as the illegitimacy of the nation-state[1] and basic community values, whether religious or social. In the Maghreb, however, the state appears more as an appropriately adjusted transfer of technology than as an alien institution. While Islamic protest is no doubt present in the region, its existence is not necessarily merely a negative factor within the political order. Although such protest is a reaction against policies of secularisation, it also – and this is what interests us most – articulates protest from the dispossessed and controls the excesses of the privileged.

Now, after long periods of political stagnation which have resulted in the ossification of these political structures established at independence, swift political and social change seems to be in the making. This is illustrated by the demise of Bourguiba in Tunisia as well as by the impending end of the Western Sahara war and the various policies of privatisation currently being carried out in the three countries of the Maghreb. These changes, which imply a new sort of awareness of civil society, do not, however, appear to be weakening the nation-state but, on the contrary, seem to be a means of strengthening its legitimacy.

The resistance of the North African[2] state in the face of religious protest or military claims to power, and its adaptation to a Mediterranean, European and international environment which is more complex than that of the Arab world, are elements which deserve careful examination. It must also be noted that North African states have successfully managed successive crises, each state doing so in its own way. Can we, then, anticipate that the Maghreb may be moving towards a democratic transition, resembling in some ways that of Mediterranean Europe? Such a change can only take place in a state which feels strong enough in its claim to legitimacy to relinquish its monopoly on popular representation and on social control which has traditionally been expressed through single-party systems. The real challenge lies in the establishment of a political pluralism based on the educated urban population.

Together with the new middle class, this population constitutes a pool of voters taking part in a political dialogue which has to be different from that of the single-party system instituted at independence. This new political process must also differ from the pluralism allowed at elite level by the Moroccan monarchy, along the lines of the old *makhzan*.

THE ORIGINS OF THE STATE IN THE MAGHREB

These perspectives of change only appear to be relevant against the background of the nature and origin of the state in the Maghreb. Such a state can be seen as a particular form of technology transfer[3] which should be understood within the context of the colonial aspects of this experience. According to Georges Balandier, the state is considered as a

> specialised, permanent and differentiated organ of political and administrative activity ... necessitating a governing apparatus capable of guaranteeing internal and border security. It manages a territory, organises political life in a way which corresponds to the hierarchy of power and authority, and ensures the implementation of fundamental decisions throughout the country under its jurisdiction. It is a means of domination held by a minority with the monopoly over political decision-making and as such, it is above the society, whose common interests it must still defend.[4]

In this sense, the state in the Maghreb is both a product of colonial heritage and the revival of endeavours which were unsuccessful in the Emir ʿAbd al-Qadir's Algeria, as well as in the Tunisia of Ahmad Bey and Khayr al-Din and in the Morocco of Hassan I.

The Algerian colonial model is of particular importance in so far as it preceded the other two and is seen as an example – in spite of the rhetoric on the nature of protectorates. When compared to standard colonial state structures it offers singularities which, although they may seem somewhat obvious, should nevertheless be recalled.

From the middle of the nineteenth century until 1962, Algeria was part of French national territory and was subject to a policy of administrative development which, despite different modes of implementation, was in fact an extension of the metropolitan model as far as education, conscription, taxes and public services were concerned.[5]

While this process of the development of the institutions of the state was carried out essentially by and on behalf of the minority population of French and Mediterranean settlers, it could not – as a matter of principle – exclude the indigenous population over which it also ruled. Its 'national' basis was developed progressively through the integration of populations of Mediterranean origin, to the exclusion of the Arab population, as well as Algeria's Jews whom the settlers wanted to exclude from this Franco-Mediterranean amalgam by eventually annulling the *Décret Cremieux*. The consequent ideological contradiction with the principles of the Third Republic, with which the European settlers ostensibly identified, was too significant to be ignored. They knew how to exploit this contradiction in parliament through their representatives in order to counter military dominance within the administration of Algeria and to obtain other advantages. They also sought to increase investments in viticulture which played a larger role than cereals within the local economy because of access to large external credits and guaranteed employment. The setting up of the *délégations financières*[6] in 1905, initiated in Algeria a regime of near autonomy designed to benefit the European minority. Thus, while sovereign expenses such as defence remained the responsibility of France, Algeria was able to manage its own income with a certain ease.

This situation made it impossible, with rare exceptions, for Arab elites to associate with the settler communities, as was the case for those territories that were united to France relatively late, like Savoy or Nice. Algeria could have moved towards a form of autonomy designed to benefit the majority group, as was the case in India or even in francophone Africa in the 1960s. But the colonisation process only managed to create a 'mamluk' caste within the Arab and Muslim population in areas like education and the military. The part played by Algerian troops, under the orders of Muslim officers and junior officers, in the colonisation of Morocco, the Rif war, both world wars and the Indo-Chinese war, shall not be forgotten, for instance. Apart from these two cases, the creation of Muslim Algerian elites never resulted in their being associated with other political or economic responsibilities in Algeria itself. At the most, some form of co-option occurred in France or in the colonial system outside the metropolis. This pattern of behaviour also spread to the two protectorates of Morocco and Tunisia despite the rhetoric of 'indirect administration'. However, the formal structures were paid more respect and the destruction of local elites was not the objective of the system. While the settlers were excluded from power during the Lyautey period, indirect administration did became a reality. Charles-André Julien has analysed the famous memorandum of 1920 which insisted that a sudden change of direction in policy was essential as a disillusioned acknowledgement of failure,[7] and of the end of 'indirect administration'.

From this point of view, therefore, the protectorate system appeared to be a convenient fiction which allowed freedom from French political and parliamentary control. It was a form of enlightened despotism over which France had little control outside the appointment and dismissal of its representative. The system worked with dedicated personalities such as Lyautey or Noguès and it even managed to persuade an important portion of the rural elite to associate itself with its administrative procedures for such processes as land registration, in which tribal land was registered in their individual names, thus turning ill-defined customary land law into a system of individual property ownership. However, this experience did not ultimately foster administrative performance at a time when a debate over the real control of power developed between the central power of the French-controlled administration, and the monarchy – itself supported by the urban middle class created by the Protectorate, and by rural discontent fostered by colonialism and the indigenous elite it had created as a partner. It was, in fact, the conflict with the king over the symbolism of state power (when he refused to countersign a law ordered by the French authorities) which was to reinforce the monarchy as the legitimate heir to power. The situation degenerated into a caricature under Juin and Guillaume as Residents-General.

The decision-making processes were actually influenced by civil servants and settler pressure groups who favoured extreme solutions which were just as unacceptable to France as to North African nationalists and the international community. Some perceived that the inevitable change would come soon after the Second World War – particularly those military officers in indigenous affairs who had held important positions in Indo-China, and who had witnessed the decolonisatian of India and liaised with their English counterparts during frequent visits to Colombo. In the course of their conversations the lack of realism prevailing in French policy at the time and in French colonial circles made the colonial enterprise appear itself as a lost cause.[8]

Ironically enough, the exile of Mohamed V revealed the king as the true holder of state power. No institution had the legitimate authority required to replace him in his absence, and political negotiations with the nationalists were limited, initially, to making his return possible. With the collapse of the administrative network in rural areas and the effects of urban terrorism, both of which jeopardised the survival of colonisation, the only possible recourse to resolve the crisis seemed to be the king. After attempting to retrieve the situation by other various means, the Edgar Faure government was forced to give the king sole power in order to guarantee in return the safety of the settlers. Before that, Mendes-France had initiated, as early as 1954, a similar process of derogation in Tunisia in favour of the Neo-Destour which took control of the state away from settlers while letting Paris retain some prerogatives of power in external affairs and security. The same kind of transfer – this time (characterised by a total and absolute derogation) of power – eventually occurred in the 1960s in favour of the Algerian FLN, when the Algerian movement agreed to respect French oil and nuclear interests in the Sahara in return. Eventually, the setting up of new states in North Africa only took place through the symbolic and real end of settler colonisation, population transfer, and political separation from the national terri-tory of France. Colonisation had served as a catalyst for nationalism and as a mould for the future states in the region. It is in this sense that it unwillingly constituted the origin of the new nation-states in the region. Independent Algeria inherited a territory deeply marked by colonisation and thus burdened with unresolved conflicts. In some respects, the pattern of decolonisation and the transfer of state power, particularly in Algeria, is closer to the Haitian example of 1804 than to the transfers negotiated in the interest of local nationalists by Great Britain, Spain or The Netherlands. Independence granted Algeria an advantage in terms of territory, oil revenues and even infrastructure, which had been built over a long period and which had been expanded just before independence by the Constantine Plan. The transfer of power did not follow the Guinean model, much to the surprise and the disappointment of neighbouring countries, who then become aware of the potential competition from Algeria created by its independence. Although France was to be constantly accused of having favoured Algeria,[9] Algeria has always insisted that it never received sufficient compensation for the length of the colonial period and the hardship involved in its termination.[10]

THE MODERN STATE

The re-appropriation of the model of the state occurred on three levels: a modern educational system fed the rise of a centralised bureaucracy – reinforced in Algeria and Tunisia by a single party, which was as much an extension of the Jacobin model of the French Revolution as it was an imitation of Communist party of the Soviet Union. In the course of 130 years of co-existence, capital transfers from Algeria were both massive and illegitimate. France's inability to integrate Algeria into the nation-state was felt as a failure of the republican synthesis, much as the Haitian revolt was perceived as a failure of the revolutionary synthesis. The break between France and Algeria has more in common with the Anglo-Irish experience[11] than with other colonial examples, whether French or not. North African states were able to establish their legitimacy with relative ease since their only standard of comparison was the previous colonial state. This gave rise to a political rhetoric reminiscent of the discourse of the Fourth Republic used by the French Resistance during the Second World War. In fact, behind this façade the leaders of the new states have integrated into their behaviour the suspicion and rejection of all public manifestations of cultural, geographic and religious specificities (including Islam itself) which had necessarily constituted the basic principle of the old colonial republican vision. This is the origin of the rejection of pluralism, expressed in various ways in the three states and particularly strongly in Algeria and Tunisia.

The Moroccan monarchy, on the other hand, hardly needed to mobilise these tactics as it was already the legitimate symbol of resistance to the colonial state. But it was also much more than that; the recovery of state power prevented it from being crushed by the single party structure which is just as inherent in Moroccan political organisation as it was in neighbouring countries. Such a development was thwarted as early as 1958 by the public liberty law, which allowed the formation of political parties, and by the Constitution of 1962 which outlawed the concept of the single party. The monarchy thus remained the sole symbol of unity, while also transcending it. It encouraged various forms of pluralism as long as it was able to retain control over them and limit their spread to the elites, thus ensuring a patron–client relationship with them in an approach which was reminiscent of the old *makhzan*.

In all three countries, regimes use coercion primarily in response to behaviour that threatens the principle of national unity, whether embodied in an individual, a group or an institution. In seeking to ensure the unity of the state, leaders use the modern notion of personalisation of power as well as the innate Muslim concept of unity. Here too, the Moroccan monarchy feels more self-assured in its legitimacy and can afford a degree of flexibility. While the very concept of monarchy, and of the boundaries of the state and of the public observance of Islam, must be respected, everything else is negotiable. But, in order to generate submissive reflexes in the political elites, the nature and timing of repressive actions vary constantly. Sanctions take the form of passport confiscation rather than prison sentence, or the grant or withholding of official approval which is, in any case, a normal part of the usual political game. The same applied for Bourguiba's Tunisia and Boumedienne's Algeria, but the level of tolerance of dissident action was lower and the official line was always more pervasive. In Morocco, the failure to play by the rules of the elite's pluralist game attracts more disapproval than the expression of dissident opinions on the functioning of the adminis-tration of the social system. Leaders also use geographic pluralism in a subtle way, including the private sector. Furthermore, the capital city, Rabat, is a city of civil servants – as was intended by Lyautey. It is therefore less likely to witness the turmoil which may affect the main economic metropolis, Casablanca. A functional distance has been established between the centre of power and the masses which does not exist in the same way in the other two countries. There, the management of geographic solidarities which pose a threat to the concept of unity is also more brutal and more threatening to the ambitions of the various clans.

The reason why the monopoly of coercion – exercised in the name of unity – has played an important role in the institutionalisation of the state, lies not so much in nation-building as in the extension of the bureaucracy, the centralised management of development and the establishment of solidarity systems linked to a particular version of the state as provider which emphasised subsidising staple consumer goods. Nationalism is an essential driving force of the system.

The establishment of huge national bureacracies in all three coun-tries played an essential role in the legitimisation of the process of state formation and nation-building. In the colonial state, public services covered mainly the needs of the European minority. For the authorities, looking after the Muslim population meant essentially safeguarding public order as Muslims often administered rural areas, notably in the areas of justice, land credit, rural employment and even control of education. The result was a lack of technical supervision, which was balanced by a refined political management of social groups. Independence soon allowed nationals to take over the bureaucracy and to extend it into these sectors neglected by the col-onial system. Education, the police, and the army benefited from this increase in control which was visible in various complementary ways in each of the three systems.

Globally, the number of jobs in the administration increased tenfold within twenty years, thus creating roles and functions which had not existed in the colonial bureaucracy and thereby developing the social basis for a new middle class. While the Maghrebi states do not offer each graduate a post in the state apparatus, as was the case in Nasser's Egypt, social practice was probably quite close to the same principles until the beginning of the 1980s. The mass of frequently underpaid civil servants established an often underestimated link between civil society and the state and sometimes contributed both to the stability of the system and to its malfunction. On the one hand they supported a large number of people through family solidarity, on the other they acted as agents, selling their services and influence, giving jobs to relatives and contributing thereby to the discrediting of the state. They were also the first to benefit from consumer subsidies, according to a system established in the 1960s essentially in the interest of urban populations. Rural populations sometimes get help in the form of state projects for reafforestation, new roads and small irrigation works. These have had some impact in economically deprived areas of Morocco. Although reductions in foreign aid, under the influence of international financial organisations, led to bread riots in Morocco and Tunisia in 1981 and 1984, order was quickly re-established and the turmoil hardly touched rural areas which were affected instead by drought and natural disasters. These natural phenomena had caused thousands of casualties after the Second World War.

Thus, on the whole, the nation-states of the Maghreb were better able to deal with difficulties than the colonial administration had been, even though populations had doubled. They were also better off than many African countries. However, in the Maghreb, official involvement with civil society never reached the same extent as in Egypt for example.[12] The state has been able to create social groups directly associated to its existence and with an interest in its survival. It has changed its social environment through education development policies and through assisting urban growth. It also initiated huge infrastructural projects and important operations for the development of industrial production. This kind of project is more closely related to the considerable 'industrialising industries' ventures undertaken by Algeria, or to Ben Salah's experiment with total socialisation of the economy in Tunisia, than to the Moroccan practice in which investment money was more scarce and the King suspicious of anything that had the potential to drastically disrupt the social balance. But the development policy of the phosphate industry (symbol of the state since Lyautey) or that of the great dams and the million hectares irrigation plan played roughly the same role.

This legitimisation through development and modernisation was enhanced by aggressive nationalism directed towards close neighbours and illustrated by border problems, which were dealt with in the manner of nineteenth-century European nationalisms. However, although nationalism may have been used as a means of creating internal tension, none of the Maghreb countries became involved in major conflicts aimed at destroying any of their neighbours. During the 1963 border war between Algeria and Morocco, the armed struggle was soon replaced by diplomatic discussions within the Organisation of African Unity (OAU). Admittedly, the Western Sahara conflict led to several long-lasting breaks in diplomatic relations and to numerous expulsions of the other party's nationals, as was the case in the conflicts between Libya and Tunisia. But direct confrontation was avoided between Morocco and Algeria, which might not have been the case if the matter had been left entirely in the hands of the military. In the long run, the purpose of the confrontation was effectively to achieve hegemony within the Maghreb, in which Algeria had a sizeable advantage in the form of resources from oil revenues and because of its dynamic management of the international environment. The Maghreb has had no conflict of the magnitude of the Iran–Iraq war or the inter-Arab consequences of the conflict with Israel. The fear of seeing the military take over in such circumstances has probably a lot to do with the cautious strategy of political leaders. Bourguiba was well known for his strong aversion to the military – which may have been inherited from his long acquaintance with the politicians of the Third and Fourth Republics.

After the 1971 and 1972 attempts against the Moroccan monarchy, the King became actively suspicious of the army and took over strategic command, an approach which failed in the first phase of the Western Sahara war.[13] None the less, Algeria was the only country in the Maghreb where a military *coup d'état* was successful, but this did not give rise to a political system run exclusively by the military. However in all three political systems the role of the military is not limited to the external defence of the state – it can also be used for internal stability. In the beginning, they tended to be involved in struggles against separatist ethnic movements as in the 1958 Rif and Tafilalt revolts and the 1963 Kabyl uprising, but gradually the army was also called in to put down urban uprisings which the police were unable to control. It started in Casablanca in 1965 with riots which already showed the rift between the state and those who had not benefited from independence. This rupture between the state and the dispossessed only widened, and riots broke out again when the state withdrew subsidies on basic foodstuffs.

Other socio-economic decisions can have unforeseen consequences, such as the increase in butane gas or petrol cost, or changes in the rules governing the education system, which may lead to mass movements that cannot always be controlled. Even important football matches can turn into violent demonstrations against the regime, according to the results. Experience shows that police forces are soon overwhelmed by the size of these mass movements and that the army alone possesses the means to intervene successfully, often involving the use of firearms if rioters do not disperse quickly enough. Thus, state power is preserved but at a cost which is difficult to evaluate in terms of the alienation of the dispossessed from the political dialogue. More important than this is the army's basically cool response to this sort of unattractive task. Thus, the Moroccan army's involvement in guaranteeing the stability of the state from 1965 was the root of the two attempts on the king's life in 1971 and 1972. If they are called in too often to repair what they believe are the mistakes, mismanagement and also the corruption of civilians, the military will feel they should be given complete power. It was the use of the Tunisian army against the UGTT in 1982 and the bread riots of 1984 which sparked off the process that led to the removal of Bourguiba. But this time another sort of responsibility was involved which only became the army's at a later stage: the fight against the Islamists. We note that the army is, within the social body, one of the groups most exposed to the Islamists' rhetoric and that, at the same time, it must provide the ultimate protection against the former's subversive activities.

THE STATE AND ISLAM

It is paradoxical that the usual apparatus of repression was for a long time geared towards the control of left-wing organisations. The 'secular' tradition of the Maghreb political apparatuses, especially in Tunisia, seems to have failed to prepare the police for the control and infiltration of Islamic organisations. There is little information on the Algerian situation but it would appear that the army and the gendarmerie were called in to storm the Laghouat mosque in 1982[14] and to intervene in the Bouali insurrection in 1986.

In Morocco, the police have always been responsible for the control of religious groupings suspected of political activism. Since the late 1970s, a number of senior officials in the interior ministry have been recruited from the *Shariʿa* schools' best students and then sent to the Kenitra management school. This type of agent, trained within the arena of official Islam, has been prepared to understand the dialectic used by the regime's adversaries and to become involved in operations involving infiltration or manipulation of religious activists in a manner that was once widely used by the *Affaires Indigènes* service. There are, of course, risks of reversal, but Islam seems to be more directly under control in Morocco than in neighbouring countries. On the whole, the problem posed by Islamic protest has been the main preoccupation of governments and observers in the region since the Iranian revolution in 1979. The image of a regime which had been perceived as powerful and fearsome only one month before, and which crumbled without resistance under the pressure of the urban masses mobilised by the *mullahs,* frightens other political leaders. The hostile popular reactions to the Shah's stay in Morocco, at the beginning of his exile, showed how sensitive public opinion was to Iranian events and persuaded Hassan II to limit his support of the deposed monarch.

But does this mean that the North African states are as vulnerable to the rise of the Islamic movement as Iran or even Egypt, as Bruno Etienne suggests?[15] Certainly the failure of the nation-state to provide for material needs or to give the urban population hope makes it alien and illegitimate for those excluded from the benefits of modernity. But it answers the needs of the elite and the middle class who live on the benefits of what was confiscated at independence, and it serves indirectly – and much more efficiently than colonisation did in its phase of decline – the interests of the market economy integrated into the international economy. 'Thus, the rise of Islamism is a reaction to anarchic modernity or rather an attempt to be with one's peers, within the group'.[16] In this global protest 'the target of the Islamists is the individual in his everyday life' and the control of female behaviour becomes a major political issue. But are we to conclude from this that 'the conflict between order and the system can only be solved by altering the system'? Is it not the case that conflict also plays a functional role in the preservation of the system? Moreover, as Bruno Etienne indicates, 'the Islamist operates a transfer of enthusiasm' which compensates for post-independence disillusion. While it is true that the Maghreb was affected by the crushing of the Arab armies in 1967, as well as by the Iranian revolution, the upsurge of Islamic movements there is more immediately due to shortcomings in the development process and to the increase in inequalities which accompanies either socialist or market economy development policies.

Considered in the context of accelerated development, which allowed the population to be doubled without any major upheaval, and taking into account very rapid urbanisation – over 50 per cent of the total population are now urban – and an increase in industrial production which, together with hydrocarbon production and emigration, puts it far ahead of agricultural production, the role of the Islamists of the 1980s can best be compared with that of the European Communist parties in the 1930s. They offer those disillusioned with modernity and rationalism an alternative which has room for dreams while at the same time persuading them to accept compromises which will strengthen the system.

The question is, in other words, will the Islamists who accept a dialogue with modernising states play the role of the tribune, defending the dispossessed and ensuring respect for innate values? Should they choose this function, which implies the renunciation, at least, of the principle of ideological hegemony, the regimes concerned will have to make concessions to them. But these concessions could also contribute to the consolidation of the system. In an economy where the population grows almost as quickly as new resources, taking Islamic values into account may help to reduce luxury consumption and pressure the privileged social strata into showing more solidarity through making them feel guilty and taxing the surpluses they may attempt to spend on western-type goods. Furthermore, it should not be forgotten that Islamic codes of behaviour offer an ideological substitute to the state's advantage because they control behaviour, thus creating reflexes of obedience which outgrow the religious domain and thus benefit the regime.

Saudi Arabia, and, to a lesser extent Morocco and Libya, know how to use legal means of coercion in order to control individual behaviour. But the concessions that the regimes will have to make towards Islamic movements in return for their legitimisation are likely to be in terms of modifications of the Code of Personal Status. A limit of what this type of compromise would involve already exists in Mubarak's Egypt and probably in Ben Ali's Tunisia as well. A global approach will be difficult as long as the state remains an authoritarian and uncontrolled power system. None of the parties can be sure that the others will respect the rules of the game in the long term and therefore none has any reason to renounce the complete implementation of its own programme.

DEMOCRACY AND THE FUTURE

An interesting variant seems to have been introduced into the political game by the perspective of democratisation. This offers interesting possibilities of compromise through the arbitration of public opinion. Of course, the Islamists have no more consideration for formal democracy than Marxist parties in the 1930s, but some currents may already be at work which might be the equivalent of what Social Democracy was to the international Communist movement. Without the revolution of 1917 and the rise of Communism in Europe, the New Deal would certainly not have had the same chances of success in the United States. In the event, the redistribution of wealth and power it made possible greatly consolidated the market economy and the rise of the federal state. Is it, then, inconceivable that the Iranian revolution and the rise of Islamism in the Middle East may play a similar role in re-integrating those excluded from the process of state-formation and nation-building by the introduction of new networks of solidarity and reviving innate inherited values which do not stem from the western model? When engaged in war with Iraq, for example, Iran showed itself more as a nation-state capable of managing modernity on an international scale than as an Islamic republic. Peace should give a greater place to civil society and maybe give more freedom to the various types of compromise mentioned earlier. Mubarak's Egypt is already well on the road to this diversity which acknowledges the role of Islamist politico-religious protest in order to control it by playing the various trends against each other. 'What appears as disorder may also be, in some sense, a phase of adaptation to another order, or of a different order.'[17]

The Moroccan monarchy has been able in the past to find its way in this kind of situation and the new Tunisian regime may be going in this direction too. However, the danger might come from a sudden decline in the resource-base, reducing the political and diplomatic flexibility of debtor states because of international pressure. But the Maghrebi states' own resources are quite significant and they are too involved in various international, Arab, European, and Western solidarity networks to fail to find the necessary credits in order to reschedule their debts and to avoid catastrophe.

While Islamic movements are still perceived as a law unto themselves, it would be more constructive to look at their potential role in a democratic context. The sudden changes which have taken place in the Maghreb since the departure of Bourguiba in November 1987, show, perhaps for the first time, democratisation as a realistic strategy which can be used by regimes trying to consolidate their power. This would constitute a less dangerous alternative than to attempt to maintain an apparent absolutism which works against government in that it puts it in competition with Islam. The Tunisian case deserves particular attention, first because it marks a sudden change in the concept of nation-building which had held to rigid assumptions since independence. The Ben Ali regime is aware it needs a new source of legitimacy and seeks a political opening which will include those Islamists who are prepared to respect the democratic process. The new president has imposed pluralism on a dominant party and on a bureaucracy which is still unenthusiastic – the loyalty of senior civil servants is not certain if democratisation is not be limited to co-option.

The Tunisian situation shows similarities both to that of Mubarak's Egypt and to Gorbachev's Soviet Union: the president will not be able to halt his strategy of democratisation without risk of having it being distorted by the ruling party apparatus. He will only be able to escape the grip of this apparatus once he has won his own legitimacy through legislative or, even better, presidential elections. But elections will only really be a source of legitimacy if they allow all currents and tendencies who accept the rules of the game to participate. This scenario assumes, of course, that on the one hand Islamic movements are recognised and on the other that they accept in return participation in an institutional game which will legitimise the state and ultimately seek to prevent them from coming to power. This can only occur if trust exists between all the parties involved, especially in the transitional phase. It also requires that Islamist leaders must have some hope of participating in an institutional process which is open to their influence providing they do not expect to obtain power immediately, by subjecting themselves to the results of universal suffrage. The alternative to this scenario is that if the actors of the Tunisian political process do not accept the risks attached to democratisation they are very likely to return to an authoritarian regime which will be increasingly forced to rely on the army.

However, the modification of the political rules in Tunisia is not the only consequence of the change which has occurred there, for it has already influenced the whole of the political scene in the Maghreb. Not only did Bourguiba's Tunisia have a very stilted internal political life, it also had become an inactive and cautious partner on the international scene. The new president appeared immediately to be a more flexible partner who could choose his own alliance structures. Algeria was trying to revive a strategy of Maghreb unity in order to be able to face the Europe of 1992 on a more equal footing and it became clear that Tunisia would not agree to become involved in such a venture if it continued to be based on the isolation of Morocco. But the reintegration of the latter into the Maghreb arena and its reconciliation with Algeria could only be achieved if the terms attached to the end of the Western Sahara conflict were acceptable to Rabat. However, this new situation also influences the Moroccan political scene which has been stable since 1975 because of the conflict. It raises the issue of the referendum and the status of the future territory within Morocco. If Morocco gains satisfaction as far as the principle of reintegration is concerned, it must also envisage the organisation of its new national territory on the basis of wide-spread autonomy. But this situation will undoubtedly influence the relationship between central power and other regions – the Rif, the Souss, the Middle Atlas and the mountain areas to the east, not to mention the old imperial cities of Fez or Marrakesh – for all will surely demand similar advantages to those granted to the Sahraoui. This change could offer the perfect opportunity for real political transition, which the Moroccan monarch has sought and feared since the attempts on his life in 1971 and 1972.

The Western Sahara conflict, accompanied by shrewd manage-ment of civil society and a real effort at decentralisation since 1976, has allowed the King to confine himself mainly to a pluralism limited to the elite and to a political system centred on himself. The King and his entourage are only too aware of the advantages and risks involved in ending the Saharan conflict, albeit in conditions which are, on the whole, favourable to Morocco. But this development eliminates the one factor which has helped maintain the unity of the political system for over ten years by turning the Western Sahara issue into a symbol of state formation and of the Moroccan state's refusal to accept a framework of regional relations dominated by Algeria. A democratic step forward along the model of the German *länder*[18] can offer a new mode of mass political participation without compromising the king's grip on central power. The logic of this process requires constitution-ally a second legislative chamber possessing real powers and subse-quently the election of the first legislative chamber without official interference. This could also involve a referendum that would modify the Constitution and also ratify concessions on the Sahara. This is the price Hassan II should expect to pay to ensure that the army returns to the barracks and to decrease his military budget with a view to channelling more resources for development. The risk in this hypo-thesis of Moroccan democratic transition lies more with the military than with the Islamists. There seems to be less of a danger in a state which has always successfully managed to keep an eye on Islam, while still granting its youth a certain degree of individual freedom give an air of Mediterranean *joie de vivre* that is hardly found in neighbouring countries. As in Egypt, sports, leisure, cinema and rock music, adapted or translated in Arabic, present a significant counterweight to the awakening of Islam.[19]

Algeria remains an enigma within this evolution, while it also influences its neighbours. Its control of the Sahara, the advantages of oil revenues, its military might and diplomatic skill, all give it a pre-eminence which would be in its interest to play down. By shifting its position on the Sahara it has allowed the Moroccan transition to take place. It would be hard to imagine Algeria not following with interest – and some anxiety – Ben Ali's pluralist drive which has signed the death warrant of the one-party state. The FLN and the Algerian military leaders were definitely not ready to follow in these steps until the 1990s. However, they cannot remain indifferent to the changes that are occurring in their immediate environment. But the Algerian political system faced Islamic protest without much anxiety and did not, until the end of the 1980s, envisage pluralism outside the party framework. It also sought to limit its effect to local echelons. On the other hand, the economy may constitute an acceptable area for liberalism, and thus be a substitute to a stagnant political life in the wake of the army takeover in January 1992. The structure of the Maghreb would encourage this development if it were organised in a coherent form, particularly in terms of tourism, agricultural production or consumer goods. Neighbouring countries possess resources which Algeria still lacks. Joint ventures can be set up even involving Eastern Arab partners who are increasingly present in the Tunisian banking system, notably through the network of Islamic banks. But these developments, which could give birth to a trans-state North African civil society, can only occur if Algeria genuinely decides to let its private sector act freely and independently, since potential Middle Eastern and North African partners in joint ventures have no wish to become involved with Algerian national companies as their majority partners. The Algerian National Assembly only recently passed a law submitted by the government which makes this sort of development possible. Those who stood to profit from the state-sponsored system of austerity may still not be ready to accept liberalisation and competition. In fact, a pan-North African economic structure may stand a better chance of being developed today. Significant private resources exist and are ready to participate if they feel they can overcome state intervention. This would also require Algeria's currency to become convertible within the Maghreb and cease to be overvalued. The Algerian regime has now embarked upon this policy, which will diminish its formal grip on civil society but increase the stability of the political environment, It must continue it if it wishes to escape from its oil-based economy in order to prepare itself for balanced relations with the Single European Market after 1992. The policy of integration with the Single European Market contains an economic priority area which Algeria is already preparing to negotiate, against a background of improved inter-Maghreb relations. The recent reopening of negotiations with Spain on the installation of a trans-Mediterranean gas pipeline going through Morocco and linked in to the European gas pipeline network constitutes a considerable commitment. Algeria will then be in a competitive position in the European market in respect of Siberian gas supplies.

But Europe is much more than an economic entity. The Maghreb states will have to manage with the outwash effects created by direct satellite broadcasts, new ideas, different cultures and the consumer society. Until now, regimes could enjoy the illusion of controlling these cultural areas and thus of maintaining an ideological monopoly. The North African community in Europe is going to create permanent links and channels whose effects will be visible in the consumer society as well as in the field of ideas. This context will make it increasingly difficult for an authoritarian regime to control the rise of individualism in the middle class. The Jacobin-style political systems put in place in the aftermath of independence are no longer appropriate to these situations. But can another type of arbitrator-state, operating between groups tempted by extreme economic individualism centred on the outside, and Islamic movements who will manage the dispossessed through religion, find legitimacy in the establishment of a democratic dialogue between these two extremes?

Seen in this perspective, the model of the state in the Maghreb, at least in Tunisia and Morocco, could present an interesting case of political stabilisation combining religious power and the integration of the masses in an open and competitive political system. Algeria, meanwhile, may remain faithful to the classic politico-military system along Egyptian or Turkish lines. How can elites, with different origins articulate their role in a phase of intensive economic development?[20] As far as the military are concerned, the structures are known from the Egyptian model. This is not so much the case for the clerics, although an in-depth study of the Iranian model could bring many surprises. A comparison is to be found in the considerable role played by *Opus Dei* in the economic development of Spain in the 1960s, which prepared, against its own wishes, the social and economic bases of democratic transition. For its part, Italian Christian Democracy continued very early on to support the economic development initiated by the previous Fascist regime. INE, the major state holding company for energy, controlled by Ettore Mattei, provides an interesting example of this pattern.

Egypt, for example, already has Islamic bankers who possess frighteningly effective skills in pious exchange speculations. Thus, are we going to see the Maghreb states follow, with a certain delay and with their own cultural variants, the democratic transition which occurred in Southern Europe and Latin America?[21] This hypothesis would appear in many ways more likely than that of the subversion of the state by Islamic movements.

NOTES

1 See, for example, Bruno Etienne, *L'Islam Radical* (Paris: Hachette, 1987).
2 The term North Africa refers here to Morocco, Algeria and Tunisia – conventionally described as the Maghreb.
3 The phrase is Bertrand Badie's. See his *Les deux états* (Paris: Fayaid, 1986).
4 Georges Balandier, *Anthropologie politique* (Paris: PUF, 1979), pp. 175–6, quoted by Abdelkader Zghal in 'L'Islam, les janissaires et le destour', in Michel Camau *et al.*, *Tunisie au present* (Paris: CNRS, 1987), pp. 379–80.
5 See *Histoire de l'Algérie contemporaine*, Tome I, Charles-André Julien, *La conquête et les débuts de la colonisation (1827–1871)*. Tome II, Charles Robert Ageron, *De l'insurrection de 1871 au declachement de la guerre de libération* (Paris: PUF, 1979).
6 This was an elected colonial assembly created on 25 August 1898 in which the European population of Algeria was able to influence government policy and to which later on a separate minority Muslim section was added.
7 Charles-André Julien, *Le Maroc face aux impérialismes 1415–1956* (Paris: Editions Jeune Afrique, 1978), p. 95.
8 Interview with General Meric, last Director of Internal Affairs under the Protectorate (1973).
9 See Hassan II's interview in *Le Monde* of 3 August 1988.
10 See Jean Leca and Jean-Claude Vatin, *L'Algérie politique, institutions et régimes* (Paris: FNSP, 1975), and Bruno Etienne, *Algérie, cultures et révolutions* (Paris: Seuil, 1977).
11 See Ian Lustick, *State Building Failure in British Ireland and French Algeria* (Berkeley: IIS, 1985).
12 See Maurice Pierre Martin, 'Etat et société civile en Egypte', *Projet*, no. 212, July–August 1988, pp. 6–12, and Nadia Khouri-Dagher, '"La fail-

lite" de l'Etat dans l'approvisionnement alimentaire des citadins: mythe ou realité', *Peuples Méditerranéens*, no. 41–2, October 1987 and March 1988, pp. 193–209.

13 William Zartman (ed.), *The Political Economy of Morocco* (New York: Praeger, 1987), p. 23.
14 See Bruno Etienne, *L'Islam Radical, op. cit.*
15 *Ibid.*
16 *Ibid.*, p. 109.
17 See M. P. Martin, *op. cit.*
18 See Hassan II's interview in *Le Monde*, 3 August 1988.
19 See M. P. Martin, *op. cit.*, p. 14.
20 See Bertrand Badie, *op. cit.*, especially p. 245.
21 See Guy Hermet, *Aux frontières de la Démocratie* (Paris: PUF, 1986), and *L'Espagne au XXe siècle*, (Paris: PUF, 1986).

16 The present and future of the Maghreb Arab Union

Mohamed Chtatou

BACKGROUND

Geographically speaking, the Arab Maghrib (*al-Maghrib al-Arabi*) is an immense territory of 6,000,000 sq. km extending on a south–north axis from the Senegal River to Tangier on the Straits of Gibraltar and on a west–east axis from the Atlantic shore to Libya's border with Egypt. This area is punctuated by mountain ranges, mainly the Atlas, which to the north runs almost horizontally through Morocco, Algeria and Tunisia. To the south, the whole of the Maghreb is continuously covered by great expanses of the Sahara.

Of the countries that constitute the Maghreb as a whole – that is, Mauritania, Morocco, Algeria, Tunisia and Libya – there is no doubt that Morocco is the one best endowed by nature in terms of water resources thanks to the Atlas mountains which not only fend off the desert climate but also constitute a formidable reservoir from which flow most of the rivers of the country.

The total population of the Maghreb is estimated today at 80 million inhabitants. The birth-rate, which conservative estimates put around 3 per cent, is undoubtedly one of the highest in the world. By the year 2000, if the birth-rate stays at what it is today, the population will reach the 100 million psychological barrier. The population would not be much of a headache for the countries of the area, considering the great potential of the region, if it were not for the problem of illiteracy which runs as high as 57 per cent and is certainly a tremendous obstacle to achieving aspirations for development of the peoples and their governments.[1]

The ethnic make-up is not as complex as in the case of the Middle East population for example.[2] Prior to the coming of the Arabs and Islam in the seventh century AD, the Maghreb was populated only by Berbers, whose origin is still a matter of heated debate and controversy. The languages used are: Classical Arabic which is the official language; dialects of Arabic used for daily communication by the people in each of the five countries; Berber, known as *Tamazight* and spoken by Berbers; and, with the exception of Libya, French is used as the language of business and communication with the rest of the outside world.

Despite the relatively diverse ethnic and linguistic pictures given above, thanks to Islam, which has for centuries acted as a unifying and binding factor, the Maghreb remains very homogeneous as a whole. Entelis argues in this respect that:

> North African Islam serves as an important common denominator transcending and mitigating the differences of tribe, language and life style. Unlike any other historical or contemporary force, Islam remains paramount in all these countries notwithstanding the different policies toward religion and religious practice adopted by the various political leaders of the Maghreb.[3]

The term *Maghrib*, currently used to designate the North African countries of Mauritania, Morocco, Algeria, Tunisia and Libya, is short for *Jazirat al-Maghrib* (The Island of the West), the name that the first Muslim Arab soldiers gave to the area when they conquered it. Today the term *al-Maghrib al-Arabi* (the Arab West) is used to contrast with *al-Mashriq al-Arabi* (the Arab East) often referred to as the Middle East. However, the designation *Afrique du Nord* (North Africa) became fashionable around 1830 with the colonisation of Algeria, and subsequently referred to the countries that were under French colonial domination in this area.

The totality of the Maghreb, until the advent of Ottoman suzerainty, shared a common historical destiny. It was the target of Phoenician commercial domination in the Mediterranean; it came under Roman colonial rule, and was for centuries ruled by Berber monarchs and chieftains (Juba II, Kahina, etc.). With the introduction of Islam around the seventh century, the new faith brought the people of the area even closer together during the reign of the Berber dynasties of the Almoravids and Almohads between the ninth and the thirteenth centuries. However, the Ottoman conquest in the fifteenth century put an end to this common historical destiny, since Libya, Tunisia and Algeria came under their domination while Morocco retained its sovereignty until the early twentieth century when the French imposed their Protectorate. Needless to say, on several occasions the Ottomans tried to conquer Morocco but failed to do so.

As stated earlier, one of the strong factors in unifying the Maghreb as a whole is undoubtedly Islam. Indeed, the people of the Maghreb are all Sunni and follow in their majority the Maliki rite, with the exception of the inhabitants of Mzab, in south-central Algeria, and those of the Island of Djerba, off the east coast of Tunisia, who are Kharejites. On this particular issue, Gellner states that:

> North African civilization does not, like the Middle East, consist of 'enclaves' – to use Dr Louise Sweet's expression – of inward – turned communities, often openly displaying their religious or cultural idiosyncracy. Such diversity as is found in North Africa is, above all, discreet: it does not underscore or advertise its idiosyncracies, which remain hidden under the newly all-embracing cloak of Sunni Islam of the Maliki rite. Of course there is de facto religious diversity, manifested in the proliferation of saint cults, religious brotherhoods, and differences in religious style of various milieux; but these differences stop short, considerably short, of an avowed separation or schism, and L. J. Duclos even claims that through their repetition of similar themes and solutions in diverse localities, these fragmented movements actually make a contribution to a sense of national unity.[4]

RESOURCES

A quick glance at the economic potentials of the member countries of the Maghreb Arab Union (Union du Maghreb Arabe, UMA) reveals that they are complementary, and that counted together they could easily create the ideal environment for the rapid development of the region.

Mauritania

Until 1960, the year of its independence, Mauritania had an economy which depended on a rural and traditional structure based on stock-breeding and agriculture. Owing to technical and financial assistance from the Arab world and the West, Mauritania has modernised its economy in pursuit of rapid development of the country. Thus, successful attempts have been made to mechanise agriculture, mainly along the Senegal River, where the arable land is located.

Over the last five years, the economic plans of the government have concentrated on developing the agricultural sector so as to counter the lasting effects of the drought of the 1970s on the population. Indeed, several schemes have been set up to improve irrigation by building dams on the Senegal River. The most important of these schemes is the Gorgol valley irrigation scheme, which necessitated an investment of $92 million, about 5 per cent of which sum was covered by loans from such Arab countries as Saudi Arabia and Libya, in addition to countries like France and institutions like the EEC and the World Bank. The scheme is expected to irrigate the equivalent of 33,000 hectares of land.[5]

Along with the southern coast of Morocco, the Mauritanian coast is considered to be the world's richest fishing area, but because the country does not have the appropriate means to exploit this resource most of it is plundered by industrialised nations such as Japan and the USSR. The potential catch of fish off the Mauritanian coast is estimated at 1 million tons annually.

Mauritania is very rich in minerals, mainly copper and iron ore. The iron ore reserves are estimated at 500 million tons with an iron content of 70 per cent. The annual production of this mineral is estimated at 10,000,000 tonnes. The country is thought to have other minerals, mainly gypsum, tungsten, petroleum, phosphates and uranium.[6]

Morocco

Because of its rich soil and abundant water resources, thanks to the Atlas and the Rif Mountains, many observers think that with the proper investment Morocco has the potential to become the breadbasket of the Maghreb of tomorrow. Indeed, even today Morocco supplies the Algerian market with most of its immediate needs of fruit and vegetables.

Thanks to a rigorous policy of dam-building (the country has over 30 major dams today and King Hassan II has taken it upon himself to build a dam every year until the year 2000) and thanks to the accelerated programme of mechanisation and modernisation, agriculture in contemporary Morocco is a rapidly developing sector though it does not yet meet national needs in cereals and sugar. With the expansion of '*culture sous serre*' (greenhouse agriculture), especially in areas known for their conservative agricultural practices, Morocco today is producing quality fruit and vegetables mainly for export to the EEC and to Arab countries.

Fisheries is another important sector of the economy that is developing rapidly. Since 1984, the annual catch has been estimated at 350,000 tonnes. This sector employs 75,000 people and the fleet consists of 2,000 boats. In 1988, Morocco exported 14,000 tonnes of canned sardines to EEC countries.[7]

Morocco holds about two-thirds of the world's known reserves of phosphate rock. It is the third largest world producer after the USA and USSR, with an annual output of about 21 million tonnes. Besides phosphates, Morocco has many other minerals, most of which are untapped, including antimony, cobalt, lead and zinc, fluorspar, barytes, copper, manganese, coal, iron ore and silver. The mining sector handles annually 26 million tonnes of ores and employs 65,000 people.[8]

Of late, Morocco has invested heavily in industry, mainly in that of downstream phosphates. Four phosphate processing plants are in operation: Maroc Chimie I, Maroc Chimie II, Maroc Phosphore I, Maroc Phosphore II; and two more are under construction: Maroc Phosphore III and IV. Another important investment was in the Nador steel rod and bar mill, built with the help of UK funds and expertise. Its annual production is estimated at 420,000 tonnes.

Morocco's food-processing and textile industry remain of considerable importance in terms of workforce, output and infrastructure, not to mention the engineering sector with four plants: SOMACA, SOPRIAM, SMEIA and Renault Maroc.

Morocco boasts very efficient banking and insurance services which are considered to be among the best in Africa; the same is also true of its network of roads, railways and seaports.

Algeria

Algeria has a major agricultural potential, with about 7.6 million hectares of arable land and 4.4 million hectares of forests; but with the exploitation of oil, especially after the sector was nationalised during the Boumedienne era, this sector took a back seat, particularly after the *Révolution Agraire* (agrarian reform).

Mineral resources are the greatest asset of the Algerian economy. Prior to the discovery of oil, the country extracted and exported antimony, lead, zinc and high-grade iron ore.

Production of crude petroleum on a commercial basis began in 1958 reaching a peak of 1.8 million barrels per day (b/d) in 1978 but, by 1986, the production had fallen to an average of 670,000 b/d. In 1987, the known reserves of crude petroleum were estimated at 8,500 million barrels. Besides crude petroleum, Algeria has other important hydrocarbons, mainly natural gas, of which its reserves are estimated at 2,950,000 million cubic metres. Algeria's production of natural gas is about 110,600 million cubic metres.[9]

Upon independence in 1963, Algeria put very strong emphasis on industrialisation and made it the keynote of its economic policy. By 1970, the state had embarked on an ambitious programme of setting up heavy industrial complexes in the belief that steel and iron industries were basic to the development of other industries. As a result, the El-Hajjar steel complex was built and in 1969 the smelter and the strip-mill were opened, followed by the steel works in 1972. It is currently operating below its capacity of 2 million tonnes per year, not to mention the production capacity of the steel-rolling mills at Baraka and Bellara. Moreover, a vast petrochemical complex was opened at Skikda and continues to produce polyethylene, caustic soda and chlorine. Also a nitrogenous fertiliser plant, utilising natural gas with an annual capacity of 800,000 tonnes, was opened at Azrew in 1970. However, Algeria suffers from a shortage of vehicles because of the closing down of the Renault assembly plant in 1970. Instead of striving to build another plant, it has since preferred to import assembled vehicles.

Tunisia

Over two-thirds of Tunisia is suitable for agriculture which, as in the rest of the Maghreb, is subject to uncertain rainfall. The main crops are barley, maize, wheat and sorghum, in addition to olives, dates, oranges, grapes and figs. However, the local production of cereals does not meet the domestic needs. Consequently, the government has been importing increasing quantities of cereals.

To give the agriculture a much-needed boost, the government embarked in the late 1970s on a massive water-supply programme for the construction of a number of dams, including the Sidi Salem dam, with a capacity of 500 million cubic metres, and the Sidi Saad dam, expected to irrigate over 4,000 hectares. Another dam, the Bou Heurtna, is under construction near Jendouba and is expected to irrigate 20,000 hectares.

Tunisia is the fourth largest producer of olive oil in the world with an output estimated at approximately 100,000 tonnes per year. Its production of citrus fruit is about 250,000 tonnes and that of dates around 70,000 tonnes per year.[10]

Tunisia has important reserves of minerals – mainly oil, natural gas and calcium phosphates. The sector employs 38,000 persons.

Tunisia's industry ranges from traditional handicraft manufacturing of leather goods, carpets and the like, to modern, complex refining of minerals. The textile sector is one of the country's most important industries, generating 29 per cent of Tunisia's export earnings. Other important sectors are the mechanical and electro-mechanical industries, construction materials, paper, wood and chemical industries.

Tunisia has a very efficient and sophisticated banking system comprising the Banque Centrale de Tunisie, the state bank that issues national currency, and several commercial and development banks.

Libya

Until the discovery of petroleum in 1950 agriculture dominated Libya's economy. More than 90 per cent of land area is desert; only 1.4 per cent of land is arable and 0.1 per cent of land is irrigated. Since the beginning of the 1970s the government has been investing steadily in agriculture: LD700 million from 1973 to 1987. The most important of the investment projects is the 'Great Man-made River'. The project involving investments totalling US $3,300 million, aims at building pipelines to carry 2 million cubic metres of water per day from the south-east Libyan natural underground reservoir to Sirte and Benghazi and to various agricultural projects along 2,000 km. In spite of these tremendous investments and until the completion of the 'Great Man-made River' project, agricultural production is likely to remain mediocre and the country will still have to import 80 per cent of its food needs.[11]

Libyan coasts are very rich in all kinds of fish, but due to the lack of the necessary equipment and infrastructure this wealth is exploited primarily by Greek, Maltese and Italian fishermen.

Petroleum is undoubtedly the most important resource of Libya. It accounts for 65 per cent of GDP and 99 per cent of export earnings, and provides employment for 10 per cent of the labour-force. In 1987, production of petroleum was estimated at 51,550,000 tonnes. According to Libyan statistics, the country has, since 1970, built a total of 21 oil refineries that produce the equivalent of 5.7 million tonnes of petroleum products per year.[12]

Libya, aware of the ephemeral duration of petroleum benefits, has been investing an important part of its earnings from oil in developing an industry which has hitherto been basically traditional. Efforts have been directed to the exploitation of iron (reserves estimated at 700 million tonnes), vehicle construction and tractor assembly plants, shipbuilding, and iron and steel works.

POLITICAL ENVIRONMENT OF THE UNION

The birth of the UMA is not the result of a historical accident but the realisation of the common aspirations of the people of the area who are bound by strong ties of belief, history and social environment. The sentiment of common identity gained strength and urgency during the struggle for independence, beginning with the opening of the Maghreb Bureau in Cairo and leading to the achievement of independence by Algeria in 1963. Maghrebi solidarity reached its apogee during the Algerian War, when both Morocco and Tunisia provided Algeria with political and military support in its efforts to achieve independence and, as a result, were the target of reprisals by the French colonial authorities.

Another important manifestation of the Maghreb's sense of common identity was the meeting in Tangier in 1958 of the political parties that led the independence movements, Istiqlal (Morocco) FLN (Algeria), and Destour (Tunisia), to develop a common post-independence strategy for the development and achievement of unity in the full sense of the word. The proposed union, however, faltered immediately after Algeria's independence owing to Morocco's dispute over the inherited colonial borders it inherited and the brief war that ensued with Algeria. This incident was followed by other attempts to realise the dream of unity; however, by 1975, with the emergence of the Sahara conflict, the dream of unity took a back seat again and Boumedienne launched his bold ideological 'Trojan Horse', the concept of the *Maghreb des peuples*, calling for the creation of the 'People's Maghreb', a kind of revolutionary union implying the dismantling of the regimes in Morocco and Tunisia and for the establishment of socialist entities on the Algerian model.

This scheme was countered by Qadhdhāfī's vision of total Arab unity, from the Gulf to the Atlantic Ocean. In the light of the vision, regional unions were to be a means of Arab unity not an end in itself. This, in a sense, jeopardised Boumedienne's claim for leadership in the area and inaugurated an ambivalent relationship between Algeria and Morocco.

With Chadli Ben Jedid in power, the idea of the Maghreb unity was once more shelved and he, instead, turned towards other forms of unity such as the *Union de Concorde et de Fraternité* (Union of Concord and Fraternity) that he first initiated with Tunisia in 1983 and was later on joined by Mauritania. In reaction to this, Morocco and Libya joined in August 1985 in an alliance called *l'Union Arabo-Africaine* (Arab–African Union) which was supposed to be enlarged to include African as well as other Arab countries.

The UMA came to life at a time when East–West relations were improving slowly but surely while a wind of *perestroika* was sweeping through the Eastern world, forcing the static political regimes to adopt much-needed reforms and undertake changes leading to democratic institutions. This international *détente* had repercussions on regional entities, one of them being the Maghreb, in which governments compromised on their principles and opted instead for dialogue and negotiations.

However, the advent of the UMA should not be credited to East–West *détente* only; other reasons were undoubtedly more relevant than the American–Soviet *rapprochement*. Among these reasons was the projected creation in 1992 of a united European market structure, an event that was greeted by the Maghreb with mixed feelings, given the challenge it would represent for the Maghrebi people, already torn apart by fratricidal quarrels. In addition, it should be pointed out that the Maghreb itself was under the grip of tremendous transformations and changes that required an immediate redefinition of regional objectives and a readjustment of priorities.

Another important factor in the swift creation of the UMA has been the increase within the individual countries of the area of internal problems that necessitated urgent solutions. In Morocco, for example, the restructuring of the economy was being carried out at a very slow pace because of bureaucratic hurdles, especially where investment was concerned. This compelled King Hassan II to intervene in the bureaucratic machine by publishing his *Letter on Investments*. This stated that if a given application for the setting up of a business was not dealt with by the administration within two months, the application would automatically be considered as being immediately authorised. In Algeria, economic difficulties resulting from a serious drop in oil reserves, coupled with the people's frustration with a government that failed to introduce political reforms, effectively led to a violent rebellion against the state and its symbols in October 1988. Tunisia, very much like Morocco, was in the throes of an economic readjustment which, notwithstanding its beneficial effects in the long term, has not immediately eased the burden of foreign debt.

Libya's problems were increasing alarmingly. Not only did it have to face the continual threat of destabilisation by the USA, irritated by Qadhdhāfi's mercurial political behaviour, but, like Algeria, it also felt the painful pinch of the reduction in oil revenues. Mauritania, like the rest of the Maghreb countries, was also suffering tremendously from severe economic problems resulting from excessively high foreign debt on top of a stagnant economy compounded by social and racial problems.

FUTURE OUTLOOK

The beneficial effects of the UMA were felt immediately on the signature of the founding documents on 17 February 1989 in Marrakesh. Individuals and goods started circulating without restrictions within the limits of the five member states of the Maghreb – something that had not happened in almost 15 years. For the man in the street, incredulous at the beginning, this was to be a significant move.

To give the event due importance and to highlight the necessity for such an institution, the heads of state exchanged visits to discuss bilateral as well as Maghrebi relations and in their declarations stressed their determination to see the UMA become an instrument capable of bringing the people of the area together and of achieving much-needed economic development. For King Hassan II, the UMA was a gift from God that all people ought to treasure:

> God, our benefactor, has granted us the honour of initiating the 'Grand Maghreb Arabe' in an international climate characterised by *détente* between the two superpowers and their respective ideologies, in a climate of coincidence between different views of social life and of socio-political management.[13]

He went on to say that, in the context of the union, the decision-makers of the Maghreb would have to play the dangerous role of educating coming generations:

> We have to understand that we are taking on the role of educators for the new generation of the Maghreb that we are training, for the essence of the Maghreb that we are trying to pass on, for the integrity and virtue of the Maghreb which we seek to enrich, and to benefit not only ourselves but also our neighbours, particularly in Africa – all are activities that follow on from our work, our faith, and our wisdom.[14]

For President Chadli BenJedid the UMA was an important factor of peace and stability in the area:

> L'UMA has essentially been conceived as an aspect of non-alignment, of peace and progress which, by its development, could create permanent stability in our region . . .[15]

and a tool for achieving economic and social development:

economic and social development is a basic parameter within the process of creating the ideal of Maghrebi unity. In this respect, the efforts which the countries of the Maghreb intend to carry out together could be a significant example for South–South co-operation.[16]

For President Ben Ali of Tunisia, the UMA was the materialisation of the aspirations of the people of the area:

The creation of the Arab Maghreb Union (UMA) reflects the profound aspirations that the region has long dreamt of realising.[17]

For Colonel Qadhdhāfī, the union of the people of the Maghreb was dictated by necessity and should be a step towards total Arab union. True to his tradition of causing controversy, he argued that the UMA should be open to such countries as Mali, Niger, Chad and Sudan to avoid the accusation of it being a racist institution:

The unity of the Arab Maghreb has been forced upon us by necessity. The world is made up of blocs, and micro-states are no longer viable. This union has been achieved by forces genuinely concerned over unity and it is the first step towards total Arab unity. If it had been undertaken by isolationist forces it would have been an act opposed to Arab unity. Finally, I invite Mali, Niger, Chad and Sudan to join the UMA so that our union can be complementary and not acquire a racist character.[18]

The treaty of 17 February 1989 giving birth to the UMA called for the establishment of a structure comprising the following components to facilitate the institution of the Union in the area:

• *The Presidential Council*: the heads of state of the five Maghreb countries. This is the highest body in the Union. The Presidency is to be held for a period of six months by each of the heads of state in turn. Its regular sessions are to be held every six months. All decisions are to be taken unanimously by the members.
• *The Committee of Ministers of Foreign Affairs*: this committee attends sessions of the Presidential Council and examines the conclusions of the Follow-up Committee and the specialised committees.
• *The Follow-up Committee*: each member-state appoints from amongst its government members, one minister who will be in charge of the Union's affairs within the Follow-up Committee.
• *The General Secretariat*: this is composed of a representative from each member-state. The General Secretariat will carry out

its activities in the country holding the presidency of the Council of Heads of State.

- *The Consultative Council*: this consists of ten representatives from the legislative bodies of each of the member-states. It holds regular and extraordinary sessions at the request of the Presidential Council. It gives its opinion on any project the Presidential Council lays before it.

- *The Judicial Institution*: each member-state delegates two magistrates to this institution. This body, whose decisions are final and absolute, will judge any disputes arising from the interpretation or application of the terms of the Treaty and agreements made amongst the member-states.

All these institutions, with the exception of the Judicial Institution, have been set up immediately after the Union was founded. The latest of these is the Consultative Council (*Majlis al-Shūra*), which was inaugurated by King Hassan II in Rabat on 19 October 1989.

The speed at which the different bodies of the union were established in the first six months seems to indicate clearly that the political will of the heads of state of the region is to set up a solid institution that will play a major role in the future of the area. This determination was further emphasised when the leaders decided to launch a vaccination campaign in all five countries at the same time – *Les Journées Maghrébines de Vaccination* – for all children under the age of 5 and their mothers, against six deadly diseases. This started on 14 October 1989.

This will to make up for the lost time was mirrored at different levels of society. Indeed, today political parties, trade unions, banks, cultural and educational institutions, following in the steps of the governments, are busy setting up activities at the level of the Maghreb and expressing the will to co-ordinate action and exchange expertise and information.

The windfall of this extensive co-operation is undoubtedly beneficial to the area and augurs a promising future to such issues as the Sahara conflict, which will hopefully be defused or, as many observers have argued, diluted in the context of the Union.

THE SAHARA CONFLICT

In the opinion of most people in the Maghreb, be they officials or just observers, the Sahara conflict has been and still is the antithesis of unity in the Maghreb. Is there room for yet another country on the map of the Maghreb? The answer to this question seems to range from a clear 'no' to an ambiguous 'well, yes, but', or statements like: 'the conflict ought to be solved within the context of the Maghreb unity'. However, the context of the Maghreb still calls for unity and consolidation of relations. So, it seems that within the map of the UMA there is no place for the Polisario Front and its state.

Following the Summit of Marrakesh, which initiated the UMA, the Polisario cadres felt a tremendous disappointment because, first, a major event had taken place without their having had even a symbolic role and, second, their staunchest ally, Algeria and their sympathiser, Libya, did not raise a finger to make even an allusion – as the case used to be in communiqués following such meetings – to the Polisario or the Sahrawi people. Instead, the Union agreement signed solemnly by the five leaders states clearly and unambiguously that any aggression against any one of the member-states is equivalent to an aggression against all the other states: 'Any attack on a member-state of the UMA will be considered as an attack on the other member-states as well'. The Treaty of Marrakesh goes even further and states that the five countries must not allow any activity on their territory aimed at destabilising another member-state: 'The five states undertake not to allow any activity on their territories which threatens the security, territorial integrity, or the political system of a member-state.'

This does not mean the end of the Polisario Front and the end of the Sahara conflict, but it surely indicates that the Treaty of Marrakesh is the first step towards a solution that does not necessarily meet the expectations of the Polisario Front and its dream of nationhood. So, little by little, even the idea of the referendum seems to fade away in favour of giving the Sahrawis some sort of autonomy within a Moroccan federal state modelled on the West German system, to which King Hassan II has referred in his interviews with the international mass media.

Robert Mortimer, a specialist of North African politics and diplomacy, argues that the Sahara conflict could find a durable solution in the framework of the Maghreb:

> After years of conflict in the region, the emerging Greater Maghreb appears to be the most promising framework within which to resolve the Western Saharan dispute. Issues of sovereignty lose a measure of salience in regional institutions. The Sahrawis are entitled to a voice in this region-building project. The precise form of their participation (as independent state or autonomous province) could be less important than the fact thay they are

recognised participants in a regional development process. But the greater Maghreb must be viewed as a viable enterprise for such an approach to success.[19]

Indeed, the creation of the UMA has had a tremendous effect on the conflict. Recently, several Polisario leaders,[20] notably Omar Hadrami, one of the founding fathers of the organisation, defected to Morocco and expressed their wish to see the conflict solved once and for all.[21]

The defection of Omar Hadrami revealed the difficulties that the Polisario Front has been encountering since the signature of the Treaty of Marrakesh. The leadership is demoralised and has almost lost hope in setting up a Sahrawi state.[22] This was shown by two Polisario suicide attacks in October 1989 upon Guelta Zemmour area in which, according to MAP (the Moroccan official news agency), several guerrillas were killed and a great amount of equipment was left behind on the battlefield.

The tendency in the Maghreb now seems to be in favour of ending this conflict – which has poisoned and still poisons relations in the context of the UMA. This would encourage the emergence of a pro-Morocco faction within the ranks of the Polisario Front.[23] This concept of 'dispersion' of the problem was underlined by Omar Hadrami in an interview with François Soudan (*Jeune Afrique*, no. 1503, 23 October 1989).

> I was, in effect, the opposition leader in the camps. In view of the improvement in relations between Algeria and Morocco, we felt that the Sahrawis should not pay the price for this situation but that they should take the initiative in trying to discuss more seriously with Morocco, because it would be with Morocco that they would have to talk eventually and, in addition, it would be inside Morocco that they would have to live. Even the Algerians themselves made it clear to Mohamed Abdelaziz in my presence that full independence would not be possible and that, as a result, Polisario would have to take the initiative itself in completely altering its vision of where the world was going and what their role in it would be.[24]

Given the determination of the Maghrebi countries to settle the Sahara conflict once and for all at their earliest convenience in order to turn to more important, mainly economic issues, it seems that two major possibilities for settlement now exist:

1 Increasing 'defections' within the ranks of the Polisario Front bring it to the point of collapse. At this point, individuals rather

than an organisation will attempt to negotiate their return to Morocco in exchange for guarantees. A few months ago this would have been the most unlikely possibility; but after the return to Morocco of Omar Hadrami and, in the light of his analysis of the situation within the Polisario Front, this possibility is to be taken quite seriously.

2   Under pressure from Algeria, the Polisario Front would give up armed struggle and settle for autonomy in a federal type of system similar to that in Germany, as King Hassan II has always suggested.

The idea of a referendum is not to be discarded. However, though Algeria, Morocco, Europe, the US and the UN still discuss the issue, no one really wants it. It will be a complicated and costly operation that the UN cannot afford and the technical problems involve factors that are complex and time-consuming: for example, the population census.

ECONOMIC INTEGRATION

Many observers argue that the UMA has had a false start in that it initially gave prominence to political content rather than economic needs and that experience has proved that unions that last are the unions in which economics take precedence over politics. This is certainly true of the EEC, which started in Rome in 1957 with a treaty that led to gradual economic integration. It was only later on, when the economic groundwork proved to be solid, that the Europeans started setting up the political structure.

Actually, the Maghreb has not taken a path different from that of the EEC. The treaty signed in Marrakesh in February 1989 was no different from the one signed in Rome in 1957; it only provides a legal platform to facilitate further action. The bodies set up since the creation of the union are more administrative than political, their mission being to regulate the necessary evil of bureaucracy. Proof of this is the fact that the union in principle, has not changed or altered in any way the political ability of the Maghreb.

The human and natural resources demonstrate that the Maghreb has the potential of achieving much-needed economic integration because its economies are fully complementary, as Sadik argues in this context: 'simply because of their differences, economic systems in the Greater Maghreb have evident possibilities for complementarity'.[25]

The *sine qua non* for the realisation of economic integration is the establishment of a common market like that in Europe; but this obviously cannot happen overnight, given the difference in the economic systems of the area. Indeed, the Maghreb is an area where two economic ideologies confront each other:

1 *Liberal (Western-style) economy.* This is true in the case of Morocco, Tunisia and Mauritania. However, in spite of the liberal tone of the economies, they are in fact a mixture of the liberal economic orientation of free enterprise and state interventionism. However, since the world recession of the early 1980s, these countries, in response to World Bank and the International Monetary Fund pressure to restructure their economies and finances, have embarked, especially in the case of Morocco, on a programme of privatisation and liberalisation of currency exchange and investment codes.

2 *Socialist economy.* This economy is typical of both Algeria and Libya with obvious differences of detail. Nevertheless, it is characterised by state control and interventionism at every level – investment, production and distribution. Because of their reliance on oil revenues since independence, these countries have neglected the tertiary economic sector and instead have invested in heavy industry. However, today, Algeria (and to some extent Libya) is slowly adopting liberal economic policies.

Initially, to undertake economic integration, the UMA has to start by destroying existing economic barriers that were erected to protect national economies (customs duties, exchange control, import–export restrictions) and adopting policies allowing for movement of goods and capital, along with tax relief schemes to encourage investment. However, the available information indicates that the Maghreb countries are seriously conducting feasibility studies to undertake some measures that will gradually lead to the establishment of a common market. There is no official word on this project, but it seems that they will in the long term attempt to achieve the following objectives:

* adoption of common customs legislation;
* adoption of common financial legislation;
* co-ordination of economic planning.

Common customs legislation

This presupposes the suppression of customs duties on internal trade and exchange of goods and the adoption of a Common Customs

Tariff applicable to third countries. The Common Customs Tariff could be applied on a preferential basis with the EEC and other regional economic communities with which the Maghrebi countries would have bilateral agreements.[26]

Common financial legislation

This entails the creation of a Maghrebi Financial Zone, a Maghrebi currency and, at a later stage, the adoption of a community budget which could finance various projects that would be beneficial to all countries. This could be financed through such taxes as VAT, or any other similar tax and any other community taxes that the financial institutions will deem it necessary to levy.

Another aspect of the common financial legislation is the establishment of a Maghrebi Fund for Development; this should be an autonomous public institution that would organise and co-ordinate investment within the community and the body that would have to raise loans from world financial institutions for specific projects in any given country of the union.[27]

Co-ordination of economic planning

The member-states of the UMA will determine the community's economic priorities and try to co-ordinate in theory and practice their economic planning as to public spending, investment, tax legislation, job opportunities, import–export policies, financial restrictions, etc. They should also adopt a unified attitude in their negotiations with the EEC and various other communities.

In the long term, the UMA will not only lead to economic integration but also solve some problems that the whole community faces – unemployment, particularly for young people. With a single market of 80 million people, production will increase, local and international investment will rise, and the integrated regional economy will gather momentum for take-off. There is a generalised willingness to adopt liberal policies and to disengage the state from the major fields of economic activity.

THE UMA AND THE WORLD

Since the UMA occupies a very important geo-strategic position in the world, the UMA could play a major role in world politics.

The UMA and Europe

Today, Europe is only a few kilometres away from the Maghreb and soon may be linked to it by bridge or tunnel between Morocco and Spain. By the turn of the century Europe will be only a few minutes away and opportunity of trade, investment, cultural exchange and human interaction will increase tremendously and will contribute to the development of the area. From the very beginning of the UMA, Europe reacted favourably because it saw in this new institution an investment for regional stability and peace, and a partner for future economic venture as well as a political mediator that could play a major role in Africa and the Middle East.

Some important signs of future links of the European Community into the Maghreb occurred in September 1989 when Spain greeted the Moroccan monarch, King Hassan II, on his first official visit since his accession to the throne in 1961. The important aspect of this visit was that the Moroccan monarch was not greeted as the head of state of Morocco only but most significantly as the President of the UMA. The discussions that ensued clearly showed the interest that Spain and the EEC have staked on the Maghreb politically and economically.

For Europe, a unified Maghreb is undoubtedly a very interesting economic partner. Indeed, Jean François Deniau, a member of the Commission for Foreign Affairs of the French parliament (*Assemblée Nationale*), describes the satisfaction of his country and that of the EEC at the creation of the UMA because of the possibilities of co-operation:

> It is quite clear, as far as issues of general orientation are concerned, that we are completely behind the UMA. As a member of the EEC we can only rejoice if there be co-operation between different structures amongst partners on the north and south coasts of the Mediterranean, whether or not they develop in the long term in the political domain of others.[28]

The same theme was repeated in a recent interview given to Mr Fenjiro, the Director of MAP (the Moroccan official newsagency), by the West German president, prior to his official visit to Morocco in October 1989. He outlined the importance of the UMA in the eyes of the EEC as to co-operation in the region:

> I believe that the Maghreb Arab Union will greatly improve the market situation for you and for your neighbours in the Maghreb as far as Europe is concerned. It will increase the volume of trade

and thus help us push the Community towards a more open-door policy.[29]

The UMA and the USA

The US views the UMA as an important step towards stability, peace and development in an area which has a vital strategic position. It also stakes hope on this institution becoming an instrument for democracy and liberalisation in the area, and serving as a means of moderating the ardour of the Libyan leader, Colonel Qadhdhāfī.

The Great Maghreb concept may be the most promising way to moderate the Libyan regime. U.S. policy to date – embargoes, military clashes in the Mediterranean, the bombing raid – has had little constructive impact on Tripoli. On the other hand, diplomatic observers report that Algeria urged Libya to normalise relations with Chad, with which it was at war during parts of 1980s; Algeria likewise encouraged Libya's rapprochement with Tunisia, thus simplifying the tasks facing Ben Ali in consolidating the post-Bourguibist order there.[30]

The UMA will also be able to play an important role in the Middle East conflict by bringing Palestinians and Israelis to the negotiating table. Prior to the creation of the UMA, neither Morocco nor Algeria spared any effort to contribute to the settlement of the conflict; the Algerians, by hosting several sessions of the Palestinian National Council (PNC), engineered *rapprochement* between different factions which cleared the way for Yasser Arafat to recognise the State of Israel and put an end to the deadlock that hindered the peace process in the area. The Moroccans for their part, through their multiple contacts with the Americans, the Europeans and with the world Jewish community, managed to moderate Israel's reaction to legitimate Palestinian national aspirations.

The UMA and Africa

Now that the Chad conflict is resolved, the UMA can play a major role in confidence-building between Sub-Saharan Africa and the Arab world. The UMA countries, because of geographic proximity and because of their experience in dealing with Africa over the centuries, can certainly actively bring the Arabs and Africans to talk to each other and help each other. The Arabs ought to play a more active role in African development and help to revive the dormant Arab-Islamic cultural traditions of which Africans are very proud.

CONCLUSION

In a world where East–West relations are improving day by day, 'region-building' is on the rise. Indeed, the European experience within the EEC has proved to the world that the weak and ageing Europe of the post-World War Two era is a thing of the past. Europe, thanks to its common market philosophy, has emerged as a giant capable of rivalling the US, the former USSR and Japan, and by 1992 it will be one country speaking several languages but talking with only one voice. The European model should gradually be emulated by the Maghreb at every level, to ensure its own development and survival. By 1992, if the Maghreb is not strong, it will be crushed by the European giant looming on the horizon, and will fall into oblivion.

The people of the Maghreb are determined to achieve this historical dream of union. Their governments are, therefore, indirectly compelled to succeed in this mission for fear of losing popular credibility and being swept away if they do not. The countries of the Maghreb have the resources and the means to achieve economic integration and unity, so there is no reason which should prevent the success of this promising undertaking.

The cultural heritage of the Maghreb is so strong that no political incident should be able to undermine such a bond, as experience has shown. The truth is that unity has always existed between the peoples of the area because of the strong Islamic heritage they share, though politically they have been separate.

The UMA in this world atmosphere of *détente* and tolerance, will mature and mellow to become a genuine reflection of the ideals of the Islamic *umma* that call for unity irrespective of colour, status, origin or wealth.

NOTES

1 *Compendium of Statistics on Illiteracy*, p. 11.
2 Ernest Gellner in E. Gellner and C. Micaud (eds), *Arabs and Berbers*, p. 11, argues in this respect: 'the Maghreb is much less diversified and pluralistic, in either an ethnic or religious sense, than is the Middle East proper'.
3 J. P. Entelis, *Comparative Politics of North Africa*, p. 6.
4 Gellner, *op. cit.*, p. 11.
5 *Africa South of the Sahara 1989*, p. 690.
6 *Ibid.*, p. 691.
7 *North Africa and the Middle East 1989*, p. 668.
8 *Ibid.*, pp. 667–8.

9   *Ibid.*, p. 306–7.
10   *Ibid.*, p. 826.
11   *Ibid.*, p. 638.
12   *Ibid.*, p. 638–9.
13   Speech by His Majesty King Hassan II on the occasion of the inauguration of the Consultative Council (*Conseil Consultatif*) of the UMA; see *Le Matin du Sahara et du Maghreb* of 20 October 1989.
14   *Ibid.*
15   Statement made by President Chadli Ben Jedid of Algeria during an interview he gave to the Yugoslav newsagency Tanjug on the eve of the 9th Summit of Non-Aligned Countries (see *L'Opinion* of 4 September 1989).
16   *Ibid.*
17   Statement made by President Ben Ali of Tunisia during an interview given to the Lebanese magazine *as-Sayyad* (see *L'Opinion* of 29 August 1989).
18   Statement made by the Libyan leader Colonel Qadhdhāfī during an interview given to the Japanese television network (see *Jeune Afrique*, no. 1496 of 6 September 1989).
19   R. A. Mortimer, 'Maghreb Matters', in *Foreign Policy*, p. 173.
20   Some of these prominent cadres are: Omar Hadrami, Noureddine Ahmed Ali, Maalainine Mrabih Rabou, and Bellali Bachir El Ouali.
21   See *Jeune Afrique*, no. 1498 of 18 September 1989, 'Sahara: le retour des égarés' by François Soudan, pp. 26–7.
22   See interview given by Omar Hadrami to François Soudan, 'Les autres finiront aussi par revenir' in *Jeune Afrique*, no. 1503 of 23 October 1989, pp. 22–34.
23   *Ibid.*, p. 22.
24   *Ibid.*, p. 30.
25   A. Sadik, *Le Grand Maghreb Arabe: intégrations et systèmes économiques comparés*, pp. 17–18.
26   *Ibid.*, p. 96.
27   *Ibid.*, p. 105.
28   Interview given to Farida Moha in *Le Matin du Sahara et du Maghreb* of 16 October 1989.
29   *Ibid.*
30   Mortimer, *op. cit.*, p. 162.

BIBLIOGRAPHY

Africa South of the Sahara 1989 (1988) London: Europa Publications. *Compendium of Statistics on Illiteracy*, 30 (1988) London: UNESCO Publications.

Entelis, J. P. (1980) *Comparative Politics of North Africa: Algeria, Morocco and Tunisia*, Syracuse: Syracuse University Press.

Gellner, E. and Micaud, C. (eds) (1973) *Arabs and Berbers: From Tribe to Nation in North Africa*, London: Duckworth.

Hart, D. M. (1976) *The Aith Waryaghar of the Moroccon Rif*, Tucson: University of Arizona Press.

Mortimer, R. A. (1989) 'Maghreb matters', *Foreign Policy*, 76, 160–75.

North Africa and the Middle East 1989 (1988) London: Europa Publications.
Sadik, A. (1989) *Le Grand Maghreb Arabe: intégrations et systèmes économiques comparés*, Casablanca: Afrique Orient.

17 The Maghreb Arab Union and regional reconciliation

John Damis

The creation on 17 February, 1989 of the Maghreb Arab Union (*Union du Maghreb Arabe*, UMA) represents a dramatic step forward toward regional integration in North Africa. It is far too soon to know whether the UMA will be the culmination of the process or merely an important milestone along the way to fuller Maghreb unity. The object of this chapter is not to determine where the UMA features in an unfinished process. Instead, this chapter has the somewhat more modest aim of examining the potential impact of the UMA on the resolution of regional disputes within North Africa.

THE BACKGROUND

The UMA forms part of an ongoing process of Maghreb integration that goes back at least to the late 1950s. It is a process and a dynamic that has been characterised by false starts, uneven progress, and unfulfilled agreements. The dynamic has been driven, at least in part, by the strong appeal that Maghreb unity has among the general populations of North Africa. What is much less clear is if Maghreb leaders have looked to regional integration as a way of resolving various disputes among and between North African states.

Even before Algerian independence, North Africans began to organise and lay the groundwork for Maghreb unity. On 27 April, 1958, the three major nationalist parties – the Tunisian Neo-Destour, the Algerian National Liberation Front (FLN), and the Moroccan Istiqlal – met in Tangier to proclaim their will to build a united Maghreb. The Tangier meeting – the first Maghreb 'summit' – reflected a good deal of popular sentiment in North Africa and was a natural outgrowth of co-operation among the nationalist movements. Decolonisation and independence brought in their wake great hopes among North Africans, and a united Maghreb seemed at the time an achievable goal.

The realities of inter-state relations in North Africa during the next 25 years made a mockery of the 1958 Tangier declaration. The period from 1958 to 1983 saw an alternation of periods of relative *détente* with periods of badly strained or even hostile relations. Arab and African divisions along radical versus moderate lines accounted for some of the bad relations. Boundary disputes added to regional tensions. Meddling by one regime in the internal affairs of another, usually in the form of clandestine subversion, also inhibited the construction of the Greater Maghreb. Finally, a natural power rivalry between Morocco and Algeria, the two leading states of the region, worked against long-term integration.

Strained relations between Morocco and Algeria during the 1960s reached a low point in the fall of 1963 when tension over their disputed joint frontier led to an inconclusive three-week border war – the 'War of the Sands'. By the end of the 1960s, however, North Africa entered a period of relative *détente* that lasted for about five years. At the western end of the Maghreb, regional reconciliation required Morocco to abandon at least some of its irredentist claims to territory recognised by the world community as belonging to Mauritania or Algeria. Morocco finally recognised Mauritania in 1969. More importantly, Morocco and Algeria were able to resolve, at least temporarily, their major bilateral disputes.

In January 1969, Morocco and Algeria signed a 20-year Treaty of Fraternity, Good Neighbourliness and Co-operation, which heralded a 'new era of friendly relations' between the two countries. A variety of bilateral agreements in the economic, commercial, and judiciary fields were signed four months later. This Moroccan–Algerian *rapprochement* culminated in 1972 with the signing of three conventions: one recognised the *de facto* Moroccan–Algerian frontier as the legal boundary; the second called for the joint exploitation of the large iron ore deposits at Gara Jebilet, 100 miles south-west of Tindouf in Algeria, through a Moroccan port on the Atlantic; and the third called for the creation of a joint company to construct and operate a cement plant in the Oujda region of north-west Morocco.

Of these three conventions, only the third, calling for a cement plant, was implemented without delay. Algeria ratified the border agreement in 1973, but Morocco would not do so as long as there were serious problems with Algeria over the Western Sahara issue; it was only in March 1989, in the context of the current Moroccan–Algerian *rapprochement*, that King Hassan finally ratified the 1972 border agreement. The second convention, calling for joint exploitation of the iron ore deposits at Gara Jebilet, has yet to be implemented. It was the dispute over the Western Sahara, more than any other factor, that badly strained Moroccan–Algerian relations in 1975 and ushered in a period of prolonged antagonism between the two countries. In March 1976, when Algeria recognised the Saharan Arab Democratic Republic (SDAR), proclaimed a week earlier by the Polisario Front, Rabat immediately broke diplomatic relations with Algiers.

At the eastern end of the Maghreb, equally impressive steps toward regional reconciliation took place in the early 1970s. In January 1970, Tunisia and Algeria signed a 20-year Treaty of Fraternity, Good Neighbourliness and Co-operation. Four years later, in January 1974, Tunisia and Libya signed a unity agreement known as the Jerba agreement. President Habib Bourguiba, however, quickly changed his mind about a union with Libya. Tunisia allowed the unity pact to lapse and it soon became a dead letter. Within two years, Libyan sponsorship of subversive activities within Tunisia badly strained relations between the two countries. In January 1980, Tunisia broke relations with Libya because of the Qadhdhāfī regime's responsibility for a commando raid against the town of Gafsa, an attack that was intended to spark a rebellion against the Bourguiba government.

PRECURSORS TO THE UNION

After several years of strained relations all across North Africa, there were several important developments in 1983 that supported regional reconciliation. Morocco and Algeria took several steps to improve their badly strained relations. Algeria and Tunisia, and subsequently Mauritania, signed a Treaty of Fraternity and Harmony. Tunisia and Libya agreed to many aspects of economic and technical integration. Libya and Algeria declared their joint interest in setting up the Greater Maghreb. And Libya and Morocco improved their generally poor relations.

The most important event for the improvement of relations among North African states was the summit meeting held on 26 February, 1983 between King Hassan and Algerian President Chadli Ben Jedid – the first top-level talks between the two countries since 1975. At this 'historic' meeting, Ben Jedid tried to use Maghreb integration as a way of resolving the Western Sahara conflict. During discussion of the Sahara issue, Ben Jedid suggested seeking a 'solution in the Maghreb framework' – a solution that would allow everyone to save face. Ben Jedid included among economic incentives such items as a gas pipeline from Algeria across Morocco to Spain, the export of Algerian iron through Moroccan ports, and joint exploitation of the Bu Craa phosphate deposits in the northern Sahara.[1] Though the Hassan–Ben Jedid summit did not achieve a breakthrough in resolving the Western Sahara conflict, it did break the ice in Moroccan–Algerian relations, and in the months that followed some important concrete steps were taken towards an improvement of bilateral relations.

In the period since the February 1983 summit, Algeria has frequently expressed its support for the establishment of the Greater Arab Maghreb. A significant step in that direction was achieved on 10 March, 1983 when Algeria and Tunisia signed a Treaty of Fraternity and Harmony which normalised relations between the two countries after several years of mutual distrust. While similar in content to the Moroccan–Algerian treaty of January 1969 and the Algerian–Tunisian treaty of January 1970, the 1983 Algerian–Tunisian treaty contained two important new aspects. First, the two parties pledges not to authorise any warlike initiative or action against the other and, further, not to authorise any organisation, activity or concentration on their territory that could harm the security of the other or its territorial integrity, or could attempt to change its regime by violence. Second, the 1983 accord was open to membership by other states of the Greater Arab Maghreb which were prepared to accept the terms of the treaty.[2]

In December 1983, Mauritania signed the Algerian–Tunisian Treaty of Fraternity and Harmony. Moroccan–Algerian differences over the Western Sahara dispute made it impractical for King Hassan to add Morocco to the growing North African bloc. When Libyan leader Mu'ammar al-Qadhdhāfī expressed his desire to join the group in December 1983, Algeria responded firmly that Libya could not participate so long as common border problems remained unresolved. Fearful of being outflanked within North Africa, Morocco and Libya responded in August 1984 by establishing their own alliance – the Treaty of Union of States – as a countermove to the Algerian-dominated pact. Thus, in a period of less than 18 months, the moderate (Morocco–Tunisia) versus radical (Algeria–Libya) alignment that had characterised North African regional relations in the two decades since Algerian independence in 1962 was replaced by an emerging polarisation along Algeria–Tunisia–Mauritania versus Morocco–Libya lines.[3]

Regional integration seemed to progess in 1983 as far as it could go at that point with the adherence of three of the five Maghreb states

– Algeria, Tunisia and Mauritania – to a single treaty grouping. The Moroccan–Libyan Treaty of Union created an Arab–African Federation that was ready to accept as members all Arab and African states. Not surprisingly, the other three Maghreb states saw no reason to join the federation. Within two years, in August 1986, King Hassan abrogated Morocco's Treaty of Union with Libya. The Qadhdhāfī regime, once again in relative isolation within North Africa, soon turned its attention back to the Algerian–Tunisian–Mauritanian Treaty of Fraternity and Co-operation. In September 1987, the Libyan General People's Congress voted to sign the treaty, but with two notable reservations: the treaty's membership should be open to all Arab states, and all boundaries among member-states should be abolished. These reservations were unacceptable to Algeria, which effectively precluded Libya's inclusion in the treaty.

RUN-UP TO UNION

Because of their relatively large populations and territory, Morocco and Algeria have long been the two dominant states in the Maghreb. Their bilateral relations are of great importance to regional integration in North Africa. When their relations are antagonistic, as they were from 1975 to 1983, little genuine progress is possible in promoting regional integration. By contrast, when Morocco and Algeria are able to mend fences and improve their relations, regional integration is greatly facilitated. Thus, the re-establishment of Moroccan–Algerian relations on 16 May, 1988, which ended a 12-year break, constituted an apparent breakthrough in stalled efforts to build the Greater Arab Maghreb.

In the joint communiqué issued at the time, the two countries reaffirmed all previous bilateral treaties, accords, and conventions, and called for a resolution of the Western Sahara conflict by means of a fair referendum. Of some significance, there was no mention in the communiqué of Algeria's long-held public insistence that direct Morocco–Polisario negotiations are a precondition for a settlement of the conflict. Outside observers, including *Le Monde*, were quick to conclude that Morocco and Algeria had agreed to a settlement of the Sahara dispute (presumably exclusive of the Polisario Front) and that this agreement had been a precondition to the re-establishment of bilateral relations.

This conclusion seemed unjustified in the spring of 1988. What appeared more plausible – at least to this author – was that Morocco and Algeria had adopted a two-track approach to their relations.

They recognised that unresolved and difficult questions over the Western Sahara could delay a settlement of that dispute for some time to come. So they agreed to disagree, at least for the time being. But they also agreed not to let the Sahara conflict interfere with the improvement of their bilateral relations.

Developments in the 18 months since May 1988 are consistent with the two-track approach. Moroccan–Algerian relations, have warmed considerably since the re-establishment of relations and bilateral co-operation has begun in a number of areas. Thus, in the weeks following 16 May, 1988, ambassadors were exchanged, the common frontier was opened, the two national airlines began regular service between the major cities of Morocco and Algeria, a number of bilateral commissions began to explore avenues of economic co-operation, commercial relations expanded rapidly, and the two governments co-ordinated their efforts to eradicate locust infestations. In July 1988, the two countries linked their electricity grids through a high-tension 20-megawatt line. Finally, during Ben Jedid's unprecedented visit to five Moroccan cities during his three-day meetings with Hassan, 6–8 February, 1989, the two leaders agreed to go ahead with the $2.2 billion Trans-Maghreb Gas Pipeline which is to run from the gas fields of north-west Algeria across northern Morocco to Spain, with a possible future extension to France and even Great Britain.

During the same 18-month period since May 1988, the Western Sahara dispute has remained unresolved. To be sure, obstacles that were considered major impediments to a settlement have been removed. First, King Hassan reversed a long-standing refusal to negotiate directly with the Polisario when he held talks in January 1989 with representatives of the front (though he denied they were 'negotiations'). Then, two months later in March, the King finally ratified the 1972 border agreement with Algeria, thus removing a festering sore that had long rankled successive Algerian governments. None the less, agreement on a referendum of self-determination for the Western Sahara is nowhere in sight. And without a referendum, the Sahara conflict will surely continue, even if the level of hostilities diminishes over time.

It is quite clear that the current Moroccan–Algerian *rapprochement* greatly facilitated the creation of the Maghreb Arab Union. When King Hassan was invited, in the spring of 1988, to attend the Extraordinary Arab Summit planned for June in Algiers, he replied that though he would like to attend, it would be difficult because Morocco did not have diplomatic relations with Algeria. The June

1988 Arab Summit thus accelerated the decision by the two governments to re-establish relations – a decision that no doubt hinged on a
number of other factors. The presence of the leaders of the five North
African countries (including Mauritania) at the Arab Summit in
Algiers allowed the convening of a Maghreb Summit on 10 June,
following the conclusion of the Arab Summit. It was at the Maghreb
Summit that the heads of state of Morocco, Algeria, Tunisia, Libya,
and Mauritania established the Maghreb Committee to discuss institutional and practical ways for further co-operation within North
Africa. In mid-July 1988, high level officials from all member countries of the Maghreb Committee met in Algiers, where they agreed to
establish five working groups to prepare the groundwork for North
African integration.

The establishment of the Maghreb Committee and the five
working groups greatly accelerated efforts towards regional integration. In January 1989, Moroccan Foreign Minister Abdellatif
Filali presented a working paper for the establishment of a Maghreb
union to a meeting of the Maghreb High Commission in Tunis. In
mid-February, King Hassan hosted the second Maghreb Summit, in
Marrakesh, and on 17 February, at the conclusion of the summit, the
five North African heads of state signed a treaty establishing the
UMA.

THE VALUE OF THE UNION

The treaty signed on 17 February in Marrakesh gives priority in the
UMA to economic issues. The decision to stress economic co-
ordination reflected the preference of Morocco and Algeria for a more
pragmatic approach to Maghreb integration. None the less, both
explicitly and implicitly, the UMA involves political co-ordination
and looks to future political integration. The structure and workings
of the UMA are consistent with the classical functionalist approach in
which economic co-operation and co-ordination among states within
a region gradually encourages political co-operation and even integration. On the political level, since the creation of the UMA,
Maghreb leaders have communicated by telephone on a frequent
basis and the Maghreb states have adopted unified positions at the
United Nations.

For the short term, however, the UMA is likely to have only a
limited effect on regional reconciliation. On the positive side, one
consequence of the first Maghreb Summit, in Algiers in June 1988,
was a warming of Morocco's somewhat strained relations with Libya.

In the other direction, the UMA has not thus far facilitated a resolution of the Western Sahara conflict, the Maghreb's most divisive dispute. Over the past two years, progress toward a settlement of the Sahara issue has been achieved either before the UMA's creation and/or strictly in the context of the current Moroccan–Algerian *rapprochement*. At present – with the resumption of large-scale attacks by the Polisario in October and King Hassan's cancellation of a second round of talks with the front – prospects for a resolution of the Sahara conflict are actually worse than they were six months earlier at the time the UMA was created.

Looking to the future, a Moroccan–Algerian agreement on the Sahara issue remains a necessary condition for a settlement of that dispute. The UMA may encourage and facilitate Moroccan–Algerian co-operation in many aspects of their bilateral relations, but it is unlikely to move these two states to resolve their differences over the Western Sahara. The stakes are high in the Sahara and, until now, some aspects of the dispute have proved intractable. A resolution of the dispute, if it occurs in the foreseeable future, will not be achieved by the UMA; rather, it will come within the context of Moroccan–Algerian relations.

NOTES

1 *Le Monde*, 1 March 1983, p. 1; *Le Matin* (Paris), 19 May, 1983, p. 12.
2 Abdelaziz Dahmani, 'Maghreb: Les Anciens et le moderne', *Jeune Afrique*, no. 1162, 13 April, 1983, pp. 28–9.
3 John Damis, 'Morocco, Libya and the Treaty of Union', *American–Arab Affairs*, no. 13, pp. 44–9.

BIBLIOGRAPHY

Bamford, David (1989) 'The Maghreb: what does "union" mean?', *Middle East International*, no. 343, 3 February, pp. 12–13.
Belhassen, Souhayr (1989) 'Libye: le Roi et le Colonel', *Jeune Afrique*, no. 1497, 11 September, pp. 14–16.
Dahmani, Abdelaziz (1983) 'Maghreb: Les anciens et le moderne', *Jeune Afrique*, no. 1162, 13 April, pp. 28–9.
Damis, John (1983) 'Prospects for unity/disunity in North Africa', *American–Arab Affairs*, no. 6, pp. 34–47.
—— (1985) 'Morocco, Libya and the Treaty of Union', *American–Arab Affairs*, no. 13, pp. 44–55.
Daoud, Zakya (1989) 'La création de l'Union du Maghreb arabe', *Maghreb–Machrek*, no. 124, April–June, pp. 120–6.
Deeb, Mary-Jane (1989) 'Inter-Maghribi relations since 1969: a study of the modalities of unions and mergers', *Middle East Journal*, vol. 43, no. 1, pp. 20–33.

Gharbi, Samir (1989) 'Maghreb: La nuit des compromis', *Jeune Afrique*, no. 1470, 8 March, p. 47.

Ka'idi, Hamza (1989) 'Maghreb: L'union dans le texte', *Jeune Afrique*, no. 1477, 26 April, pp. 43–4.

Parker, Richard B. (1985) 'Appointment in Oujda', *Foreign Affairs*, vol. 63, no. 5, pp. 1095–110.

Romdhani, Oussama (1989) 'The Arab Maghreb Union: toward North African integration', *American–Arab Affairs*, no. 28, pp. 42–8.

Soudan, François (1989) 'Grand Maghreb: une étape décisive', *Jeune Afrique*, no. 1467, 15 February, pp. 13–14.

Index